Personnel and Human Resource Management

Gerald Cole

Fifth edition

continuum
LONDON • NEW YORK

Continuum

The Tower Building   370 Lexington Avenue
11 York Road   New York
London SE1 7NX   NY 10017-6503

www.continuumbooks.com

First edition published 1986 by Letts Educational
Second edition 1988
Reprinted 1991
Third edition 1993
Reprinted 1993, 1995
Fourth edition 1997
Fifth edition 2002

British Library Cataloguing-in-Publication Data
A catalogue record for this book is available from the British Library.

ISBN: 0-8264-5862-9 (hardback)
      0-8264-5863-7 (paperback)

Typeset by YHT Ltd, London
Printed and bound in Great Britain by Biddles Ltd, Guildford and King's Lynn

CONTENTS

ACKNOWLEDGEMENTS

I am grateful to the following for permission to reproduce examination questions:

Chartered Institute of Personnel Management
Institute of Chartered Secretaries and Administrators
Hotel Catering and Institutional Management Association
The Institute of Bankers
Association of Business Executives

I am also indebted to Jinny McDonald-Matthews of Toyota Motor Manufacturing (UK) Ltd for her help in developing the case study of the Burnaston plant.

PREFACE TO FIFTH EDITION

This new edition has been given the more comprehensive title of *Personnel and Human Resource Management*, and a number of changes have been made throughout the text to reflect this somewhat broader concept of managing people in organisations. Since the previous edition, the debate about what is, and what is not, Human Resource Management (HRM) has been more thoroughly explored, and a greater consensus of opinion is apparent. This is reflected in this new edition, where the opening chapter focuses on the differences and similarities between the two concepts.

There has been considerable change in the realm of employee relations in recent years, and the chapters on trade unions and individual employment law have been rewritten. The chapters dealing with collective disputes and individual grievances have been updated.

The emphasis on performance management has led to numerous changes in the chapter on pay and benefits (Chapter 21).

The effects on personnel and human resource management of the increasing reliance on IT-related measures are reflected throughout the book. Data protection measures are a major issue here, and the provisions of the new Data Protection Act have been included, superseding the details of the previous legislation (see Chapter 17).

Globalisation is another pervasive concept affecting personnel and human resource management, and whilst this is acknowledged in Chapter 3 on the international aspects of personnel and HR management, it has implications for a range of core activities in the profession.

The leading professional bodies holding examinations in the area of personnel and human resource management have moved away from traditional essay-type answers towards a preference for short case-study analyses plus short-note answers to a range of specific topics. The essay answers used in the previous edition are nevertheless retained here on the basis that getting students to think about a question, and then answer it in good written English, are important learning skills, which will help individuals when they come to be employed, or seek promotion.

The glossary has been retained with one or two additional items. A novel feature is the list of useful websites, reflecting the growing use of the Internet to access official data sources and other useful material in the public domain.

The author always welcomes constructive feedback on the contents of the book.

Gerald Cole
West Sussex
February 2002

GLOSSARY OF MANAGEMENT TERMS

The following glossary contains short working definitions of a number of important terms used in personnel management. It is hoped they will be useful to readers who are unfamiliar with the language and jargon of the subject-area of personnel management and human resources.

Arbitration A device for settling disputes where the parties concerned fail to agree; the key feature is that the person acting as arbitrator makes the decision for the parties. (See also **conciliation, mediation** and **pendulum arbitration**.)

Assertiveness Behaviour in which the individual states his or her needs and wishes in a way that does not overrule the rights of others to express their needs and wants, in contrast to **aggressive behaviour**, which ignores or dismisses the rights of others.

Attitude A predisposition in an individual to make certain kinds of judgements about external events and other people's behaviour, usually based on deeply-held personal values.

Authority This refers to the formal power to act conferred on individuals to enable them to fulfil their responsibilities. It is usually fairly well-defined in order to limit the powers available to any one individual.

Basic pay Pay which is guaranteed from one period to the next; it excludes bonus earnings, overtime, etc.

Behavioural science The study of the individual and the group in the working environment; subjects of study include motivation, communication, organisation structure, decision-systems, and organisational change; as a science it is still in the development stage, relying considerably on the contributions of psychology and sociology.

Benchmark jobs In job evaluation, these are the representative sample of jobs which are precisely written up and measured so as to provide a satisfactory range and standard of jobs upon which to base the evaluation of the remainder.

Benchmarking Comparing the organisation's standard of performance in one or more key aspects of strategy (or operations) against that of a first-class competitor or comparable organisation.

Benefits Items such as pensions, sickness payments, company cars etc., which are additional to earnings; sometimes known as 'fringe benefits'

Body language Non-verbal indications of behaviour, usually involving body movements and gestures, sometimes made deliberately but more often subconsciously.

Bonus A payment in addition to basic pay, usually given for results achieved beyond an agreed norm; can apply to managers as well as to other employees.

Bureaucracy A term used by Max Weber to describe what he called 'rational-legal' authority, in which an individual's power arises from the nature of his or her position, as prescribed by the organisation's rules and procedures. Can be contrasted with (1) *traditional authority*, in which power arises from customary practices usually based on family or tribal connections, and (2) *charismatic authority*, which arises principally from the force of an individual's personality.

Business process re-engineering A method of raising organisational efficiency by questioning every stage of key operational processes to see if they still achieve what is required of them in terms of cost, quality, service and speed.

Certified trade union A trade union which, under procedures now incorporated into the Trade Union and Labour Relations (Consolidation) Act, 1992, has been granted a certificate of independence by the Certification Officer.

Change agent An external person, usually a behavioural scientist, who acts as a facilitator or catalyst in the process of change in an organisation and who provides key analytical skills designed to give the client organisation's members an insight into what is going on in terms of people's reactions to change in themselves, their colleagues and their environment.

Classical management theory A body of theory about managing organisations which claims to provide universal principles on which good practice can be modelled.

Coaching A form of employee development, usually applied to managerial staff, in which an experienced and skilled individual helps a colleague to apply knowledge and techniques in practice.

Collective agreements The results of collective bargaining are expressed in agreements; these are principally procedure agreements and substantive agreements; they are not legally enforceable in the UK. (See also **procedure agreement** and **substantive agreement.**)

Collective bargaining The process of negotiating wages and other working conditions collectively between employers and trade unions, it enables the conditions of employees to be agreed as a whole group instead of individually. (See also **negotiations.**)

Committee A formally-established group for the purposes of *decision-making*, incorporating explicit roles (e.g. chairholder, secretary) and rules of procedure (agenda, minutes, voting).

Competence Refers to a person's ability to perform a task to an externally-agreed standard, whether set by the organisation or some third party. Competencies are derived from key job roles and are usually described in terms of their context (e.g. a 'range statement') and specified performance criteria.

Conciliation A process whereby a third party attempts to promote an agreement between the parties in a dispute by exploring any common ground which may lead to a settlement being achieved by the parties themselves; unlike an arbitrator, a conciliator does not aim to make the decision for the parties. (See also **arbitration** and **mediation.**)

Conflict A condition that arises when two or more individuals or groups perceive their own interests as being challenged by the other(s), and where strong feelings can be aroused. Conflict can be dealt with in several different ways leading to one of the following outcomes: win–lose, compromise or lose–lose.

Counselling A skilled activity in which the counsellor helps the 'client' to understand their problems, take responsibility for them and develop ways of overcoming them using their own inner resources.

Culture (organisation) This is essentially the collection of shared values which provide employees with explicit and implicit signposts to what has come to be regarded as preferred behaviour in the organisation; organisation cultures are likely to be greatly influenced by national cultural characteristics.

Decision A commitment to a particular course of action, sometimes taken unilaterally but usually following discussion and negotiation with others.

Deductive learning Refers to learning in which new ideas or concepts are tested out in practice and conclusions drawn from the results. Sometimes referred to as 'Rule-E.g.'

De-layering Reducing the number of layers (levels) in a job hierarchy.

Differentials Differences in earnings between groups of workers, usually based on skills, responsibility or custom and practice.

Disciplinary procedure A set of rules or guidelines for dealing with instances of bad behaviour or rule-breaking amongst employees; the most common sanctions are warnings, suspensions and dismissals.

Discrimination Usually refers to unfair treatment of an individual or group on grounds of their sex, race or disability.

Dismissal The termination of an employee's contract of employment either by the employer, or by the employee himself in circumstances where the employer's conduct justifies such a step (constructive dismissal); dismissal may be with or without notice.

Downsizing Reducing the scale of an organisation, especially in terms of reducing the headcount/labour force. Often accompanied by **de-layering** (see above).

Earnings The total monetary remuneration received by an employee, including overtime, commission, bonuses, etc.

Empathy Refers essentially to a person's ability to see a situation from the point of view of another and letting them know it. It does not imply agreement with the other, but merely non-judgmental acceptance of the latter's viewpoint.

Employer's association An organisation of employers set up for the purposes of collective bargaining and/or for advising and assisting members with industrial relations problems; some also deal with trading interests as in a 'trade association'.

Empowerment A term used to describe the process of granting employees greater discretion over how their jobs are done or their responsibilities fulfilled, and usually involving a genuine attempt to increase people's *authority* and *responsibility* at the appropriate level.

Environment Usually refers to the external context in which an organisation operates, including the activities of stakeholders and other external sources of change, but can also be used to refer to internal conditions within an organisation, such as management styles, employee attitudes, technical environment

and financial situation. External environments can be stable or dynamic and simple or complex.

Flexitime Flexible working hours: A system enabling employees to vary their working hours in a particular period, provided they do attend during certain 'core hours', e.g. 1000 hours – 1600 hours.

Glass ceiling Expression used to denote a subtle barrier to women's promotion to senior posts in an organisation, and usually implying that it is kept in place by men's innate prejudice against women in senior management positions.

Grievance Complaint made by an employee about wages, conditions of employment, or the actions of management; most organisations have a special procedure for handling grievances.

Group, formal A number of people brought together in fairly well defined roles and inter-relationships by the management of an organisation. Such groups are formally recognised within the organisation, given appropriate resources, and usually possess a degree of authority.

Group, informal A group which is not formally recognised by the management of an organisation, but which has been formed by a group of employees *for their own purposes*, and has the power to work against organisational goals as well as to collaborate with them. Informal groups are usually less permanent than formal groups.

Hawthorne Effect Term used to describe changes in productivity and motivation arising primarily from the attention given by management to the employees concerned, rather than by any other changes in employment conditions, such as bonuses or hours of work.

Human resource management (HRM) This expression refers to decisions about the deployment and treatment of personnel taken by line units as well as personnel specialists. HRM implies an approach which recognises that employees are only one group among several, such as customers and shareholders, who have a claim on the resources of the organisation. In practice, HRM cannot be considered different from a **Personnel management** approach (see below) operating in a competitive environment.

Human resource planning A technique aimed at securing and improving an organisation's human resources to meet present and future needs; three prin-cipal stages can be distinguished: evaluation of existing resources, forecast of future requirements and, finally, action plan.

Hygiene factor According to Herzberg, this is an element of work motivation which arises from the environment or context of the individual's job, such as status and incentive payments, in contrast to **motivators**, which arise from the person's experience of the job, such as achievement and intrinsic job interest. Hygiene factors do not trigger motivated behaviour, but can cause individuals to become demotivated.

Increment Refers to an increase within a pay scale, usually of a fixed amount and paid annually; incremental scales are especially common in the public services.

Induction The process of introducing new employees into their jobs with the aim of integrating the newcomers as quickly and effectively as possible.

Inductive learning Learning manifested in the ability to form concepts or make generalisations as a result of observing or experiencing external events. Sometimes referred to as 'E.g.-Rule'.

Investors in People (IIP) Brand name of a national UK quality standard aimed at encouraging organisations to invest in employee development within the context of business goals; award of the standard is only granted after a successful assessment of company policy and practices by independent, licensed assessors.

Job The name given to a particular set of tasks allocated to a particular individual or position, for which the job-holder will be held accountable. The arrangement or revision of tasks allocated to a job is called *job design*.

Job description A statement of overall purpose and scope of a job, together with details of its tasks and duties; the description is a product of job analysis.

Job enlargement The horizontal increasing of job responsibility, i.e. by the addition of tasks of a similar nature to be distinguished from **job enrichment**.

Job enrichment Usually refers to the enhancement of a job by the addition of motivating factors, such as job interest and responsibility. Is different in kind from **job enlargement**, which is essentially the addition of extra tasks to an existing job.

Job evaluation A technique for determining the size of one job compared with another, and the relationship between the two; job evaluation schemes can broadly be divided into analytical and non-analytical; the technique forms the basis for wage and salary administration.

Labour turnover Percentage figure which indicates the rate at which employees move in and out of employment with the organisation; usually expressed as follows:

$$\frac{\text{Number of employees who left during year}}{\text{Average number of employed during year}} \times 100$$

Leadership A process within groups in which one person, either by virtue of position or personality or both, obtains sufficient commitment of the other members to facilitate the achievement of group goals.

Leadership style A term used to describe the manner in which a person exercises leadership, especially in relation to their treatment of people and tasks.

Learning A process by which individuals acquire knowledge, understanding, skills and values, and usually described in terms of demonstrable behaviour (i.e. evidence of learning). Often described as **deductive learning** or **inductive learning** (see above).

Line and staff A reference to an organisational configuration which embraces *line functions*, which contribute directly to the provision of goods or services, and *staff functions*, which contribute indirectly by supporting the line functions; should be distinguished from line and functional organisation structures, in which functional, i.e. staff specialist, managers can exercise considerable power over other managers, including line managers.

Management development A systematic process for ensuring that an organisation meets its current and future needs for effective managers; typical features include manpower reviews, succes-sion planning, performance appraisal and training, both on and off the job.

Mechanistic organisations Refers to organisations which are not only highly-structured but whose processes are seen as serving the structure. Thus the operation of the organisation is seen as a machine process which sustains the balance between the different parts. In this situation people's needs are seen as secondary to the needs of the structure. Contrasts with **organic organisations** (see below).

Mediation A process whereby a third party makes specific proposals to both sides in a dispute in order to promote a mutually acceptable solution; sometimes regarded as a 'halfway house' between conciliation and arbitration. (See also **arbitration** and **conciliation**.)

Mentor An expression which refers to a mature and experienced person – other than an individual's line manager – who is entrusted with the personal development and workplace learning of one or more less experienced persons in the organisation.

Motivation The processes, both instinctive and rational, which occur in an individual when seeking to satisfy perceived needs and wants.

Motivators These are factors arising from a person's experience of a job, such as achievement and intrinsic job interest, and which cause that person to become motivated to put effort into the job. Motivators usually have a positive effect on a person's drive, unlike **hygiene factors** (see above).

Negotiations Term used to describe the bargaining between employers and trade union representatives on the subject of terms and conditions of employment; the object of the negotiations is to obtain mutual agreement to improved conditions. (See also **collective bargaining**.)

Norms Essentially collective values, usually manifested in the form of (1) explicit rules, laws and codes of practice, and (2) implicit group attitudes or culture.

Organic organisations Refers to organisations which are designed so as to reflect the dynamism of all the relationships between people, tasks, technology and environment. Organic organisations achieve a degree of flexibility that does not exist in **mechanistic organisations** (see above).

organisation behaviour A reference to the study of the way individuals and groups behave at work, including the analysis of the interrelationships between individuals and groups, their interaction with their environments and the conduct of change.

organisation development A long-range, or strategic, approach to change involving the whole organisation, or a major part of it, and aimed at improving organisational processes and cultural development as a major contribution to the organisation's mission and goals.

organisation structure A term used to describe the intangible network of relationships between jobs, job-holders, roles and organisational groupings by which organisations achieve sufficient differentiation and co-ordination of human effort to meet their strategic goals.

Outsourcing This usually refers to the decision to sub-contract some aspect of work that has previously been conducted in-house, for example, salary adminis-tration or training.

Overtime A period of work, in excess of normal or standard hours, which is paid at an enhanced rate.

Pendulum arbitration A form of arbi-tration where an arbitrator (or arbitra-tion panel) is asked on behalf of the disputing parties to choose between either the management's last offer, or the trade union's final demand.

Perception Usually refers to a person's distinctive understanding of a situation, which may or may not reflect the objective truth of the situation. Is con-siderably influenced by such factors as intelligence, awareness of facts, and past experience.

Personality The unique pattern of atti-tudes, predispositions and behaviour possessed by an individual.

Personnel management The expression 'personnel management' refers primarily to the activities of *specialist* staff respon-sible for implementing the key objectives of the organisation in respect of its use of people (employees). Personnel staff have always had responsibilities towards the workforce, for an important part of their role is a concern for fair treatment, equitable payment and other aspects of importance to the *employee* stakeholders in the organisation. Thus, the personnel role is distinguishable from the team leadership role, which is essentially about the harnessing of people's efforts in the pursuit of organisational goals. (See also **human resource management**.)

Picketing Trade union activity where groups of workers in dispute with their employers attend at their own place of work for the purpose of peacefully persuading other workers not to leave or enter the premises for work; the persons in attendance are the pickets and the area they are picketing is called the picket line.

Policy A statement of the manner in which work activities are to be pursued, thus contributing to the development and implementation of a set of dominant values in an organisation (i.e. its **culture**).

Power The ability to achieve results through people's acquiescence, whether encouraged by the organisation or not. Can be distinguished from **responsibility** and **authority** (see separate entries).

Procedure agreement A collective agree-ment setting out the procedures to be followed in the conduct of management–union relations with particular reference to negotiating rights, union represen-tation, disputes and grievance proce-dures. (See also **substantive agreement**.)

Psychometric tests Tests applied to human beings aimed at measuring in-dividual performance, usually by com-parison with others, on the basis of objective and standardised questions. Usually assessed in terms of individual aptitudes, abilities and personality traits.

Recognition issue A situation where an employer and a trade union disagree about the extent to which the employer is prepared to recognise the union for the purposes of collective bargaining; unions may seek the help of the Advisory, Conciliation and Arbitration Service, but employers are not obliged to grant recognition.

Redundancy The loss of a job on the grounds that it is no longer required or no longer available at a particular place of employment; it is regarded as a form of dismissal.

Responsibility This refers to an individ-ual's formal accountability to a superior in the organisation. Unlike tasks it cannot be delegated to another, as it is personal to the job-holder.

Role Essentially, role refers to the expectations that the members of a role-set have about the nature of the job and the way it should be carried out; the individual may or may not agree with this perception of the role and role-conflict may thus occur.

Role-set All those jobs/roles that directly impinge on the job-holder's own job/role to form a small job/role network in which context the job-holder undertakes his or her work and role.

Scientific management A phrase coined by F.W. Taylor to sum up his analytical and rational methods of measuring work and the subsequent design of work to produce the most efficient way of working in the circumstances.

Seven point plan A guide to selection interviewing, enabling interviewers to assess candidates under seven headings: physical make-up, attainments, general intelligence, special aptitudes, interests, disposition and domestic/family circumstances.

Shop steward A union member elected by work-place colleagues to represent them to management; shop stewards are appointed under arrangements agreed collectively between the employer and the recognised trade union(s); they are not full-time, nor are they paid for their union work.

Socio-technical system A term used to describe work systems which combine the demands of technology and production requirements with the interpersonal needs of people as individuals and in groups.

Stakeholder An individual or group having a clear interest in the outcomes of an enterprise, and potentially able to influence future decisions, either directly or indirectly.

Strategy Essentially a long-range plan for an organisation comprising a statement of mission and goals, company policies and resourcing provisions, which provides the organisation's employees with direction, guidance and support in the conduct of the organisation's affairs.

Stress Refers to the bodily changes that can take place when the external pressures on an individual reach an intolerable pitch causing weakened job performance and ill-health. The level of stress depends on several factors, especially the individual's personality and perceptions of his or her ability to cope with the external pressures.

Substantive agreement A collective agreement dealing with terms and conditions of employment, e.g. wages, hours of work, holiday's etc. (See also **procedure agreement**.)

Synergy A term used to describe the extent to which the deployment of a range of resources produces results in excess of the sum of the resources invested. Often referred to as the '2 + 2 = 5 effect'.

Systems, open Usually refers to an entity (e.g. an organisation) which takes in inputs from its environment, processes them by means of human efforts, the application of finance and the use of technology, in order to produce outputs in the form of goods and services. A key feature of an open system is that it interacts with its environment, and thus a crucial aspect of the processing activities is to generate feedback on results.

Theory Z An expression coined by Ouchi to describe a process of organisation, modelled on Japanese practices, that encourages management to focus on the co-ordination of people's efforts rather than technological requirements in the pursuit of enhanced productivity.

Trade union An organisation of employees whose principal purpose is to negotiate with employers about terms and conditions of employment and other matters affecting the members' interests at work. (See also **certified trade union**.)

Training needs analysis A rational approach to assessing the training or development needs of groups of employees, aimed at clarifying the needs of the job and the needs of individuals in terms of training required.

Unfair dismissal A statutory definition of dismissal which states that every employee shall have the right not to be unfairly dismissed; remedies for unfair dismissal must be pursued via an industrial tribunal, which may award compensation or reinstatement (in previous post) or re-engagement (employment in some other comparable post).

Work design Refers to the analysis and subsequent restructuring of the activities in which people engage in a work situation. Work design is manifested in the clustering of such activities into jobs, which themselves are designed to achieve change and/or effectiveness in the pursuit of organisational goals.

PART I

THE SCOPE OF PERSONNEL AND HUMAN RESOURCE MANAGEMENT

The three chapters of this opening section of the book set the scene for the all the other sections. Chapter 1 engages in a short discussion of the subject matter of personnel and human resource management, and in particular examines to what extent there may be distinguishing features between them. The overall conclusion is that there are no substantive differences between the two, and that each concept can operate at strategic, operational and intermediate levels in an organisation. Chapter 2 outlines the different levels at which personnel/HRM work in practice, and provides some introductory examples. The chapter also summarises the principal accountabilities that might be expected from persons carrying out specialist personnel/HR roles in the organisation. Chapter 3 summarises some of the international aspects of personnel/HR.

The subject matter of all three chapters gives rise to issues of theory and practice that are examined in greater detail throughout the rest of the book. At the outset it should be stated that the key issues facing personnel and human resource practitioners at the present time are as follows:

- Economies are global in every sense of the word, and there is always a global dimension to business activities

- Strategic considerations have never been so important

- Niche markets requiring specialised products and services demand appropriate employee skills

- Competitive advantage is based more on the knowledge and skills of the workforce than any other factor

- Life-long learning is consequently vital for employees at all levels in organisations

- Flatter organisation structures demand better leadership at the grass roots in order to gain employees' commitment and trust in achieving corporate goals

1

- Flexible working arrangements which respect the law and employees' proper wishes are a challenge to be met

- The use and adaptation of information technology is a critical support factor in facilitating the added value that employees can bring to their work

- Achieving excellence in customer satisfaction will henceforth be a permanent feature of any strategic plan

- The human resource function in any organisation must understand that it is responsible for creating the conditions in which people make the greatest contribution to the success of the enterprise.

CHAPTER 1

Personnel and human resource management

INTRODUCTION

1. The changed title of this edition reflects the growing use of the expression 'Human Resource Management' (HRM) in the management of people in work organisations. The title also reflects the continuing use of the expression 'Personnel Management' to describe the same genre of management activity in such organisations. Both expressions are used, often interchangeably, in practitioner and academic circles. It is clear over the past decade that, in the United Kingdom at least, the debate still rages about whether, or what, differences may separate the two concepts. This chapter examines some of the arguments put forward by both sides in this debate, and concludes with the view that there is insufficient evidence to indicate substantial differences between the two concepts. The assumption in this book is that the two expressions are so closely related *in practice* that they are, in effect, interchangeable.

2. Personnel and human resource management activities are carried out by all those in a leadership role in an organisation. Every manager or team leader is necessarily involved in concerns about the *way* in which people are employed as well as about what they need to be doing, and how well. In most situations such leaders fulfil their personnel/HR responsibilities within a clear framework of HRM policy. These responsibilities will, of course, form part of the focus of this book. However, the principal focus here will be on the work and responsibilities of *practitioners* in the field of personnel and human resource management.

3. An illustration of the congruence between 'Personnel' and 'Human Resources' can be gleaned from a quick examination of job advertisements in this field. For example, the Chartered Institute of Personnel and Development's journal *People Management* for 9 October 1997 showed that references to '*Personnel Manager/ Adviser/Officer*' represented 31 per cent of the total compared with 39 per cent referring to '*Human Resource Director/Manager/Adviser/Officer*'. Three years later (12 October 2000) the references to '*Personnel*' had decreased to 21 per cent, whilst those to '*Human Resources*' (HR) had increased to 49 per cent. It seems that, in the practical world of people management, organisations are expressing a preference for describing personnel specialists as '*HR specialists*'. An examination of the job profiles of all these advertisements, however, reveals that there are no significant differences in their content between '*Personnel*' and '*HR*'.

4. Typically, jobs at Director or Senior Manager level sought experience and personal qualities that would enable a person to fulfil a strategic role, in which personnel/ HR policies and plans are developed to meet business goals and conform to legal and cultural norms. Posts seeking a functional head of department, whether called 'Personnel' or 'Human Resources', looked for someone able to ensure that the organisation's needs for recruitment and staff training and development were met, and supported by adequate compensation and benefits, and attention to employee relations matters. Posts at Adviser level were generally seeking an internal consultant able to advise the board on the personnel/HR implications of business decisions or plans. Such posts may have been seeking individuals capable of making a *proactive* contribution to business policy as well as a *reactive* one, but this was not necessarily so. The more junior posts advertised were as likely to be named 'HR Assistant' as 'Personnel Officer'. The tasks were essentially the same — to undertake the administration of the procedures required to recruit, train, retain and, where necessary, dismiss employees.

PERSONNEL MANAGEMENT OR HRM – BACKGROUND TO THE DEBATE

5. Over the last 50 years or so, the term '*Personnel Management*' has been used to describe that function of management that deals with the recruitment, employment, training, redeployment, safety and departure of employees. The former *Institute of Personnel and Development* described the personnel function as follows:

> It is that part of management which is concerned with people at work and with their relationships within an enterprise. Personnel management aims to achieve both efficiency and justice ... It seeks to bring together and develop into an effective organisation the men and women who make up the enterprise, enabling each to make his own best contribution to its success ... It seeks to provide fair terms and conditions of employment, and satisfying work for those employed. (IPM, 1963)[1]

Notable aspects of this definition of the personnel/HR function are its reference to justice as well as efficiency, implying a caring role for the management in its relations with its employees. As well as referring to fair terms of employment, the definition goes further by including satisfying work, implying management's responsibility for enabling employees to experience job satisfaction. Today's approach would be more likely to stress the contribution of satisfied employees to achieving corporate goals such as customer satisfaction, cost-effectiveness and profitability.

6. Until the 1990s, personnel management in practice was as much about handling collective relationships with employees and their representatives as about mediating individual employment relationships. In terms of stakeholder relationships (see Figure 1.1), the main pressures on a typical Personnel Manager in those days came principally from the managing director, trade union representatives, and line management colleagues. The capacity for the senior management to introduce change and flexibility in operations was hampered at this time due to such factors as:

- government economic policy was directed towards full employment

- industrial and public sector organisations were heavily unionised, often with a multiple array of trade unions

- employment legislation encouraged collective bargaining as the best means of (a) settling pay and conditions, and (b) resolving disputes between employees and their employers.

7. The network of relationships that surrounded a senior personnel manager in the mid-twentieth century was predominantly as shown in Figure 1.1. The board, and especially the chief executive, would be looking to the personnel manager to ensure that employee relations were both peaceful and predictable – in other words, no unpleasant surprises by way of unexpected strikes or other employee sanctions, such as a ban on overtime working. Senior line managers were particularly keen to ensure that there would be no disruption to their output schedules. Shop stewards were always keen to ensure that they had ready access to the personnel manager if there was any problem with their own line manager. They would also be pressing for frequent consultation meetings on a wide range of shop-floor issues, in addition to negotiating meetings about basic pay and conditions, where they would often be accompanied by trade union officials. The latter would be in frequent contact with the personnel manager when negotiations were in progress or when a dispute was imminent. Their influence was more powerful when they knew they had members in other plants or offices owned by the firm, with whom they could engage in company-wide action, if necessary. Junior personnel officers and their staff were often forced to refer to the personnel manager, because the tightly written rules concerning relations with the unions meant they usually had very limited discretion to act. Bodies such as ACAS, the Advisory, Conciliation and Arbitration Service, could intervene with the personnel manager on behalf of individuals or groups, where grievances or disputes were involved. Finally, the individual employees always had access to the personnel manager through the organisation's grievance procedure.

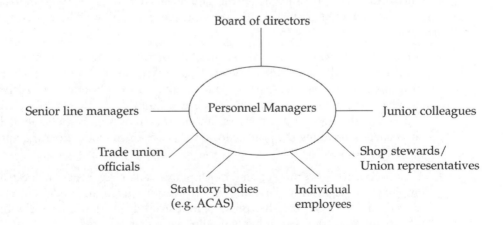

Figure 1.1 *Personnel management's stakeholders (industrial relations era)*

8.   The conditions therefore in which personnel management was conducted in those times could usefully be described as highly regulated, dominated by considerations of relative power between management and trade unions, and inflexible in terms of labour mobility. Line managers had to be constantly aware that a strike, or other collective employee sanction, could disrupt their production targets at a moment's notice. Personnel managers in this situation were called upon to ensure that, so far as possible, such disruption did not occur by acting as mediators between union representatives and the line management. Specialists in *employee relations*, as the management of collective bargaining came to be known, became the doyen of the senior management. They were treated rather like highly-respected company *lawyers* advising senior management teams on how best to avoid, or minimise conflict, and how best to handle the consequential legalities that a face-to-face confrontation would entail. It was left to the company accountant to expose the relative financial costs and benefits of whatever course of action was proposed.

9.   It is not surprising that against this background *personnel management* came to acquire a reputation for defending the *status quo*. Personnel managers in the 1970s and 80s were much more concerned with the smooth-running of operations than with making proposals for change. During those same decades the concept of *Organisation Development* (OD) had emerged (see Chapter 10). OD is the name given to a collection of techniques aimed at improving organisational effectiveness by stimulating *collaborative* efforts at both strategic and operational levels, thus minimising conflict and reducing inflexibility in the labour force. The introduction of OD was aimed at change, albeit as envisaged by the top management, sought and planned on a mutual rather than arbitrary basis. However, such theoretical concepts can only work if they are introduced in the right organisational climate. At that time most organisations, whether in the public or private sector, had to negotiate change with the trade unions, and this had the effect of putting personnel managers on the defensive. Any changes that were agreed had their price in terms of extra concessions to the workforce. It took a number of important external factors in the UK to bring about the required sea change in the conduct of employee relations.

10.   The situation changed radically in the late 1980s when several external factors combined to make a major impact on workplace relations. These factors were primarily:

- trade union power in one of its most conservative areas – printing – was challenged by the newspaper owner, Rupert Murdoch, who was prepared to print his daily newspapers abroad, if unable to do so in London; the early signs of what we now call *globalisation* were beginning to emerge; the challenge caused much anger and bitterness among the trade union movement, but it succeeded in breaking the print unions' veto over the introduction of computer-led technology

- a Conservative government under Margaret Thatcher began to restructure employment legislation so that the protection given to trade unions and unionised workgroups in the course of industrial disputes was severely limited, whilst the protection for individual employees was boosted

- the so-called *closed shop* arrangement whereby employees were obliged to join a trade union as a condition of employment was outlawed, and this had the effects of reducing the power of shop stewards in the workplace, and of slowing down trade union recruitment in the workforce

- a collapse in the UK's domestic and overseas markets led to a huge increase in unemployment, which weakened the position of the unions even further, as the policy of full employment was set aside by the government

- when the economy began to improve, and as the effects of new employer-friendly legislation began to take hold, businesses everywhere were able to place the *customer* at the forefront of their stakeholders rather than their *employees*; thus developed the concept of *customer relations* that is now so pervasive in the UK economy.

11. The 1990s came to be seen as the '*decade of the consumer*' (customer, client, patient or other end-user of goods and services); this situation brought forth a need to redefine '*personnel management*' so that it better reflected the contemporary focus on (a) customers and their needs, and (b) the need to adapt to changing conditions in the external marketplace; there was now less focus on either the concerns of employees or the need for *formal* communication structures within the organisation. The 1990s was also the decade that saw a major attack on organisational hierarchies, leading to considerable de-layering of structures and a greater delegation of accountability to work-team leaders.

12. The last decade of the twentieth century has sought to change the emphasis of '*personnel management*', so as to be more concerned with primary *business* goals, and less with the implications for employees of the consequences of pursuing those goals. The work environment today has changed from the confrontational mixture of mid-century employee relations, with its emphasis on highly regulated personnel procedures, to collaborative approaches based on small work-teams dedicated to customer satisfaction, where workplace learning is paramount and the need for centralised procedures less relevant. At the same time the external environment for all of the private sector, and parts of the public sector, has become much more competitive. Not only are customers and their requirements important, but so too are the actions of competitors. It is in this new environment that the term '*Human Resource Management*' sits more comfortably for many people than '*Personnel Management*'.

PERSONNEL MANAGEMENT OR HRM – SOME OF THE ARGUMENTS

13. Much of the debate about whether there are significant differences between these two concepts is of interest only to academics. Nevertheless, given that significant numbers of business and government organisations have taken the step of renaming their personnel function as the HRM function, it is fair to assume that they are making some kind of statement about how they view people management. It could be argued that it has become fashionable to speak of HRM, and that this is why many organisations have adopted the expression. The term is also the preferred way of describing the personnel function in the United States, and is thus

employed by the most influential management 'gurus'. Use of HRM language also helps to bypass 'politically incorrect' terms used in the past, such as manpower planning. However, these are not very convincing answers so far as the UK is concerned. It is significant that in July 2000, when the professional body for personnel management in the UK was awarded chartered status, it decided *not* to change its title to Human Resource Management but to continue as the *Chartered Institute of Personnel and Development*.

14. There has to be some other set of justifications, therefore, for describing '*personnel*' activities as '*human resource*' activities. What are the principal distinctions that might underlie these two expressions? There are no pat answers to this question, but the following points have been made in recent debates on this topic:

Personnel Management implies	HRM implies
• Reactive, servicing role	• Proactive, innovative role
• Emphasis on implementation of procedures	• Emphasis on strategy
• Specialist department	• General management activity
• Focus on employees' needs in their own right	• Focus on employee requirements in the light of business needs
• Employees seen as cost to be controlled	• Employees seen as investment to be nurtured as well as cost to be controlled
• Presumption of union–management conflicts	• Conflicts dealt with by team leaders within their teams
• Preference for collective bargaining of pay and conditions	• Management-led planning of people resources and employment conditions
• Emphasis on settling pay more in terms of the organisation's internal market	• Emphasis on competitive pay and conditions to stay ahead of competitors
• Serving other departments/units	• Contributing 'added value' to business
• Supporting change	• Stimulating change
• Challenging business goals in light of effects on employees	• Total commitment to business goals
• Less flexible approach to staff deployments	• Completely flexible approach to staff deployments

15. The strength of the arguments for or against the two concepts, as indicated in the above lists, depends considerably on whether one takes a '*hard*' or '*soft*' view of Personnel Management or HRM. A '*hard*' view of Personnel Management would see the function as essentially procedural, reactive and, where necessary, protective of employee needs against the harshness of business goals. This viewpoint would place Personnel Management at some distance from any concept of HRM. However, a '*soft*' view of Personnel Management might see the function as supporting change, even helping to define it, supplying and developing relevant employee skills in accordance with the business aims of line units, and providing a framework for pay and conditions that achieved competitive advantage for the organisation. Such a view would come very close to any definition of HRM. It would certainly be close to a '*soft*' view of HRM, where employee commitment to challenging business goals was fostered by encouraging personal initiative within teams under sensitive leadership. It would be less close to a '*hard*' view of HRM, where the emphasis on total commitment to business goals and competitive advantage would override individual needs and aspirations, where successful

employees were seen as an investment, but poorer performers seen as a liability. The key phrase here is *added value*. Employees are judged primarily on whether they are seen to be adding value to the business. Unlike the mid-twentieth century when over-manning was a chronic British weakness, the emphasis now is on 'lean' structures with minimum numbers employed.

16. A recent commentator on this debate, Ulrich (1997)[2], sees four possible routes for HRM. First, and minimally, he suggests, it could aim for just a servicing function, which he calls the *work organisation* approach. Second, he sets forth the idea of the HR practitioner acting as spokesperson for the employees in situations where conflict is involved, the so-called *employee champion*. These two approaches compare well with our '*hard*' view of personnel management. They would provide only a very restricted role for the HRM practitioner. Ulrich's third possibility for HRM is that it could fulfil an active change management role in the organisation, where personnel/HR practices bring added value to the business. This approach corresponds closely to our '*soft*' views of both personnel management and HRM. The fourth approach suggested by Ulrich is that of *business partner*, where the HR practitioner participates fully in the strategic processes of the organisation, and is wholly committed to concepts of added value and competitive advantage. This approach corresponds to the '*hard*' view of HRM expressed in the previous paragraph.

17. What we are seeing at the start of the new century is a merging of the 'softer' elements of the respective approaches to personnel management and HRM, and a greater willingness to subordinate employees' concerns to overall business goals. The dominant stakeholders now are the customer and the shareholder (see Figure 1.2). This process has been accelerated in the UK by the development of employment legislation over the past decade. This has had the effect of taking much of the internal conflict out of work organisations, enabling them to be dealt with at a distance by tribunals or government agencies, such as ACAS. The sea change in trade union attitudes, away from the strongly pluralistic and adversarial stances of the 1970s to the generally unitary and collaborative approaches of the 1990s, has also been an important factor. It has enabled personnel/HR practitioners to associate themselves more closely with their organisation's business aims than in the past.

18. Another key factor has been the change in the competitive environment of business organisations, where global considerations are now paramount. Competition for the manufacture of products and the provision of services can come from almost any direction nowadays. Competitors have become very significant players in a business organisation's network of relationships. Few businesses apart from tourism and bread-making are purely 'home-grown' these days, but on the contrary rely on international suppliers to an extent that greatly increases the inter-dependence of businesses and nations. Thus, suppliers also loom large in any business network and, indeed, '*outsourcing*' of services has become a fact of life for many businesses in the past decade.

THE ROLE OF PERSONNEL/HRM TODAY

19.   In the contemporary situation, the prime role of personnel/HR practitioners is that of developing the organisation's staff resources so as to enable people to make a flexible, multi-skilled contribution to the overall aims of the organisation, be it a business or in the public sector. In earlier decades it was the customer or supplier who often had to suffer in order to meet the requirements of the workforce. Rigidity in job and employment structures meant that line managers could not deploy employees to the best production advantage. Managers' relations with their workforce were based as much upon fear of upsetting them as upon respect for their skills and know-how. Nowadays this situation has changed. The customer's needs are the focus of attention today. The *external* marketplace – be it a competitive market or a public service market – is the battlefield, rather than the *internal* one of workplace relations. This shift of focus calls for a different role for personnel and HR practitioners, but always one which endeavours to procure, deploy, train and motivate people in the service of their organisation.

20.   The complex web of stakeholder relationships that make up the role-set of the personnel/HR manager in the twenty-first century are depicted in Figure 1.2. This gives an indication of the various groups of people within the organisation who can make a legitimate claim on the time, competencies and energy of the senior personnel/HR job-holder. It also indicates those external groups who can exert pressure from outside the organisation.

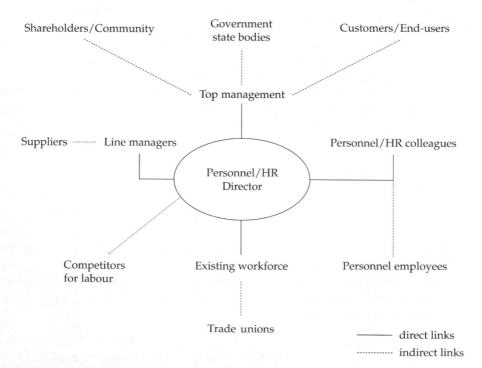

Figure 1.2   *A stakeholder view of personnel/HRM (the contemporary situation)*

21. The relative influence on the personnel/HR practitioner of each of the above relationships can be analysed under two broad categories: those that exert a *direct* influence on the job-holder, and those exerting *indirect* pressure. The directly influential are as follows:

   - *Top management* – here there is pressure on the personnel/HR practitioner to devise and implement effective human resource policies that will contribute to corporate goals, including strategies for achieving workforce flexibility and underpinning the management of change.

   - *Line managers* – the principal expectations here will be for personnel/HR support for recruitment, staff training, competitive salaries, advice on employment law, and effective personnel administration.

   - *Personnel/HR colleagues* – the senior person's own staff will have expectations of clear direction and effective leadership of the HR function, including having an interesting and demanding job, opportunities for learning and promotion, and adequate backup arrangements.

   - *Existing workforce* – the chief expectation of the organisation's employees is likely to focus on fair treatment at work, opportunities for training and development, and the effective administration of pay and conditions; where a trade union is recognised by the employer, some of these expectations will be met by means of negotiations between employer and union.

22. Those stakeholders who do not have a direct relationship with the personnel/HR director, but who nevertheless affect what the jobholder may or may not do, include:

   - *Customers/end-users* – in service industries, in particular, where employees come face to face with their customers, there are ample opportunities for the latter to experience poor levels of service; their reactions can bring great pressures to bear on those responsible for staff training and competence; customers can affirm a business's reputation, or they can destroy it; if customers go elsewhere, the very existence of the business could be in doubt; most end-users want an effective and reliable service (or product) at an attractive price, and the personnel/HR function has a key role to play in making this happen.

   - *Shareholders/the community* – in a business the shareholders will expect to see competitive outcomes from the management: a healthy balance sheet, growing revenues from sales, stable or even reducing costs, adequate profits and dividends, and a rising share value; where public services, such as health and education, are concerned the community will expect adequate public funding to ensure access to facilities and a fully satisfactory outcome.

   - *Government/state bodies* – such bodies are expected to reflect public priorities for key services, including providing adequate information about choices and performance; they may press for performance standards, seek 'league tables' of comparable providers, and stress public accountability.

   - *Trade unions* – external trade union officers have an ever-present interest in the employment conditions of organisations; they can exert pressure for the

11

recognition of a union, where there is no independent representation of employees; they have a more direct involvement in the affairs of an organisation if they have representation rights for one or more groups of employees.

- *Potential employees* – these as yet non-members of the organisation will have expectations of relevant information about the organisation, the jobs on offer, the training and promotion opportunities available, and fair treatment at interview; such matters have a direct bearing on the reputation of the employer in the labour market.

- *Competitors for labour* – this group has a close interest in the recruitment activities of others, watching for changes in pay levels, employee benefits and recruitment techniques; in a tight labour market, a competitor's actions in 'poaching' staff from another employer, or offering extra inducements to reduce staff turnover, can challenge a personnel/HR manager to improve existing arrangements, with the inevitable knock-on effect on costs.

23. In a situation where a 'hard' approach to HRM is adopted, the most influential stakeholders on the personnel/HR specialists will tend to be the customers and the shareholders. Figure 1.3 suggests that a high level of care for customers, regardless of employees' needs, will result in a stressed and unhappy workforce. In a 'softer' approach, the influence of customers will still be considerable, but is likely to be tempered by a concern for employees' needs in meeting customers' demands. Where a traditionally 'hard' view of personnel management is taken, the needs of the workforce and the requirement for management–union harmony are likely to predominate over the customers.

24. In the scenario suggested by Figure 1.3 it can be seen that a high level of concern for employees can have either disastrous or optimum outcomes for customers. Where the concern for employees is matched by the concern for customers, then it is likely that customers will get excellent service of a sustainable kind from a well-

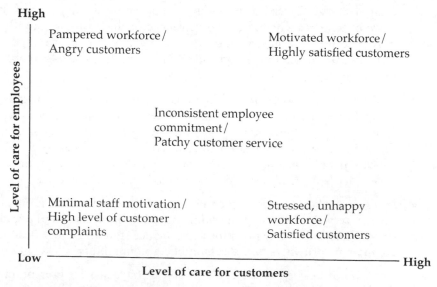

Figure 1.3 *Employees and customers – a matrix of personnel/HRM care*

motivated workforce seeking proactively to further customers' satisfaction. If there is less concern for customers than for the workforce, the result is likely to be poor or indifferent service producing a lot of angry customers! In situations where the level of concern for customers is high, but where *employees* are not cared for, then there is likely to be a good deal of 'clenched teeth' service to customers, which is only likely to be maintained in the short-term, before employee dissatisfaction boils over into customer relations. If an HRM approach does not cater for employee needs whilst asking for full commitment to excellence and customer satisfaction, then it is less likely to produce a successful outcome than an approach adopting a policy of high concern for both sets of stakeholders. The danger for traditional personnel management is that it may err on the side of employee needs at the expense of customer satisfaction, while the danger for an HRM approach is that line managers will pay inadequate attention to employee needs in their rush to satisfy their customers.

25. Other things being equal, there are always certain factors that tend to strengthen the standing of personnel/HRM, and others that tend to weaken it. These can be summarised as shown in Figure 1.4.

Strengthening factors	Weakening factors
• Political/visionary skills possessed by personnel/HR practitioners	• Inept personnel/HR practitioners
• Perceived competence of personnel/HR staff	• Personnel/HR function performing only a servicing role
• Top management support	• Lack of top management support
• Involvement in strategy-making	• Personnel/HR managers not involved in strategy process
• Ongoing need for staff development and training	• Training undertaken by line units
• Large-scale reorganisation in train	• Stable organisation with little demand for change
• Expansion of business requiring emphasis on recruitment and training	• Static business conditions
• Crisis in employee relations, especially where trade unions involved	• No challenge from workforce
• Business critically reliant on people as opposed to technology (e.g. services)	• Role of people less important than that of technical considerations

Figure 1.4 *Factor influencing standing of personnel/HRM specialists*

26. Generally speaking, personnel/HR specialists come into their own when the following conditions apply:

- they have the encouragement and support of top management

- they are fully involved in the strategy process (i.e. they become part of top management themselves)

- they are perceived as fully competent in their specialism

- there is a high level of movement of people throughout the organisation

- there is a continuing need for staff development at all levels

- the function is headed by a manager who has a good grasp of the politics of the corporate role of management, and can exploit it.

27. In historical terms the dominant role of personnel practitioners in the UK has gone through a number of changes over the last 70 years. In the 1930s the key role was that of staff welfare officer, mainly carried out by women. In the postwar years of the 1950s, the need was for recruitment specialists and manpower planners, people who could staff up the organisation. Then, in the following two decades, the role of industrial relations negotiator was called for to help counter the claims for better conditions demanded by trade unions. Often this led personnel practitioners to compromise on issues such as over-manning and demarcation in order to achieve a settlement and head off strike action. Towards the end of the twentieth century personnel practitioners were being expected to act as internal lawyers, advising their fellow managers of the requirements and implications of new employment laws, many of which arose from decisions made in the European Parliament. As we move into the new century, the specialism has acquired some of the 'harder' elements of human resource management, and is gradually shifting practitioners towards an integrating role where employees' rights and needs are dealt with in the context of the competitive situation and the perceived needs of customers.

28. What now seems to be emerging is a model of personnel/HRM as an integrator of business-wide goals, such as delivering customer satisfaction and obtaining competitive advantage, with the needs of employees for challenging work and fair conditions of employment. This new synthesis of personnel/HRM with the competitive forces at work in the organisation has gradually been developing over twenty years or more.

29. Moss Kanter (1983)[3], in a seminal work on organisational change, commented on the modernisation of the personnel system at General Motors in the 1970s, which was transformed from a series of multiple divisional systems lacking coherence and controls into 'a brand-new, state-of-the-art human-resource-management (HRM) system' headed by a vice-president and a corporate Personnel Administration and Development Unit, which both guided and worked with the line divisions on personnel matters. The HRM system referred to in this case is perhaps the optimum model, containing the best of traditional personnel management with the sharp-end focus of the line human resource activities. Moss Kanter described the GM system as

> a brilliant and innovative move. It not only developed coherence, equity, and an integrative element to personnel service, but provided a vehicle in each facility that gave line managers responsibility and accountability for personnel decisions. Furthermore there was now a mechanism for monitoring these actions and for helping people move across as well as within divisions and levels. (p. 325)

The new system employed by General Motors could be described as a 'fully supported Human Resource Management system', i.e. one where the line units supply their own personnel services, but in the context of corporate personnel policies designed and supported by personnel specialists. Such an approach would fit well with Peters' and Waterman's (1982)[4] idea of developing simultaneous 'loose-tight' controls, empowering devolved units to carry out personnel activities (see below), but within the discipline of a coherent personnel strategy and its associated policies.

30. In a survey reported by Purcell (1985)[5] there were signs of a move in large organisations towards dismantling the corporate personnel department and devolving its duties to operational levels rather along the lines of a weakly supported HRM model. This dismantling of the central personnel core has the effect of reducing personnel to a devolved servicing function. Purcell suggested that there were nevertheless a number of 'core' activities 'which could form the heart of the corporate personnel department's role'. Significantly these included references to 'corporate culture and communications'. 'If corporate philosophies are important', commented Purcell, 'it must be the personnel department's function to cultivate and disseminate them, or at least those which relate to the management of people.' Thus an emergent role for the personnel manager could be as the custodian of the corporate culture or value-system. While this would be a key strategic role for personnel, at least in respect of the organisation's values, it would probably not make much impact on the quality of day-to-day employee relations. The nature of the organisational culture is discussed further in Chapter 4 below.

31. In a similar vein to Purcell, Hunt (1984)[6], in an article in *Personnel Management*, argued that if personnel specialists were to maintain any credibility in the organisation they must associate themselves closely with the corporate image and culture of the organisation:

> ... [so as] to relate personnel practices to beliefs, to link each ... process of the recruitment, induction, training, appraisal, rewarding of individuals to an overall set of articulated beliefs of that organisation.

Personnel specialists, it can be argued, may frequently be in a key position to influence the nature of an organisation's beliefs. Their role, therefore, need not be merely to accept the status quo, but is capable of being turned to the advantage both of the organisation collectively and its employees individually.

32. The professional body for personnel managers in the UK, the Chartered Institute of Personnel and Development, in its current Code of Professional Practice (1996)[7], includes under its charitable objectives 'to establish, promote and monitor standards of competence, good practice, conduct and ethics for those engaged ... in the practice of management and development of people, for the public benefit'. The Code implies an HRM approach towards employees, and an inclination towards involvement in strategic matters, as the following extracts indicate:

> Although they often have a professional responsibility for personnel at the place of work, [human resource practitioners'] ultimate responsibility is to their employer. Where such responsibilities conflict, they may seek the advice of the Institute ...

> Along with a total commitment to the overall goals of the organisation, they need a detailed understanding of the economic, financial, political and social factors so they can play a full role in decision making ...

They must encourage self-development and seek to achieve the fullest possible development of employees in the service of present and future organisation needs ...

33. In carrying out their responsibilities, CIPD members are also expected under the Code to respect a number of standards *in relation to employees*. These include:

... maintain high standards of accuracy in the information and advice they provide to employers and employees ...

... ensure that all personnel information ... remains private ...

... must be prepared to act as counsellors to individual employees, pensioners and dependants or to refer them ... to other professionals or helping agencies ...

... maintain fair and reasonable standards in their treatment of individuals ...

Personnel professionals are also expected to 'endeavour to enhance the standing and good name of the profession'.

34. An analysis of personnel management roles undertaken by Storey (1992)[8] looked at developments in what he termed the management of human resources. He considered two major dimensions of personnel management: (1) a strategic-tactical dimension and (2) an interventionist-non-interventionist dimension. The first dimension served to highlight personnel management styles in terms of whether the approach was primarily strategic/long-term or tactical/short-term. The second dimension distinguished between interventionist/proactive and non-interventionist/ passive styles of personnel management. The resulting quadrant of dominant styles produced the following four types.

Type	Dominant style
1 *Changemakers*	Strategic and interventionist
2 *Advisers*	Strategic and non-interventionist
3 *Regulators*	Interventionist and tactical
4 *Handmaidens*	Non-interventionist and tactical

The 'changemakers' were personnel managers who saw their role as proactively helping to integrate personnel policies and practice with the dominant business needs of the organisation. 'Advisers' were those who saw their role predominantly in terms of acting as internal consultants, albeit at a strategic level. 'Regulators' were concerned to ensure that rules and procedures were set and followed, including those concerned with maintaining harmonious relations with employees and trade unions. The so-called 'handmaidens' basically saw themselves at the service of (and to a certain extent at the mercy of!) their colleagues.

35. The range of roles that can be exercised by personnel/HR practitioners depends, in the final analysis, on the following factors:

- the nature of the competitive business environment

- the nature and extent of other external factors, such as the legal framework

- the extent to which top management is prepared to involve personnel/HR practitioners in the business planning of the organisation

- the degree of professional competence and political skill possessed by the senior personnel/HR practitioners

- the way in which power and authority is dealt with in the organisation
- the extent to which change is a consistent feature of organisational life.

These factors are very similar to those we have seen in Figure 1.4 above. Ultimately, roles can only be played out in a context that is framed by the strategies and policies adopted by the senior managers of the organisation. It is to these aspects together with their operational implications that we turn in the following chapter.

REFERENCES

1. IPM (1963), 'Statement on Personnel Management and Personnel Policies', *Personnel Management*, March.

2. Ulrich, D. (1997), *Human Resource Champions: The Next Agenda for Adding Value and Delivering Results*, Harvard Business School Press

3. Moss Kanter, R. (1983), *The Change Masters*, Unwin.

4. Peters, T. and Waterman, R. (1982), *In Search of Excellence*, Harper & Row.

5. Purcell, J. (1985), 'Is Anybody Listening to the Corporate Personnel Department?', *Personnel Management*, September.

6. Hunt, J. W. (1984), 'The Shifting Focus of the Personnel Function', *Personnel Management*, February.

7. Institute of Personnel and Development (1996), *Code of Professional Conduct*, IPD.

8. Storey, J. (1992), *Developments in the Management of Human Resources*, Blackwell.

TER 2

Personnel/HRM in practice: policies, strategies and operations

INTRODUCTION

1. This chapter outlines the nature and process of policy-making and strategic planning in HRM, and summarises the areas in which operating plans flow from the strategic framework. It briefly describes typical HRM activities that might be carried out by *line* managers, and then summarises the main distinctions between all the different specialist personnel/HR roles, including their various levels of accountability. The fulfilment of these roles is what the rest of this book is about. In essence, the activities of specialist practitioners in HRM are all geared to the organisation's need for adequate investment in, and deployment of, people and their skills. This requires effective action in the following areas:

- human resource planning in the light of business goals

- recruitment and selection of employees

- facilitating the movement of employees between jobs and units (labour flexibility)

- decisions about outsourcing selected activities, or the employment of short-term contractors in key operations

- creation of a sustained learning environment throughout the organisation

- advice on competitive pay, salaries and other conditions of employment

- provision of efficient administration of routine personnel/HR matters

- advice on legal matters affecting all aspects of employment.

POLICY-MAKING IN HRM

2. Policy-making is a key part of strategic planning in an organisation. It is especially important when developing responses to key personnel/human resource management issues. What is a policy? Put simply it is a statement of intended conduct, or a rule of behaviour, which is intended to apply across the organisation. A policy is an expression of the organisation's values and beliefs concerning all the major functions of the enterprise. A policy states not *what* the organisation intends to do

(i.e. overall objectives), but the manner in which the organisation intends to achieve its objectives. A policy has to be distinguished from a strategy, which is essentially a statement of long-term objectives to be achieved, and the principal mechanisms intended to enable this. Strategic objectives provide a framework within which detailed operational plans can be made while policies provide the ethical or behavioural context of this framework.

3. Examples of personnel policies, which it will be noted are expressed in quite general terms, are as follows:

    - 'the company will conform to the spirit as well as to the letter of the law in employment matters'

    - 'all vacancies will be advertised within the organisation'

    - 'all posts will be filled on grounds of merit only, and no one will be discriminated against in terms of sex, ethnic origin, age or any factor other than ability to fulfil the job competently'

    - 'the company will always negotiate in good faith with trade union representatives'

    - 'no organisational changes will be implemented without thorough consultation with all those directly affected by them'

    - 'pay levels will be maintained so as to compete with the best in the industry'

    - 'employees will be expected to participate in training and development activities in order to develop their skills

    - 'every employee will have the right to fair treatment in matters of discipline'.

4. Policies such as the above express the organisation's long-term view of how it intends to conduct its employee relations. Once these rules of behaviour have been established, whether in written form or through custom and practice, it is possible to develop strategies that are consistent with them. Ideally, strategic goals should be measurable, but only in general terms. If they are capable of being expressed in detailed terms they are not strategic, but operational, or short-term, objectives. Personnel/human resource management strategies are the product of discussion and agreement between all the senior managers of the organisation and not just between the personnel specialists. Naturally, the first objectives to emerge will be those related to the organisation's principal business or service. Thus for any commercial enterprise the primary objectives will be concerned with identifying its markets and setting its production aims.

5. Once the essential product-market strategy has been agreed, then the personnel and other strategies can be developed. In simplified form the process can be depicted as shown in Figure 2.1. The overall purpose and policies outlined in the diagram give rise to a product-market strategy out of which all the other key strategies, including the organisation's personnel strategy, are developed. Each strategy initiates a number of short/medium-term plans which are monitored and reviewed. The results of the review process are fed back to the earlier stages of the planning process. The rest of this chapter highlights the key features of this process as applied to the personnel function.

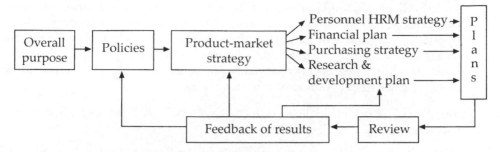

Figure 2.1 *Personnel strategy in corporate planning*

STRATEGIC GOALS FOR PERSONNEL/HRM

6. Examples of the kind of long-term goals to be found in a statement of personnel/ HR strategy include the following:

    *   ensure that the organisation's human resource needs for the next five years are met both in terms of numbers and categories of employees

    *   maintain wage and salary levels sufficient to recruit, retain and motivate staff at all levels in the organisation

    *   ensure top priority given to development of leadership skills for key personnel

    *   ensure effective training and development opportunities for all staff to improve skills and develop flexibility of roles

    *   develop effective communication systems between management and other employees and between departments and functions

    *   provide mechanisms for enabling the organisation to cope with the human consequences of change

    Such strategic goals can only be evaluated in qualitative terms. A judgement has to be made as to the degree to which a strategy is successful. This is not to say that it is not capable of being measured quantitatively in some respects. So, if the management were to assess the relative achievement of the strategy on wages and salaries it would have to make a judgement based partly on personnel statistics (labour turnover, vacancy levels, etc.) and partly on general observations and conclusions about the level of motivation of staff. The important point is that enough evidence should be obtained for the management to assess the relative achievement, or non-achievement, of a particular goal.

7. Strategic goals are stated very broadly because they are intended to express long-term aims and have to stand the test of time. As Figure. 2.2 indicates, there are considerable external influences on the way in which a personnel strategy may be implemented. These include legislative changes, actions by competitors (especially in personnel matters) and technological developments, as well as the more obvious influences such as the level of demand for the organisation's goods or services and the state of the local or national labour market.

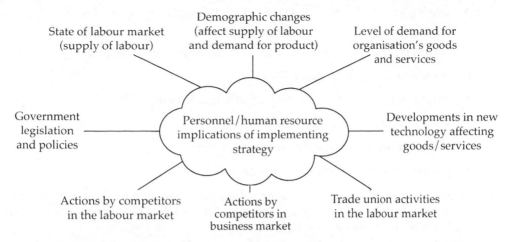

Figure 2.2 *External influences on personnel strategy*

8. Some of the alternatives that might flow from the impact of the above factors on personnel/HR strategy include the following:

- *either* buy in trained and experienced staff *or* hire inexperienced staff and train them in-house

- *either* increase numbers in line units to meet extra demand *or* contract out

- *either* increase *or* reduce the proportion of staff on part-time contracts

- *either* seek to attract skilled labour to the area (e.g. by offering subsidised housing) *or* expand production facilities by moving to a better labour-market

- *either* continue recognising one or more unions for bargaining purposes *or* revoke existing recognition agreements (with due notice).

All the above alternatives are possible responses by personnel managers to changing conditions. They can be evaluated, largely in quantitative terms, but also qualitatively. So, for example, it would be possible to assess with some accuracy the cost of increasing staff numbers or of contracting out, but would be more difficult to assess the benefits of either, especially the contracting out element.

OPERATING PLANS

9. Given personnel/HR strategies such as the above, a head of human resource could seek agreement for year-on-year operating plans designed to achieve the long-term objectives. The subject-matter of such plans appears throughout this book, and would be likely to comprise the following:

- basic human resource planning (see Chapter 11)

- recruitment planning (see Chapter 14)

- wage/salary administration (see Chapter 21)

- negotiating arrangements with employee representatives (see Chapter 35)

- establishment of adequate grievance and disciplinary procedures (see Chapter 38)

- the establishment of joint consultative machinery (see Chapter 39)

- training plans (see Chapter 28)

- management development programmes (see Chapter 32)

- health and safety arrangements (see Chapter 22)

- employee welfare arrangements (see Chapter 23)

- personnel administration (see Chapter 17).

10. Operating plans contain the detailed statements, including budgets, which set out the means by which the organisation intends to achieve its strategic objectives. Such plans are intended to produce and resource the actions that are required for intentions to be turned into reality. They typically contain references to quantity, quality, time and cost, as well as identifying those responsible for achieving the required results. They are therefore quite capable of being evaluated quantitatively as well as qualitatively.

HR ACTIVITIES IN LINE MANAGEMENT

11. Regardless of any differences of interpretation concerning personnel management and HRM, and setting aside the question of personnel roles, it is clear that any organisation whatever its size undertakes personnel/HR activities. Every person with a direct responsibility for the performance of others has a human resource function to fulfil. Much of the focus of attention in recent years has been on 'leadership', i.e. gaining the commitment of staff to the organisation's objectives at the level of the work-team. This is an important aspect of managing people, but it is not the only one. Much of the pressure nowadays comes from top management's insistence on meeting customers' needs first, and co-ordinating team efforts with that goal in mind before all else. There is also increasing pressure on managers to achieve goals with minimum staff costs. Taylor-type efficiency is the order of the day in white-collar occupations just as much as in factory situations. Also, the sheer bureaucracy involved in managing people should not be underestimated. Issues such as sexual and racial equality, health and safety at work requirements, employee rights to detailed grievance and disciplinary procedures, all combine to make modern management a more codified business than in earlier times.

12. Against this background appropriate HR policies and procedures are as important to the line manager as they are to the personnel/HR specialist. Also, as if these factors alone were not enough, there is also the matter of employee development to be considered. Team managers are nowadays expected to do their bit towards helping the organisation to grow its own talent. In a fast-changing environment, where many office processes are software based, employees increasingly have to learn by doing, and they learn with the support of their team. Team members in any case expect their managers to provide opportunities for learning and personal growth at work, especially since de-layering has removed many of the traditional

career moves once open to individuals. This is no small task for the managers concerned, who have to fulfil their human resource responsibilities in the midst of their principal operational duties.

13. Typical HRM activities that might be carried out by a line manager could include the following:

- staff selection

- induction of new staff

- training and development (especially on-the-job training)

- staff performance appraisal

- job structuring

- implementation of grievance and disciplinary machinery

- implementation and control of bonus/incentive payments

- team motivation

- establishment of adequate communication systems

- implementation of the organisation's safety policy

- planning for the effects of change on staff.

14. These are complex tasks in their own right, and they have to be undertaken in association with equally complex tasks related to all the processes required to achieve team goals – workflows, materials resourcing, computer facilities, budgeting and others. Not surprisingly, in such conditions a line manager is likely to meet his or her business goals more effectively if supported and assisted by specialists. What kind of support and assistance can personnel/HR departments provide? Much, of course, depends on the size of the department and the influence it carries within the organisation.

SPECIALIST PERSONNEL/HRM ACTIVITIES

15. The activities contributed to an organisation by its personnel/HR department can be summarised under three main headings:

- strategic activities (i.e. HR policy-making, long-term planning and innovation)

- advisory activities (i.e. assisting managers in key aspects of HR management)

- day-to-day operational activities (e.g. staff recruitment, salary administration, record-keeping, etc.)

The strategic activities may be considered as directive and creative, the advisory activities are essentially consultancy, and the operational activities provide a servicing function. Most personnel departments provide help at the operational level, but the extent of their involvement at the advisory or strategic levels depends on the stature of the department in the organisation.

PERSONNEL/HR DEPARTMENTS

16. Personnel departments usually contain three main categories of specialist staff, as follows:

   - *Personnel/HR directors/managers*, whose main role is to develop corporate personnel/HRM policy and implement it; they may also have a major responsibility for facilitating change throughout the organisation.

   - *Personnel/HR advisers/personnel officers*, who provide specialist knowledge and skills within the context of the organisation's personnel/HRM policy.

   - *Personnel/HR administrators*, whose task is to develop and maintain the procedures and routines connected with employment.

   The principal roles and activities carried out by these three categories of personnel specialist are summarised below. The assumption in each case is that the personnel specialists are working in collaboration with their line colleagues at each level of responsibility in a fully-supported HRM system. For the purpose of consistency, and to avoid unnecessary repetition, the senior positions referred to subsequently will be given an HR title, while the junior roles will continue to be termed 'personnel officers'.

HUMAN RESOURCE DIRECTORS/MANAGERS

17. Human resource directors and managers are the senior representatives of the HRM specialism in an organisation. Their principal role is to formulate, gain acceptance for, and implement agreed HRM policies and strategies. They are expected to advise senior colleagues when the latter themselves are carrying out human resource responsibilities in their own divisions or sections. In certain situations, the senior HR director may be expected to make known the views of employees, or their trade union representatives, on matters affecting their job security and other important employment matters. The manner in which the senior HR post is carried out will influence the overall reputation of the specialist function throughout the organisation. Where the senior person is seen as the architect of effective human resource management policies, or as someone able to give constructive advice in solving 'people problems', then the department's reputation will be high. Conversely, if the advice given frequently leads to further problems then the personnel/HR team's reputation will be poor. Human resource specialists often have to tread a delicate path between offering helpful, if sometimes unpopular, advice to colleagues and yet not seeming to teach them how to run their departments. Although line managers have considerably more freedom of action now than in the former industrial relations era, they still have to abide by the law of the land. Many employment issues still need to be pursued jointly with the HR staff in order to avoid tribunal or other legal actions being taken against the organisation.

HUMAN RESOURCE ADVISERS

18. An HR adviser, in the context of this book, refers to any experienced personnel professional, whose role is predominantly that of internal consultant rather than company executive. HR advisers tend to be found in such specialist aspects as employee relations, human resource planning, change management and training. The responsibilities of such advisory positions, especially in large organisations, frequently include the following:

    - the provision of relevant and up-to-date assessments of matters within their particular specialism, e.g. an employee relations adviser would be expected to give a reliable assessment of the impact on the organisation of the latest changes in employment law

    - advice on training needs, assessment of external providers, and development of outline programmes (training adviser)

    - insights into change programmes, facilitation of cross-border communications in the organisation, and preparation of proposals for planning change programmes (change management specialist)

    - assessment of internal labour requirements and of external labour market (human resource planner)

    - in each case the ability to conceptualise the organisation's business needs and tailor advice or develop programmes to meet those needs.

19. Advisers may also be found in small and medium-sized enterprises, usually on a part-time basis, since such organisations either do not need, or cannot afford, a full-time personnel/HR manager. In these instances the advisers are more likely to act as generalist practitioners rather than specialists, and their title reflects their consultancy role.

    In many of the larger organisations personnel advisers play a central role in supervising developments in their particular specialism. For example, where a management development adviser has agreed with senior management that selected younger managers should be given opportunities to engage in collaborative projects as part of their general business development, then it is usually the adviser's job to ensure that an appropriate framework is devised and the necessary procedures put into place.

PERSONNEL OFFICER

20. A personnel officer, in this book, refers to any junior or middle-ranking personnel specialist responsible for providing a range of general personnel services. These are likely to include most of the following services, which may be provided by a central personnel/HR department or jointly in conjunction with key staff from line units:

    - recruitment (including designing and placing advertisements, conducting initial interviews, short-listing, etc.)

- staff selection (interviewing, arranging terms of offers, etc.)

- staff induction (procedures, programmes, etc.)

- administration of basic terms and conditions of employment (hours of work, pay rates, etc.)

- wage and salary administration (including benefits)

- human resource planning (in close collaboration with line units)

- maintenance of staff records (including sickness absence, holiday entitlements, etc.)

- administration of disciplinary and grievance procedures

- co-ordination of relations with employee representatives (including trade unions)

- administration of redundancy and dismissal procedures

- job evaluation (including job analysis) in collaboration with the line units

- administration of welfare services.

In some cases the personnel department is also responsible for planning and implementing employee training programmes; in other cases training and development activities are delegated to a separate unit.

PERSONNEL ADMINISTRATORS

21. In a typical personnel/HR department, the most numerous staff are those engaged in administrative and clerical tasks. This is because decisions on employment matters have generally to be open to public scrutiny, and tend therefore to generate a variety of procedures and documentation, so that detailed written records are available should a dispute arise between the organisation and one or more of its employees. A relatively minor change in a company's policy on sickness pay, for example, will lead to the amendment of all the relevant documents and statements in the organisation. In cases such as the revision of an organisation's safety policy, individual copies of the revised statement may even be sent out to every employee via pay packets and salary slips. If the personnel department is responsible for administering the pay/salary system, then it is crucial that its systems are accurate and efficient.

22. Although personnel administration deals only with the routine aspects of human resourcing, it is nevertheless extremely important to user departments precisely because it takes charge of the detailed arrangements of such activities. User departments need handle only the minimum amount of paperwork, leaving personnel staff to record, amend, file and retrieve the necessary files and other information. Accuracy in recording information is paramount here, as is confidentiality in maintaining individual's records, and in this situation it is preferable to have a group of specialist staff to undertake the necessary administration. Chapter 17 provides examples of typical records handled by personnel administrators.

CHAPTER 3

International aspects of personnel/ HR management

INTRODUCTION

1. Human resource managers in a major trading nation such as the United Kingdom cannot afford to ignore the international influences on their work. For several decades, large US multinational companies have established operations here, bringing with them their own management attitudes and business styles. More recently, a number of important Japanese companies have established production and marketing operations here, and in so doing have succeeded in introducing a number of their production methods and personnel practices to the British workforce. Now they have been joined by Malaysian and Korean companies.

2. However, it is the European dimension of human resource management that is likely to have the greatest influence on UK policies over the next decade. January 1993 saw the opening of the Single European Market, which has enormous implications for the British economy, particularly for the management of business and public sector organisations. Britain's participation in the European Union (EU) means that its laws (and customs) are affected by EU laws, guidance, codes of practice and administrative decisions. Although individual countries are permitted to retain or develop certain local practices (the notion of subsidiarity), the overall intention of the underlying legislation (the Treaty of Rome) is to work towards the harmonisation of business and economic practices between all the EU nations. The key issue for every nation, and not just Britain, is how to balance local (i.e. national) wishes with acceptance of European-wide policies and practices at a time when there is increased competition in home markets as a direct result of the lifting of trade barriers in the EU. However, the overall size of the EU economy is of great benefit to its members. In 1997 the EU was the world's largest exporter, accounting for nearly 20 per cent of world exports, larger than the comparable exports of its trading partners in the USA and Japan.

3. The EU is playing a key role in changing legislation, e.g. equal opportunities, in its member states. This is because EU law takes precedence over national law on such issues. There are two main categories of output from EU legislation – (1) Articles and (2) Directives. Under EU law, an Article is directly binding on member states, e.g. Article 119, which states that men and women should receive equal pay for work of equal value, 'pay' in this context meaning not only basic pay but also any other consideration whether in cash or kind (e.g. pensions), which the employee receives. A Directive is not directly binding, but has the effect of requiring member

states to introduce their own legislation. The Equal Pay directive (75/117) was made following a complaint to the European Court that the Equal Pay Act was inadequate in its treatment of work of equal value. As a result of the Directive, amending legislation – the Equal Pay (Amendment) Regulations, 1983 – was passed by the UK Parliament in order to bring Britain into line.

4. Article 117 of the main Treaty aims to promote improved living and working conditions for workers so as to facilitate harmonisation. Discussions have particularly centred on the EU's so-called 'Social Charter', the social chapter of the as-yet unratified Maastricht Treaty, which the UK government has not fully ratified on the grounds that it is too prescriptive in certain areas, such as vocational training, employee involvement, and social benefits. Management organisations in Britain also have some reservations about the charter, especially on the issue of harmonisation of employee relations matters. The fact is that whilst there are several common problems to be faced by personnel managers in the EU (e.g. coping with greater job flexibility in production/service areas, managing employee relations in times of economic and technological change, achieving greater efficiency with smaller workforce, etc.), the solutions to them are quite varied as each country follows its own preferred pattern of handling competitiveness, productivity and employee relations, as well as social support for the unemployed, families and the elderly. In general, Britain has developed a more confrontational approach to employee relations than most of its EU partners, and has a weaker framework of state support for collective bargaining, including fewer provisions of a social security nature (e.g. family benefit, nursery provision, etc.). The emphasis in the enterprise economy has been to break down large organisational structures in favour of smaller units with delegated powers, and to encourage individual initiative and responsibility. Whilst some decentralisation has taken place in many EU countries, there is nevertheless a greater sense of partnership between governments, employers and trade unions than in the UK. Thus there are several issues on which British and other EU opinions are likely to vary.

THE SOCIAL CHARTER

5. The Social Charter includes among its aims the following:

- social aspects of the developing European Market must be accorded the same importance as the economic

- a key priority is to promote employment and combat unemployment

- the completion of the Market must offer EU citizens improvements in the social sphere, particularly in relation to freedom of movement within the EU, living and working conditions, social protection, education and training

- it is important to combat every form of social discrimination, including on grounds of race, colour and religion.

6. Within these broad aims there are several specific rights conferred on EU citizens, which are referred to shortly. There are some reservations among UK management

professions concerning the prescriptive nature of certain elements of the Charter, but also an acknowledgement that there is much in it which represents 'good practice'. Whatever the final outcome, there is no doubt but that personnel managers throughout the EU will be deeply involved in the implementation of the revised terms and conditions of employment that will be expected of their organisations. A look at some of the leading rights contained in the draft Charter will confirm this point:

1   The right to freedom of movement

- Every citizen of the EU will have the right to freedom of movement throughout the territory subject to certain restrictions relating to public order or health

- A citizen shall be able to engage in any occupation or profession on the same terms as those applied to nationals of the host country ...

2   Employment and remuneration

- All employment shall be fairly remunerated whether by law collective agreement or other practice

- A decent wage shall be established especially at the basic level

- Every individual shall have free access to public placement services ...

3   Improvement of living and working conditions

- A maximum duration of working time will be established

- Improvements should also cover seasonal, part-time and temporary workers as well as issues such as night work, shift work, etc.

- Every worker shall have the right to annual paid leave and to a weekly or other agreed rest period ...

4   Right to social protection

- All workers whatever their status, and whatever the size of their undertaking, shall enjoy adequate levels of social benefits proportional, where appropriate, to their length of service pay and personal contribution to the social security system ...

5   Freedom of association and collective bargaining

- Employers and workers shall have the right to form associations for the defence of their economic and social interests, and to have the right to join or not to join such associations

- Employers' and workers' organisations shall have the right to make collective agreements under the conditions laid down by national legislation and practice

- The right to resort to collective action in case of a dispute shall include the right to strike, subject to national regulations and collective agreements

- Appropriate levels of conciliation, mediation and arbitration procedures should be encouraged to facilitate settlements ...

6 Right to vocational training

- Every EU worker shall have the opportunity to continue his/her training during working life

- Every EU citizen shall have the right to enrol for occupational training on the same terms as nationals in the country where the course is held ...

7 Right of men and women to equal treatment

- Equal treatment for men and women shall be assured, and equal opportunities developed, especially in relation to remuneration, access to employment, social protection, education and training, and career development

- Such action shall imply the development of facilities to enable those concerned to reconcile their occupational and family obligations more easily ...

8 Right of workers to information, consultation and participation

- Information, consultation and participation for workers must be developed taking account of national laws and practices

9 Right to health protection and safety at the workplace

- Every worker must enjoy satisfactory health and safety conditions ...

10 Protection of children and adolescents

- The minimum employment age shall not be lower than the minimum school-leaving age, and, in any case, not lower than fifteen years

- Young employees must receive equitable remuneration in accordance with national practice

- The duration of work must be limited and night work prohibited for those under eighteen years

- Following the end of compulsory education, young people must receive initial vocational training of sufficient duration during working hours ...

11 Elderly persons

- Every person in retirement shall be able to enjoy a decent standard of living ...

12 Disabled persons

- All disabled persons shall be entitled to additional measures aimed at improving their social and professional integration.

7. Many of the above rights are already contained within UK law and/or collective agreements. Most are within the scope of collective bargaining between employers and employees, and could be introduced or extended by the parties concerned, but some are the prime responsibility of the Government, which must act before employers can introduce further improvements. However, it will clearly be some time before all the nations of the EU achieve parity in their provisions for people at

work. Performance in meeting the commitments of the Social Charter are monitored by the European Committee of Social Rights, which highlights shortcomings in national legislation. In a report published in February 2001, the Committee found fault with the UK's levels of maternity pay and maternity leave, both matters which the government is seeking to remedy.

FOREIGN INVESTMENT IN BRITAIN

8. There are numerous reasons why foreign companies, especially from Asia, are currently investing huge amounts of capital in the United Kingdom. Some of these are purely commercial reasons, such as developing globalisation of operations in the wake of competitors, gaining entry to the massive economic market of the European Union and taking advantage of tax incentives and other inducements offered by the authorities. Others are to do with key features of the UK's economic infrastructure, such as varied transport facilities, high-quality telecommunications systems and a first-class banking and financial services sector. However, several of the reasons are undoubtedly personnel-related:

    1   British employees have a wide range of knowledge and skills in many high-tech industries.

    2   They have shown themselves to be pragmatic, capable of making the transition between one type of industry and another, including taking advantage of retraining to develop new skills.

    3   There is a steady flow of young people leaving the nation's schools and colleges, many with sound basic IT skills and most able to learn the skills necessary for new businesses.

    4   Against the background of relatively high unemployment of recent years, employees are motivated to perform well at their jobs in order to sustain stable employment as well as to achieve a degree of satisfaction in what they do.

    5   Labour costs (i.e. wages and social costs) are relatively low compared with competitors.

    6   Employee relations are generally stable with low levels of industrial strife.

    7   Last but not least is the influence of the English language – the UK's native tongue – which has established itself as the *lingua franca* of the commercial world, and which provides a competitive edge over other European competitors, as well as enabling foreign managements to communicate comparatively easily with their British employees.

9. Inevitably, when foreigners invest huge sums of money in projects abroad they expect to be able to exert considerable influence on the way their developments are operated, whilst at the same time making the best use of local talent and attitudes as well as other resources. The projects established in the UK by Asian companies, in particular, have been of such a size that they have usually been offered so-called 'greenfield' sites, where they can build factories and offices from scratch. Personnel

systems, and other cultural aspects of organisation, can be drawn up from new. Thus, there is no history of poor employee relations and no experience of disappointments on either side. Most terms and conditions of employment, including single-union recognition, can be set out at the beginning and the arrangements for recruiting staff can include tests for trainability, for example. In this way, considerable control can be exerted over selection, which enables concepts such as job flexibility to be assumed at the outset rather than having to be negotiated later.

CULTURE DIFFERENCES BETWEEN NATIONS IN THE CONTEXT OF EMPLOYMENT

10. In a study that has become a classic in the study of cultural differences, Hofstede (1980)[1] investigated value differences between over 11,000 employees in some 40 countries employed by a single multinational company (IBM). Hofstede's study focused on the influence of *national* culture on the sub-cultures of the worldwide organisation, which he investigated by questioning and observing employees. His conclusions have shed valuable light on key cultural differences between nations in the way they conduct themselves at work. It is especially important to consider such differences when investing in a foreign country, since an awareness of others' cultural preferences provides the basis for either accepting their way of doing things, or of finding a compromise which meets everyone's basic requirements.

11. Drawing on his data, Hofstede identified four key dimensions against which to distinguish between the differing values and attitudes that emerged in each of the cultures towards work-related issues. The four dimensions can be summarised briefly as follows:

1 *Individualism versus collectivism* – i.e. where *individualism* is a national cultural attribute that favours people looking to themselves and their families as their first priority, and where *collectivism* is an attribute that favours people giving their prime loyalty to, and finding protection in, the wider group.

2 *Power distance* – i.e. the extent to which different cultures accept different distributions of power within the society; thus, a *high* power distance society accepts wide differences of power between those at the top of society and those at the bottom, while a *low* power distance society sees power as being shared much more equitably, leaving less of a power gap between the top and the bottom ranks.

3 *Uncertainty avoidance* – i.e. the extent to which a society is tolerant of uncertainty, and which therefore feels either *less* need to avoid it (*low avoidance*) or feels threatened by it (*high avoidance*).

4 *Masculinity versus femininity* – i.e. where a nation either has a tendency to prefer assertiveness and materialism (*masculinity*), or has a higher concern for relationships and the welfare of others (*femininity*).

12. When comparing the results obtained from the 40 different countries against the

criteria of the framework, Hofstede found that it was possible to categorise them to eight *'culture clusters'*, each of which had a particular profile of characteristics under the four dimensions. These clusters were labelled primarily according to geographical area (Asian, Near Eastern and Nordic) or language (Latin, Germanic and Anglo), but in some cases in terms of economic development (less developed or more developed). The clusters, which are here compared in couplets, and not with each other, can be summarised as shown in Figure. 3.1.

13.　From his research Hofstede concluded that it was *impractical to produce a unified managerial approach that could be adopted worldwide to meet the needs of individuals and groups, their structures and the requirements of change*. The conclusion to be drawn from this study is that a contingency approach to management is called for in these circumstances. This means that organisation structures, management styles, organisation cultures and change programmes have to be adapted to *the dominant cultural attributes of the host nation*. This is of major significance to multinational organisations and others that employ, or collaborate with, nationals of a foreign country. Japanese companies investing in the UK, for example, have learned to work with British managers and workers by accepting their high sense of individualism (which does not come easily to the Japanese) whilst at the same time seeking some compromise on uncertainty avoidance (where the Japanese prefer certainty). Such international collaboration may well hold important clues to future developments, as each nation's managers learn to adapt their cultural values in the light of their experience of working together.

14.　An individual who has made an important contribution to our understanding of the international dimension is Ouchi (1981)[2], who studied the characteristics of Japanese and American organisations, principally to see if selected practices from Japanese industry could be translated to the United States. Among the findings from his research, Ouchi discovered several differences in the behaviour of Japanese and American organisations, as the following list demonstrates.

Japanese organisations	American organisations
• Offer lifetime employment (Core workers only)	• Offer (generally) short-term employment
• Promote from within	• Recruit from outside
• Career paths are non-specialised	• Generally specialised career paths
• Shared decision-making	• Individual decision-making
• High degree of mutual trust/loyalty between managers and employees	• Varying degrees of trust/loyalty between managers and staff
• Importance of collective responsibility	• Individual responsibility for results
• Long-term performance appraisal	• Short-term performance more important
• Success seen in terms of co-operative efforts	• Success seen in terms of individual achievements

15.　Ouchi proposed what he called 'Theory Z' (i.e. as opposed to McGregor's Theories X and Y)[3] as a means by which American companies could imitate certain features of the Japanese approach to managing people. He argued that American firms could make changes in the following areas of human resource management:.

I – *More developed Latin*
High power distance
High uncertainty avoidance
High individualism
Medium masculinity
Belgium   France
Argentina   Brazil
          Spain
          (Italy)

II – *Less developed Latin*
High power distance
High uncertainty avoidance
Low individualism
Whole range of masculinity
Columbia   Mexico
Venezuela   Chile
          Peru
          Portugal

The principal difference between these two groups lies in their different attitudes towards individualism with the less developed nations preferring collective approaches.

III – *More developed Asian*
Medium power distance
High uncertainty avoidance
Medium individualism
High masculinity
          Japan

IV – *Less developed Asian*
High power distance
Low uncertainty avoidance
Low individualism
Medium masculinity
Pakistan   India
Taiwan   Philippines
Thailand   Singapore
Hong Kong

There are several differences between Japan and many of its Asian competitors, in particular its preference for certainty in its affairs, a lesser willingness to accept wide differences in power, and a greater assertiveness than the others.

V – *Near Eastern*
High power distance
High uncertainty avoidance
Low individualism
Medium masculinity
          Greece
          Iran
          Turkey
          (Yugoslavia)

VI – *Germanic*
Low power distance
High uncertainty avoidance
Medium individualism
High masculinity
          Austria
          Israel
          Germany
          Switzerland

Both groups here are intolerant of uncertainty, but the Germanic nations do not favour a high power differential in their organisations, and are generally more assertive.

VII – *Anglo*
Low power distance
Low–medium uncertainty avoidance
High individualism
High masculinity
Australia   New Zealand
Canada   USA
Great Britain
Ireland   (South Africa)

VIII – *Nordic*
Low power distance
Low–medium uncertainty avoidance
Medium individualism
Low masculinity
Denmark   Norway
Finland   Sweden
Netherlands

The striking features of the Anglo nations are their preference for individualism and assertiveness, which are in strong contrast to their Nordic counterparts.

Figure 3.1 *Cultural clusters arising from Hofstede's research (adapted from Hofstede 1980, p. 336)*

1   they could offer more secure employment prospects and better prospects of a career

2   they could extend employee participation in decision-making

3   they could place greater reliance on team-spirit and on recognising the contribution of individuals to team effort

4   they could encourage greater mutual respect between managers and their staff.

Such an approach would have to be supported from the top, and would require appropriate consultation measures and a substantial training commitment, especially for managers and supervisors.

16.   It should be pointed out that Ouchi's analysis was carried out at time when the Japanese economy was expanding rapidly and they could afford to employ their core workers on a permanent career basis. As the twentieth century came to its end, the Japanese economy was beginning to suffer a downturn. In August 2001 the economy was reported as suffering an unemployment rate of about 5 per cent, as major companies shed staff to reduce their costs. The electronics industry in particular has been badly hit with firms such as Hitachi, Toshiba, Fujitsu and NEC cutting thousands of jobs worldwide, including their own nationals. Not all Japanese companies are in difficulties, however. In the UK, for example, motor vehicle manufacture continues to boom, and both Honda and Toyota have expanded their production facilities in the past year.

17.   Given the difficulties of developing careers in today's business organisations, where reducing the number of job levels, as well as minimising the number of jobs is commonplace, it seems unlikely that firms can offer their employees guarantees of long-term prospects. The other three points in the above list (para 15) can be, and are being, adopted in many companies and indeed would be regarded as merely following 'good practice' by many successful British and American firms. What, perhaps, is different is that the Japanese companies concentrate on *collective* responsibility and *collaborative* effort, whilst their British and American counterparts instinctively prefer to acknowledge *individual responsibility and achievement*, even within the context of a team approach.

JAPANESE MANAGEMENT PRACTICES IN BRITAIN

18.   Despite the competitive difficulties currently being suffered by many Japanese companies, there is still much interest in the UK in their approach to human resource management. The main features of Japanese management practices in manufacturing industries that have been highlighted by foreign observers include the following:

- They offer lifetime employment (but only for core workers).

- They rely considerably on temporary workers, mostly women.

- They insist on retirement of core workers at age 55.

- They develop non-specialised career paths for core workers, and job flexibility is a key feature of this.

- Pay is based on seniority.

- Considerable attention is paid to employee selection and training.

- Collaboration and team-working are seen as essential.

- There is an egalitarian culture in which single-status predominates (at least for core workers).

- Promotion is invariably from within the workforce.

- Employees are only able to join the company union.

- Meticulous attention to production planning and quality.

- Importance of customer requirements is seen as paramount.

All these features take place against a background of loyalty to the company, and identification with its products and its ultimate success – in other words a strong adherence to company culture.

19.   Some of the above practices have been incorporated into the personnel policies of Japanese companies that have established production units in Britain, and appear to have worked. The principal features of employment conditions in Japanese-owned companies such as Toshiba, Nissan and Toyota that have factories in Britain are as follows:

- Each company will only grant recognition (with full negotiating rights) to one union – admittedly an independent trade union not a company union. Toyota Motor Manufacturing (UK) Ltd recognises the AUEE as the sole trade union. This union was formed following a merger of the principal unions representing engineering and electrical workers.

- Terms and conditions of collective agreements are held to be binding on both sides.

- There is a 'no-strike' clause in procedure agreements.

- In the case of a dispute which cannot be resolved internally, there is resort to 'pendulum arbitration' by an external arbitrator who has to decide in favour of one side or the other (see Chapter 37).

- Single status applies – i.e. all employees are staff, receive annual salaries and share the same facilities.

- Selection is rigorous and training is thorough (e.g. new recruits sent to Japan for part of their basic induction and job training).

- Employees expected to accept complete job flexibility once trained.

- Full participation in company as well as shop-floor decisions expected as well as encouraged by management.

- Overall sense of teamwork and commitment to company business goals encouraged.

- Great attention paid to quality of work and efficiency of systems.

20. Japanese firms investing in Britain over the past decade benefited from a situation where investment in manufacturing was low, unemployment was high, and generous government grants were available to investors. Employees were motivated to use their latent skills and seek employment in the new state-of-the-art factories that were being established. Being free of the combative, and often unproductive, culture of British industrial relations was also an important factor. British workers adapted smoothly to the Japanese way of doing things to produce high quality products, be those electronic goods, motor vehicles or pharmaceuticals. The efficient paternalism of Japanese companies is not always sufficient to quell British workers' sense of independence, however. The Honda car plant at Swindon only recently recognised a trade union after sixteen years in the UK, following a successful ballot of its workforce after the AEEU (engineering and electrical union) won the right to test employee opinion on the subject.

21. In the final analysis, the effects of Japanese approaches to human resource management have been beneficial to Britain. They have provided a stimulus to changed employment attitudes, as well as practices, in the UK. This has been consolidated by the adoption of a range of other management practices aimed at achieving more effective outcomes from organisations composed of flatter structures with greater responsibility resting on grass-roots team leaders. Changes in UK employment law have also helped to improve the industrial climate, whilst the ever-present possibility of unemployment casts its shadow over the whole situation.

REFERENCES

1   Hofstede, G. (1980), *Culture's Consequences: International Differences in Work-related Values*, Sage Publications.

2   Ouchi, W. (1981), *Theory Z: How American Business can meet the Japanese Challenge*, Addison Wesley.

3   McGregor, D. (1960), *The Human Side of Enterprise*, McGraw-Hill.

QUESTIONS FOR DISCUSSION/HOMEWORK

1. To what extent is it possible, or even desirable, to distinguish *personnel management* from *human resource management (HRM)*?

2. In what specific ways might line managers/supervisors be said to engage in HRM activities?

3. Why are personnel/HRM policies important? For whom do they provide the greatest benefit?

4. In a typical industrial or commercial situation, which stakeholders tend to exert the greatest influence over the personnel/HR department?

5.   What external and internal factors might be considered as enhancing the status of personnel/HR specialists in an organisation?

6.   How might the roles of personnel/HR specialists in the public sector (local or central government) differ from those of colleagues working in the commercial sector?

7.   In what ways might foreign investors be said to be benefiting now from the massive changes in much of British industry over the last twenty years?

8.   What human resources issues are likely to be the focus of problems of adjustment when Japanese companies are set up in Anglo nations? How can such issues be overcome?

EXAMINATION QUESTIONS

EQ1   Discuss the effects of social change on a company's personnel policies.

(ABE)

EQ2   Bearing in mind the view that it has been said 'personnel management is largely a collection of incidental techniques without much internal cohesion', discuss the role of personnel management in the catering industry.

(HCIMA)

EQ3   At the annual conference of the Institute of Personnel Management, Sir Michael Edwardes claimed that a good chief executive would welcome 'a more robust approach' from the personnel function. Why do you think he made that remark, and what would be entailed in practical terms (in your judgement) by 'a more robust approach'?

(ICSA)

CASE STUDY 1: LION OFFICE SYSTEMS PLC

BACKGROUND:

Lion Office Systems is a small but growing business in office machinery and services. It has been formed over the years by acquisition and merger, but is now intent on consolidating rather than expanding its present base. Some 165 employees work in the three divisions and at head office. The numbers employed at each site are indicated on the organisation chart opposite. The head office is located in North London in premises which are shared with the Office Machinery and Microcomputer Division. The Office Supplies Division is located in a town some 10 miles north of London, while the Printing Division is located in Essex.

The firm is organised on a divisional basis as follows:

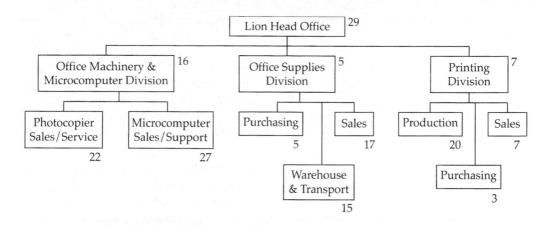

STAFFING

The company is staffed as follows:

- Head Office: Managing director, Finance director, Administration manager, Personnel manager (just appointed) and 25 admin/clerical staff.

- Office Machinery/Microcomputer Division: Divisional director plus 15 specialist and admin staff; 22 staff in photocopying department (sales office, representatives & service engineers); 27 staff in microcomputer department (sales office, representatives & technical support staff).

- Office Supplies Division: Divisional manager plus 4 admin staff; 5 staff in purchasing; 17 in sales (incl. 2 representatives); and 15 warehouse staff (incl. 4 drivers).

- Printing Division: Divisional manager plus 6 clerical/admin staff; 20 production staff (printing, binding etc.); 7 sales staff (incl. 1 representative); and 3 purchasing staff.

BUSINESS AND PERSONNEL CLIMATE

The state of business and employee relations in each of the firm's main units are as follows:

- Head Office: in an effort to achieve greater integration of the total business, the directors have increased the role of head office in developing financial and administrative procedures applicable throughout the organisation. The Personnel function has been strengthened by the appointment of a full-time Personnel Manager, whose task will be to introduce uniform procedures on key matters such as pay, disciplinary and grievance matters and manpower returns. The admin/clerical staff are mostly local people, and turnover is very low. Salaries are competitive without being generous.

- Office Machinery, etc., Division: photocopier sales/servicing are maintaining their market position, but at an increasing cost to the company. Salaries are moderate, although commission for sales staff can be attractive. Admin/clerical staff are paid at competitive rates. Turnover is low among the latter, but higher among the representatives and the service engineers. The Microcomputer sales department is still expanding in terms of sales, and commission rates are good. Office sales salaries are modest. Although morale seems high, there is nevertheless a relatively high level of turnover of representatives and technical support staff, most of whom are young, ambitious and highly marketable in a very competitive market.

- Office Supplies Division: business is expanding for consumable office supplies, and the company has increased its market share in the London area. Wages and salaries are lower than in the other divisions, but staff turnover is quite low, except on the sales side. The warehouse and transport employees are all members of the General Workers' Union.

- Printing Division: business is just being maintained in the face of fierce competition from High Street franchise operations. Wages on the production side are high in comparison with other sections of the company, but average in sales and purchasing. The workforce is very stable and the employees are generally older than in other divisions. The machinery in use is modern. All employees are in their appropriate union.

CURRENT STRATEGY

Key strategic targets include:

- increase the competitiveness of every division.

- speed up the introduction of computerised systems

- reduce costs in relation to sales/output by necessary restructuring, even if this means compulsory redundancies.

QUESTIONS

1. What personnel problem are likely to face the newly appointed Personnel Manager during the next few months?

2. What immediate operational aspects of personnel management would you select as being the most urgent for the Personnel Manager? Explain why.

3. Taking a longer-term view, say over the next 1–2 years, what aspects of personnel management should receive the Personnel Manager's special attention, and why?

4. How much authority should the Personnel Manager be given by the directors, and how do you think this authority should be exercised?

PART II

THE ORGANISATIONAL CONTEXT

The purpose of the seven chapters in this part is to describe the organisational context in which personnel management activities take place. Chapter 4 introduces the reader to important features of organisations (purpose, people, tasks, technology, culture and environment) and outlines some of the theories that have been proposed to make sense of the interrelationships between these various features. Chapter 5 follows with an introduction to the task structure of organisations and considers some of the alternative choices available.

Chapters 6, 7 and 8 provide an outline of major issues and theories in the closely related areas of leadership, groups and motivation. Chapter 9 deals with the design of jobs, and Chapter 10 examines organisational change.

CHAPTER 4

Organisations, cultures and perspectives

INTRODUCTION

1. The context of personnel management is the work place, which is strongly influenced by the nature of the host organisation – its overall purpose, its structure, the people it employs, its work processes and technology, and above all its culture, or dominant values. This chapter looks at the meaning of the word '*organisation*' and considers some of the important issues that have been identified by leading theorists of organisational behaviour, especially that of organisation culture.

THE MEANING OF ORGANISATION

2. The word '*organisation*' can be used in a number of different ways. For our purposes, the most important distinction to make is between the use of the word 'organisation' to mean the process of ordering and co-ordinating activities (e.g. drawing up detailed arrangements for a recruitment programme), and 'organisation' to denote a social entity formed by a group of people. In this chapter we are concerned only with the latter meaning.

3. There is no widely accepted definition of the term 'organisation' as applied to a social entity. The variety of positions that can be taken are indicated in the following quotations of leading writers on organisations:

    > Organisations are intricate human strategies designed to achieve certain objectives. (Argyris, 1960)[1]

    > Since organisations are systems of behaviour designed to enable humans and their machines to accomplish goals, organisational form must be a joint function of human characteristics and the nature of the task environment. (Simon, 1960)[2]

    > ...organisations are complex and paradoxical phenomena that can be understood in many different ways. Many of our taken-for-granted ideas about organisations are metaphorical ... by using different metaphors to understand the complex and paradoxical character of organisational life, we are able to manage and design organisations in ways that we may not have thought possible before. (Morgan, 1986)[3]

4. What can be said here is that there is only limited agreement as to the major

components of an organisation but, in terms of work organisations, the basic components are likely to be the following:

- they have a purpose, or *raison d'être*

- they are composed of people

- they have a degree of structure

- they utilise technology

- they operate in the context of an external environment

- they develop their own dominant value-system, or culture.

5. These six components are interrelated, so that change in any one has repercussions on the others. The interrelationships are shown in diagrammatic form in Figure 4.1:

Figure 4.1 *Basic components of an organisation*

6. The basic model can be enhanced to include a number of sub-components, which will be considered in this and subsequent chapters throughout the book. These sub-components, under their appropriate headings, are as follows:

1   Purpose/Goals

- mission statements

- organisation policies

- organisation strategies.

2   People

- knowledge, skills and competencies

- different perceptions and meanings

- in groups and as individuals.

3   Technology

- machines (office, factory, etc.)

- information processing.

4 Structure

- corporate structure (e.g. functions/divisions, etc.)

- task structure

- roles allocated,

5 Culture

- dominant organisation values

- management style

- sub-cultures (e.g. R&D, Marketing, etc.).

6 Environment

- social, political, technological, market and economic pressures

7. Some aspects of the first component – purpose/goals – have been mentioned already in Chapter 2 (e.g. personnel strategy). There have also been references to environmental issues in Chapter 3 (e.g. impact on personnel of foreign investment). Culture has already been mentioned in the context of differing national attitudes towards behaviour in organisations and will be referred to again later in this chapter. Most of the other components of organisations will be discussed in subsequent chapters. First, however, it may be useful to summarise very briefly some of the key ideas about organisations expressed by theorists over the past century. Most of the theories of organisation are concerned with the *formal*, that is the officially recognised, organisation established by the senior management to achieve organisational objectives. The formal organisation has to be distinguished from the *informal* organisation, which is any grouping formed by individuals for their own sectional or social purposes. In this book the context of personnel management will be taken primarily as the formal organisation, while recognising the influence of informal organisational groupings.

ORGANISATION THEORISTS

8. The overwhelming majority of organisation theorists subscribe to the view that some degree of structure is an essential part of every organisation. The arguments between the different theorists thus tend to devolve around the extent to which structure either is present, or should be present. In the industrial period between the two World Wars, the dominant figures of organisation theory were mostly practical managers whose approach to the management of organisations was a prescriptive one, based on practical experience. The essence of their theories was that organisational effectiveness depended on having a suitable structure of jobs and relationships. These theorist-managers have been called the 'Scientific Management School', or the Classical School. Typical exponents of these theories were F.W. Taylor, Henri Fayol, and L.F. Urwick.

9. After the Second World War, an alternative approach appeared. This approach focused on attention to people as a way of improving organisational effectiveness, and was based not on personal experience but on observation, i.e. on social research. The theorists adopting this approach have been labelled the Human Relations School or Social Psychological School. Typical exponents have been Elton Mayo, D. McGregor and F. Herzberg.

10. The Social Psychologists remained supreme for some 30 years before their theories were significantly modified by the ideas of the so-called Systems Theorists, whose research-based theories showed that what was actually happening in organisations was the result not only of peoples' needs and structural issues, but of a combination of these and the effects of technology and environment.

11. The most recent approaches to organisation theory tend to prefer a contingency view, that is to say they take several organisational variables into account, but especially environment and culture, in deciding what might be the most appropriate form for an organisation in the light of circumstances. Exponents of the Contingency approach include Lawrence and Lorsch, the Aston School and Henry Mintzberg.

SUMMARY OF ORGANISATION THEORISTS

12. A summary chart of the leading theorists of organisation over the last 50 years or so is given below. References will be made to most of these theorists in the course of the next few chapters. For those who wish to follow up the ideas of particular theorists, there is a bibliography at the end of this chapter.

Theorist	Dates (or key text)	Dominant Viewpoint
Henri Fayol[4]	1841–1925	Rational, structured approach to management of organisations.
F.W. Taylor[5]	1856–1917	The measurement and control of jobs by 'scientific management'.
Frank & Lilian Gilbreth[6]	1868–1924	The use of Method Study to find the one best way of doing a job.
L.F. Urwick[7]	(1947)	Achieving the most efficient form of organisation structure by the adoption of certain 'principles'.
E.F.L. Brech[8]	(1946)	A combination of Fayol and Urwick.
Max Weber[9]	1864–1920	Organisational efficiency by means of a 'rational-legal' system of authority, i.e. 'bureaucracy'.
Elton Mayo[10]	1880–1949	Social needs at work are as important as economic and physical needs.
Joan Woodward[11]	1916–1971	Technology, and the technical demands of production make a significant impact on organisational choice.
Abraham Maslow[12]	(1954)	People are primarily motivated by a range of needs arranged in an ascending hierarchy.

Douglas McGregor[13]	1906–1964	Underlying managerial behaviour are two basic sets of assumptions: Theory X – people need to be coerced and controlled to perform; Theory Y – people can be self-directing and self-motivating.
F. Herzberg[14]	(1959)	People need to find motivating factors in their jobs if they are to experience job-satisfaction.
Victor Vroom[15]	(1964)	People will be motivated to the extent that they can perceive links between effort, performance and rewards available.
Tavistock Group[16, 17]	1946–	Organisations are socio-technical systems interacting with their external environment.
The Aston Group[18]	1967–1974	Factors such as size, technology, location and type of ownership affect the structure of organisations.
Lawrence & Lorsch[19]	(1967)	Different states of differentiation (specialisation and attitudes) and integration (quality of collaboration) produce different possibilities of success in achieving economic objectives.
Mintzberg[20]	(1979)	Organisational choice can be reduced to *five* major structural forces in the light of certain contingency and other factors.

ORGANISATION CULTURE

13. The expression 'culture', when applied to organisations, has come to mean the predominant system of beliefs and values held in an organisation by its members. Schein (1985)[21] defines 'culture' as follows:

> ... a pattern of basic assumptions – invented, discovered, or developed by a given group as it learns to cope with its problems of external adaptation and internal integration – that has worked well enough to be considered valid and, therefore, to be taught to new members as the correct way to perceive, think, and feel in relation to those problems.

A key feature of Schein's definition is its focus on assumptions, that is on *implicit* behaviour, rather than on *explicit* or overt behaviour. He also stresses that culture is learned as a result of experience and suggests that it can be changed if we know the dynamics of the learning process.

14. It is probably useful to consider 'culture' as a two-tier set of shared values, norms and beliefs within an organisation. On the surface is the *explicit culture*, which manifests itself in the way management itself is structured and in the rhetoric of bulletins, notices, etc. Beneath the surface lies an *implicit culture*, probably closer to reality, which resides in the assumptions made by management and staff about what really *is* important. The point can be illustrated in the following examples.

1   An organisation can claim to be an Equal Opportunities Employer in its literature, advice to staff and in its job advertisements (*explicit* culture), and yet in reality women and racial minorities fail consistently to get promotion and men are rarely considered for posts typically held by women (cashiers,

secretaries, etc.). In this case, the *implicit* culture predominates over the explicit and public culture.

2   A retail organisation might announce improvements to customer service at all levels and revise relevant procedures (*explicit* culture). However, it is not prepared to spend time and money on what it considers as backup activities, such as staff training (*implicit* culture), and therefore much of what it offers in the way of improvements is likely to be cosmetic.

15.   A strong culture is one where the implicit and explicit assumptions are in harmony. A weak culture is one where the implicit and explicit dimensions are at odds with each other. The whole point of cultural change strategies is to achieve harmonisation between the two tiers. Schein (*op.cit.*) makes the interesting point that 'The function of culture in the life of the group changes as a group matures.' He adopts the idea of a culture life-cycle in discussing how culture changes. As he puts it: 'The forces that can unfreeze a given culture are also likely to be different at different stages of organisational development . . .'.

His view is that organisations pass through three major periods of this life-cycle:

- *birth and early growth* followed by a *succession phase*

- *organisational mid-life*

- *organisational maturity* followed by an alternative between *transformation* or *destruction*.

16.   At each major period the culture has a different function to perform. For example, at the birth stage culture is 'the "glue" that holds the organisation together'; at the succession stage, culture becomes the 'battleground between conservatives and liberals'; at organisational mid-life the dominant culture begins to weaken, providing an opportunity for change; at organisational maturity culture 'becomes a constraint on innovation'. After the maturity stage, culture can be transformed in an evolutionary way, or can be destroyed and completely replaced 'through a massive replacement of key people'.

PERSPECTIVES ON ORGANISATIONS

17.   The culture of an organisation may often spring primarily from the assumptions and attitudes of its owners or directors. Farnham (1984)[22] suggests that organisations can be typified in terms of two key parameters: their capital ownership (public or private) and their orientation (profit/revenue or welfare). This produces the model shown in Figure 4.2.

18.   A rather different, and much more theoretical, analysis of organisations has been conducted by Burrell & Morgan (1979)[23] who suggest that there are two key dimensions to assumptions about organisations and what they stand for. These dimensions are as follows:

1   subjective reality *versus* objective reality

2   regulation of status quo *versus* radical change.

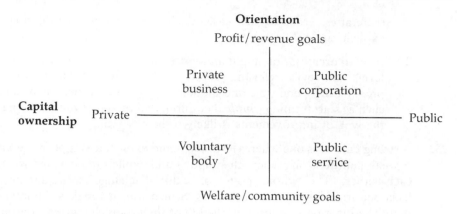

Figure. 4.2 *Organisation types by ownership and orientation*

The authors conclude that people's perspective on organisations, including the values and assumptions they hold, depends considerably on the position they take on these two dimensions. Burrell and Morgan explain their dimensions as follows:

Subjective dimension	Reality is the product of one's mind.
	Things are relative.
	People are free.
Objective dimension	Reality is 'out there' in the world.
	Things can be true or false.
	People are creatures of their environment.
Regulation dimension	The emphasis is placed on the status quo.
	Stability, social order and integration are preferred.
Radical change	The emphasis here is on structural conflict, disintegration and alienation.

19. Their explanations are treated from a sociological perspective, and are thus more suitable as a study for students of sociology than of personnel management. However, in the theoretical model that they derive from the above dimensions, what they term the *functionalist perspective* is the nearest to most of the organisation theories advanced in management textbooks. The *functionalist perspective* on organisations spans the objective dimension and regulation and regards organisations as essentially stable social systems that can be examined and measured so that social affairs can be explained rationally. Burrell and Morgan point out that:

> Whilst superficially there appears to be a dazzling array of different kinds of theory and research, in point of fact the subject tends to be very narrowly founded indeed. ... Most [theories] are located within the context of ... the functionalist paradigm [conceptual standpoint].

20. The principal assumptions of functionalist theories of organisation are (1) that organisations are objective phenomena existing in their own right, (2) that they are capable of being analysed, and (3) they require stability, equilibrium and order. This book adopts a functionalist perspective throughout, for in the final analysis personnel and human resource management are basically about practical issues of maintaining equilibrium and controlling change.

21. It is appropriate, therefore, to end this chapter with a consideration of some of the choices and implications of the key components of organisations mentioned in Figure 4.1 above. Each of the key elements that were noted gives rise to a number of alternative decisions and value positions at corporate level and/or has implications for courses of action by management. The list in Figure 4.3 provides examples of both the range of choices available to decision-makers and the possible implications for managerial decisions.

Organisational feature:	Choices available/alternative scenarios	Implications for
Purpose/goals	• Profit/Growth • Non profit-making • Social service • Voluntary service	Policy-making Strategy
People	• Trained professional • Skilled craftsmen • Unskilled/untrained personnel • Predominantly manual • Predominantly white-collar staff	Motivation Individual effectiveness Leadership Team-working
Structure	• Tall or flat • Centralised or decentralised • Hierarchical or organic • Matrix	Communication Promotion prospects Decision making Efficiency Motivation
Technology	• High or low-level machine technology • High or low-level information technology • No technology	Organisation design strategy Knowledge/skills required Productivity
Environment	• Turbulent/changing • Stable/relatively unchanging	Success (however measured) Organisation change
Values/culture	• Financial success • Product quality/reliability • Production or people orientation • Market-orientation • Efficiency • Scientific research • Self-sufficiency • Altruism	Reputation Policy-making Planning Organisation design Collaboration Motivation Management style Decision-making

Figure 4.3 *Organisational choices*

REFERENCES

1. Argyris, C. (1960), *Understanding Organisational Behaviour*, Tavistock.

2. Simon, H.A. (1960), *Administrative Behaviour*, Macmillan.

3. Morgan, G. (1986), *Images of Organisation*, Sage.

4. Fayol, H. (1949), *General and Industrial Management*, Pitman.

5. Taylor, F.W. (1947), *Scientific Management*, Harper & Row.

6. Gilbreth, F.B. & L.M. (1917), *Applied Motion Study*, Sturgis & Walton.

7. Urwick, L.F. (1947) *The Elements of Administration*, Pitman.

8. Brech, E.F.L. (1946) *Management: its Nature and Significance*, Pitman.

9. Weber, M. (1947) *Theory of Social and Economic Organisation*, Free Press.

10. Mayo, E. (1933) *The Human Problems of an Industrial Civilisation*, Macmillan.

11. Woodward, J. (1965) *Industrial Organisation: Theory and Practice*, OUP.

12. Maslow, A. (1954) *Motivation and Personality*, Harper & Row.

13. McGregor, D. (1960) *The Human Side of Enterprise,* McGraw-Hill.

14. Herzberg, F. (1966) *Work and the Nature of Man*, World Publishing.

15. Vroom, V. (1964) *Work and Motivation*, Wiley.

16. Trist, E. *et al* (1963) *Organisational Choice*, Tavistock.

17. Rice, A.K. (1963) *The Enterprise and its Environment*, Tavistock.

18. Pugh, D.S. *et al* (1968) *Dimensions of Organisational Structure*, Administrative Science Quarterly.

19. Lawrence, J. & Lorsch, P.(1967) *Organisation and Environment*, Harvard UP.

20. Mintzberg, H (1983) *Structure in Fives: Designing Effective Organisations*, Prentice Hall.

21. Schein, D. (1985), *Organisation Culture and Leadership*, Jossey Bass.

22. Farnham, D. (1984) *Personnel in Context*, IPM.

23. Burrell, G. & Morgan, G. (1979) *Sociological Paradigms and Organisational Analysis*, Heinemann.

CHAPTER 5

Organisation structures

INTRODUCTION

1. As mentioned in the previous chapter, structure is a key element in the nature of organisations. Indeed, the classical management theorists saw it as *the* key to organisational effectiveness. The modern view, as exemplified by the contingency approach, does not give structure the same degree of prominence as the classical theorists, but nevertheless accepts that it is one of the principal variables to be considered when designing organisations. Issues of structure are not only important for theorists, but also for practitioners. This chapter examines some of the alternative structures available to managers in their search for the most appropriate means of harnessing their resources to achieve the objectives of the enterprise.

ORGANISATION DESIGN

2. Child (1977)[1], writing about organisations and their structures comments:

    The design of its organisation is one of management's major priorities. This entails creating a structure which suits the need of the particular enterprise or institution, achieving consistency between the various aspects of the structure, and adapting it over time to changing circumstances.

    There are several points that can be made from these comments. Firstly, organisations are designed by managers, and this implies that structures will reflect *managerial* intentions and values, rather than those of other stakeholders in the enterprise (employees, customers, etc.). Secondly, the structures that are created are primarily there to promote *corporate* interests rather than individual or sub-group interests. Thirdly, no structure can be considered as permanent, and must be adaptable in the light of changes brought about by external circumstances.

3. Generally speaking, before designing an appropriate structure, managers have to ask themselves a number of basic questions. For example:

    *   What is the best basis for dividing up the work? By specialist function? By product? By geography?

    *   How much specialisation should be encouraged? How closely should individual tasks be defined in relation to other tasks?

    *   How much standardisation of procedures should be encouraged?

- How much discretion (freedom to act) should be permitted to individuals?

- What is the best way to achieve co-ordination and integration across the specialisms?

There are no simple answers to such questions. Each set of circumstances produces its own constraints and opportunities for the designers of organisations. Ultimately managements have to exercise their judgement as to the best configuration for their particular situation.

4.   Apart from the very small business in which the owner-manager controls all the major functions (marketing, production, etc.), most organisations, whether commercial, public sector or voluntary, require some degree of specialisation, or differentiation, of functions. Specialisation breaks down the overall purpose of the organisation into manageable functions, shared out amongst the senior members of the organisation. Specialisation is essentially a disintegrating process, and when joined with processes of co-ordination and integration produces a constant source of tension in the organisation.

5.   Specialisation is effected initially by the grouping of key activities, and subsequently defining tasks, which are clustered together and allocated to individuals as jobs. Specialisation is usually achieved on the basis of one or more of the following factors:

1   common function (e.g. production, accounting, personnel)

2   product, or service

3   geographical location.

Examples of structures that enable specialisation to be achieved in one or more of these ways are given later in the chapter. They include hybrid versions such as divisional and matrix structures.

ORGANISATION STRUCTURES

6.   Mintzberg (1979)[2] has made a major contribution to ideas about organisation structure, based on intensive studies of the research literature on organisations. He sets his ideas out in four basic parts, in which he identifies the following underpinning features of organisation structure:

1   *The foundations of organisation* – these are (1) the basic parts, (2) the co-ordinating mechanisms and (3) the system of flows.

2   *Design parameters* – these are:

- job specialisation

- behaviour formulation

- training and indoctrination

- unit grouping

- unit size

- planning and control systems

- liaison devices

- *vertical* decentralisation

- *horizontal* decentralisation.

3   *Contingency factors* – Mintzberg identifies four factors which consistently feature in considerations of structure, which are as follows:

- age and size

- technical system

- environment

- power.

4   *Structural configurations* – Mintzberg sees five alternative configurations, which he describes as follows:

- simple structure

- machine bureaucracy

- professional bureaucracy

- divisionalised form

- adhocracy.

7.   The foundations of an organisation, according to Mintzberg, comprise firstly the basic parts of the organisation, which he identifies as follows:

- *the strategic apex* – i.e. the directors, chief executive and staff

- *the middle line* – i.e. the operational/ line managers

- *the operating core* – i.e. the operators and other direct staff

- *the technostructure* – i.e. the specialist staff (including Personnel)

- *support staff* – i.e. those who provide direct services to the line.

The foundations also include the co-ordinating mechanisms and what he terms the system of flows, both of which are explained below.

8.   Mintzberg concludes that there are five principal co-ordinating mechanisms that organisations used in operating their structures, as follows:

1   *Mutual adjustment,* which 'achieves the co-ordination of work by the simple process of informal communication' (e.g. as in 'organic' systems).

2   *Direct supervision,* where co-ordination is achieved by 'having one individual take responsibility for the work of others' (e.g. as emphasised by the classical management theorists).

3   *Standardisation of work processes,* where co-ordination is built-in to the

various work activities by specifications, set procedures, programmes, etc. (i.e. essentially a 'scientific management' idea).

4   *Standardisation of work outputs*, where co-ordination is achieved by means of output targets and specifications (e.g. as in Management by Objectives).

5   *Standardisation of worker skills*, where co-ordination is achieved by training staff in specified knowledge and skills.

9.   Mintzberg argues that a simple organisation can achieve co-ordination largely through mutual adjustment, but as the organisation increases in size, a higher degree of specialisation is required, and then direct supervision is necessary to facilitate co-ordination. With increasing complexity of operations, direct supervision is not enough, thus standardisation is required, first of work processes, then of outputs, and where neither of these is practicable then the employees themselves must be standardised through their training. Mintzberg suggests that organisations mostly achieve co-ordination by employing several of the five mechanisms.

10. His description of the system of flows in an organisation focuses on:

- *flows of authority* – i.e. the allocation of formal authority throughout the management structure

- *flows of work material* – i.e. the regulated flow of work materials in a production process

- *flows of information* – a central feature of organisational life; these are primarily flows of formal communication, but include important elements of informal methods

- *decision processes* – every organisation is itself a system of decision flows.

11. Of Mintzberg's nine design parameters (see para 6) some are more or less universal, but one or two need further comment. *Behaviour formulation*, for example, refers to the standardisation of work roles, content and rules. The overall effect is to regulate human behaviour. *Training and indoctrination* is concerned with (1) the required level of knowledge and skill sought by the organisation (i.e. obtained by prior training or in-company provision), and (2) the process by which organisational norms (i.e. 'culture') are acquired by employees (what Mintzberg calls 'indoctrination'). The intention is to ensure the internalisation of appropriate behaviours by the workforce. *Liaison devices* are a range of integrating devices including specific liaison posts, task forces, committees and matrix organisation. *Decentralisation* refers to the extent of devolution of *power to make decisions*. Devolution down the chain of line authority is called *vertical decentralisation*, while devolution to specialists in the technostructure and support services is called *horizontal decentralisation*.

12. The first two of the contingency factors identified by Mintzberg can be elaborated as follows.

Age and size of organisation – these affect organisation structure in a number of ways. Older and larger organisations, for example, tend to be more formalised than younger and smaller organisations. Organisations tend to change their structure with age and size, and this change is rarely smooth, usually creating disruption.

Technical system – this can be seen from two perspectives: first, a *regulation dimension* (e.g. technical controls over operators); second, a *sophistication dimension* (i.e. technical complexity). When the technical system is highly regulated, operating work becomes more formalised and the structure becomes bureaucratic. When the technical system is sophisticated, the administrative structure increases, there is an increased dependence on liaison devices and an increased tendency to decentralise authority. The technical system has its greatest impact on the operating core of the organisation.

13. Age, size and the technical system are all internal factors. The *environment*, however, represents the external world of the organisation. Mintzberg sees four principal characteristics of environments as follows:

    1 *stability*, ranging from stable to dynamic/unpredictable

    2 *complexity*, ranging from simple to complex (i.e. sophisticated)

    3 *market diversity*, ranging from integrated (i.e. single product/single customer) to diversified (i.e. multiple products/global market)

    4 *hostility*, ranging from munificent (i.e. benevolent) to hostile (i.e. competitive/unpredictable/requiring rapid response).

    Mintzberg comments that 'it is not the environment per se that counts, but its specific impact on the organisation's ability to cope with it ... '.

14. The contingency factor of *power* is seen by Mintzberg as an issue of control by groups and individuals. Attempts to control important decision-making outcomes arise, according to Mintzberg, from three main sources:

    1 *outside groups*, such as shareholders, owners, parent organisations and governments

    2 *members of the organisation*, notably top, middle line and specialist managers

    3 *social/cultural norms*, that is to say fashions and trends in the external environment.

15. The general effect of the first source is to 'concentrate decision-making power at the top of the organisational hierarchy and to encourage greater than usual reliance on rules and regulations for internal control'. When such outside groups seek control over the organisation, the outcome is a structure that is centralised and formalised, i.e. bureaucratic. The justification of such control is '*accountability*', i.e. the chief executive is accountable to the parent company, the owners, or the taxpayer etc. The effect of the second source, in the case of top management and senior line managers, is to encourage centralisation. The effect when originating in the technostructure or support areas is to encourage *decentralisation*, i.e. to draw power *away* from the line. The third source – social and cultural trends outside the organisation – may cause firms to adopt an inappropriate structure in their haste to keep up with competitors. Mintzberg concludes that the impact of power as a contingency factor is to 'exert significant influence on the design of organisational structure, sometimes encouraging organisations to adopt structures that the contingency factors of age, size, technical system, and environment deem inappropriate'.

16.   The conclusion to Mintzberg's research on organisation structures is the
      production of a set of five clusters, or configurations, that can serve as focal
      points for the study of organisations. The five configurations reduce the separate
      influences of the design parameters, contingency factors and other key organis-
      ational features into manageable concepts that can be used in studying
      organisations. In Mintzberg's own words

> In each structural configuration, a different one of the co-ordinating mechanisms is
> dominant, a different part of the organisation plays the most important role, and a
> different type of decentralisation is used.

The five configurations – in highly summarised form – are as shown in Figure 5.1.

Configuration	Prime co-ordinating mechanism	Key part of organisation	Main design parameters	Contingency factors
1. *Simple structure ('non-structure')*	Direct supervision	Strategic apex	Centralisation Organic	Age: young Technical: simple Environment: simple/dynamic
2. *Machine bureaucracy*	Standardisation of work processes	Techno-structure	Behaviour formalisation Specialisation Centralisation	Age: old Size: large Technical: simple and regulated Environment: stable/external control
3. *Professional bureaucracy*	Standardisation of skills	Operating core	Training Horizontal specialisation Decentralisation	Environment: complex Technical: simple, non-regulated
4. *Divisionalised form*	Standardisation of outputs	Middle line	Unit grouping (markets) Performance control	Environment: diversified markets Age: old: Size: large Power: middle managers
5. *Adhocracy*	Mutual adjustment	Support staff Operating core	Liaison devices Organic Unit grouping (functional/ markets)	Age: young Technical: automated Environment: complex/dynamic

Figure 5.1   *Mintzberg's five structural configurations*

17.   The choice of configuration made by an organisation's senior management has
      considerable implications for a wide range of personnel and human resource
      management activities, especially recruitment, staff selection, employee motivation
      and all aspects of training and development.

SPECIALISATION BY COMMON FUNCTION

18. By far the commonest method of specialisation is to allocate activities and responsibilities on the basis of common function, as illustrated in Figure 5.2. Thus, all production matters are unified under a production manager, and all personnel matters become the prime responsibility of a personnel manager. What functional specialisation does is to give all staff from top to bottom the opportunity to devote their energies to ensuring the success of their own functional group. While this enables the development of experience and the encouragement of expertise, it also carries within it the seeds of conflict between one functional group and another. A feature of functional specialisation is that line relationships (i.e. where direct authority is exercised over employees) not only derive from the operational management chain but also from the functional management chain. Senior functional managers usually have qualified authority over staff in the line operations, in respect of their functional duties, as well as full authority over their own staff. Functional authority does not apply so readily to managers of *service* functions, such as payroll, security, etc. (who are in effect support staff). Functional grouping often provides better career and promotion opportunities than other structural forms, but is less adaptable in meeting the challenge of product diversification or geographical dispersion, for example.

Figure 5.2 *Functional Organisation Structure*

19. The main advantages of a functional organisation structure are as follows:

1 staff are grouped according to their technical or specialist expertise

2 the use and deployment of such staff is facilitated

3 career and promotion paths are created

4 control of functional activities is more or less centralised.

The main disadvantages are:

1   functional specialisms tend to encourage the development of sectional interests which may become at odds with corporate intentions

2   it is difficult to adapt this form of organisation so as to reduce reliance on strong central functions and encourage lateral links between them.

SPECIALISATION BY PRODUCT OR SERVICE

20.   Where grouping is arranged around specified products or services, each group has its own specialist functions provided at the operational level. This leads to a situation where the specialist function such as personnel or finance will tend to have less power over events on the shopfloor or at the point of sale. For example, in Figure 5.3 below, taken from the pharmaceutical industry, the Divisional Personnel Manager is directly responsible to a Divisional Manager, but at the same time has a 'dotted-line' relationship to the Personnel Director. This means that he is accountable for his day-to-day actions to the divisional Manager, but is accountable for his discharge of Company personnel policy to his Personnel Director. This dual responsibility may well cause some tensions within the job, since his two senior managers will almost certainly take a different view of the role required to be fulfilled in the job.

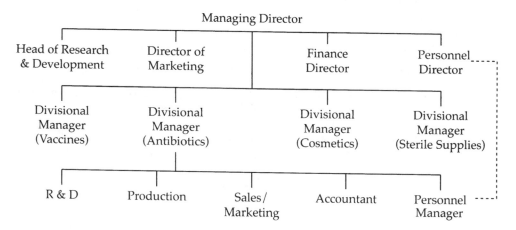

Figure 5.3   *Product-based structure*

21.   The above organisation chart shows a structure in which the 'line' activities, i.e. the principal production activities, are organised on a product-grouping basis. Each product division pursues its objectives with a full team of functional specialists, which serves its line interests first rather than the company's corporate interests. The company's corporate interests are handled by senior functional specialists at director level. These directors ensure that a framework of policies and strategies is established within which the product divisions can operate. Such a structure gives

line managers a powerful position in the organisation since four of them report directly to the chief executive.

22.   The advantages of a product-based structure are:

1   it enables the company's major product-groups to concentrate on their own priorities, within the total business plan

2   it provides a mechanism for supplying the major groupings in the company with their own specialist resources

3   it enables the major groupings to develop their own preferred culture

4   it encourages the senior specialists at director level to focus on corporate issues, leaving production matters within product-groups much more in the hands of the senior line-managers concerned.

The main disadvantage of this kind of structure is that individual divisions may seek to promote their own objectives so forcefully as to endanger wider, corporate strategies. Thus, the senior directors need to be capable of exercising sufficient control over corporate intentions, but without robbing the line managers of their motivation to obtain the optimum results for their divisions.

GEOGRAPHICALLY-BASED STRUCTURE

23.   A division of work on the basis of geographical location is common among organisations providing goods or services over a wide area. Transport and retail are two industries where geographically based structures are to be found. In such industries individual operating units – depots or shops – are grouped together on a regional basis and supplied with specialist support as necessary from a regional office. An example of this form of structure can be taken from a large haulage company (Figure 5.4).

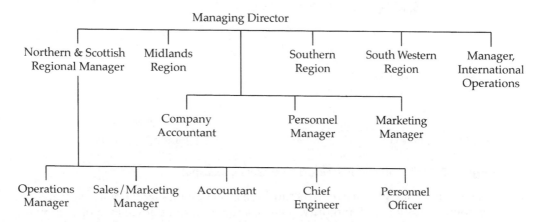

Figure 5.4   *Regional structure in road transport*

24. The chief advantages of this form of structure are:

    1 widely-spread markets can be catered for

    2 local knowledge of customers, the labour market and routes can be utilised

    3 the provision of a service at the point of delivery is better controlled on a geographical basis than on a centralised basis.

    The disadvantages, as with any attempt to provide decentralisation, are associated with the inevitable tension that develops between 'Head Office' and the Regions concerning priorities for action and priorities for scarce company resources.

MATRIX STRUCTURES

25. These are relatively new types of structure, which have come about as a result of co-ordination problems in highly complex industries such as aerospace, where the functional and product types of structure have not been able to meet the demands of the variety of activities and relationships created by the work. A matrix structure usually combines a functional form of structure with a project-based structure. Thus, for the purpose of a two-year project, for example, one project manager co-ordinates, and is accountable for, the work to be undertaken by the project team, and he is the person who deals with the client. However, although reporting to his own line manager, he is functionally involved with one or more functional managers, depending on the complexity of the project. The functional managers provide technical expertise and organisational stability. The project manager provides the leadership required to steer the project through during its relatively temporary lifetime. An example of a matrix structure is shown in Figure 5.5.

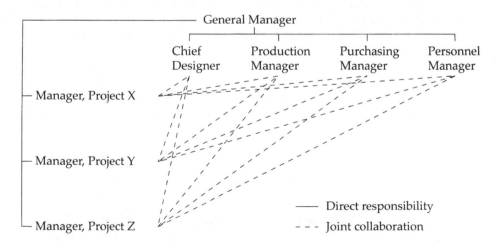

Figure 5.5 *Typical matrix structure (engineering industry)*

26. The main feature of a matrix structure is that it combines lateral with vertical lines of communication and authority. This has the important advantage of combining the relative stability and efficiency of an hierarchical structure with the flexibility

and informality of an organic form of structure. A matrix form focusses on the requirements of the project group, which is in direct contact with the client. It helps to clarify who is responsible for the success of the project. It encourages functional managers to understand their contributive role in the organisation's productive efforts, and thus offsets one of the principal disadvantages of the purely functional form, i.e. individual empire-building by the functional heads. However, like all organisational forms, matrix structures do have their disadvantages. The most important are:

1   the potential conflicts that can arise concerning the allocation of resources and the division of authority as between project groups and functional specialists

2   the relative dilution of functional management responsibilities throughout the organisation

3   the possibility of divided loyalties on the part of members of project teams in relation to their own manager and their functional superiors.

Despite these disadvantages, the matrix form probably offers us the best answer to date to the issue of handling the tension between the need to differentiate and the need to integrate the complex activities of modern organisations.

CENTRALISATION AND DECENTRALISATION

27.   The inevitable push towards specialisation in all but the smallest of organisations leads to the diffusion of accountability. The need to structure activities develops logically into the need to allocate appropriate amounts of authority to those responsible for undertaking those activities. As we have seen in the organisation charts in this chapter, the issues are as much about power and authority as they are of grouping activities and deploying key roles. Thus, every organisation of any size has to consider how much authority to delegate from the centre, or the top. Only the small entrepreneurial organisation can sustain what Handy calls the 'power culture' where effective authority is firmly retained at the centre. Most organisations have to decide how, and how much, to delegate to managers and others throughout their total operation.

28.   The concept of decentralisation, as it is being considered here, is not referring to the physical dispersal of an organisation, but to the organization's authority to commit the organisation's resources. The *physical* deployment of an organisation may or may not reflect genuine power-sharing. In our definition, therefore, a highly decentralised organisation is one in which the authority to commit people, money and materials is widely diffused throughout every level of the structure. Conversely, a highly centralised organisation is one where little authority is exercised outside a key group of senior managers. In practice, some functions are more easily decentralised than others. Production and marketing/sales functions are more amenable to extensive delegation than planning and R & D, for example. So, even highly decentralised organisations usually reserve certain key functions to the centre. As well as planning and research, it is usually the finance and personnel functions that are least decentralised.

29.   The advantages of decentralisation are chiefly:

1   it prevents top-management overload by freeing them from many potential decisions and enabling them to concentrate on their strategic responsibilities

2   it speeds up operational decisions by enabling line units to take actions without reference back all the time

3   it enables local management to be flexible in their approach to decisions in the light of local conditions, and thus be more adaptable in situations of rapid change

4   it focuses attention on to important cost and profit-centres within the total organisation, which sharpens management awareness of cost-effectiveness as well as revenue targets

5   it can contribute to staff motivation by enabling middle and junior management to get a taste of responsibility, and by generally encouraging the use of initiative by all employees.

30.   The main disadvantages of decentralisation are:

1   it requires an adequate control and communication system if major errors of judgement are to be avoided on the part of operational management

2   it requires greater co-ordination by senior management to ensure that individual units in the organisation are not working against the interests of the whole

3   it can lead to inconsistency of treatment of customers, clients or public, especially in service industries

4   it may encourage parochial attitudes in subsidiary units, who may be inclined to look more to their own needs than to those of colleagues in the organisation

5   it requires a plentiful supply of capable and well-motivated managers, able to respond to the increased responsibility that decentralisation brings about.

31.   On balance, the advantages outweigh the disadvantages, but this is principally because of the enormous pressures on modern business organisations to concede more and more authority to staff at executive and specialist levels. Ultimately, all organisations have to live with the conflicting forces of central control on the one hand, and delegated responsibility on the other. Some companies and institutions prefer the bias to be towards centralised direction and control; others prefer loose central direction and strong devolvement of decision-making and action. On balance, the larger and more complex the organisation, the more likely it will incorporate strong central functions. Very small businesses also exercise tight control from the centre through their owner-managers. Only highly-professional groups such as business consultancies, accountancy firms and legal practices will generally tend to be highly decentralised within a broadly-agreed framework of company policy.

JOBS AND WORK-ROLES

32. The basic unit of any organisation structure is a job. Taken at its simplest level a job is a collection of tasks assigned to a position in an organisation structure. In bureaucratic organisations, tasks are assigned to a position more or less regardless of the job-holder's particular strengths and weaknesses. In less bureaucratic organisations, jobs will tend to be varied in accordance with the strengths and weaknesses, and sometimes even the personal preferences, of the job-holder. Junior jobs tend to be more rigidly defined than senior jobs, where the job-holders are expected to exercise their own discretion in fulfilling their duties.

33. The allocation of tasks to a job may be a rational exercise, based on 'natural' groupings of activities or, on the basis of convenience. In the latter situation, it is possible for individuals to be saddled with a job which chafes them at every possible point. There is a good deal of research evidence to suggest that people prefer not only a variety of tasks, but also a comfortable variety. An illogical or downright conflicting set of tasks can only lead to frustration and stress on the part of the job-holder. A major element of any work design programme (see Chapter 9) is to assemble tasks into an acceptable job for an individual, as well as to ensure that work-objectives are attained efficiently.

34. Jobs, however established, are subjected to various forms of analysis in organisations. Individual tasks may be analysed for the purposes of improving efficiency, analysing training needs and reallocating work, for example. Whole jobs may be analysed to identify key tasks, measure relative importance and provide a basis for organisational change. Some jobs are explicitly described in job descriptions, others are intuitive understandings made between different people in the organisation. Whether written or unwritten, however, there has to be some agreement in any organisation about how to deal with apparent overlaps of tasks or duties, and, more importantly still, to minimise situations where no-one is apparently responsible for certain tasks.

These issues will be looked at in greater detail in the next part of the book, and especially in Chapter 12.

35. It has been said above that a job is basically a collection of tasks. This, however, represents a somewhat narrow view, since it focuses only on the *action* required of the job-holder. Tasks imply action, but jobs imply more than just action. Jobs imply results and duties. A job description (see Chapter 12) invariably includes references to the overall purpose and principal responsibilities of a job as well as to particular tasks that need to be performed. However, even a comprehensively described job description does not entirely match the reality of a particular situation, for the job description only sets out what the job-holder is expected to perform. It usually says nothing about how the job is to be performed, that is to say it does not shed any light on the role required of the job-holder. The job-holder's *role* consists of all the expectations that various people, the job-holder included, have concerning the manner in which the job should be carried out. So, for example, a personnel officer in a factory may see his or her primary function as acting as a legal adviser to line management, whereas the personnel director sees the role in terms of preventing conflict with the unions, and the line managers see

the role primarily in terms of the provision of an efficient recruitment service. An individual in such a post would be unfortunate indeed! The degree of role conflict could prove to be very stressful.

36. Job descriptions represent the letter of the law, so to speak, whereas roles represent the spirit of the law. Both need to be taken into account when planning organisation structures.

REFERENCES

1. Child, J. (1977), *Organisation*, Harper & Row.

2. Mintzberg, H. (1979), *The Structuring of Organisations – a Synthesis of the Research*, Prentice Hall.

CHAPTER 6

Leadership in organisations

INTRODUCTION

1.   Leadership is a vital element in the social relationships of groups at work. Groups need leaders and leaders need followers. This chapter outlines some of the major contributions to the theory of leadership, and indicates some of the practical implications of theories that have been developed.

LEADERSHIP

2.   Leadership is a concept that many people have written about but few have defined. However, a working definition is suggested as follows:

> Leadership is a dynamic process at work in a group whereby one individual over a particular period of time, and in a particular organisational context, influences the other group members to commit themselves freely to the achievement of group tasks or goals.

3.   This working definition encompasses several important features of leadership:

   1   Leadership is a dynamic process, influenced by the changing requirements of the task, the group itself and the individual members. The implication of this is that there is no 'one best way' of leading, and leaders need to be able to exercise a *range* of behaviour to maintain their role effectively.

   2   Leadership is not necessarily confined to one person, but may be shared between members. Usually, an appointed leader (e.g. manager) is nominally in charge of a group, but he or she may not always be the leader in practice. Some leaders are mere figureheads, and Mintzberg (1973)[1] specifically sees this function as a bona fide management role. The significant point is that whoever exercises influence is the leader.

   3   The leader's principal role is to influence the group towards the achievement of group goals. In an official group, such as a production team, goals are set mainly, if not exclusively, by senior management. In an informal (unofficial) group, composed of people who have got together as friends and workmates, group goals are much more likely to be agreed on a consensus basis. Either way, the leader's task is to gain the group's commitment to these goals.

   4   Leadership is exercised in, and influenced by, the particular set of circumstances which form the organisational context. This context, as Fiedler

(1967)[2] points out, has important implications for the degree of power possessed by the leader.

4. Research studies conducted over the last 30 years have suggested that there are at least four key variables which are crucial in any analysis of leadership. These are:

    1 the attributes (knowledge, skill, attitudes) of the leader

    2 the nature of the task or goal

    3 the nature of the group or team

    4 the climate, or culture, of the organisation.

    As the following diagram suggests (Figure 6.1), each of the four variables is closely related to its neighbours.

Figure 6.1 *Key leadership variables*

5. The most recent researches suggest that a contingency approach to leadership is likely to achieve the most productive balance between the needs of the team, the requirements of the task, the nature of the organisation climate and the pressures exerted by the situation or context. A contingency approach is one where the leader adapts his or her behaviour to suit the needs of the situation. Clearly, such a view makes leadership somewhat problematic in practice. How many people are capable of this kind of flexibility? We shall return to this point later in the chapter on Management Development (Chapter 32). In the meantime, we shall look at each of the key variables in more detail, commencing with the attributes of the leader.

LEADER ATTRIBUTES

6. The earliest studies of leadership focused on the personal qualities, or traits, of leaders. The thinking behind this approach was that the secret of leadership lies in some innate 'qualities of leadership' possessed by selected members of society. Indeed, since most of the leading early exponents of 'management' such as Henri Fayol and Frederick Taylor were themselves lively personalities as well as successful entrepreneurs, it is not surprising that personal qualities were the focus of attention. It is true that personal qualities – or 'charisma' – can play a part in the exercise of leadership. Nevertheless, the so-called 'trait theories' of leadership produced such varied accounts of the key characteristics that Handy

$(1976)^3$ mentions that by 1950 over 100 studies into leadership qualities could only find common features in about 5 per cent of the cases studied.

7. Adair $(1968)^4$ quotes lists of leadership qualities supplied by various military groups. Three groups of examples are shown below (Figure 6.2). As can be seen, the differences are more noteworthy than the similarities!

US Marine Corps	Royal Naval College	RAF College
Integrity	Faith	Efficiency
Knowledge	Courage	Energy
Courage	Loyalty	Sympathy
Decisiveness	Sense of duty	Resolution
Dependability	Integrity	Courage
Tact	Humanity	etc
etc	etc	

Figure 6.2 *Leadership qualities (adapted from Adair, 1968)*

The inevitable conclusion is that charismatic leadership, founded on inborn traits or qualities, is no basis for any feasible theory of leadership. It is altogether too rare and exclusive.

8. Although trait theories are largely discredited as an instrument of leadership theory, the qualities approach can have some useful applications in management training and development. For example, Pedler, Burgoyne & Boydell $(1978)^5$ describe a list of attributes which were found to be possessed by successful managers and not possessed by less successful managers. Their idea of success, and their use of the list of key qualities is discussed later in the chapter on Management Development (Chapter 31).

STYLE THEORIES

9. Since the 1950s, much of the study of leadership has centred on the behaviour, or style, of the leader. If leadership is not so much about personal attributes, the argument goes, then perhaps it is about the way in which the leader exercises leadership? The 'Style Theorists', as they have been called, were influenced by an earlier study by Lewin, Lippitt & White $(1939)^6$ in which the effects of three different styles of leadership on the performance of groups in a boys' camp were studied. It was found that in terms of both goals achieved and member satisfaction, a democratic style was preferred to autocratic or laissez-faire styles. The Style Theorists have taken dimensions such as autocratic – democratic and employee-centre – task-centred in order to test ideas about leadership style and leadership effectiveness. We shall consider the meaning of leadership effectiveness first, and then go on to outline some of the classic leadership studies into leadership style.

10. Leadership effectiveness, or 'success', refers to performance that leads to:

    1 the achievement of organisational goals

    2 a high degree of commitment to those goals by the group

    3 a high level of group member satisfaction.

    Reddin (1970)[7], in a discussion on managerial effectiveness distinguishes three types of effectiveness:

    1 *Apparent effectiveness* – i.e. the extent to which the manager gives the appearance of being effective by maintaining a high input into the job, but where, in reality, his or her achievements are disappointing.

    2 *Personal effectiveness* – i.e. the extent to which the manager achieves his or her own objectives, as opposed to those of the organisation.

    3 *Leader effectiveness* – i.e. the extent to which the leader influences his or her followers to achieve group objectives.

11. The concepts of leadership that we are concerned with in this chapter are those associated with leader effectiveness, as defined by Reddin. That is to say, they are concerned with the results of leadership rather than the inputs; they are concerned with the achievement of organisational rather than personal goals, and they are intimately concerned with the relationships between the leader and his or her group. The way in which the leader approaches the task and people needs of the situation is commonly referred to as 'leadership style'. There have been several well-known studies into styles of leadership and these are summarised briefly below.

THE MICHIGAN STUDIES

12. In a series of studies carried out in the early 1950s, Rensis Likert and his colleagues studied the behaviour of supervisors of both high- and low-producing groups. The object was to see if they could identify any significant pointers to optimum leadership style. The researchers observed that supervisors of high-producing groups tended to be employee-centred in their approach. That is they paid considerable attention to relationships within the group, exercised less direct supervision, and encouraged participation in decision-making. By comparison, supervisors of low-producing groups tended to be more directive in their behaviour, and appeared to be more concerned with the demands of the task than the needs of people in their groups.

13. It appeared to the researchers that the two different approaches represented two alternative orientations along a single continuum. Thus, a supervisor was either employee-centred or task-centred (see Figure 6.3).

    The members of the groups concerned clearly preferred working under a leader who was employee-centred. This preference was an important factor in the nature of the groups themselves.

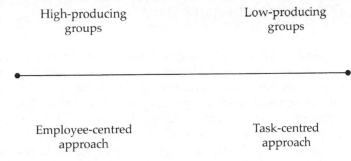

Figure 6.3   *The Michigan continuum*

THE OHIO STUDIES

14.   These were also conducted in the early 1950s, but from a slightly different perspective from the Michigan studies. The basis of the Ohio researches (Stogdill & Coons, 1957)[8] was a Leader Behaviour Description Questionnaire of some 150 items. When the responses to this questionnaire were analysed, two distinct behaviour patterns emerged – one emphasised employee relationships and feelings, and was termed 'Consideration' by the researchers; the other emphasised the organisation of the task, and was termed 'Initiating Structure'. The analysis also suggested that, unlike the Michigan conclusions, the two approaches represented *separate* dimensions. That is to say, people could be scored both on Consideration and on Initiating Structure (see Figure 6.4).

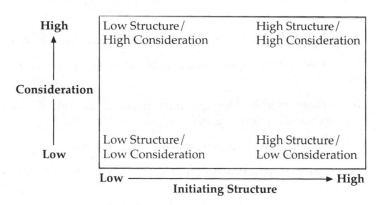

Figure 6.4   *The Ohio matrix*

The researches found that employee satisfaction was greatest under leaders who were rated high on Consideration. However, the context had a bearing on responses, since military groups tended to discount Consideration in favour of Initiating structure.

MCGREGOR AND LEADERSHIP

15. Douglas McGregor (1960)[9], reflecting on leadership and motivation at work, took the available literature on organisations and examined contemporary managerial policy and practice. His conclusions were that there were two contrasting sets of assumptions about people underlying managerial attitudes and behaviour. He gave these two sets of assumptions the deliberately neutral labels of 'Theory X' and 'Theory Y'. McGregor's achievement lay in drawing attention to two contrasting types of managerial attitude. The assumptions embodied in the two approaches are explained below.

16. Theory X assumptions are as follows:

1   The average human being has an inherent dislike of work and will avoid it if he or she can.

2   Therefore, people must be coerced, controlled, directed and threatened with punishment to get them to put in adequate effort.

3   The average human being prefers to be directed, wishes to avoid responsibility, and has little ambition, wanting security above all.

These are the assumptions of Scientific Management. They have much in common with the task-centred behaviour described in the Michigan Studies and the Initiating Structure approach described by the Ohio researchers. In 1960 McGregor saw them as 'predominant throughout our (USA) economy'. It might be said with some justification that the situation has not altered very much since then, given the numerous controls to which most employees, managers included, are subject.

17. In contrast to Theory X are the assumptions of Theory Y. These are that:

1   The expenditure of physical and mental effort at work is as natural as play or rest.

2   The average person does not only respond to controls and threats, but exercises self-direction and self-control.

3   Effort can produce intrinsic rewards for individuals

4   Under proper conditions people not only accept but actively seek responsibility.

5   People are able to exercise imagination, ingenuity and creativity in the solution of organisational problems.

Theory Y assumptions are those of the humanist-manager, who takes an optimistic view of people's attitudes and skills. These assumptions have much in common with Consideration and employee-centred approaches to leadership.

18. McGregor's views represented his personal commentary on the world around him. They were not the results of research. They have been applied to managerial practices rather than to further the ends of research work. The biggest single disadvantage of Theory X and Theory Y is that they are put forward as competing

sets of assumptions – a manager is either motivated by Theory X or by Theory Y. Yet, recent studies (e.g. by contingency theorists) suggest that Theory Y is not necessarily an enlightened alternative to a dismal Theory X. Both sets of assumptions may be valid, depending on the circumstances of the situation.

RENSIS LIKERT

19. Another model of managerial behaviour has been devised by Rensis Likert on the basis of his researches and reading. This distinguishes four categories of management styles, which he calls System 1 to System 4. They are described as follows:

System 1 – Exploitive-authoritative.
This is where power and direction come from the top downwards, where threats and punishment are employed, where communication is poor and teamwork non-existent. Productivity is mediocre.

System 2 – Benevolent-authoritative.
Similar to System 1, but allows some opportunities for consultation and delegation. Productivity is fair to good, but at the cost of considerable absenteeism and labour turnover.

System 3 – Consultative.
Goals are set or orders issued after discussion with subordinates. Communication is both upwards and downwards, and some teamwork is encouraged. Rewards are preferred to threats. Productivity is good.

System 4 – Participative.
This is the ideal system. The keynote is participation, leading to commitment to organisational goals. Communication is good and higher-level needs are catered for. Productivity is excellent.

20. All four systems are a variation on the task-centred versus employee-centred approach of the Michigan and Ohio studies. Another related model is that put forward by Blake & Mouton (1978)[10] and originally called The Managerial Grid. This model is more appropriately discussed under management development (see Chapter 32).

TANNENBAUM AND SCHMIDT

21. These two academics, in an influential article (1958)[11] proposed a continuum of leadership styles, as shown in the diagram (Figure 6.5).

Like several of their contemporaries they used two polarised dimensions. In this case Authoritarian versus Democratic. However, their model is considerably more flexible than many others. It demonstrates that managers have a choice in selecting a leadership style. They acknowledge that this choice is affected by 'forces', of which they identify three – the manager himself, his subordinates and the situation.

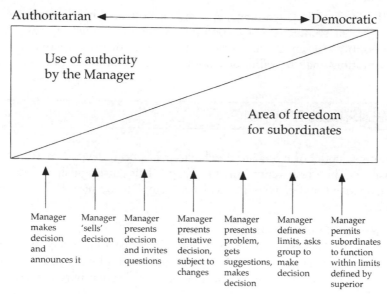

Authoritarian ◄───────────────► Democratic

Use of authority
by the Manager

Area of freedom
for subordinates

| Manager makes decision and announces it | Manager 'sells' decision | Manager presents decision and invites questions | Manager presents tentative decision, subject to changes | Manager presents problem, gets suggestions, makes decision | Manager defines limits, asks group to make decision | Manager permits subordinates to function within limits defined by superior |

Figure 6.5 *A continuum of leadership styles*

They recommend a flexible style depending on the manager's perception of the strength of the three forces.

22.   The continuum has been utilised for management development purposes as a useful way of getting managers to think about flexibility of style. A simplified version of the continuum that is often used for such training purposes is shown in Figure 6.6.

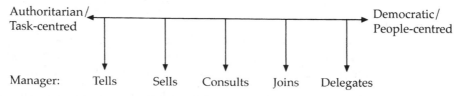

Authoritarian/ ◄──────────────────► Democratic/
Task-centred   People-centred

Manager: Tells   Sells   Consults   Joins   Delegates

Figure 6.6 *A range of management styles*

The work of Tannenbaum and Schmidt helped to promote further research into situational variables, much of which has been labelled the 'contingency approach" to leadership. Basically, a contingency approach is one that sees leadership as a *relative* process, i.e. 'good' leadership is whatever is appropriate for the situation.

CONTINGENCY THEORIES

23.   The so-called 'Contingency Theorists' of leadership have broken away from the strait-jacket of one or two-dimensional models of leadership behaviour to explore a wider range of variables. The first theorist to use the expression 'contingency' was Fiedler (1967)[2], whose important contribution to leadership theory will be summarised below.

24. *F.E. Fiedler.* On the basis of his researches, Fiedler came to the conclusion that group performance was contingent upon (dependent upon) the leader adopting an appropriate style in the light of the relative favourableness of the situation According to Fiedler, favourableness depended on three key variables:

    1   leader-member relations

    2   the degree of structure in the task, and

    3   the power and authority of the position.

    Fiedler found that these three variables could produce eight possible combinations of situations. The most favourable of these was when:

    1   there were good leader-member relations

    2   the task was highly-structured, and

    3   the leader had strong position power.

    The least favourable situation was when:

    1   the leader was disliked

    2   the task was relatively unstructured, and

    3   the leader had little position power.

25. By isolating position power as a key variable, Fiedler introduced an important element into the situational aspect of leadership, and his ideas have stimulated a number of further research studies. As Handy (1976) comments: 'No leadership style, no process, no motivation principle, can work in an impossible situation'. He suggests that more effort needs to be expended on identifying what he calls the 'givens' in the leadership situation. The 'givens' are the short-term constraints that cannot be changed in the immediate situation. Handy sees them as follows:

    1   the nature of the group (size, composition, etc.)

    2   the nature of the task (type of task, performance standards, etc.)

    3   the environment (organisation norms, leader position, etc.).

26. Another model of leadership which takes a contingency perspective is Adair's (1973)[12] concept of Functional, or Action-centred, Leadership. As Figure 6.7 shows, Adair sees three main variables at work in the leadership situation. These are: task needs, group needs and individual needs. Like the earlier American studies, Adair takes 'task' and 'people' to be the most important factors, but makes the distinction between people in groups and people as individual team members.

27. Adair suggests that providing adequate leadership means creating the right balance between the three sets of needs in the light of the total situation. The circumstances of each situation determine the priority that the leader needs to allocate to each of the three variables. An effective leader is one who sees this priority and who acts on it. For example, in a situation of great danger an airline captain must consider the safety of his passengers before all else. In a minor emergency, he must also pay attention to preventing damage to the aircraft as well. In a quite different situation, such as building up a team of Antarctic explorers, the leader's emphasis will be on

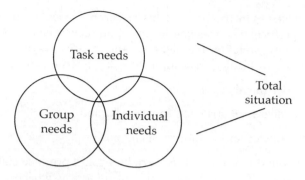

Fig. 6.7 *Functional leadership model*

team-building and attention to individual needs. The model thus encourages a flexible approach to leadership.

28. Task functions, according to Adair, can include setting objectives for the group, planning tasks, allocating responsibilities and setting standards of performance. Group maintenance functions can include team-building, communication, group motivation and disciplinary activities. Another important function is to act as spokesman for the group in its relations with others. Individual maintenance functions include coaching, counselling and motivation. Adair's model has been useful as a management training device because of its emphasis on skills development in leadership.

LEADERSHIP AND ORGANISATION CULTURE

29. Handy (1976)[13] develops the idea of the environmental element in leadership. He sees six key aspects in this:

   1 the power position of the leader

   2 the relationship between the leader and the group

   3 organisational norms (i.e. culture)

   4 structure and technology of the organisation

   5 the variety of tasks

   6 the variety of subordinates.

   In Handy's view, leadership is basically a question of achieving the 'best fit' between the leader's personal attributes, the expectations and needs of the subordinates, the needs of the task, and the environment in which the events take place.

30. Handy is particularly interesting on the topic of organisational culture – 'the deep-set beliefs about the way work should be organised, the way authority should be exercised, people rewarded, people controlled.' He describes four possible cultures, which can be summarised as follows:

Role culture, or bureaucracy, where position power is the major source of authority and where rules and procedures are the tools of control exercised by a narrow band of top management. Visually, this is seen as a Greek temple.

Task culture, where the emphasis is on getting the job done, and where expert power is more important than position power. People work in teams, and the organisation structure is often in matrix form. It is represented as a net.

Power culture, where power emanates from one or two persons at the centre. Resource power is the dominant influence here, and emphasis is on achieving results. This culture is represented as a web.

Person culture, where individuals do what they are good at. Power tends to be expert power, but this is a culture for individualists, and the organisation exists to sustain individuals rather than the other way around. This is depicted as a cluster, or 'galaxy of individual stars'.

31. Leadership is exercised against a background of one or other of the above cultures, and this fact has important implications for the amount of power assigned to leaders as well as on the range of styles that will be permitted. This is not to say that all leaders in any one organisation will adopt the same style. Personnel managers or R & D managers, for example, will tend to adopt a less task-centred style than line managers, because their particular sub-cultures may be sufficiently different from the organisation's as a whole. A sub-culture is a 'culture within a culture' – it is the value-system of one part of an organisation which is at variance with the dominant value-system of the organisation. The variance may not be great, but it will be significant. For example, whilst the R & D department are supporting future products and developments in the long-term, their immediate concerns are not to be hurried, not to be over-conscious of costs, and above all to be assiduous in their pursuit of innovation.

CONCLUSION

32. We now know enough about leadership to understand that it is not just a straightforward choice between this or that style. It is principally a question of balancing a number of key factors, such as the nature of the task, the composition of the group, the degree of authority available and the personal attributes of the leader. This balancing act is not achieved in a vaccum, but in the context of a living organisation, composed of ordinary people, and shaped by their dominant values.

REFERENCES

1. Mintzberg, H. (1973), *The Nature of Managerial Work*, Harper & Row.

2. Fiedler, F. (1967), *A Theory of Leadership Effectiveness*, McGraw-Hill.

3. Handy, C. (1976), *Understanding Organisations*, Penguin.

4. Adair, J. (1968), *Training for Leadership*, Macdonald.

5. Pedler, M., Burgoyne, J. & Boydell, T. (1978), *A Manager's Guide Self-development*, McGraw-Hill.

6. Lewin, K., Lippitt, R. & White, R. (1939), 'Patterns of Aggressive Behaviour in experimentally created social climates', *Journal of Psychology*, Vol 10.

7. Reddin, W. J. (1970), *Managerial Effectiveness*, McGraw-Hill.

8. Stogdill, R.M. & Coons, A.E. (1957), *Leadership Behavior: Its Description and Measurement*, Research Monograph No. 88, Ohio State University.

9. McGregor, D. (1960), *The Human Side of Enterprise*, McGraw-Hill.

10. Blake, R. & Mouton, J. (1978), *The New Managerial Grid*, Gulf.

11. Tannenbaum, R. & Schmidt, W. (1958), 'How to Choose a Leadership Pattern', *Harvard Business Review* Mar/Apr.

12. Adair, J. (1973), *Action-centred Leadership*, McGraw-Hill.

13. Handy, C. (1976), *Understanding Organisations*, Penguin.

CHAPTER 7

Groups and teams at work

INTRODUCTION

1. Work-groups have been the focus of considerable research ever since the celebrated Hawthorne Investigations (see below) conducted in the United States over the period 1924–36. Typical areas of interest to researchers have been the following:

    *   formal and informal groups at work

    *   leadership

    *   group cohesiveness

    *   inter-group competition

    *   roles played by individual members of groups

    *   team-building.

    This chapter examines all these areas of interest except for leadership, which was considered in the previous chapter.

THE HAWTHORNE STUDIES

2. The early results of these studies, conducted at the Hawthorne plant of the Western Electric Company, were popularised by Professor Elton Mayo (1933)[1], who had been partly involved in the research work. The official research findings, however, were not published until 1939, when the authors Roethlisberger & Dickson[2] finally completed the account of the experiments they had led practically from start to finish. The principal conclusion reached by the researchers was that social factors play a key role in people's behaviour at work. This finding had major repercussions for those who subscribed to the Scientific Management school, with its emphasis on the structuring of work and the development of controls. This 'scientific' approach was now seen to be insufficient as a means of enhancing productivity. Task-centred approaches began to give way to employee-centred approaches in management.

3. The main stages of the research can be summarised as follows:

    Stage One (1924–7). Under the direction of two of the Company's staff, an investigation was conducted into the effects of lighting on production and morale. Two groups of employees of comparable performance were isolated from the rest and located in a separate part of the plant. One group, the control group, received a consistent level of lighting; the other group, the experimental group, had its lighting varied. To the surprise of the researchers, the output of both groups increased. Even when the lighting for the experimental group was reduced to a very low level, production still went up! Clearly some other, unidentified, factor was at work in the groups. The Company decided to call in Mayo and his Harvard colleagues.

Stage Two (1927–9). This was known as the Relay Assembly Test Room stage. Its objective was to make a closer and more detailed study of the effects of differing physical conditions on productivity. There was no deliberate attempt at this stage to examine social relationships or employee attitudes. For the purposes of this study, six women workers in the relay assembly section were segregated from the other members of the section and located in a room of their own. Over a period of time numerous changes were made in working conditions, and their effects were observed by the researchers. Rest pauses were introduced and varied, lunch times were varied both in timing and in length. In most cases the women were consulted about the changes before they were implemented. The researchers found to their surprise that productivity went up whether the changes were for better or for worse! The researchers concluded that far from just being involved with the effects of changing physical conditions at work, they were also involved in a study of employee attitudes and values. The response of the women appeared to be influenced by their sense of being a special group – the centre of attention. Their reaction has since been called 'the Hawthorne Effect' by social scientists.

Stage Three (1928–30). Before the end of the Stage Two experiments the Company had already decided to bring the issue of attitudes out into the open. They set up an interview programme designed to find out about employee attitudes towards working conditions, supervision and jobs. Initially the interviews were conducted on a structured basis, half-hourly, by selected supervisors. Subsequently, the interviews became less structured and more time was allocated to them. Over 20,000 people had been interviewed by the end of the programme, and a wealth of material gained about employee attitudes towards their work, the supervision they received and their physical working conditions. Of one thing the researchers were left in little doubt – relationships with people at work were important to employees.

Stage Four (1932). This stage was known as the Bank Wiring Observation Room. In this study fourteen men on bank wiring were separated out from the main wiring area and located in an observation room with basically the same working condition as in the main area. The intention in this case was to observe people working under more or less normal conditions for a period of some six months. The observers began to notice that the group was setting its own rules and values. It restricted production in accordance with its own standards, it short-circuited the company wage-incentive scheme and in general protected its own interests as a group. The supervisors concerned appeared powerless to stop this situation. The group had developed its own, unofficial, organisation and was able to protect itself from outside influences as well as to control its internal relationships.

Final Stage (1936). This stage was based on the lessons drawn from the earlier studies. Its focus was firmly on employee relations and took the form of employee counselling. Counsellors encouraged employees to discuss their problems at work, and the results led to improved employee-supervisor and employee-management relationships and to improvements in personal adjustment at work.

4.   The main conclusions drawn from these pioneering studies were as follows:

    1   individual workers cannot be treated in isolation, but have to be seen as members of a group

    2   group membership and the status that goes with it, is more important to individuals than monetary incentives or good physical working conditions

    3   informal, or unofficial, groups in the work-place exercise a strong influence over employee behaviour

    4   supervisors and managers need to be aware of these social needs if they are to obtain commitment to organisational goals.

5.   By modern standards of research the Hawthorne studies were less than rigorous in many respects. Nevertheless, they stand as the first major attempt to undertake genuine social research, and they redirected the attention of industrial psychology away from studies of fatigue and the effects of physical working conditions to a consideration of the human factors operating in the workplace.

GROUPS

6.   The two pioneering efforts into the study of groups were (i) the Hawthorne studies and (ii) the experiments conducted by Lewin and colleagues (1939)[3] into the behaviour of groups in a boys' camp, and which were referred to briefly in Chapter 6.

7.   A key finding of the Hawthorne studies, in particular, was to confirm the existence of informal groups in the workplace. Hitherto, groups had been seen only in terms of the groupings of tasks required as part of the division of labour in a work organisation. It is now customary to describe groups forming a part of the organisation structure, established by management as 'formal', or official, groups. Those which are established by the employees themselves, for their own purposes rather than to fulfil organisation ends, are known as 'informal', or unofficial, groups. Informal may not be a particularly helpful label to describe all groups within firms. For example, trade union groups are highly structured and formal. The term 'unofficial' is nearer to the truth for such groups, and will be used from now on.

8.   What is a group? It is obviously not one person, but is it two, three or more? And when do sheer numbers transform a group into a crowd? There are no easy answers to these questions. Optimum size for a group depends very much on circumstances, as we shall see shortly. Schein (1965)[4] defines a group as 'any number of people who (1) interact with one another, (2) are psychologically aware of one another, and (3) perceive themselves to be a group.' In his view, these three conditions need to be fulfilled if a group is to be distinguished from a random collection of individuals. Schein also assumes that groups share some common aim or purpose.

Workgroups, for example, have a clear purpose, spelt out in the nature of the tasks assigned and the standards to be achieved. Such groups are formed for a variety of purposes:

- to process tasks

- to solve problems

- to take decisions

- to share information

- to develop new ideas.

9. Unofficial groups also have their purposes, which are generally to meet the social and security needs of the employees. The purposes of these unofficial groups may fit in fairly well with organisational objectives, but more than likely will be opposed to them. Burns and Stalker (1961)[5] make the interesting point that in 'mechanistic' (hierarchical) organisations loyalty is to the concern, and obedience is to superiors. In this kind of organisation, there is every possibility of open conflict between the behaviour of people in their unofficial groups as compared with their behaviour as members of official groupings. Burns and Stalker found that in 'organic' organisations, which were stratified but not hierarchical, the collaborative nature of the organisation made it '... far less feasible to distinguish "informal" from "formal" organisation' (op.cit.).

10. Reviewing the research that has been conducted into groups and group behaviour it is possible to summarise the key variables involved. These are as shown in Figure 7.1.

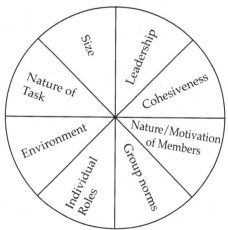

Figure 7.1 *Key variables in group behaviour*

11. We have already considered several aspects of leadership in groups in the previous chapter (Chapter 6). The rest of this chapter, therefore, will concentrate on the remaining factors and some of the important issues arising from them.

GROUP SIZE

12. There is no magic formula for arriving at the optimum size for a group. In one situation three persons in a group could be ideal for the performance of group goals; in another situation three could be totally inadequate. Much depends on other variables, such as the nature of the members, the task they are required to perform and the appropriateness of the leadership. However, as a general rule we can say that 'the size of any group should be sufficient to provide enough resources from within its membership to enable the achievement of its goals both to the satisfaction of the organisation and to that of the members'.

13. Where speedy action is required, a small group of three or four persons may be preferable. Where the quality of discussion is important then a larger group, representative of different interests and skills, may be more effective in achieving its goals. Effective groups (see below) seem to be those where there is active participation by all the members. If a group is too large to enable such involvement, it is likely that both performance and group satisfaction will suffer.

    Smaller groups tend to be more cohesive than larger groups, and encourage fuller participation, but may suffer from lack of talent. Smaller groups may be easier to control, from the leader's point of view. Larger groups, by comparison, may develop sub-groups, which often make leadership more difficult since internal conflicts may develop. In practice the size of work-groups has been reduced in many industrial situations from groups of as many as 100 (motor manufacturing) to about twenty on average.

14. The question of assessing the optimum number of persons that any one manager or supervisor can control in the overall hierarchy of jobs has been called the 'span of control'. Specifically, this has been used to describe the maximum number of subordinates reporting directly to a superior. Such a question was meat and drink to the classical theorists! Probably the most famous 'theory' concerning the span of control was that put forward by V.A. Graicunas, a French management consultant, who attempted to demonstrate mathematically the relationship between the number of subordinates supervised and the total number of relationships the leader would be faced with. Graicunas's formula was as follows:

$$R = n \left(2n{-}1 + n{-}1\right)$$

    (n = number of subordinates)

    It showed that, where a manager had two subordinates, for example, the total number of possible relationships was six, but where six subordinates were supervised, the number rose rapidly to two hundred and twenty-two!

15. Graicunas's idea was highly theoretical, and bore little relationship to what actually happened in practice. However, it did draw attention to the complexity of managing group relationships. One classical theorist, Lyndall Urwick (1947)[6], who had a major influence on management practices, suggested in his Principles of Management that the span of control of any one manager should not exceed five or six subordinates who work interlocked. This is the kind of situation that would be found in a project team, for example. Where the nature of the work involves little or no collaboration between the members, then larger spans are perfectly possible.

So a production team working on routine manufacturing tasks could be considerably larger than six without causing undue problems of control for the supervisor.

GROUP NORMS

16. All groups establish some sort of standards of behaviour (norms) for themselves. Workgroups, as the Hawthorne studies indicated, develop their own standards of social and work behaviour. These standards develop within groups as a response to the influence of key individuals, the style of the manager concerned, the nature of organisation procedures and other environmental issues. Once norms are established they tend to be enforced. For example, there have been numerous cases cited where a member of a group has been 'sent to Coventry' by the other group members for failing to observe some group standard.

17. Norms set by the group members may or may not correspond to those of the organisation. For example, the organisation, through its management, may want higher output from faster working, whereas a group may have decided to pace out the work, so as to ensure their future livelihood. Where work-norms are concerned, it is clearly in the interests of the management to ensure, so far as possible, that the employees' standards mirror those of the organisation. Where non-work norms are concerned, it may be advisable not to interfere with social standards set by groups, e.g. permitting the office to be draped in potted plants.

18. B. Tuckman (1965)[7] described groups as moving through four key stages of development to which he later added a fifth – adjourning (Tuckman & Jensen, 1977)[8]. The five stages are shown in Figure 7.2.

Stage 1 – Forming. Finding out about the task, rules and methods; acquiring information and resources; reliance on the leader.
Stage 2 – Storming. Internal conflict develops; members resist the task at the emotional level.
Stage 3 – Norming. Conflict is settled, co-operation develops; views are exchanged and new standards (i.e. norms) developed.
Stage 4 – Performing. Teamwork is achieved, roles are flexible; solutions are found and implemented.
Stage 5 – Adjourning. The team disperses. Members prepare themselves for new roles.

Figure 7.2 *Stages in group development (Tuckman, 1965)*

19. Newly-formed groups take time to develop their own norms. Tuckman sees them as initially taking stock of their situation, then attempting to tackle tasks in a head-on fashion before moving into the more considered stage of 'Norming'. In progressing to the 'Performing' stage, groups have abandoned or modified many of the norms imposed on them by the organisation at large and their leader in particular, and have effectively demonstrated a degree of 'ownership' of the task and the methods required to achieve it.

20. Tuckman's analysis of group development can be compared with that of Woodcock (1979)[9], who has made a particular study of teams and their development. Woodcock also sees a four-stage sequence of development as follows:

   1   *The Undeveloped Team* – feelings are avoided, objectives are uncertain, the leader takes most of the decisions.

   2   *The Experimenting Team* – issues are faced more openly, listening takes place, the group may become temporarily introspective.

   3   *The Consolidating Team* – personal interaction is established on a co-operative basis, the task is clarified, objectives agreed and tentative procedures implemented.

   4   *The Mature Team* – feelings are open, a wide range of options considered, working methods are methodical, leadership style is contributory, individuals are flexible and the group recognises its responsibility to the rest of the organisation.

21. The key point made by these analyses of team or group development is that effectiveness (see below) is an outcome which develops over time, as the group begin to understand what is required of them and how they can utilise the knowledge, skills and attributes of the individual members in fulfilling group and individual goals. On the way to achieving effectiveness groups will undoubtedly face uncertainty, if not conflict, but these processes have to be seen as necessary costs of achieving both harmony and purposeful behaviour.

GROUP COHESIVENESS

22. The cohesiveness of any group is the extent to which the group members develop strong ties to each other and to the group as a whole ('team spirit'). It is also a measure of the ability of the group to attract new members. A very cohesive group is one that demonstrates strong bonds of loyalty within its membership and strict adherence to the established norms of the group. As Tuckman suggests, cohesiveness develops with the life of a group. New groups lack it, whereas old-established groups are typified by it.

23. Factors encouraging cohesiveness include:

   • similarity of work

   • physical proximity

   • system of work

   • task structure

   • group size (especially small size)

   • external threats

   • prospect of rewards

   • leadership style of manager

- common social features (age, sex, etc.).

24.   Where a high level of cohesiveness has been achieved in a group, external forces will play a significantly reduced role in bringing about change in the group. Change in such a situation will only be realised if key members of the group agree to adopt the new ways. Less cohesive groups are more easily changed from without. Hence the strategy of 'Divide and rule' aimed at preventing cohesive groups from forming.

ROLES IN GROUPS

25.   The reference to 'key members' in the previous paragraph highlights a very important aspect of groups – the roles played out by the members. A role may be defined as

> the set of expectations held by the individuals concerned and those about them concerning how a job or task is to be performed.

A role needs to be distinguished from a position, or job, which is primarily a statement of the duties an individual has been allocated. The job description is merely the script, but the role is the way the script is acted out.

26.   In fulfilling a role the role-holder does not act in isolation. He or she interacts with other members of their own organisation and with people from outside. These are the other members of the cast, and are called the 'role-set'. A typical role-set for a personnel manager is shown in Figure 7.3. The role-set amounts to a network of relationships that exerts a significant set of pressures on the role-holder.

Figure 7.3   *Personnel manager's role-set*

27.   The diagram shows that several members of the role-set have positions in the job hierarchy which place them in an influential position in relation to the personnel manager. Others, however, have no place in the internal hierarchy, but represent external stake-holders in the role-holder's success. The implications of the diagram are also considered in the discussion in Chapter 1 (see especially Figures 1.1 and 1.2).

28.   Belbin (1993)[10] suggests that there are six factors that determine team-role behaviour. These are as follows: personality, mental abilities, personal values and

motivation, environmental constraints (e.g. as implied in the role-set diagram above), personal experience, and role learning (e.g. as acquired through team skills training/team-building exercises). The extent to which an individual exploits a team-role has considerable implications for the degree of influence or power that he or she is able to wield in the group. The range of team-roles identified by Belbin on the basis of earlier research and now modified are described later in the chapter.

ROLES AND POWER

29. An understanding of role is vital to the effective performance of any job, because it enables the job-holder to assess his or her power position.

Power is a key aspect of any managerial post, and springs from a variety of sources. Legge (1978)[11] describes power as '... (the) capability of exercising influence over the attitudes and/or behaviour of other individuals or groups.' This is a useful definition since it emphasises the *capability* of exercising influence. In other words, power does not necessarily rely on formal authority, i.e. power granted by the organisation to a particular position-holder. Power is more a matter of what a person does, or is potentially capable of doing, to influence others. Thus, a trade union representative who successfully persuades a group of workmates to stop work has exercised power, regardless of whether he had any authority to do so under his union's rules.

30. Exercising influence over others depends on factors, which are valued by the others-knowledge and rank, for example. The degree of value of such factors depends on circumstances.

For example, a personnel manager whose role is seen by line colleagues as essentially a servicing (servile) function, and whose position power is thus rather weak, may find his or her situation transformed by the onset of a mass of employment legislation to which the firm must respond. Overnight, almost, the personnel role has become the custodian of the company's approach to the new laws, with the responsibility for ensuring consistency of behaviour throughout all functions. The role has been enriched by dint of external events. The way in which the personnel manager perceives this improved position determines the extent to which he or she utilises the newly-won power available to him or her. (See discussion in Chapter 1).

31. The various forms of power that are available to managers have been described by Handy (1993)[12] as follows:

- *Physical power* – this is the capability of using physical force to achieve influence. An unlikely source of power for a manager, but a lockout is one such manifestation.

- *Resource power* – 'the possession of valued resources', as Handy puts it. Examples include control over salary and promotion prospects. This form of power is less available to managers in large bureaucracies, where such issues are dealt with in accordance with centrally-directed procedures. (For individual entrepreneurs, the scope is considerable, and merits the word 'patronage').

- *Position power* – this is the power of the office, or position, as described by Weber. It refers to the rights written into the particular position (to allocate work, assess performance, etc.). Position power relies closely on resource power. However, it does give access to what Handy calls 'invisible assets', i.e. information, rights of access to key groups, and the right to organise work.

- *Expert power* – this arises from the possession of acknowledged expertise. This is power which, in effect, is given to a position by those over whom it is to be used. Expert power only exists if other people recognise it and value it.

- *Personal power* – this is the power of personality (charisma). Like expert power, it is only effective when it is recognised by those concerned.

- *Negative power* – this is the power to stop things happening, for example. Even lowly members of an organisation may have this form of power. It finds expression in the filtering or distorting of information. It tends to surface at times of low morale.

32. The possession of power, however achieved, is one thing. The use of power is another. As Legge (*op.cit.*) puts it:

> ... he (the manager) also needs sufficient political sensitivity to know how to relate the resources available to him to interests that are salient to those he wishes to influence.

This political sensitivity represents the subjective dimension of power and on this the perception of one's role is crucial.

GROUP EFFECTIVENESS

33. In considering the effectiveness of a group, there are two major criteria for measuring success:

1 how effectively were group tasks accomplished?

2 what was the level of individual satisfaction with membership of the group?

The first question looks at effectiveness from the point of view of organisational goals, the second considers personal goals. Organisations seek success in terms of tasks accomplished, targets achieved, solutions rendered and other benefits. Individuals seek personal satisfaction from membership of the group, opportunities to perform a role and to gain status within the group. Sometimes both sets of goals can be achieved. Generally, however, there is some dissonance between organisational goals and expectations and those of group members, and a key part of every leadership role is to minimise the negative consequences of this conflict.

34. If we were to examine the effectiveness of groups in terms of their *processes* rather than in terms of their end-results, then McGregor's perceptive account of the differences between effective and ineffective groups is illuminating. Some of the most important distinctions noted by McGregor (1960)[13] can be summarised as follows:

Effective groups	Ineffective groups
• The atmosphere is informal and relaxed	• The atmosphere suggests boredom or tension
• There is much relevant discussion in which most members participate	• Discussion is dominated by one or two persons, and is often irrelevant
• The group task is clearly understood and people are committed to achieving it	• No common objective is apparent
• The members listen to each other	• Members tend not to listen to each other
• Conflict is not avoided, but brought into the open and dealt with constructively	• Conflict is either avoided or is allowed to develop into open warfare
• Most decisions are reached by consensus	• Simple majorities are seen as sufficient for group decisions
• Ideas are expressed freely and openly	• Personal feelings are kept hidden for fear of criticism
• Leadership does not always reside in the chairman, but is shared as appropriate	• Leadership is retained by the chairman
• The group examines its own progress and behaviour	• The group avoids discussion of its own behaviour

35. McGregor's description of effective groups matches the behaviour described by Tuckman in his Stages 3 and 4 – Norming and Performing. These might be described as the behaviour of mature groups. Ineffective groups, by comparison, correspond closely to Tuckman's first two Stages – Forming and Storming. These represent the behaviour of immature groups. McGregor seems to imply that any one group is either effective or ineffective. Tuckman takes the view that a group can change as it gains experience. McGregor, however, sees training in group membership as the key factor in improving the performance of groups.

36. The study of how people behave when they are in groups has been aided greatly by the work of R.F. Bales (1950)[14] who drew up a list of categories of verbal behaviour identified during numerous studies of small groups. This was an important attempt to categorise frequently occurring behaviour so that the descriptors developed could be applied to other groups in a relevant and consistent way. Typical examples of the descriptors were:

- shows solidarity

- agrees

- gives opinion

- asks for suggestion

- shows antagonism.

Bales grouped his descriptors according to whether they furthered task functions or aided interpersonal relations.

37.   These categories have attracted the attention of several British researchers, notably Rackham & Morgan (1977)[15] who have used their version for training people in interpersonal skills. Their list of descriptors includes the following:

- proposing (concepts, suggestions, actions)

- building (adding to others' proposals)

- disagreeing

- defending/attacking

- blocking

- testing understanding

- summarising

- seeking information

- shutting-out behaviour

- bringing-in behaviour.

38.   Although it is by no means easy to apply these behaviour categories consistently in the course of observing group behaviour, they can provide a useful way of permitting groups and their members to assess their behaviour together. The two key issues, according to Rackham & Morgan, are the reliability of the behaviour analysis, and the manner of giving feedback. They suggest a number of ways by which reliability, i.e. consistency, of analysis may be achieved, and for being able to recall the content of what was said as well as being able to classify the behaviour in accordance with the chosen behaviour categories. On the topic of feedback, they comment that 'The adage, "practice makes perfect" is a half-truth. It is practice allied with feedback that makes perfect, or at least enables people to learn and improve.'

39.   The role of feedback in improving group effectiveness is to mirror the activities of the group, to enable it to hear and, using closed-circuit television, to see what went on during a particular group activity. It enables the group members to stand back from the process in which they were participants in order to obtain an outsider's perspective on their behaviour.

NATURE OF TASK

40.   One of the key variables mentioned in Figure 7.1 above was the nature of the task, which we shall consider next. The nature of the task can affect group behaviour in several ways:

1   A specific or clearly-defined task requires a different leadership style from that required for an unstructured, possibly ambiguous task (Fiedler, 1967)[16].

2   A task requiring close co-operation makes team development a key priority, whereas in a situation where people can work at their own task in a group, individual needs will tend to be more important than team needs (Adair, 1973)[17].

3   The importance, or salience, of the task will have a decisive effect on the motivation of group members. It will also attract greater attention from management, possibly implying the use of tighter controls.

4   Problem-solving tasks will require a different leadership style and different roles from, say, work-allocation tasks (Handy, 1993 op.cit.).

5   In manufacturing, different production systems make different demands on groups. In jobbing, or one-off, production, groups have to be flexible and imaginative in approach. These conditions will create very different demands for groups working on a mass-production line, where tasks are narrowly-defined and controls tight (Woodward, 1965)[18].

6   Where the nature of the work leads to people working on their own, for example in transport or power stations, workgroups are very loosely-knit associations. To compensate for this, employee-groups, i.e. unofficial groups, may be formed to provide some degree of social support for individuals.

7   Time can be an important factor in group behaviour. Urgent tasks, or emergencies, will clearly require a task-oriented approach. Non-urgent tasks can permit a more employee-centred approach.

NATURE OF GROUP MEMBERS

41. Another important variable in groups is the nature of the membership. The effectiveness of a group in achieving personal as well as organisational goals depends partly on the range of skills and attitudes possessed by the individual members. The most important issues here may be summarised in the following questions:

1   How much relevant knowledge is possessed by group members?

2   What level of skills can individuals contribute?

3   What personal characteristics are available to the group? Is there a balance between different personality types?

4   How well do the group members relate to each other?

5   To what extent do individuals share each others sense of values or priorities?

6   How effective is the group leader? How far is he or she accepted by the group?

7   How well do group members communicate with one another?

8   How experienced are the group at working together? How aware are they of group processes?

42. Schein (1965 op.cit.) suggests that for effective work to occur there must be 'a certain amount of consensus on basic values and on a medium of communication'.

Where values or status differ markedly, groups may find communication difficult. A junior person may not wish to say something critical of their boss, for example. Schein suggests that training in group working can help to remedy problems of this type. Handy *(op.cit.)*, in a discussion on groups, mentions the 'hidden agendas' that individual members bring to a group. These hidden agendas are the personal aims that individuals seek to pursue – for example, the desire to impress one's boss, or to make a particular alliance. Unless these covert motives are controlled by mutual agreement, implicit or explicit, there is little hope of getting a collaborative spirit within a group. The group's development will be stuck at the Storming stage. Successful collaboration between the individual members of a group will ultimately depend on (a) the commitment to group goals, and (b) the degree of trust that is generated within the group.

ENVIRONMENT

43. Finally we turn to the environment or context in which group behaviour takes place. This context can be seen from two principal perspectives – the physical and the social.

   The physical aspects of environment are important because they can permit proximity or isolation between people. The closer people are physically, the greater the interaction between the group members. Conversely, as mentioned above under the nature of the task, relative isolation acts as a barrier to interaction. Hence the strenuous efforts of head-office managers to hold regular meetings with off-site personnel (sales staff, site personnel officers, etc.). Sometimes physical surroundings are changed deliberately to emphasise a change in approach, for example, when a Director decides to hold a forward planning meeting at a country house instead of at head office. The implication being that this will be an occasion for less formality and urgency, but with more time spent on creativity and reflection.

44. The social environment is even more influential than physical, for we are concerned with the very culture, or lifestyle, of the organisation and its constituent groups. Key questions for assessing the social environment are as follows:

   1 What are the dominant values relating to 'success'? Are they to do with return on capital, levels of sales, efficient provision of a service, establishing good employee relations, or maintaining market leadership?

   2 What is the basic orientation of the top management – task-centred or people-centred?

   3 How is motivation achieved – by threats and rewards, by attention to individual needs, or by providing satisfying work?

   4 What is the shape and structure of the organisation? Relatively flat, or multi-layered?

   5 How much reliance is placed on formality of relationships in the structure?

   6 How are rules and procedures handled, and what purposes are they intended to serve?

7   How important is the individual in the organisation?

8   What degree of participation in decision-making is permitted by senior management?

45. There is no easy way of describing the ideal social environment. Ultimately, it is the extent to which people adapt their behaviour in order to cope with internal conflict and external pressures that determines the success or failure of any organisation.

TEAMS AND TEAM-BUILDING

46. A team, according to Adair (1986)[19], is more than just a group with a common aim. It is a group in which the contributions of individuals are seen as complementary. Collaboration, working together, is the keynote of a team activity. Adair suggests that the test of a good (i.e. effective) team is:

> whether ... its members can work as a team while they are apart, contributing to a sequence of activities rather than to a common task, which requires their presence in one place and at one time.

What we have described in this chapter are the key variables that determine the relative effectiveness of groups in achieving their goals and satisfying the needs of their members. These variables, which have to be addressed if there is to be any chance of building a successful team, are worth summarising again. They are:

- the size of the group
- the nature of the task
- the environment in which the group operates
- the leadership requirements of the group
- the roles played by individual members
- the knowledge, skills, motivation and other attributes of the group-members
- the potential for/desirability of group cohesiveness
- the work and social norms of the group.

47. What, then, to sum up, are the characteristics of effective teamwork? Woodcock (*op.cit.*) states that the characteristics of good teamwork are:

- clear objectives and agreed goals
- openness and confrontation
- support and trust
- co-operation and conflict
- sound procedures
- appropriate leadership
- regular review

- individual development

- sound inter-group relations.

Adair (*op.cit.*) emphasises the importance of careful selection of team members. The key factors here for individuals are not only technical or professional competence, but also the ability to work as a team member, and the possession of 'desirable personal attributes' such as willingness to listen, flexibility of outlook, and the capacity to give and accept trust.

48. Belbin (*op.cit.*) in his important researches into team roles originally identified eight such roles in which individuals' key contributions and allowable weaknesses were described. The original list has been revised slightly and one further role identified. The current list of team-roles that follows gives some interesting comparisons in role behaviour (see Figure 7.4).

Fig. 7.4 *Summary of Belbin's team roles*

Role title	Key contribution	Allowable weaknesses
Plant	Creativity, imagination, able to solve difficult problems	Ignorance of details, often too pre-occupied to communicate effectively
Resource investigator	Enthusiasm, communication, looks for opportunities, makes contacts	Over-optimistic, easily loses interest
Co-ordinator (previously Chairman)	Chairmanship, clarification of goals, decision-making skills, delegation	Can be manipulative, may delegate personal work
Shaper	Dynamism, drive, courage to overcome obstacles, copes with pressure	Being provocative, hurting other people's feelings
Monitor evaluator	Discernment, constructive criticism, strategic thinking	Inability to inspire others, being overtly critical
Teamworker	Co-operation, diplomacy, perceptive approach, averting friction	Indecisive at times, easily influenced
Implementer (previously Company worker)	Discipline, reliability, efficiency, generating practical action	Inflexibility, slow to see new possibilities
Completer	Conscientious approach, finds errors and omissions, timely delivery	Worrier, reluctant delegator, nit-picker
Specialist (additional role)	Single-mindedness, self-starting capacity, provision of scarce knowledge and skills	Narrow contributor, dwells on technical details, fails to see the wider picture

49. Belbin's nine team-roles provide us with enough distinctive attributes to see the range of roles that can be performed in a team. The precise pattern of strengths and weaknesses of individuals can be determined fairly accurately from group exercises and feedback. Belbin points out that executives are 'seldom strong in all nine team roles' (p. 23). The important point is that most people have a range of individual strengths to contribute to a team and this does not detract from the fact that these strengths are invariably accompanied by some weaknesses. Recognition of both is required if successful teams incorporating the whole range of roles are to be developed.

CONCLUSION

50. Since the majority of employees in organisations are employed in groups of one kind or another, attention to team-roles, group working and/or team-development is a crucial activity for management. As the Japanese experience has shown, the development of highly cohesive teams imbued with the organisation's culture, has brought considerable benefits both to individuals and the economy at large. As such improvements are intimately associated with personal values and self-esteem, the training provided in this area needs to be undertaken with sensitivity and an understanding of the relative power position of the individuals concerned.

REFERENCES

1. Mayo, E. (1933), *The Human Problems of an Industrial Civilisation*, Macmillan, New York.

2. Roethlisberger, J. & Dickson, W. (1939), *Management and the Worker*, Harvard UP.

3. Lewin, K. *et al* (1939), 'Patterns of Aggressive Behaviour etc.', *Journal of Psychology*, Vol. 10.

4. Schein, E.H. (1965), *Organisational Psychology*, Prentice Hall.

5. Burns, T. & Stalker, G.M. (1961), *The Management of Innovation*, Tavistock.

6. Urwick, L.F. (1947), *The Elements of Administration*, Pitman.

7. Tuckman, B. (1965), 'Developmental Sequence in Small Groups,' *Psychological Bulletin*, 63.

8. Tuckman, B. & Jensen, N (1977), 'Stages of Small Group Development Revisited', *Group and Organisational Studies,* Vol 2, pp. 419 et seq.

9. Woodcock, M. (1979), *Team Development Manual*, Gower.

10. Belbin, R.M. (1993), *Team Roles at Work*, Butterworth Heinemann.

11. Legge, K. (1978), *Power, Innovation, and Problem-solving in Personnel Management*, McGraw-Hill.

12. Handy, C. (1993), *Understanding Organisations* (4th edn), Penguin.

13. McGregor, D. (1960), *The Human Side of Enterprise*, McGraw-Hill.

14. Bales, R.F. (1950), *Interaction Process Analysis*, Addison-Wesley.

15. Rackham, N. & Morgan, T. (1977), *Behaviour Analysis in Training*, McGraw-Hill.

16. Fiedler, F. (1967), *A Theory of Leadership Effectiveness*, McGraw-Hill.

17. Adair, J. (1973), *Action-centred Leadership*, McGraw-Hill.

18. Woodward, J. (1965), *Industrial Organisation – Theory and Practice*, OUP.

19. Adair, J. (1986), *Effective Teambuilding*, Gower.

CHAPTER 8

Motivation theories

INTRODUCTION

1. The aim of this chapter is to summarise the leading theories that have influenced management's attempts to achieve a motivated workforce.

   Motivation theory attempts to explain *why* people behave in the ways they do. This is not an easy task, as Vroom & Deci (1970)[1] put it: 'The question of what motivates workers to perform effectively is not an easy one to answer.' The difficulty is that the researchers involved have to make assumptions about the motives for behaviour that they have observed or recorded. There is always an element of subjectivity, therefore, in any judgements made about motivation.

2. The link between motivation theory and the practice of management is crucial to management's success. People are the greatest single asset available to an enterprise. In fact an organisation is people! Unfortunately, however, people are the only asset that can actively work *against* the organisation's goals! It is, therefore, only by collaborative efforts that people can find a release for their latent energy and creativity in the service of the enterprise.

MOTIVATION

3. For our purposes here, the following working definition of motivation is proposed:

   Motivation is a process in which people choose between alternative forms of behaviour in order to achieve personal goals.

   Such a definition excludes the operation of instinctive or reflex behaviour and focuses on individual choice. Exercising choice is not just a rational process, but one which is considerably affected by the emotions and deeply held values of the individual.

4. The goals sought by individuals can be relatively tangible, such as monetary reward or promotion, or intangible, such as self-esteem or job satisfaction. The rewards available to an individual are generally classified under two headings – intrinsic and extrinsic rewards. Briefly, intrinsic rewards are those that derive from the individual's own experience; extrinsic rewards are those are conferred on a person from outside. An intrinsic reward would be a sense of achievement or a feeling of self-esteem; an extrinsic reward would be a pay rise or a promotion. Whilst motivation as such is essentially a personal experience, managers, in particular, are

keen to find reliable links between individual motivation and effective performance. They are also concerned to create the conditions under which organisational
and personal goals may be harmonised.

5. Put simply, motivation can be described as behaviour caused by some stimulus but
    directed towards a desired outcome, as indicated in Figure 8.1.

    Stimulus ⟶ Appropriate ⟶ Goal/Desired
                behaviour   outcome

Figure 8.1 *The basic motivation model*

In this model, the stimulus could be a need, drive or incentive of some kind, e.g. the
need for food. Appropriate behaviour would be to pull into a motorway restaurant
or go to the larder. The goal or desired outcome would be, at the very least, the
relief of hunger pangs and, at best, the enjoyment of a satisfying meal.

6. In relation to Figure 8.1, a researcher would want to ask the following questions:

    • What stimulus prompted the observed behaviour?

    • What is the nature of the perceived stimulus? (e.g. a basic appetite? its
       attractiveness?)

    • What was the response to the stimulus?

    • Why was this particular behaviour chosen?

    • What goal appeared to be sought by the person?

    • Why was this goal chosen?

    • How effective was the behaviour?

    • How appropriate was the goal?

Theories that focus on the stimulus, i.e. on what specifically causes motivation,
have been called content theories. Exponents include such well-known names as
Maslow, Herzberg and McGregor. Theories that focus on the behaviour have been
called process theories. Exponents of this approach include Skinner (see Chapter
25) and Vroom.

7. Effective performance at work does not just depend on motivation. Numerous
    other factors, such as individual knowledge and skills, the nature of the task, the
    management style adopted and the organisation climate, all play a part in the
    results people achieve.

    The key feature of motivation is that it determines the extent to which an
    individual *desires* to place his or her knowledge and skills at the disposal of others,
    and, more than that, to shrug off the effects of obstacles and difficulties in so doing.

8. Let us now look briefly at some of the leading theories of motivation that have been
    put forward over the last 30 years. The theories suggested by Maslow, Alderfer,
    Herzberg and McClelland are content theories. Those that come under the labels of
    Expectancy Theory, Equity Theory and Goal Theory are primarily process
    theories.

MASLOW'S HIERARCHY OF NEEDS

9. Maslow (1954)[2] suggested that human needs operate at a number of different levels, from basic physiological needs such as hunger, to higher-level needs such as self-development and self-fulfilment. These levels can be arranged in a hierarchy as shown in Figure 8.2.

Figure 8.2 *Maslow's hierarchy of human needs*

10. Maslow's general argument was that, other things being equal, people tend to satisfy their lowest level of felt need before moving on to higher-level needs. As Guest's (1984)[3] review of motivation theories comments, however, research studies conducted in the 1960s and early 1970s 'showed little or no support for the theories of Maslow'. The major difficulty associated with Maslow's model lies in its apparent rigidity. Whilst few people would deny that there are lower-level and higher-level needs, many would dispute that people do tend to satisfy their needs in a relatively systematic way from the bottom to the top, as it were.

ALDERFER'S THEORY

11. Clayton Alderfer (1972)[4] followed up Maslow's idea with some studies which led him to propose his so-called ERG theory of motivation. This suggested that people's needs are arranged along a continuum, rather than in an hierarchy, and that there are three rather than five groups of needs, viz Existence, Relatedness and Growth. Existence needs correspond to Maslow's lower levels, Relatedness corresponds to Maslow's social needs, while Growth corresponds to Maslow's higher-level needs. Alderfer's model is altogether more dynamic than Maslow's. It allows for people to deal with two sets of needs at once, and it also distinguishes between chronic, or long-lasting needs, and episodic, or occasional, needs.

HERZBERG'S MOTIVATION-HYGIENE THEORY

12. Frederick Herzberg (1966)[5] took the view that Man lives at two levels, the physical level and the psychological level. His original study into the good and bad experiences at work of 200 engineers and accountants was designed 'to test the concept that man has two sets of needs: his need as an animal to avoid pain and his need as a human to grow psychologically'. The respondents in the study were asked to recall times when they had felt exceptionally good about their jobs, and then to recall negative feelings they had experienced.

13. His interpretation of the results led him to state his two-factor theory, or Motivation-Hygiene theory, of motivation. As Figure 8.3 indicates, several factors led persistently to employee satisfaction, while some others led persistently to dissatisfaction. The satisfiers were called 'motivators' and the dissatisfiers 'hygiene factors'. Motivators appeared to be closely connected to the job, whilst hygiene factors were connected with the environment. Motivators appeared to produce motivated behaviour. However hygiene factors produced either dissatisfaction or a nil response.

14. To take a motoring analogy, hygiene factors can be considered as filling up the petrol tank, i.e. the car will not go, if there is no fuel, but refuelling of itself does not get the vehicle under way. For forward movement, the car electrics must be switched on and the starter operated – this is the effect created by the motivators. As a theory of motivation, Herzberg's ideas have been effectively discredited mainly on the grounds that there is no evidence to support his concept of two independent sets of factors in motivation. Critics (e.g. Campbell *et al.*, 1970)[6] have claimed that, in an empirical sense, Herzberg's work has been concerned more with job satisfaction/dissatisfaction than job behaviour. Nevertheless, his work has led to what might be called the 'job enrichment movement' (adding motivators to jobs) and, more recently, to the 'quality of working life' movement.

ACHIEVEMENT MOTIVATION

15. Achievement motivation is generally associated with the work of D. McClelland and colleagues at Harvard University. Working from a list of some twenty needs identified by an earlier theorist, H.A. Murray, McClelland focused his attentions on three particular needs:

    1 the need for achievement (n Ach)

    2 the need for affiliation (n Aff)

    3 the need for power (n Pow).

    Of these three, the need for achievement received the greatest emphasis in the research. This was because this motive was perceived as having a relatively stable tendency, and was activated by external events in the individual's situation.

16. McClelland (1961)[7] found that individuals with a high n Ach factor tended to display the characteristics listed on p. 100.

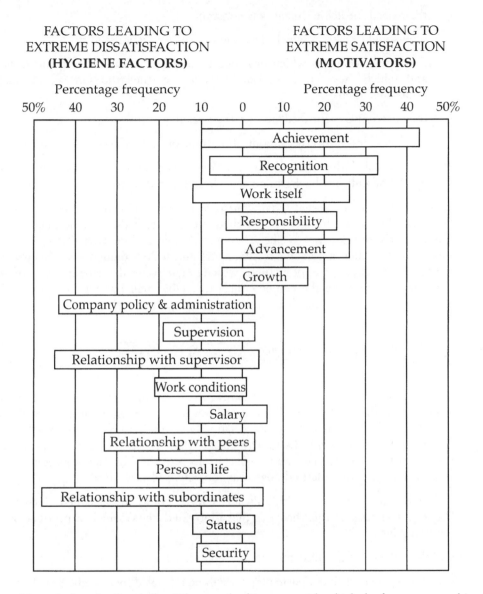

FACTORS LEADING TO
EXTREME DISSATISFACTION
(HYGIENE FACTORS)

FACTORS LEADING TO
EXTREME SATISFACTION
(MOTIVATORS)

Percentage frequency

Percentage frequency

50%   40   30   20   10   0   10   20   30   40   50%

Achievement

Recognition

Work itself

Responsibility

Advancement

Growth

Company policy & administration

Supervision

Relationship with supervisor

Work conditions

Salary

Relationship with peers

Personal life

Relationship with subordinates

Status

Security

Note the length of each 'box' denotes the frequency with which the factor occurred in the situations described by the respondents. The depth of each 'box' denotes the relative duration of the good or bad feelings about the job:

a)   that motivators have their negative aspects, e.g. lack achievement can lead to dissatisfaction, and

b)   that hygiene factors have their positive aspects, e.g. salary can be a source of satisfaction.

Figure 8.3 *Factors affecting job attitudes (Herzberg, 1966)*

1   their need for achievement was constant

2   they sought tasks in which they could exercise responsibility

3   they preferred tasks which provided a challenge without being too difficult, and which they felt they could master (i.e. they did not set themselves impossible goals)

4   they actively sought feedback on their results

5   they were less concerned about affiliation, or social, needs.

McClelland concluded that n Ach was developed more by the experiences of childhood and cultural background than by inherited factors.

17.   In view of the suggested characteristics of the achieving type of person, McClelland's ideas have been applied in the selection of managers. The psychometric test known as the Thematic Apperception Test (TAT) has been widely used to elicit a person's n Ach, n Aff and n Pow tendencies. This test asks subjects to look at a series of pictures, which they have to describe in terms of what is happening, who are the people concerned, what will happen, and so on. The strength of individuals' needs are inferred from their descriptions.

V.H. VROOM & EXPECTANCY THEORIES

18.   Vroom (1964)[8], in an influential work, focused his attention on individual behaviour in the workplace. He observed the work behaviour of individuals with the object of explaining the *processes* involved. He assumed that much of the observed behaviour would be motivated, i.e. that it was the result of preferences among possible outcomes and expectations concerning the consequences of actions. His principal methodology was 'objective observation'.

19.   The essential elements of Vroom's ideas have come to be called 'Expectancy Theory'. The crux of this theory is that motivated behaviour is a product of two key variables:

1   the valence of an outcome for the individual, and

2   the expectancy that a particular act will be followed by a predictable outcome.

Valence is the anticipated satisfaction from an outcome. This distinguishes it from the *Value* of the outcome, which is the actual satisfaction obtained. *Expectancy* is a momentary belief concerning the likelihood that a particular act will be followed by a particular outcome. The product of Valence x Expectancy is Force. *Force* is used in the sense of pressure to perform an act. Thus the basic formula designed by Vroom can be stated as follows:

$$\text{FORCE (Motivation)} = \text{VALENCE} \times \text{EXPECTANCY}$$

20.   Vroom's ideas have been pursued by numerous other theorists to the extent that in his review of motivation theory, Guest (1984)[3] concluded that 'Expectancy theory continues to provide the dominant framework for understanding motivation at work'. Lawler & Porter (1967)[9], in particular, have extended Vroom's ideas by

developing a model which attempts to address two major issues:

1   What factors determine the effort a person puts into his job?

2   What factors affect the relationship between effort and performance?

21.   The variables selected by Lawler & Porter were as follows:

- effort

- the value of rewards

- the probability that rewards depend on effort

- performance

- abilities

- role perceptions.

Underlying their basic model (see Figure 8.4) is the assumption that people act on the basis of how they perceive situations. This subjective aspect of the model is crucial.

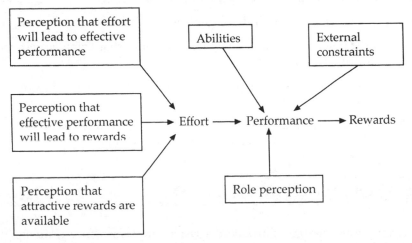

Figure 8.4   *Simplified model of expectancy theory (based on Lawler & Porter, 1967)*

The model indicates clearly how effort is determined by individuals' perception of their situation. It also shows that performance is qualified by individuals' own abilities and understanding of their role, as well as by the constraints in the environment (e.g. company policy).

22.   The rewards that individuals will find attractive, that is to say those which have a high valence for them, may be intrinsic or extrinsic rewards. Vroom (1964)[8] considered the question of job satisfaction as an aspect of motivation. The term 'job satisfaction' was regarded as 'the conceptual equivalent of the valence of the job or work role to the person performing it'. In his opinion, the main variables affecting job satisfaction were:

1   supervision

2   the work group

3   job content

4   wages

5   promotional opportunities

6   hours of work.

In concluding his discussion on job satisfaction, Vroom comments that:

> People's reports of their satisfaction with their jobs are ... directly related to the extent to which their jobs provide them with such rewarding outcomes as pay, variety in stimulation, consideration from their supervisor, a high probability of promotion, close interaction with co-workers, an opportunity to influence decisions ... and control over their pace of work.

23. In practical terms, therefore, managers who wish to make use of the ideas embodied in expectancy theory will need to consider the following:

- How can employee values and preferences be identified?

- What rewards are most likely to be valued by employees?

- In what ways can rewards be tied to performance?

- How can available rewards be publicised?

- What training resources are required to ensure that employee effort can result in effective performance?

- How can jobs be re-designed so as to incorporate the rewards sought by employees?

24. Job re-design, including reference to its motivational aspects, is a topic which is dealt with in its own right (see Chapter 9 – Job Design).

PERFORMANCE-RELATED PAY

25. Organisations that have introduced a system of performance-related pay, partly as a form of employee motivation, may not always see the benefits of this approach. This may be because the rewards concerned (bonuses, etc.) are too small to be attractive, and/or the rewards are paid too long after the effort that brought them about has been recognised. Individual performance-related pay often seems to suffer from rather restricted rewards, even when all targets have been met. Where profit-related pay is concerned, the rewards – usually confined to a few senior managers – can be considerable, and probably large enough to satisfy individuals even though paid out many months after being achieved. Studies such as the CIPD report into performance-related pay (see Chapter 21 paras 52–55) suggested that rewards related to profits were perceived as having little to do with individual effort, and seemed to have only a marginal effect on employee performance. Where team-based incentives were available there was some small improvement noticed in employee performance and commitment.

OTHER MOTIVATION THEORIES

26. Locke (1976)[10] put forward a theory of motivation based on goalsetting. This so-called Goal Theory suggested that it is the goal that an individual is aiming for which motivates, rather than just the satisfaction of attaining it. Locke's view is that what a person values or desires determines the goals he sets for himself, but that what actually drives him (motivates him) are the goals themselves.

27. Locke's own researches indicated that individual performance was better when people had been set specific goals of a challenging or difficult nature, and when they received feedback on their performance. This approach clearly has implications for the practice of management-by-objectives, or target-setting, which relies for its success on the mutual agreement of specific goals between a manager and his subordinate.

28. Another motivation theory is Equity Theory, or Social Comparison Theory, which suggests that people at work compare themselves with others doing similar work in similar circumstances and judge whether they are being fairly treated by comparison. Adams (1964)[11] and his colleagues found that if employees thought that they were being treated equitably, their work effort was sustained; if they thought they were not being treated equitably in relation to other comparable employees, then their effort declined.

29. So far the theory has not been supported by research findings, but it does have links with Expectancy theory. Lawler (1971)[12], for example, notes that in considering rewards, the satisfaction gained by an individual is governed by the difference between 'the amount of some valued outcome that a person receives and the amount of that outcome he feels he *should* receive. Moreover, the amount a person feels he should receive ... (is) ... strongly influenced by what he perceives others ... are receiving.' The implications for management of these comments are that organisations do need to provide a system of equitable payment for their employees. Regardless of any negotiations with trade unions, if managements want a motivated workforce, then they must ensure that the rewards for effort, other things being equal, are seen as fair by all employees.

30. Edgar Schein (1988)[13], in a leading text on the behavioural sciences, identifies a number of assumptions that have been made about motivation. These can be summarised in order of historical appearance as follows:

Rational-economic view. This view of individual behaviour has its roots in the economic theories of Adam Smith in the 1770s. It suggests that people are primarily motivated by self-interest and the maximisation of gain. It stresses people's rational calculation of self-interest, especially in relation to economic needs. Ultimately, says Schein, all human beings can be placed into two categories, if this approach is adopted – (1) the untrustworthy, money-motivated, calculative masses, and (2) the trustworthy, more broadly-motivated, moral elite, whose task is to organise and manage the masses. This approach corresponds to McGregor's Theory X view of motivation. It is the approach which dominated the classical school of managers (Taylor, the Gilbreths, Urwick, etc.). It is still an important assumption made in many organisations today.

Social view This view of motivation sees people as motivated primarily by their social needs. Historically, the initiators of this approach were the Hawthorne researchers. This view also forms part of socio-technical systems theory as propounded by Trist & Bamforth (1951)[14], in their study of British coalminers at work. Acceptance of this view by managers implies a close attention to people's social needs with less emphasis on task considerations.

Self-actualising view. This view of motivation sees people as motivated more by self-fulfilment needs than by any others. Self-actualising people need challenge, responsibility and a sense of pride in their work. Exponents of this approach to motivation are McGregor (Theory Y), Maslow and Argyris. Research studies indicate a good deal of support for the Self-actualising view amongst professional and skilled grades of employee, but the situation regarding unskilled workers is somewhat less clear.

Complex view. This view of motivation sees it as an altogether more complex matter than previously conceived. People are complex and variable; they respond to a variety of managerial strategies; and are affected by different tasks and different work-groups. Schein sees motivation here as a form of 'psychological contract' based on the expectations that the respective parties have of each other and the extent to which these are fulfilled. This approach does not exclude the previously-mentioned approaches but encompasses them in its viewpoint.

CONCLUSION

31.   Human motivation is an issue which is as complex as it is important for management in organisations. In considering the different theories which have been advanced, it is possible to summarise the main factors currently of interest to researchers and practitioners alike. Figure 8.5 sets out a basic model for the purposes of concluding this chapter.

32.   The model suggests that successful performance is the outcome of two major sets of factors-firstly, an individual's aptitudes, abilities and knowledge, which need to be combined so as to produce the best fit for the achievement of intended outcomes; and secondly, the attitudes, motives, needs and expectations that an individual brings to the situation in selecting appropriate behaviour. Learning influences knowledge and skills (see Chapter 25). The criterion of what represents successful performance varies between individuals and organisations, with the former preferring the satisfaction of various intrinsic and extrinsic rewards, and the latter seeking economy in the achievement of targets.

33.   Most of the factors both influence, and are influenced by, job performance. Other, external, factors also influence performance, involving risks for both parties, and possibly leading to unintended outcomes. Finally, the inclusion of researchers' criteria serves to remind us that there is always the perspective of the observer to be considered when assessing academic studies in the social sciences.

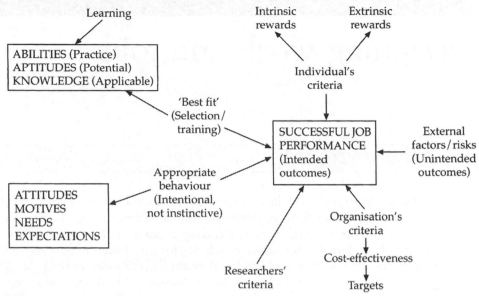

Figure 8.5 *Summary of motivation models*

REFERENCES

1. Vroom, V.H. & Deci, E.L. (1970), *Management and Motivation*, Penguin.

2. Maslow, A. (1954), *Motivation and Personality*, Harper & Row.

3. Guest, D. (1984), 'What's New in Motivation?', *Personnel Management*, May 1984.

4. Alderfer, C.P. (1972), *Existence, Relatedness and Growth: Human Needs in Organisational Settings*, Collier and Macmillan.

5. Herzberg, F. (1966), *Work and the Nature of Man*, Staples.

6. Campbell, J.P. *et al* (1970), *Managerial Behaviour, Performance, and Effectiveness*, McGraw-Hill.

7. McClelland, D. (1961), *The Achieving Society*, Van Nostrand.

8. Vroom, V.H. (1964), *Work and Motivation*, Wiley.

9. Lawler, E.E. & Porter, L. (1967), 'Antecedent Attitudes of Effective Managerial Performance', in Vroom, V.H. & Deci, E.L. (1970) *op.cit.*

10. Locke, E.A. (1976), 'The Nature and Causes of Job Satisfaction', in Dunnette, M. (ed) (1976) *Handbook of Industrial & Organisational Psychology*, Rand McNally.

11. Adams, J.S. & Jacobsen, P.R. (1964), 'Effects of Wage Inequities on Work Quality', *Journal of Applied Psychology*, No. 67.

12. Lawler, E.E. (1971), *Pay and Organisational Effectiveness*, McGraw-Hill.

13. Schein, E. (1988), *Organisational Psychology* (3rd edn), Prentice Hall.

14. Trist, E.L. & Bamforth, K.W. (1951), 'Some social and psychological consequences of the longwall method of coal-getting', *Human Relations*, 4.1.

CHAPTER 9

Designing work and jobs

INTRODUCTION

1. All work organisations can be thought of as networks of jobs. These networks may be relatively rigid or flexible, depending on the extent to which the boundaries between jobs are adapted to meet changing conditions. Jobs are fundamental to organisations. They are the principal vehicles for the allocation of tasks, duties and roles to the various personnel employed by the organisation. In their classic work, *The Management of Innovation*, Burns & Stalker (1961)[1] drew some important distinctions between rigid and flexible organisations, which they termed 'mechanistic' and 'organic' respectively.

2. Mechanistic organisations were typified by:

    1   specialist tasks performed in isolation from others

    2   precise definition of methods and duties

    3   vertical interactions within management

    4   operational behaviour governed by superiors

    5   vertical communication flows.

    A mechanistic system of organisation appeared to be 'appropriate to an enterprise operating under relatively stable conditions.'

3. By comparison, an 'organic' system was seen to be adapted to 'unstable conditions, when problems ... arise which cannot be broken down and distributed among specialist roles within a clearly defined hierarchy.' The outstanding features of organic systems were seen as:

    1   specialist tasks seen in the context of the whole enterprise

    2   jobs loosely defined and subject to change

    3   interaction and communication are performed laterally as well as vertically

    4   knowledge is seen as distributed throughout the organisation.

4. Whether organisations see themselves as 'mechanistic' or as 'organic', the fact remains that most of them will be faced by change in one form or another. Organisation development, or adapting the organisation to respond adequately to change, is a growing focus of attention in business and public services. Ultimately, organisation development (see Chapter 10) is implemented at the level of the

individual job. That is to say, job design is a key element in responding to changing conditions.

JOB DESIGN – KEY ISSUES

5. The questions faced by those seeking to adapt jobs can be summarised as follows:

    1   What tasks need to be done?

    2   How should these tasks be divided between people, computers and machines?

    3   What are the optimum tasks for people, in terms of (a) efficiency, and (b) personal satisfaction?

    4   How ought tasks to be grouped to form individual jobs?

    5   What mechanisms are required to facilitate changes to jobs in response to new conditions?

    6   What priority should be given to organisational efficiency over individual job satisfaction?

6. The answers to these questions will depend largely on the attitude of the senior management to the issue of organisation structure. If a mechanistic approach is preferred, then it is likely that people's jobs will be designed around machines and work-systems rather than the other way round. In an organic approach, it is much more likely that individual needs will be given precedence over those of the production process.

7. The reasons why the above-mentioned questions are important are basically as follows:

    1   They enable the management of an organisation to consider how they ought to approach the problem of allocating tasks throughout the organisation.

    2   They focus attention on how to obtain optimum potential performance from the organisation's employees.

    3   They highlight the issue of how best to combine human and material resources to attain organisation goals.

    4   They are the pointer to steps that might be taken to achieve a high level of employee job satisfaction.

    5   They raise the issue of how far employees' needs should be sacrificed to considerations of 'efficiency'.

8. Looking at job design as a whole, the most widely applied approaches can be summarised in Figure 9.1.

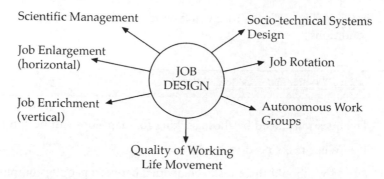

Figure 9.1 *Approaches to job design*

The above approaches will be described briefly in the rest of this chapter, and their implications considered. The impact of Information Technology is a significant factor in current personnel management and job design, and will be considered towards the end of the chapter.

JOB DESIGN AND SCIENTIFIC MANAGEMENT

9. The dominant rationale for job design over the past 50 years has been the need to achieve optimum output. This is the rationale of 'scientific management', in which human work and effort is seen in terms of its relationship to machines and the systems created for them. As Davis & Taylor (1979)[2] put it:

    > What we have seen is the rationalisation of man, inappropriately called the rationalisation of work, and, in the 1960s, the rationalisation of systems.

    The hallmarks of job design according to the scientific management approach are as follows:

    - maximum degree of job specialisation
    - minimal levels of skill
    - minimal time for completion of tasks
    - minimal learning time
    - maximum use of machines
    - minimal degree of flexibility or discretion in the job
    - measurability of job tasks.

10. The production systems resulting from such an approach have undoubtedly led to many improvements in efficiency and productivity at work. Taylor's (1911)[3] application of work study in the Bethlehem Steel Works produced a convincing case for improving productivity by designing a job rationally and then fitting the worker to it. In postwar conditions, however, many businesses and public services have experienced something of a disappointment in the results of the rational approach to work. Labour turnover has been high, absenteeism and lateness have

been widespread, attention to quality has been poor, and flexibility of labour has been difficult to achieve. In effect, man has rebelled against much of the rigidity imposed on his working conditions by the 'technological imperative', as someone has called the demands for people to fit in with machines. Davis & Taylor (1979)[2] consider that:

> We have been unequal to the task thus imposed on us of designing jobs and roles that appropriately relate man, with his needs and unique capabilities, to technology ...

It is because we have been unequal to the task that, in the last ten years in particular, greater efforts have been made to look at job design from the point of view of the employee as well as from the perspective of the production system.

JOB DESIGN

11. The concept of 'job design' is ascribed to Davis & Canter (1955)[4], who saw job design as

> the organisation (or structuring) of a job to satisfy the technical-organisation requirements of the work ... and the human requirements of the person performing the work.

Davis's work led him on to identify a number of design problems relating to the structuring of jobs. These were:

a)   identifying job boundaries

b)   identifying the factors at work in jobs

c)   determining methods of estimating and controlling these factors

d)   developing systematic design methods

e)   developing criteria for evaluating designs.

(Davis, 1957)[5]

12. In facing up to these problems, Davis concluded that, in order to achieve more effective performance and greater job satisfaction on the part of the employee, it was necessary for jobs to be 'meaningful' to the individual concerned. This idea has since become a dominant feature of modern approaches to job design summed up in the 'quality of working life' movement (see below).

SOCIO-TECHNICAL SYSTEMS

13. In the 1960s, the focus of job design moved away from the perspective of seeing jobs as the basic organisational units in a work system towards a perspective that saw jobs as part of a wider socio-technical system. From this latter viewpoint jobs are seen as arising from, and dependent on, the way in which the management approaches the technical and social features of the organisation. The implication of the socio-technical systems approach is that managements can choose what

configuration of social and technical systems seem the most appropriate to them. Jobs, therefore become inventions to meet particular sets of conditions at any one point in time, and are always liable to change.

14. The classic case on which socio-technical systems theory is based is that of the British coalmining study carried out by Trist & Bamforth (1951)[6]. The key features of this important study are summarised in the following paragraphs.

15. During the 1940s, Trist and Bamforth of the Tavistock Institute of Human Relations, carried out a lengthy study into the effects of mechanisation on social and work organisation at the coalface. Before mechanisation the coal had been extracted by small closely-knit teams of men working more or less as autonomous groups. They worked at their own pace, sharing the work between the group members and making their own decisions, invariably isolated in the darkness from other work-teams. Conflicts between groups were frequent and sometimes violent, but always contained. Bonds developed within groups were maintained outside work and carried over into the men's social life. This system of working was known as the 'shortwall' method of coal-getting and was the system that operated before the introduction of mechanical coal-cutters and conveyors.

16. The mechanised system which replaced it was known as the longwall method. This system required a long coalface which called for teams of between 40 and 50 men, together with supervisors, all spread out over a distance of some 200 yards. The new system was in effect a mass-production system based on a high degree of job specialisation. This specialisation was enhanced by the fact that the work was divided up between three shifts. This meant that the first shift would cut the coal, the second shift would clear it onto the conveyors and the third shift advanced the coalface along the seam. Under the earlier system each team had performed all of these basic functions.

17. The social consequences of the longwall method were observed to be as follows:

    1   there was a complete breakdown of the closely integrated social structure underground

    2   there was increased haggling over pay

    3   competition between shifts became intense

    4   absenteeism increased noticeably.

18. The conclusion drawn by Trist and Bamforth was that effective work was a function of the interdependence between technology and social needs. They realised that it was not enough to regard the work environment as *either* a technical system or a social system, but as a combination of the two, that is a 'socio-technical system'. Eventually a 'composite longwall method' was introduced with the help of the researchers. This composite system enabled the social needs of the underground workers to be met, whilst at the same time utilising the benefits of the new machinery. Tasks within shifts were no longer exclusively directed to any one basic function, e.g. coal-cutting, but could range over all the basic functions. These and other changes enabled the revised method to achieve higher productivity, lower absenteeism and fewer accidents.

19. Socio-technical systems theory, according to Davis & Trist (1974)[7], rests on two

major assumptions. First, that in any work system output is achieved through the joint operation of social as well as technical systems. Second, that every socio-technical system is affected by the culture and values of its environment, with which it interacts. The first assumption acknowledges the existence of two separate, but interdependent, variables in organisation design. These can be shown diagrammatically as in Figure 9.2.

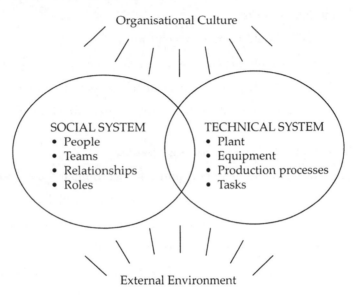

Figure 9.2 *Socio-technical system*

The 'social system' embraces both formal and informal groups for example, official work-teams and unofficial groupings based on friendships and other informal relationships. The 'technical system' encompasses tasks and production processes as well as visible features such as plant and equipment.

20. The second assumption of socio-technical systems theory suggests that there is no such thing as the 'technological imperative'. i.e. that everything is subordinate to technical considerations. On the contrary, technical systems are as much influenced by culture and environment as social systems. We do not *have* to devise jobs around machines. We do have the alternative of assuming that machine-based systems can be adapted to meet the important needs of human beings. The 'new technology' according to Davis & Taylor (1976)[8] works in favour of increasing social considerations, since the new processes have pre-empted people's roles in respect of energy provision and the guidance of tools, but have left open the crucial role of controller or regulator of work systems.

THE QUALITY OF WORKING LIFE

21. In Britain the former Work Research Unit of the Department of Employment has made work design its major focus. As a result of case studies analysed by the WRU

111

together with the findings of others engaged in work research, the WRU produced a guide to good practice in work design. Much of this work has acquired the label of 'the quality of working life movement', as its main thrust is towards creating conditions in which employee-needs are given a high priority compared with the requirements of technology. In a typical paper by White (1982)[9], the WRU guidelines suggested the following approach to the design of work:

1   In relation to tasks:

    a)   tasks should form a coherent job

    b)   tasks should provide some variety of pace, method, location and skill

    c)   tasks should provide for feedback on performance

    d)   tasks should allow for some degree of discretion by the person concerned.

2   In relation to job and work organisation:

    a)   there should be opportunities for learning and development

    b)   some sort of desirable future should be available

    c)   people should be able to contribute to decisions affecting their job

    d)   work goals should be clear, and provide a degree of challenge

    e)   adequate resources should be available to the job-holders.

3   In relation to the work context:

    a)   industrial relations procedures should be jointly agreed between management and employees

    b)   payments systems should be seen to be fair and should be related to contribution made

    c)   personnel policies should be fair and adequate

    d)   physical surroundings should be reasonable.

22.   The above guidelines represent something of an ideal view of what should be done to enhance job satisfaction and human dignity at work. In practice, several contrasting approaches have been adopted over recent years, all of which contain some of the elements of the WRU's suggestions. The most widely known efforts have been:

- job enrichment

- job enlargement

- job rotation

- autonomous groups.

These different approaches are summarised in the next few paragraphs.

JOB ENRICHMENT AND JOB ENLARGEMENT

23.   One of the ways of tackling the issue of employee performance and satisfaction is to enhance the motivating factors in jobs. The term 'job enrichment' was coined by Herzberg (1968)[10] to denote the vertical enlargement of a job by adding responsibility and opportunity for personal growth, for example. Job enrichment needs to be distinguished from 'job enlargement' which generally involves only the horizontal extension of the job, i.e. 'more of the same thing'. Herzberg put it thus: 'Job enrichment provides the opportunity for the employee's psychological growth, while job enlargement merely makes a job structurally bigger.'

24.   In job enrichment the emphasis in redesigning jobs is directed towards individual job satisfaction rather than towards increased efficiency. There have been two major influences on job enrichment:

●   Herzberg's (1959)[11] motivation-hygiene theory.

●   Expectancy theory (see Chapter 8 above).

Herzberg suggested that there were several factors at work which could lead to employees' experiencing job satisfaction and thus, in Herzberg's view, be motivated. These factors included achievement, recognition, responsibility and opportunities for personal growth. Herzberg (1968)[10] proposed 'seven useful starting points' adopting principles of vertical job loading, i.e. job enrichment. These seven points are as follows:

1   Remove some controls while retaining accountability.

2   Increase the accountability of individuals for their own work.

3   Give a person a complete unit of work.

4   Grant additional authority to an employee.

5   Make periodic reports back to employee rather than to his or her supervisor.

6   Introduce new and more difficult tasks.

7   Assign individuals tasks which enable them to become experts.

As will be seen shortly, many of these points have indeed been adopted by job designers in order to meet human needs at work.

25.   The other influence on job enrichment has been that of Expectancy theory. In a nutshell, expectancy theory states that if an employee can see links between his or her efforts and performance, and between performance and rewards, and if those rewards are personally valuable to him or her, then he or she will be motivated to put in the required effort. The relevance of this theory to job design is considered by Lawler (1969)[12] as follows:

> ... if changes in job design are going to affect an individual's motivation they must either change the value of the outcomes that are seen to depend on effort, or positively affect the individual's beliefs about the probability that certain outcomes are dependent upon effort. The argument ... is that job design changes can have a

positive effect on motivation because they can change an individual's beliefs about the probability that certain rewards will result from putting forth high level of effort.

Lawler, in fact, uses Maslow's list of needs to illustrate the application of the theory to job design. He considers extrinsic rewards as mostly satisfying lower level needs, whilst intrinsic rewards seem to satisfy higher level needs. The key rewards, or motivators, according to Lawler are the intrinsic rewards, since they derive from the job itself. In terms of job design factors, Lawler favours the following:

1   the job should allow for meaningful feedback

2   the job should test the individual's valued abilities

3   the job should permit a great amount of self-control.

26.   These ideas have been taken a stage further by Hackman (1977)[13], who suggests that meaningfulness, responsibility and knowledge of results do contribute to increased motivation and performance at work. As Figure 9.3 indicates, certain task characteristics are observed to lead to 'critical psychological states', which in turn produce a number of desirable personal and work outcomes.

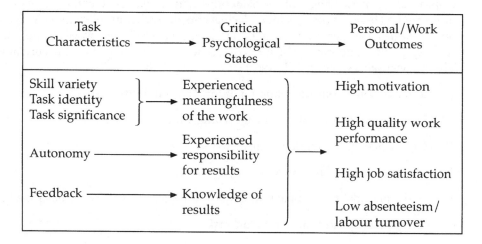

Figure 9.3   *Task characteristics and work motivation (adapted from Hackman 1977)*

27.   Whilst accepting that there will be gains both to individuals and to organisations from implementing job redesign, it is worth noting the cautionary, if not sceptical comments on the quality of working life movement made by Burrell & Morgan (1979)[14]:

> [This movement] . . . is based upon a philosophy of piecemeal social engineering which seeks to solve the problems posed by the transition from the industrial to the post-industrial society. (p. 182)

They further comment that:

> Although committed to humanitarian concern for the development of human growth and potential through the satisfaction of 'higher-level' psychological needs, their

'selling pitch' is invariably geared to the contribution this will make to the stability and survival of the system as a whole.

Their conclusion is that 'the quality of working life movement stands as the contemporary equivalent of the industrial psychology and human relations movements.' They clearly see current job design as firmly rooted in a culture that is based upon an essentially managerial view of organisations.

JOB ENRICHMENT IN PRACTICE

28.   Several studies have been carried out on the application of job design principles over the past decade or so. One of the earliest British studies concerned the application of job enrichment in ICI during the late 1960s. In this study by Paul & Robertson (1970)[15], job enrichment was defined as follows:

> ... to improve both task efficiency and human satisfaction by building into people's jobs, quite specifically, greater scope for personal achievement and recognition, more challenging and responsible work, and more opportunity for individual advancement and growth.

As their definition suggests, they were strongly influenced by the earlier work of Herzberg (Motivation – Hygiene Theory), who emphasised motivators such as achievement, recognition and responsibility.

29.   The subjects of the ICI research were drawn from a number of different employee categories: sales representatives, design engineers, production and engineering foremen and others. Each group of subjects was divided into an experimental group (in which job changes were made) and a control group (in which jobs remained unchanged).

In the case of the sales representatives, disappointing sales throughout the Company appeared to be due to insufficient effort on the part of the sales representatives. This was despite the fact that an attitude survey had shown that these representatives appeared well-satisfied with their current jobs. It was decided to introduce several changes into the working practices of the experimental group in order to stimulate greater effort on their part, and thus bring about increased sales. The perspective here was definitely managerial and output-oriented!

30.   The theme of the changes, according to Paul and Robertson, was 'to build up the sales representative's job so that it became more complete in its own right'. Examples of the changes introduced were as follows:

1   Responsibility for determining call-rates was placed wholly on the representatives themselves.

2   Representatives were given a discretionary range of about 10 per cent on the prices they could charge on most of the product sold, and had to report any quotations at other than 'list price'. The results of the changes were that sales in the group gradually increased, whilst those of the control group fell considerably. Turn around time on customer complaints was speeded up, and individual job satisfaction increased even further.

31. Taking their study as a whole, Paul & Robertson concluded among other things that:

    1 job enrichment led to improved performance by employees, and not once led to poorer performance

    2 reactions to job enrichment were an increase in enthusiasm for work, and did not reduce a person's level of interest

    3 the gains from job enrichment were significant financially, and were more related to effective job performance than to individual satisfaction

    4 the effects on management and supervision were generally beneficial, for example:

        i)   'production foremen's supervisors found themselves playing an altogether more managerial role'

        ii) 'The hidden agenda in all job enrichment studies is managers' fear that they will lose control, authority, prestige and power. In fact they don't: they may lose the semblance, but they gain the substance.'

32. In the ICI studies increased employee job satisfaction did not appear as one of the dominant outcomes of job enrichment. In other cases (see Bailey (1983)[16] greater job satisfaction has been one of the key gains quoted by the organisation, along with other indicators of human satisfaction such as reduced absenteeism, reduced lateness, reduced labour turnover and improved quality of work. Strauss (1976)[17], in a review of the literature on job redesign, expressed his doubts as to the effects of job redesign as follows:

    Ironically, although job restructuring has been presented as a motivator, in practice it may work more like a hygiene. Turnover, absenteeism, and satisfaction have improved. But as far as production is concerned, the clearest gain seems to be that the work force is more flexible, not that it is more highly motivated.

AUTONOMOUS WORK GROUPS

33. In several examples of job redesign the emphasis has been on group work rather than on individual jobs. The most well-known studies into group working are those conducted at Volvo, Saab-Scania and Philips. The idea of autonomous work groups is an extension of job enrichment to a collection of jobs. Such groups tend to be typified by the following characteristics:

    1 they permit full labour flexibility by job rotation

    2 they have a considerable degree of autonomy in the allocation of work between members

    3 they have considerable discretion to plan their production schedules, within broad management guide-lines

    4 they organise their own rest periods

5   they may elect their own team-leader

6   they encourage full participation in group decision-making.

34.   The extent of discretion granted by management to a work group determines whether it is 'autonomous' or 'semi-autonomous', but this distinction is nothing when contrasted with the difference between group working and the 'assembly-line approach' to production. According to Emery (1979)[18], in reviewing his work at the Volvo plant and elsewhere, the revolution of introducing semi-autonomous work groups

> has not been that of throwing out the assembly line. The revolutionary change began with the eradication of an organisational principle of 'one man-one shift-one station' a principle that had no intrinsic relation to the design of the assembly lines.

In effect, what Emery is describing is a series of production clusters, each of which is performing typical assembly line operations.

JOB DESIGN – SOME CONCLUSIONS

35.   The evidence for the success or otherwise of job design is still emerging. What evidence is available has come mainly from a few widely publicised studies, whose common ground has been the enthusiasm for the results achieved rather than 'hard' evidence of common relationships between studies. On the evidence so far, it is possible to make a number of tentative conclusions about the design of jobs. These are as follows:

A.   In relation to job performance:

1   limited improvements in job performance are likely

2   considerable improvements in quality are likely

3   labour flexibility is vastly increased

4   significant cost-savings are likely to be achieved by reductions in absenteeism and labour turnover

5   change may be easier to introduce due to the enhanced level of labour flexibility.

B.   In relation to employee motivation and satisfaction:

1   some increase in job satisfaction

2   removal of several causes of dissatisfaction (repetitive work, excessive supervision, etc.).

36.   Strauss (1976)[17] sums up the prevailing opinion concerning employee motivation that

> ... it is fair to conclude that most blue-collar workers and perhaps many white-collar workers as well – (1) would prefer some increase in challenge and autonomy in their jobs, or would learn to like these if they had them, but (2) are not prepared to give up much in the way of material benefits ... to obtain challenge and autonomy, nor (3)

would they give higher priority to challenge and autonomy than to various hygienes such as higher pay, safety, flex-time ... and the like.

If what he suggests is true, then job redesign programmes may continue to be relatively small-scale affairs rather than major forces for change in organisations.

37. An important current issue involving all the problems of work design is the introduction of new technology into offices, and we shall end this chapter by considering some highlights of this issue.

THE IMPACT OF INFORMATION TECHNOLOGY IN OFFICES

38. Within the last decade we have seen a great leap in the application of new technology to office work. For the first time in the history of office work, investment in machinery is reaching a stage where issues of boredom, work fragmentation, redundant skills and unemployment are having to be faced on a scale never previously experienced. Offices may prove to be the battleground of a renewed struggle between the quality of working life and scientific management. The current situation has been triggered by the arrival of 'Information Technology' (IT). IT is a combination of three related technologies:

- computing

- electronics

- telecommunications.

IT has applications in industrial settings, where it is employed for process control, machine control and for monitoring. However, it is in the office setting that IT truly comes into its own, for the very reason that offices are, above all else, centres of information processing, storage and distribution.

39. In offices IT takes such forms as word processing, personal computing, electronic data storage and retrieval, electronic mail and local area networking (internal communications systems using IT). Birchall & Hammond (1981)[19] indicated the changing nature of office systems by means of a wheel diagram, which provides the basis for Figure 9.4.

Probably the most significant feature of the wheel is the fact that all the different office systems have converged into a combined system sustained and supported by microelectronic technology. This feature has considerable implications for the organisation of offices, for the skills required in them, and for the numbers of personnel required to operate them. It also raises issues of security and discipline in respect of employee records, use of email and the Internet (See Chapter 17 for details of data protection, and Chapter 38 for disciplinary aspects of email and Internet use).

40. In a Report by APEX (1980)[20], a white-collar trade union pointed out the dangers to staff of being unprepared in the face of the rapidly changing office technology:

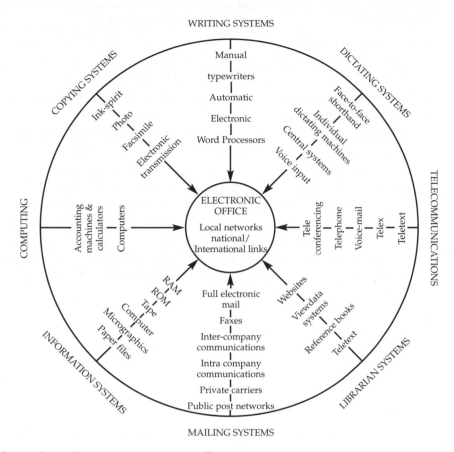

Figure 9.4 *Changing technology in office systems*

Microelectronic technology has a number of distinctive features. It is flexible, instantaneous and can be rapidly modified ... It is reliable ... available ... and most important of all, it is cheap ... The new technology poses a challenge to trade union representatives ... If ... questions of job content, skills, training and grading are neglected (by the union) there is a danger that ... a large proportion of the office workforce will find itself in more routine and less satisfying jobs.

41. The capacity of IT to combine several functions into one unit, such as a word processor, can lead to major structural changes in jobs. For example, in the past a personal secretary not only fulfilled a number of different tasks (typing, filing, reception work, etc.), but did so in a variety of work modes (sitting, standing, moving around). Now, with the onset of IT, the secretary has fewer options in terms of work modes, because most of his or her office functions can be channelled through a computerised workstation, at which he or she must sit for most of the day.

42. Like other technological marvels, Information Technology presents opportunities as well as threats to employees. Briefly, the advantages and disadvantages of IT are as follows:

Advantages	Disadvantages
• Learning new skills	• Fewer jobs will be required
• Tedious jobs can be delegated to machines	• Office workers might become 'machine minders'
• Possibility of upgrading	• Individuals may become tied to their workstations
• Easier and quicker access to information	• Health problems associated with VDUs*/printers, etc.
• Easier means of remedying typing errors/amending text	• Difficulties of learning to operate electronic machines
• More jobs for those who are skilled in maintenance of electronic equipment	• Strong competition between employees for available jobs
• More jobs for those engaged in manufacturing office machines/ equipment	• Loss of personal contact as information is passed by machine instead of by mouth
• More jobs for programmers and software designers	
• Opportunities for shorter working day/week	* Visual display units

43.   For employers there are few disadvantages and many advantages.

The disadvantages include:

- time/disruption caused on transferring from manual to electronic systems

- software may not necessarily meet operational needs, and may have to be custom-made

- considerable upheaval amongst existing staff.

Advantages include:

- substantial savings on salaries due to fewer staff required

- relative cheapness of new technology (e.g. a word processor may cost as little as £1000 compared with £15,000 plus benefits for a secretary)

- substantial reduction in office space required as disk storage replaces filing cabinets, etc.

- speed of obtaining, processing, storing and retrieving information

- vastly increased productivity in offices

- flexibility of working due to variety of equipment available, all or most of which can be operated by existing staff

- less reliance on other services (e.g. printing)

- improved communications between individual executives and offices.

REFERENCES

1. Burns, T. & Stalker, G.M (1961), *The Management of Innovation*, Tavistock.

2. Davis, L E & Taylor, J.C. (1979), *Design of Jobs* (2nd edn), Goodyear.

3. Taylor, F.W. (1911), *Principles and Methods of Scientific Management*, Harper.

4. Davis, L.E. & Canter, R.R. (1955), 'Job Design', *Journal of Industrial Engineering*, Vol. 6, p. 3.

5. Davis, L.E. (1957), 'Toward a Theory of Job Design', *Journal of Industrial Engineering*, Vol. 8, p. 19.

6. Trist, E. & Bamforth, K. (1951), 'Some Social and Psychological Consequences of the Longwall Method of Coal-getting', *Human Relations*, Vol. 4, No. 1.

7. Davis, L.E. & Trist, E. (1974), 'Improving the Quality of Working Life: Socio-technical Case Studies, in O'Toole, J. (ed), *Work and the Quality of Life*, M.I.T Press.

8. Davis, L.E. & Taylor, J.C. (1976), *Technology and Job Design, in Design of Jobs* (2nd edn), Goodyear.

9. White, G.C. (1982), 'Technological Changes and Employment', *WRU Occasional Paper 22*, WRU.

10. Herzberg, F. (1968), 'One More Time: How do you Motivate Employees?', *Harvard Business Review*, XLVI, p. 53–68.

11. Herzberg, F. *et al.* (1959), *The Motivation to Work*, Wiley.

12. Lawler, E.E. (1969), 'Job Design and Employee Motivation', in Gruneberg, M. (ed), *Job Satisfaction*, Gower Press.

13. Hackman, J.R. (1977), 'Work Design', in Hackman & Suttle (eds), *Improving Life at Work*, Goodyear.

14. Burrell, G. & Morgan, G. (1979), *Sociological Paradigms and Organisational Analysis*, Heinemann.

15. Paul, W.J. & Robertson, K.B. (1970), *Job Enrichment and Employee Motivation*, Gower Press.

16. Bailey, J. (1983), *Job Design and Work Organisation*, Prentice Hall.

17. Strauss, G. (1976), 'Job Satisfaction, Motivation and Job Redesign', in Strauss *et al.* (eds), *Organisational Behaviour: Research and Issues*, Wadsworth.

18. Emery, F.E. (1979), 'The Assembly Line – Its Logic and our Future', in *Design of Jobs* (2nd edn), Goodyear.

19. Birchall, D. & Hammond, V. (1981), *Tomorrow's Office Today*, Business Books.

20. APEX (1980), *Automation and the Office Worker*, APEX.

CHAPTER 10

Organisational change

INTRODUCTION

1. The subject-matter of this chapter is organisational change. As Lawrence & Lorsch (1969)[1] put it: 'When we talk about organisation development, we are implying that we want to find ways to change the organisation from its current state to a better-developed state.' What is 'Organisation Development (OD)'? This is not an easy question to answer. In his survey of OD in a small number of British companies, Thakur (1974)[2] commented 'In a sense OD defies precise definition since it is a concept rather than a specific technique.' In Thakur's study, the firms concerned were asked to select which of four 'definitions' from the literature they felt was closest to their own understanding of OD. The biggest single preference was for Beckhard's (1969)[3] definition as follows:

    An effort:

    (a) planned

    (b) organisation-wide

    (c) managed from the top, to

    (d) increase organisation's 'processes', using behavioural science knowledge.

2. Beckhard's definition was one of the first to emerge at a time when OD was a very new concept. A fuller, and in some respects much clearer, definition is that of French & Bell (1978)[4] as follows:

    In the behavioural science, and perhaps ideal, sense of the term, organisation development is a long-range effort to improve an organisation's problem-solving and renewal processes, particularly through a more effective and collaborative management of organisation culture – with special emphasis on the culture of formal work teams-with the assistance of a change agent, or catalyst, and the use of the theory and technology of the applied behavioural science, including action research.

    This version incorporates a number of important issues in OD: organisation renewal, culture, collaboration and change agents. These and other aspects of organisation development will be dealt with in the paragraphs which follow.

KEY ISSUES IN ORGANISATION DEVELOPMENT

3.   Organisation development is an approach to change which embraces the organisation as a whole, unlike many other, localised efforts to promote change. OD is fundamentally a strategic activity, which is founded on a systems-concept of organisations. Therefore, change is seen as a function of (a) the external environment (economic, social and political), and (b) the internal transactions between the various sub-groups within the organisation.

Several writers see OD principally in terms of a strategy for learning. Thakur *et al.* (1978)[5], for example, described it as

> fundamentally a learning process that comes about through attempting to resolve task, organisational and human issues. The aim of OD is not just to bring about the transformation of individuals, groups and organisations but rather to get each of these social units to learn how to develop themselves in their work.

4.   We can summarise the key issues of organisation development diagrammatically as shown in Figure 10.1.

Figure 10.1   *Key issues in organisation development*

The above issues are all closely interrelated, but a useful way of understanding them is to consider firstly what a typical OD programme might look like in practice.

OD PROGRAMMES IN PRACTICE

5.   The typical stages of an OD programme are indicated in Figure 10.2.

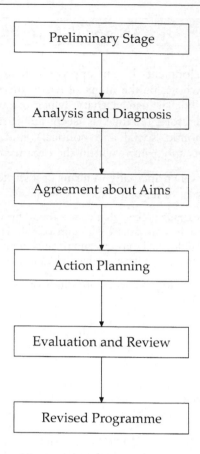

Figure 10.2 *Stages of an OD programme*

6.   The Preliminary Stage consists of establishing that there is a need for an organisation-wide change. The senior management have to ask themselves why they want such a programme. What problems have arisen? What opportunities have presented themselves? If they are satisfied that change is needed, for example, to be able to harness the efficiencies of new technology in the face of intense competition from overseas manufacturers, then discussion can begin to identify the scope and aims of a possible programme. At this point the management concerned will need to appoint a person to act as the co-ordinator, or facilitator, of the programme. This is the role of 'change agent' that is more or less essential to the success of OD activities. The change agent may be some relatively neutral and impartial senior manager, perhaps from the personnel department, or an outsider. Thakur and colleagues (1978)[5] suggested that: 'If there is no one inside the organisation who can fulfil this role of 'internal consultant' or 'change agent', it will be necessary to bring in someone from outside ... A change agent from outside the organisation will be usually less constrained by any organisational politics and 'conditioning'.

7.   One of the key elements of the preliminary stage is to decide the role to be played by the third party, and his or her relationship to the senior management team. Some situations may call for a third party to act as an 'expert adviser' or as a

'catalyst' for new ways of thinking and acting. Other situations require the third party to be more of a 'soundingboard' or a 'facilitator'. In another situation the prime role is that of 'educator' or 'analyst'. A preferred role is the one of 'process consultant' as described by Schein (1969)[6] in an influential book on organisation development:

> The process consultant seeks to give the client 'insight' into what is going on around him, within him and between him and other people.

8. The range of roles expected of a third party, be that an individual change agent or a team of consultants, depends considerably on the extent to which the client organisation wants to be directed. Many organisations want to be given clear direction as to what is the best way forward at a time of change; others want to be supplied with ideas or inspiration but wish to take the initiative themselves and thus look for a non-directive approach from their change agent. In between these two broad approaches are various options which may be sought by organisations, as suggested in simplified form in Figure 10.3. The diagram indicates that there is a range of roles that can be adopted by change agents, and these can be plotted on a continuum of relative directiveness from a highly directive approach to a substantially non-directive one. There are no clear boundaries in practice between the different roles depicted, which should be seen as merging and overlapping with their neighbours.

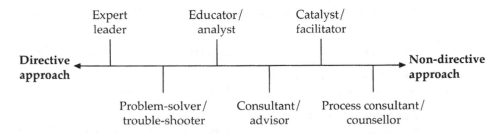

Figure 10.3 *Range of third party/change agent roles in OD*

9. Once the scope and aims of the OD Programme have been agreed, the focus of activities is on analysis and diagnosis, i.e. on 'finding out'. At this stage the change agent usually takes the initiative in proposing and designing appropriate and acceptable means of acquiring relevant information. This may be done by using questionnaires, conducting interviews, observing day-to-day activities and locating relevant documentation and statistics. As French and Bell (1978)[4] put it:

> An OD programme thus starts with diagnosis and continuously employs data collecting and data analysing throughout. The requirement for diagnostic activities – activities designed to provide an accurate account of things as they really are stems from two needs: the first need is to know the state of things, or 'what is'; the second need is to know the effects or consequences of actions.

10. An example of the kind of questionnaire that might be used at the diagnostic stage is shown in Figure 10.4, which indicates the sort of questions that are often put to employees to assess their views about the way the organisation operates. This enables managements to get a better awareness of the organisation's internal strengths and weaknesses. The results obtained from such a questionnaire also give

clues as to the current climate, or culture, of the organisation. Since most of the questions tend to be put simply and briefly, it is often necessary to follow up the replies by randomly asking a selection of employees to supply further details. In this situation the questioning is done by the external change agent and not by management in order to maintain confidentiality and thus encourage employees to be truthful about how they feel.

In the following pairs of statements please indicate which answer is nearest to your experience of this organisation by circling one of the three choices available. There are no right or wrong answers, only your view of which is the most appropriate answer to describe how things are for you. All replies are anonymous. Please feel free to answer as frankly as possible.

1	In this company communication between management and staff is	Excellent	Fairly good	Poor
2	Work tasks and targets are made clear	Always	Sometimes	Rarely
3	My manager is helpful when I have a problem	Always	Sometimes	Rarely
4	Team-working is encouraged	Always	Sometimes	Rarely
5	Conflict is handled constructively	Always	Sometimes	Rarely
6	I feel I have a share in decision-making	Often	Sometimes	Never
7	I feel that my work is recognised	Often	Sometimes	Never
8	There are good career opportunities in this company	Yes	No	Unsure
9	Training for new IT systems is always available	Always	Sometimes	Rarely
10	I feel I am adequately rewarded for my work (i.e. salary, benefits, etc.)	Yes	No	Partly

Figure 10.4 *Organisational climate questionnaire*

11. From the information received in the diagnostic stage, the management team and the change agent consider the implications of what has been revealed about the organisation and its various activities. Eventually an agreed diagnosis is made, which enables the next stage to be implemented – the revised aims of the programme.

These revised aims could be one or more of the following:

1   enable the Company to establish a more appropriate and effective structure following the acquisition of our new partner

2   obtain the commitment of all managers to an open and democratic style of leadership

3   enable the organisation to introduce new electronic equipment into all its major offices with the minimum of disruption to its client services and with optimum co-operation of all the staff concerned

4   achieve the complete restructuring of all our communication and decision-making mechanisms between Head Office and the branches.

12.   Once agreement has been reached about Aims, the Action Stage can commence. Action planning requires decisions to be made about:

- What OD activities should be considered (e.g. team-building, MBO, work structuring)?

- What sequence of events should be followed?

- How should necessary consultation be conducted?

- What resources are required (e.g. training staff, secretarial)?

The majority of OD activities, or interventions as they are sometimes called, are directed towards one or more of the following:

- bringing about change in individual behaviour

- changing organisational structures/mechanisms

- aiding problem-identification and analysis

- changing the culture of the organisation.

OD ACTIVITIES/INTERVENTIONS

13.   Examples of activities aimed at changing behaviour are:

1   Sensitivity training or interpersonal skills training. This usually involves small groups in exploring the feelings and relationships present in the group, in order to help individuals to be aware of them, and to learn to cope adequately with them. This training usually involves quite high levels of stress.

2   Coaching and counselling activities, in which individuals can explore particular aspects of their work-relationships with their immediate superior or an outside counsellor.

3   Transactional Analysis. This is a form of training in which the way people communicate with each other is examined with a view to helping participants to communicate more clearly and tactfully than at present.

4   Team-building activities, designed to help groups to examine how they work together and what they need to improve to achieve better collaboration.

5   Management development activities, such as leadership training (e.g. the Managerial Grid).

14.   Activities aimed at changing structures include:

1   Role Analysis, where individuals examine the roles they are required to perform in their jobs, and subsequently matching their role situation with their job responsibilities and making appropriate changes by agreement with their superiors.

2   Job Redesign (see previous chapter). This refers especially to job enrichment, but may also encompass job rotation and horizontal job enlargement.

3   Organisation Analysis, in which the entire structure of the organisation is examined with a view to reassembling it to form more 'natural' groupings of activities or more efficient ways of achieving corporate objectives.

15.   Activities aimed at aiding problem-identification and analysis include:

1   Diagnostic questionnaires aimed at pin-pointing problem areas (as in Figure 10.4 above).

2   Process consultation, where a third party helps client groups to gain an insight into the various human interactions involved in order to select appropriate behaviour to deal with conflict, competition and complexity, for example.

3   Planning and objectives-setting activities designed to improve identification of priorities, decision-making processes and planning.

16.   The sequence of activities in an OD programme usually commences with problem-analysis and moves on either to structural issues or to behavioural matters, depending on the aims of the programme. Practically every OD programme highlights problems of human relations, whether at a group or individual level, and so behavioural exercises are a dominant feature after the initial diagnostic work.

17.   One major problem faced by change agents is how to deal with resistance to change by many of those involved. Inertia and apathy on the one hand, and fear and prejudice on the other, are all forces resisting change in the organisation. We shall turn briefly to consider some significant techniques for promoting change.

RESISTANCE TO CHANGE

18.   Lewin (1951)[7] contributed his classic notion of 'force-field' theory as a way of demonstrating what process is at work in the move from one state of equilibrium to another. Basically, Lewin's theory states that behaviour is the result of an equilibrium between two sets of forces – driving forces and restraining forces. Thus in any organisation, at a particular point in time, a number of factors will act as driving forces (e.g. top management's desire to save the business) and others will act as restraining forces (e.g. employee disillusionment with management). The basic 'force-field' model can be summarised as shown in Figure 10.5.

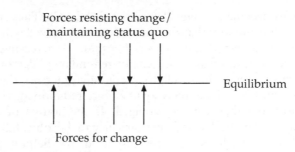

Figure 10.5 *Force-field theory*

19. The 'force-field' model can be used to map out conflicting issues in a changing situation. Figure 10.6 gives examples of the kinds of factors that can emerge on both sides of the line of equilibrium when a management team decides to introduce new ways of working involving multi-skilled activities.

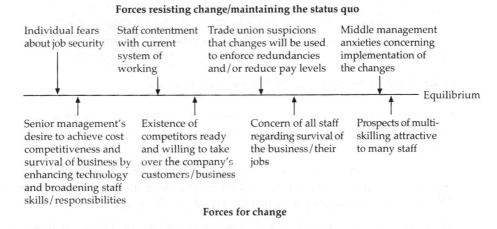

Figure 10.6 *Applying force-field analysis*

The opposing forces in Figure 10.6 represent the reality of the situation as it appears to those concerned. The most productive way forward for the senior management is to tackle *both* sides of the line at once, building on the forces for change by exploiting people's desires for survival and possible new challenge, and reducing the effects of resistance by allaying fears and anxieties.

20. The important point about the opposing forces is that they exist to the extent that individuals perceive them as existing. For example, if the management believe that their employees are resistant to the idea of implementing new technology in the offices, they will conduct their proposals for introducing change in a rather different way than if they believed that the employees were generally in favour of the new technology. Hence the emphasis in OD programmes on using diagnostic aids to help individuals to gain a better awareness of the forces that are operating in their environment.

21. The natural tendency among humans appears to be to utilise driving forces to implement change. However, this approach all too easily causes the restraining

forces to become stronger ('resistance hardens'). Thus in an OD programme, the greatest likelihood is that the change agents involved will aim to focus on removing or weakening restraining forces rather than on increasing the driving forces. So, for example, instead of using threats of redundancy, demotion and top management sanctions to persuade people to adopt new practices, the change agents will try to identify the obstacles in the way of embittered individuals or unhelpful procedures, and see how they can be changed. If the source of discontent of embittered employees can be located, perhaps it can be obviated or at least mitigated. If unhelpful procedures can be displaced by helpful procedures, or removed altogether, then another source of restraining forces has been removed, or at least seriously weakened.

22. Lewin developed a three-stage approach to changing behaviour, which was adopted and elaborated by Schein (1964)[8]. This approach involves 'unfreezing' present behaviour, 'changing' or developing new behaviour, and, finally, 'refreezing' or reinforcing the new behaviour (see Figure 10.7).

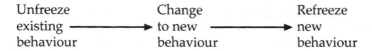

Figure 10.7   *Three-stage approach to changing behaviour*

23. Unfreezing is mainly concerned with providing individuals or groups with a motive for change, i.e. they must be able to see that change is not only necessary, but is also desirable.

Changing is mainly a question of identifying (with a change agent) what is more appropriate behaviour and then acquiring 'ownership' of this changed behaviour. The role of the change agent is usually crucial at this stage.

Refreezing implies consolidating the new behaviour by providing various rewards from the organisation (pay, promotion and praise, etc.).

Of the three stages, the unfreezing stage is probably the most difficult to bring about successfully, since it is this stage that requires real motivation to move away from the status quo.

24. Assessing the prospects for introducing change involves a full analysis of current conditions and attitudes within the organisation concerned. Tynan (1980)[9], in an article on the quality of working life, suggests that there are some conditions which do favour the change process. These may be summarised as follows:

1   the enterprise is financially viable, and seen as secure by the employees

2   there is significant room for changes to jobs and work organisation

3   an awareness of the value of a participative approach to problem-solving

4   a considerable degree of trust exists between management and employees

5   effective systems of negotiation and consultation are in operation

6   there is a high degree of commitment to change by the senior management

7   there are no serious deficiencies in conditions of employment

8   there is provision for action on manning levels, job security and pay considerations.

25.   The above list suggests strongly that implementing change relies on a higher-than-average level of trust and collaboration between management and employees. A good deal of trust can be built up by involving employees widely in the change process, for example by enabling them to complete opinion questionnaires and participate in group discussions. Collaboration, or active co-operation, requires managements to consider the consequences of change for their employees and to find ways of softening some of the unpleasant results of change for certain individuals.

26.   Chin & Benne (1976)[10] described three categories of change strategies:

1   *Empirical-rational*, in which it is assumed that people will follow their rational self-interest, and thus will accept change if they can see that this is advantageous to them.

2   *Normative-re-educative*, in which change comes through a re-education process in which old norms (standards of behaviour) are replaced by new norms.

3   *Power-coercive*, in which change is pushed through by those with the power to force compliance from others.

27.   Organisation Development is firmly located in the normative-re-educative category on account of its commitment to an open and collaborative approach to change. The empirical-rational category is more likely to apply in organisations where a unitary view of employee relations is dominant (e.g. in many Japanese companies). The power-coercive category is more likely to be seen in situations where survival is at stake and management can be ruthless in pursuing their objectives.

CONCLUSION

28.   As the previous paragraphs have indicated, the processes involved in achieving change are complex and far-reaching. Organisations that utilise Organisation Development programmes as their principal means of effecting change are implying that openness, mutual trust and participation will be the hallmarks of their approach. However the techniques available in OD, whilst giving full consideration to individual sensitivity, are nevertheless basically aimed at revealing weaknesses as well as strengths, and conflicts as well as collaborative efforts. OD, therefore, can never be a comfortable exercise for most people in the organisation. Hence the importance of top management support for such a programme if it is to weather the inevitable stormy periods in order to realise the benefits of increased participation, better team-working, more effective problem-solving and other benefits of planned change.

REFERENCES

1. Lawrence, P.R. & Lorsch, J.W. (1969), *Developing Organisations: Diagnosis and Action*, Addison-Wesley.

2. Thakur, M. (1974), 'OD: The Search for Identity', *Information Report No. 16*, IPM.

3. Beckhard, R. (1969), *Organisation Development: Strategies and Models*, Addison-Wesley.

4. French, W.L. & Bell, C.H. (1978), *Organisation Development* (2nd edn), Prentice Hall.

5. Thakur, M. *et al.* (eds), (1978), *Personnel in Change*, IPM.

6. Schein, E.H. (1969), *Process Consultation: its Role in Organisation Development*, Addison-Wesley.

7. Lewin, K. (1951), *Field Theory in Social Science*, Harper.

8. Schein, E.H. (1964), 'The Mechanisms of Change', in Bennis, W.G. *et al.* (eds), *Interpersonal Dynamics* (1964), Dorsey Press.

9. Tynan, O. (1980), 'Improving the Quality of Working Life', *WRU Occasional Paper 16*, Work Research Unit, London.

10. Chin, R. & Benne, K., 'General Strategies for Effecting Changes in Human Systems', in Bennis, W.G. *et al.*, *The Planning of Change* (3rd edn) (1976), Holt, Rinehart & Winston.

QUESTIONS FOR DISCUSSION/HOMEWORK

1. How might you distinguish a commercial enterprise (business or industrial) from a public-sector service (local or national) in terms of:

   a) organisational culture?

   b) overall purpose/goals?

   c) organisation structure?

   d) use of technology?

2. What would you describe as a 'contingency approach' to organisations?

3. How reasonable is it to discuss organisations as if they exist in their own right?

4. Why do you think that organisation theorists have adopted a managerial perspective in their analysis of organisations?

5. What is the justification for specialisation in organisations?

6. What are the essential differences between jobs and roles?

7. How would you measure success in leadership?

8. What variables, in addition to the personal attributes of the leader, are important in the leadership situation?

9. Why are groups significant in the workplace?

10. What kinds of factors contribute to the development of team spirit in a group?

11. What is power and what forms can it take?

12. How might Expectancy Theory be applied to improve the motivation of employees in either a public authority, or a commercial undertaking?

13. What examples of the scientific management approach to job design can you supply from modern organisations?

14. What specific factors are likely to motivate professional staff, in your opinion?

15. In what situations would you expect a change agent to adopt an expert role rather than say a counselling role?

16. What are the pressures on managements when it comes to selecting people for redundancy in a situation where some employees have to leave, whilst others remain?

EXAMINATION QUESTIONS

EQ4 'Rational-economic man', 'social man' and 'self-actualising man' are theories that have been advanced successively about the motivation of employees at work. How useful are they in indicating how to manage employees?

(ABE Diploma)

EQ5 What factors determine the form of organisation structure that is appropriate in a particular situation?

(IPM Stage 2)

EQ6 You have been studying staff turnover rates in a region of the bank where you are employed as a personnel manager. You notice that the turnover of clerical staff is much higher in the regional head office than it is in a busy branch in a suburb of the same town.

What are likely to be the key factors which would explain the difference and what might be done to lower the clerical staff turnover rate in the regional head office?

(IOB-NOM)

EQ7 a) Offer a workable definition of leadership and identify what are currently accepted as the most important types of leader.

b) Define 'trait theory' and discuss whether there is still some merit in this approach.

(HCIMA)

CASE STUDY 2: THE GWYN VALLEY RAILWAY

BACKGROUND INFORMATION

The Gwyn Valley Railway is an important tourist attraction located near the Snowdonia National Park. In addition to a substantial museum of steam engines and old railway equipment, the GVR offers visitors excursion rides in authentically-restored locomotives over some 16 miles of track. The railway was founded fifteen years ago by a small, but dedicated, group of railway enthusiasts, who appointed Ron Bailey as full-time General Manager. Under Bailey's management the railway has grown from an archaeological rubbish-tip to a much-loved centre for tourists, and locals too. Financially, the GVR operates as a company limited by guarantee. Its objectives are to develop the railway as a leisure and educational activity on a non-profit-making basis. Due to this position, it has not been possible to borrow large sums to finance the operation, and has had to rely (a) on takings from visitors, and (b) on donations from wealthy patrons or commercial undertakings. Despite these limitations, the railway has improved year by year, partly because of Bailey's shrewd understanding of marketing and finance, and partly because of the vast amount of restoration work carried out by volunteers.

ORGANISATION

The organisation structure of the GVR is as follows:

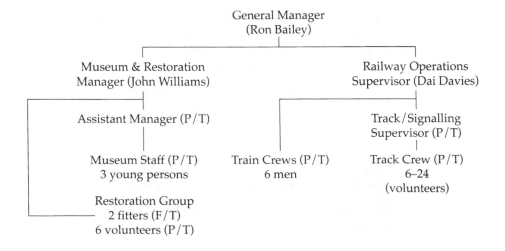

Bailey, as General Manager, is responsible to a Board of Trustees for the overall planning and success of the venture. Above all, he is charged with never allowing the operation to fall into debt. Otherwise he is free to run the railway according to his best judgement.

John Williams is responsible to Bailey for the operation of the museum, which is open for nine months of the year. This entails preparing and mounting the exhibition, staffing it, and collecting the admissions charges. Williams is also responsible for the restoration of locomotives and coaches, work which continues throughout the whole year, except for Christmas and the New Year. Apart from an assistant manager, employed on a part-time basis to help with the management of the museum, Williams has two full-time, permanent fitters working on the rolling stock. Dai Davies' responsibilities are to ensure that the excursion trains are operated safely in accordance with agreed timetables, and that the track and signalling equipment are both safe and in good condition. For this work, Davies has no full-time workers, but several part-timers, who worked a rota system for the nine months of railway operations. The key person in Davies' team is the part-time track/signalling supervisor, who has taken early retirement from similar work with the national railways.

All the full-time staff, Bailey included, receive a modest wage for their efforts together with free meals on duty and low-rent accommodation, if required. Apart from Williams, who has an income from a small farm in the area, the remaining full-time staff are pensioners.

The part-time staff receive a sum per eight-hour shift worked. Rates of pay are low, but meals on duty are free, and caravan accommodation available on a temporary basis.

Volunteers receive no pay, but are provided with free meals and temporary caravan accommodation.

Everybody works hard, but morale is very high.

PROBLEM

Bailey wants to give up his post, and the trustees are therefore looking for a successor. Much of Bailey's success is due to his quiet charisma. He does not need to make an issue of leadership, it comes to him quite naturally. It will be difficult to find someone to follow in his footsteps.

QUESTIONS

1. How would you describe the culture of the Gwyn Valley Railway?

2. What attributes would you look for in a replacement for Bailey?

3. If you were appointed to the post of General Manager what changes would you make to the structure of jobs, and why?

4. Bearing in mind the age profile of the key supervisory and managerial staff, what suggestions would you make to secure the future of the Railway?

5.   What are the implications for management of having a significant number of volunteer staff employed in the organisation?

6.   If you were offered the opportunity to take on, for up to six months, a small number (maximum six) of long-term unemployed persons available under a government-sponsored scheme, what conditions would you want to insist on to the government agency concerned?

PART III

PLANNING THE ORGANISATION'S HUMAN RESOURCES

People represent the most flexible resource available to the senior managers of an organisation. Deploying people in the right numbers, with the right skills and in the right place is fundamental to success. Personnel specialists can play a central role in assisting with the planning of the organisation's human resource requirements. Chapter 11 introduces human resource planning as a systematic approach to the acquisition, use and deployment of people in an organisation. Human resource planning is viewed as a corporate activity arising from the business objectives of the organisation, and leading to specific plans for recruitment, training, promotion, etc. Since human resource planning is essentially about placing people in jobs, Chapter 12 deals with Job Analysis, considering why it is important, how it is carried out, and what typical job descriptions look like. Chapter 13 follows with an outline of the closely related topic of Job Evaluation. Chapters 14 and 15 look at some of the practicalities of acquiring sufficient and suitable new staff. The final two chapters deal with the movement of people out of the organisation (Chapter 16) and with personnel administration (Chapter 17).

CHAPTER 11

Human resource planning

INTRODUCTION

1. Planning the resources of the organisation is a key responsibility of every senior manager. Arguably the most important single resource is people. It is important, therefore, to ensure that sufficient numbers of the appropriate calibre of people are available to the organisation in pursuit of its objectives. Every organisation has to make some attempts to acquire, train, re-deploy and dismiss employees in the course of its activities. Not all of these attempts can be regarded as human resource planning, for they are much too haphazard. Human resource planning, in the sense used here, is a much more rational exercise. One well-respected definition of human resource planning is as follows:

    > ... a strategy for the acquisition, utilisation, improvement and retention of an enterprise's human resources. (Department. of Employment, 1974)[1]

    This particular definition sees human resource planning as a strategic activity, i.e. one that is concerned with securing resources on a long-term basis. It is interesting to note that there is no mention of staff disengagement in this definition, which was written at a time of full employment, unlike the present.

2. For our purposes, human resource planning will be taken to mean any rational and planned approach for ensuring:

    1   the recruitment of sufficient and suitable staff

    2   their retention in the organisation

    3   the optimum utilisation of staff

    4   the improvement of staff performance

    5   the disengagement of staff, as necessary.

    Thus, human resource planning is not just a numbers game, even though labour statistics are an important element in it. Human resource planning is as much, if not more, concerned with the quality of personnel and with their deployment throughout the organisation.

3. At its simplest, human resource planning is concerned with identifying the organisation's demand for human resource and devising means to ensure that a sufficient supply of labour is available to meet that demand. The context of human resource planning is dominated by (a) the state of demand for the organisation's

goods or services, (b) the supply of people in the labour market, and (c) the time-scale involved (at least six months to a year, and quite possibly over a two to five year period).

THE HUMAN RESOURCE PLANNING PROCESS

4.   There are four categories of staff that are important in human resource planning. These are as follows:

- existing staff

- new recruits

- potential staff

- leavers.

Each of these categories requires different decisions to be made by the managers concerned, and some of these are set out below:

Category:	Decisions required about:
Existing staff	Performance appraisal
	Productivity
	Deployment
	Equal opportunities
	Training
	Remuneration
	Promotion/career development
New recruits	Recruitment methods
	Selection procedures
	Induction
	Training
	Terms of contract
Potential staff	Recruitment methods
	Public relations
	Wage/salary levels
	Employee benefits
Leavers	Dismissals for poor performance
	Retirements
	Redundancy procedures
	Labour turnover

5.   The above list indicates some of the far-reaching implications of human resource planning activities. Clearly, we are considering a process which affects every aspect of personnel/human resource management: recruitment, training, remuneration, performance assessment, termination of employment and so on. More than this, it

is a process which is linked inextricably both to the corporate aims of the organisation and to the economic, social and political environment.

6.   The Institute of Personnel Management in its statement on human resource planning argues that the personnel function's role in the activity is as follows:

- To stimulate awareness amongst management of the importance of planning human resource policies and programmes for the future well being of the enterprise.

- To encourage the allocation of appropriate resources to training, retraining and development of staff to meet organisational and individual needs, rather than relying mainly on external recruitment or on 'ad hoc', unplanned internal moves.

- To work closely with management and advise on the development and implementation of up-to-date approaches to planning the human resource.

- To monitor and adapt plans on a continuing basis with corporate and line management.

7.   By comparison, the IPM statement sees line management's role in the activity as:

- To give systematic consideration to the factors likely to affect their part of the organisation over coming years and the likely impact of these factors on the numbers and skills of the people employed.

- To identify the training and development needs of staff in the light of performance, potential and likely positions to be filled.

- To ensure that employees clearly understand the standards of performance required of them and how these link to the reward system.

- To discuss training and development needs with employees in the light of the organisation's objectives and to implement the human resource plan.

- To establish regular and relevant systems of communication with employees and to monitor their effectiveness.

8.   Diagrammatically, the process of human resource planning can be summarised as in Figure 11.1, which shows that human resource planning begins and ends with a review of the organisation's corporate objectives. The most important areas of study will be those concerning marketing and production, since these represent the organisation's intentions about where it will direct its goods or services, and at what level of activity. If, for example, a transport organisation makes a corporate decision to buy out a similar operation on the European Continent, there will be human resource implications of various kinds – What kinds of knowledge and skills will be required'? Should we recruit local staff or install British managers? How many staff speak French, German and other key European languages? What local specialist services (legal, accountancy, etc.) should we purchase?

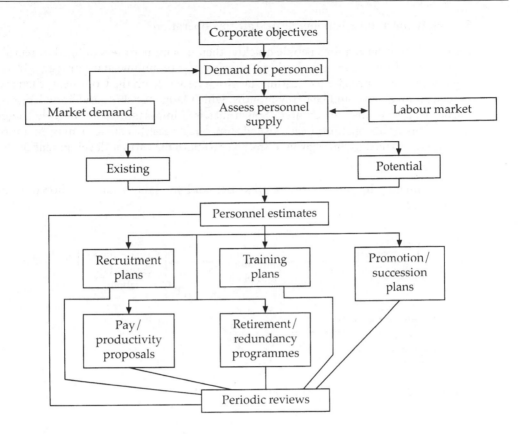

Figure 11.1 *The human resource planning process*

9. Having come to some interim understanding about what kinds of people might be required, the managers responsible for implementing this new strategy have to decide the level of activity to be entered into. How many routes will he operated? How many services per route? How will vehicles be serviced or repaired? How many drivers will be needed, taking into account the legal restrictions on drivers' hours?

ASSESSING THE DEMAND FOR LABOUR

10. Questions such as the above help the organisation to estimate the effective demand for labour. Some existing employees undoubtedly could be used in such a venture, some new recruits would also be required from amongst the local populations, and some jobs could be put out to third parties such as leasing sub-contractors and professional advisers. Three other questions can be raised at this stage:

1   Should we train our own staff for selected key posts?

2   Should we buy in experienced people from outside?

    3   How much time is required to staff this operation?

11.   If the organisation requires people quickly, then it is more or less obliged to recruit trained staff from other organisations, possibly at a premium salary or wage. If the organisation is to prepare its existing staff for a new role on the Continent, then the time-span involved could be many months, whilst language skills and knowledge of European operations are acquired. Sometimes it is important to act quickly to get the nucleus of an operation established, but once past this stage it may be more economical to feed in 'homegrown' staff to promote the further development of the business.

12.   At its simplest, the organisation's *gross* demand for labour can be shown as in Figure 11.2.

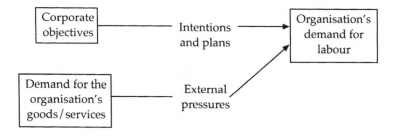

Figure 11.2   *Gross demand for labour*

The objectives of the organisation are translated into intentions and plans for assessing and securing sufficient manpower resources, whilst the state of economic demand represents a collection of external pressures on the organisation's awareness of its labour requirements.

13.   At a more detailed level, the *net* demand for labour, that is the requirement for additional personnel, can be demonstrated as shown in Figure 11.3.

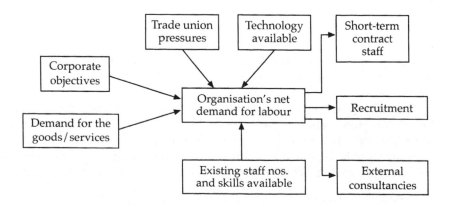

Figure 11.3   *The net demand for labour*

At this level of detail, several other factors are introduced, notably trade union pressures and the effects of technology. These points are discussed below.

14. Bramham (1982)[2] made the useful point that one important question to ask is whether certain work is needed at all, and suggested that 'Systems and procedures tend to last longer than the purpose for which they were intended . . .'. The fact that certain tasks have been performed in a particular way by a particular number of people does not necessarily mean that working methods and numbers involved should remain unalterable. Old practices die hard, as the experience of railway operations shows. In the days of steam, two men were required on the footplate – one to drive the engine, the other to maintain the steam. When diesel and electric locomotives took over, it seemed natural for many of those concerned to assume that two men were still required in the driver's cab, when all that was needed for the safe operation of the locomotive was the driver. In this case, it was trade union pressures to maintain employment in the occupational group concerned that enabled over-manning to continue.

15. Another factor in assessing the organisation's effective demand for labour is technology. To what extent could tasks be carried out by machines or electronic devices? In a transport situation it might be thought that a driver is always a necessary requirement, but in relation to metropolitan railways there are perfectly adequate services using driverless trains (e.g. Docklands Light Railway). In offices, to take another example, there has been a reduction in the demand for clerical and administrative posts because of the advent of computers and word-processors, which are able to undertake a far greater volume of work than any manual system. Such changes have not obviated the need for people but have certainly had a major effect on reducing the demand for particular categories of job.

16. The accuracy of an organisation's forecasts of its demand for labour depends considerably on the state of its external market for goods or services. If the organisation is operating in a relatively stable market, where demand is consistent, the product is efficient and reliable, and there are few competing products, then forecasting for all purposes becomes relatively straightforward. Examples of such situations might be found in the education services and in the manufacture of baby clothes.

If, however, the external market is a turbulent one, where demand fluctuates wildly, where technological innovation is commonplace, and where the competition is intense, then forecasting becomes an extremely difficult affair.

ESTIMATING PERSONNEL REQUIREMENTS

17. Estimating the numbers of people required is usually undertaken in one or more of the following ways:

   1   by exercising managerial judgement

   2   by using Work Study techniques, and

   3   by using statistical techniques.

Bowey (1974)[3] noted that manpower planning

> is not a clearly defined practice ... To some it is a statistical technique in which rates of wastage (etc.) ... are incorporated into a ... computerised model, and predictions made about required rates of recruitment ... But social scientists have pointed out that trends in statistics are only the result of social processes ...

We shall comment briefly on the relative merits of qualitative and quantitative approaches to human resource planning.

18.   In a typical work organisation, as opposed to a research organisation, the single most important element in forecasting personnel requirements is managerial judgement. Individual managers, in the light of (a) their knowledge of events and (b) personnel in their own areas of responsibility, draw up their own estimates of their requirements. They do not always question their own assumptions in making their judgement, and that is why most organisations have one or two senior personnel involved in reviewing submissions from individuals and 'editing' the final document that sets out the organisation's requirements. In large organisations it is invariably the head of the personnel function who has the responsibility for this final review and co-ordination. Much personnel forecasting is carried out when unit managers are working out their draft budgets for the coming year. The personnel budget is an important feature of any unit's budgetary control activities, and it has the advantage of being considered in the context of financial and other targets which are central to the attainment of corporate objectives.

19.   The use of statistical techniques in human resource planning is largely the concern of research organisations and Government statisticians. However, many organisations make use of analyses of labour turnover, labour stability and similar ratios, which are described below (see paras. 26 et seq).

20.   The application of Work Study techniques, such as Work Measurement, Method Study and O & M, can be helpful in identifying the numbers of people required to achieve certain tasks. By definition these have to be tasks that are capable of realistic measurement, such as many manual and clerical operations. Supervisory, specialist and managerial tasks are not easily measured and in these categories it is much more likely that judgement will have to be exercised. Work Measurement is basically a technique for establishing a standard time in which a qualified worker can carry out a specified task at a defined standard of performance. Method Study, by comparison, aims to establish whether a task is being performed in the most efficient and economical manner. Method Study normally precedes Work Measurement. O & M, or Organisation and Methods, is the name given to a range of Work Study techniques applied to an office situation for the purposes of improving administrative and clerical procedures.

ASSESSING THE SUPPLY OF LABOUR

21.   In assessing the supply of labour available to the organisation, there are two major areas to be reviewed:

1   the existing workforce (the internal labour market)

2   the supply of potential employees (the external labour market).

Under each of these areas a number of important questions need to be asked, relating to key aspects of manpower requirements and utilisation. A typical analysis of supply will focus on the following:

Existing Staff

- Numbers
- Categories
- Skills
- Performance
- Flexibility
- Promotability

Potential Staff

- Location
- Categories
- Skills
- Trainability
- Attitudes
- Competition

Less leavers:

- Retirements
- Wastage rates
- Redundancies
- Dismissals

22.   First, we shall examine the existing workforce. No workforce is completely static – there are always some people leaving and entering the organisation, even if the bulk of the workforce is stable.

Typical questions that managers need to ask when assessing the state of their internal labour market are as follows:

- *Job categories* – What categories of staff do we have (e.g. engineers, process workers, etc.)?

- *Numbers* – How many people do we have in each category?

- *Skills* – What skills are available amongst existing employees?

- *Performance* – What levels of performance are we getting from our various categories of employee?

- *Flexibility* – How easy is it to transfer employees between jobs? Are individual skills transferable? What about trade union views on this point?

- *Promotability* – How many of our employees are ready for promotion into more demanding roles? What training could be reasonably provided to assist promotions?

- *Age profiles* – Do we have any age-related problems due to imbalances between experienced and inexperienced staff?

- *Sex distribution* – Have we an appropriate balance between the sexes, given the requirements of our business?

- *Minority groups* – Are minority groups properly represented in the workforce?

- *Leavers* – What is our labour turnover rate by staff category and/department? How many people are due for retirement? Are any redundancies likely? How many people left for reasons of dissatisfaction? Are any trends noticeable?

23. Answers to the above questions can provide a reliable picture of the state of the organisation's own labour force. The resulting information can be matched with the demand forecast for labour in the various categories identified by the management. The overall outcome is likely to fall within one of three possibilities:

    1 the supply available more or less matches the forecast of demand by staff category

    2 the supply exceeds forecast requirements in one or more categories

    3 the supply falls short of requirements in one or more categories.

    The first outcome is unlikely for all except small or very stable workforces. The second outcome is more likely in an industry that is contracting, as in the European coal and steel-producing industries, or that has suffered some short-term economic disaster, such as an international boycott. The third outcome is likely to apply to most organisations most of the time, that is to say, they are always short of appropriately qualified personnel in one part or another of their business.

24. Another aspect of the supply side of the workforce equation is that of the organisation's ability to attract new recruits and to retain them as effective members of the workforce. Recruitment is a major concern of personnel management in its own right (see Chapter 14), but so far as manpower planning is concerned it is crucial for ensuring a supply of fresh blood into the organisation. Almost as important, to pursue the physiological analogy, is to prevent the loss of blood. If people are constantly leaving, it is not possible for the organisation, or its units, to achieve an acceptable level of stability to ensure the continuity of operations.

LABOUR TURNOVER

25. A common index of labour performance used in organisations is Labour Turnover. This provides information about the ratio of leavers to the average numbers employed during the course of a year. It is usually expressed as follows:

$$\frac{\text{Number of employees leaving during the year}}{\text{Average numbers employed during the year}} \times 100$$

A turnover rate of 25 per cent would be considered perfectly satisfactory by most firms. A turnover rate of 100 per cent would be considered a major problem.

Whilst the labour turnover index is useful in broad terms, it has some distinct disadvantages:

1   it does not indicate in which areas of the organisation the rate of leavers is high

2   it does not identify the length of service of the leavers

3   it does not indicate any sudden changes in the numbers employed from one year to the next.

These disadvantages mean that further questions have to be asked about the movement of people through and out of the organisation. For example, which units are experiencing a high turnover of staff? How long have the leavers served in the organisation? Are the numbers employed in the year concerned typical or do they represent an increase/decrease on previous years?

26.   In addition to the labour turnover index, some organisations make use of a Labour Stability Index, which links the leaving rate with length of service. The index is usually expressed as follows:

$$\frac{\text{Number of leavers with more than one year's service}}{\text{Number employed one year ago}} \times 100$$

The results of applying this measure of performance are to identify the extent to which new recruits leave, rather than longer-serving employees. However, it still does not identify which units are producing more early leavers than most. It is also not very satisfactory to have a figure which includes as 'long-serving employees' people with only just over one year's service!

27.   In this latter case, it would be more informative to produce a straightforward analysis of leavers by length of service, as indicated in Figure 11.4.

Period – 1 January to 31 December

Employee Category	Less than 6 months	6 to 12 months	1 to 2 years	3 to 5 years	6 to 10 years	Over 10 years
Unskilled						
Skilled						
Clerical						
Supervision						
Management						

Figure 11.4 *Leavers by length of service*

If required, such an analysis could be further refined to show leavers by department or unit as well as by length of service.

147

28. Staff turnover has a number of advantages and disadvantages. These are briefly as follows.

Advantages:

- it provides an incentive to recruit fresh staff

- it enables organisations to shed staff more easily when redundancies are planned (i.e. through 'natural wastage')

- it opens up promotion channels for longer-serving employees

- it introduces an element of 'self-selection' among new employees, which may save dismissals at a later date.

Disadvantages:

- additional costs of replacement recruitment

- disruptions to production of goods or services caused by leavers

- additional training costs, especially induction and initial job training

- wasted investment in people

- may lead to difficulties in attracting new staff.

On balance, a small amount of turnover is a positive benefit, as the above-mentioned advantages suggest, especially when an organisation is going into decline. For most organisations, however, the extra disruption and recruitment required to offset more than a small amount of turnover are unwelcome.

THE EXTERNAL LABOUR MARKET

29. Most organisations need to tap the external labour market at regular intervals in order to make up for shortfalls of labour in the existing workforce. What is the external labour market? At its simplest, it is that particular group of potential employees, locally, regionally or nationally, who possess the skills and knowledge required by an organisation at a particular point in time. The size and nature of this labour market at any one time depends on a variety of economic and social factors (see Figure 11.5).

30. For example, if there is a slump in economic activity with its associated high level of unemployment, then from the employers' point of view the market is easier. Conversely, if the economy is booming, there will be a shortage of most categories of labour and employers will regard the labour market as being difficult. Social factors tend to have a more gradual effect on the labour market, but it has been noticeable over recent years that fewer school-leavers have sought a career in industry. Indeed the Confederation of British Industry introduced a campaign in schools to make industry more attractive as a career. Political factors also play a part, especially in terms of the level of State benefits, taxation policies and labour legislation.

31. Changes in the nature of the labour market can be seen in the following comment

Figure 11.5 *Factors affecting nature of external labour market*

made by Bramham (1982)[2], which reflects a very different picture of employment in Britain compared with today:

> Today, increasingly the initiative rest with the employee, or rather with organised groups of employees. Technology has increased the skill and therefore the scarcity of many jobs ... Time and the scale of unemployment and social security benefits has blunted some of the fear of unemployment ...

The labour market situation in the 1990s, in contrast to the 1970s, is that of a buyer's market with the initiative firmly in the hands of employers – quite unlike the seller's market of twenty years ago.

32. Even when there is high unemployment overall, there is invariably a shortage of employees with particular skills. Thus there are high-technology firms who cannot find enough engineers or software designers. For these particular categories of employee competition will be fierce, for these are the people who have to be bought in already trained to a high standard. To develop one's own staff to such a standard would take three or four years at least, and for many firms this is just not a practicable proposition.

33. When the labour market is extremely competitive, firms have to sharpen up their recruitment and selection processes, reconsider their salary policies, and focus extra attention on methods of retaining skilled categories of staff. As ever, if something is in short supply its value to the user is enhanced.

34. Another factor in deciding whether to make use of the external labour market is technology. Can the organisation do without more people merely by increasing its investment in new machinery and equipment? The increasing use of computers in industry and commerce serves to dampen down demand for certain categories of employee, since the machines are capable of processing the work previously performed by several people. Investment in new technology also changes the nature of the demand for labour, since different skills are required. In some situations organisations use new technology to expand the business as a whole. In such cases, new investment does not lead to fewer jobs, but only to increased output. This, of course, can only be realised in a situation of growth in demand for the organisation's goods or services.

35. Any organisation that regularly draws on the labour market needs to be aware of its current and short-term status, at the very least. Changes in population densities, new developments in skills training, occupational choice trends amongst school and college leavers are all factors which have to be considered. On top of these points, the recruitment activities of competitors also need to be kept under observation.

36. One final factor to be considered is the attitude of trade unions to the labour market. If the organisation is in an industry where former skills have been superseded by new technology, then a good deal of opposition to 'labour flexibility' may be expected from the unions concerned. In such a situation, human resource planning will have to allow for cautious estimates of the savings that might be achieved from the introduction of new technology. In an entirely different situation, where the industry is in decline, then clearly the trade unions are in a far less powerful position when it comes to bargaining about new working practices, since the employers will have the ready sanction of redundancies to deploy, if their overall policy is not met.

CONCLUSION

37. Planning for a rational approach to the demand and supply of labour to meet the organisation's objectives is not easy. People are the most volatile resource available to organisations, and they are recruited, employed and rewarded against a complex background of economic and social forces, which make firm decisions problematic for human resource planning. What can be said, however, is that organisations which do adopt a rational approach to manpower planning will be better able than their competitors to maintain and renew a viable workforce capable of ensuring the success of the enterprise.

38. The possible benefits from a planned approach to the acquisition, use and deployment of people throughout the organisation include:

- appropriately skilled and flexible workforce
- ability to respond to change
- stability in the core of the workforce
- reduced need to recruit externally
- improved morale and employee relations
- improvement in quality of products/services
- higher productivity.

REFERENCES

1. Department of Employment (1974), *Company Manpower Planning*, HMSO.
2. Bramham, J. (1982), *Practical Manpower Planning*, IPM.
3. Bowey, A. (1974), *Manpower Planning*, Heinemann.

CHAPTER 12

Job analysis

INTRODUCTION

1. In an earlier chapter (Chapter 5 para 33) we defined a job as 'a collection of tasks assigned to a position in an organisation structure.' We commented that this was a very narrow view of a job, since it omitted to consider the responsibility for results required by the job-holder. We also suggested that an individual's job was intimately linked with the role he or she is expected to perform in the job. This particular chapter is concerned with the process that leads to written descriptions of jobs, covering not only key tasks, but responsibilities and work context as well. The question of the job-holder's role is secondary here.

CREATING A JOB

2. Most jobs are allocated on a fairly crude basis. The manager of a unit sees a number of tasks that need to be done and allocates them to individuals on the strength of his or her own judgement. A new job may well be discussed with his or her superior manager, and possibly with someone from the personnel department, but invariably it is the unit manager's perception of the need for, and the nature of, the post that exerts the greatest influence on the decision to add the job to the structure. As the requirements for tasks change, so jobs change, mainly in response to the demands of the immediate management concerned. Only certain kinds of jobs are created in a completely rational way. These are the jobs composed of routine, easily-measurable tasks to be found in many production and clerical departments. Most other jobs, and certainly those requiring a high degree of judgement or discretion, cannot be created in a once-and-for-all manner. Such jobs have to develop and grow as they are performed. Naturally, over a period of time, a job can change quite considerably without anyone really noticing it. Thus, when a review of the organisation takes place, the managers concerned have to take steps to redefine the job in the light of the changed circumstances. This is where job analysis comes in.

JOB ANALYSIS – DEFINITION

3. Job analysis is the term used to describe a process of examining jobs in order to identify their main features, in particular the duties they fulfil, the results they are

expected to achieve, the major tasks undertaken, and the job's relationships with other jobs in the organisational hierarchy. The product of job analysis is a job description. This may take one of several forms, depending on the nature of the job. Routine jobs of a junior kind are best described with an emphasis on the tasks to be achieved, whereas managerial jobs require the emphasis to be on the results to be achieved.

JOB DESCRIPTIONS – THE BASIC FRAMEWORK

4.   It is customary for a job description to be written up so as to cover the following features of the job:

Job title	Location	Date of analysis
		Numbers supervised
Immediate superior		
Relationships with other jobs		
Overall purpose of job		
Main duties/responsibilities (i.e. key tasks)		
Authority granted		
Resources available to job-holder		
Principal qualifications required for job		

If a job is to be described with any accuracy, then adequate coverage of these features is vital.

5.   By working within a framework of key job features, important issues can be addressed. For example:

1   What is the reason for the existence of this job?

2   What end-results are expected from the job?

3   What key tasks have to be carried out?

4   How much formal authority does the job carry?

   • authority to commit financial resources?

   • authority to recruit staff?

   • authority to dismiss/suspend staff?

5   What resources does the job command?

   • £x,000 budget?

   • x numbers of staff?

- equipment/plant/buildings/vehicles?

6   What formal qualifications and what experience is required to perform the job satisfactorily?

(NB This information is often kept on a separate document; see reference to Personnel Specifications in Chapter 14).

6.   An example of a typical managerial job description is given in Figure 12.1.

Job Title: Personnel Manager	Date of Analysis: Dec. '02

Location: Site A
Reports to: Works Director
Functional responsibility to Company Personnel Director

Other regular relationships:

- Production Manager
- Departmental Managers
- Packing Shop Superintendent
- Works Convenor
- Shop Stewards
- Headquarters Personnel Advisers
- Local Trade Union officials
- Local Jobcentre officials

Immediate subordinates:

- Personnel Officer
- Safety Officer
- Site Training Officer
- Security Supervisor
- Works Nurse

Overall purpose of job:

Within the limits of company personnel policies, to provide a full personnel service to line management, and to provide a framework for maintaining good relationships between management and staff (including staff representatives).
Principal Responsibilities:

1)   Ensure the efficient recruitment of suitable and sufficient staff to meet vacancies identified by departmental management.

2)   Implement the company's payment policy in accordance with laid-down procedures.

3)   Advise line managers on employee relations and legal matters during negotiations with trade union representatives.

4) Establish and maintain a regular programme of joint consultation with employee representatives.

5) Ensure regular safety inspections throughout the works and feedback of results to departmental managers.

6) Provide adequate training programmes for the induction of new staff, for job training and for supervisor training.

7) Advise departmental managers on management development matters.

8) Maintain adequate records for all staff.

9) Provide a routine health service for all employees on site, including arrangements for giving first-aid.

Limits of authority:
1) May commit company's financial resources for recruitment within agreed budgets.

2) May recruit own staff within budget limits.

3) May decide individual salary/wage levels in accordance with agreed scales.

4) May suspend staff without pay in cases of alleged serious misconduct.

Resources available:
1) Factory health centre

2) Security vehicles

3) Company car

Qualifications required:

Several years experience in personnel or line management in an engineering environment. Previous experience of negotiating with trade union representatives. Professional qualifications, including membership of the Chartered Institute of Personnel and Development.

Figure 12.1 *Job description – Personnel Manager*

WRITING JOB DESCRIPTIONS

7. In writing up a job description such as the one above, the most difficult sections to describe accurately and concisely are (a) the overall purpose, and (b) the principal duties. The difficulties arise, in the author's experience, because firstly there is always the problem of translating events or concepts into lucid English, and secondly because the analyst concerned has to identify the key tasks from a welter of less relevant information obtained from interview or questionnaire. A useful way of minimising such difficulties is to tackle the principal duties before attempting to describe the overall purpose of the job. After all, these duties represent the key areas of the job, and, if they are pinpointed accurately, they can provide an ideal basis for arriving at the main purpose of the job.

8. Writing up the principal duties can be helped by making use of lists of appropriate verbs to describe the nature of what the job-holder is expected to do or achieve. As Figure 12.2 shows, verbs vary in their relevance to particular levels of jobs. Senior specialist jobs are expected to 'advise', 'propose', etc., whereas clerical jobs are expected to 'produce', 'maintain', etc.

Line management	Senior specialist	Clerical
Plan	Analyse	Check
Direct	Proposed	Make available
Establish	Interpret	Operate
Implement	Advise	Provide
Achieve	Appraise	Maintain
Ensure	Recommend	Submit
Maintain	Develop	Present
Set		
Review		

Figure 12.2 *Relevant verbs by job category*

9. Some typical examples of each of the above categories are as follows:

- Line Manager – 'set and maintain high standards of product quality and reliability'.

- Senior Marketing Manager – 'propose marketing strategies designed to optimise sales of laptop computers to new and existing customers'.

- Records Clerk – 'produce accurate and timely records in response to requests from departmental managers'.

BENEFITS OF JOB ANALYSIS

10. At this point it might be well be asked how can job analysis be justified. As Ungerson (1983)[1] puts it:

> Job descriptions, like all other products and activities of the personnel function, must be useful to line managers and be seen ... to contribute to efficiency and profit or they will fail in their purpose.

This is a somewhat uncompromising view of personnel's role in job analysis. Even if one took a less subservient view of personnel's role, it would be necessary to recognise the importance of winning and maintaining the confidence of line managers in work of this nature, which, as Roff & Watson (1961)[2] point out '... is dealing with a subject on which the pride of many ... people is sensitive'.

11. The main grounds on which job analysis can be justified are as follows:

1 it clarifies posts for which new recruits are sought

2 it produces job descriptions which can provide essential evidence for selection interviewers

3   it enables personnel or role specifications to be drawn up for the purpose of selection or training

4   it can provide the basic material on which performance assessment can be based

5   it is a prerequisite for any analytical attempt at job evaluation

6   it can aid the review of organisation structures by clarifying the basic units of the organisation (i.e. jobs)

7   it can aid an assessment of training needs.

12.   The benefits just described are directed towards management, and especially towards line management. There are also benefits to individuals from job analysis:

1   they can be given a clear idea of their main responsibilities

2   they are provided with a basis for arguing for changes or improvements in their job (e.g. job redesign)

3   they are provided relevant information in respect of any appraisal they may have

4   they have an opportunity to participate in setting their own short-term targets or objectives.

CARRYING OUT JOB ANALYSIS

13.   Roff & Watson (1961)[2] describe the job analyst as an 'intruder' and emphasise that 'care must be taken ... to make sure that he wins the confidence of the people with whom he is dealing'. Clearly job analysis is a sensitive issue. What steps need to be taken to ensure that it is conducted effectively? A suitable checklist follows:

1   Decide aims and objectives of the analysis, e.g. job evaluation, organisation planning, etc.

2   Submit outline plan to senior management.

3   Gain support of senior management.

4   Discuss plan with line managers and specialists and modify if necessary.

5   Seek co-operation of employee representatives.

6   Draw up detailed plan with timetable.

7   Select and train job analysts, if applicable.

8   Notify all staff affected.

9   Implement pilot stage.

10   Review results, discuss any problems.

11   Proceed with final plan.

12   Review results.

As in any other personnel activity, a good deal of preparation has to be put into any job analysis programme, even before it is discussed with senior and other managers. Once initial responses from management groups have been noted or acted upon, then it is important to discuss the proposals with employee representatives, either through trade union channels or through some other joint consultative body. Following discussions with employee representatives it is quite likely that a number of changes may need to be made in the way the programme is implemented. For example, as a result of representations by employees, the selection of analysts may be amended to enable the selection of a jointly approved list, subject, of course, to the ability of persons named to fulfil the duties required.

14. Where job analysts are employed to conduct interviews and write up job descriptions on the basis of their notes or recordings, it is important to select appropriately skilled staff for such an enterprise. Producing accurate, clear and concise job descriptions is no easy task. It requires interviewing skills of a high order, it requires the ability to exercise judgement about what to include and what to leave out, and it requires competent writing skills. As Roff & Watson (1961)[2] comment: 'The job analyst has to use his judgement to make sure that he obtains all the detail he needs without encumbering himself with unnecessary detail.'

A personnel specification for a job analyst would include the following features:

Knowledge – 1 acceptable knowledge of the organisation
2 general grasp of the types of jobs likely to be encountered in the analysis
3 understands the framework of analysis to be employed.
Skills – 1 ability to create rapport with interviewees
2 adequate questioning technique
3 analytical abilities
4 writing and editorial skills.
Attitudes – 1 should be able to exhibit a helping role
2 tactful and diplomatic approach
3 should be able to describe the truth as he or she sees it (integrity)
4 able to pay attention to detail.

15. Job analysis is usually implemented using one or more of the following methods of data collection:

1 by interview between analyst and job-holder (usually semi-structured)

2 by questionnaire

3 by analysing existing documents

4 by observation.

We shall look at these briefly in turn.

THE JOB ANALYSIS INTERVIEW

16. The analyst may commence the interview by reassuring the jobholder that it is the job and its scope that is being analysed, and not the performance of the job-holder. It is also useful to inform the job-holder of the approach intended to be taken and the time-scale of the interview. Once the interview is under way, the analyst can begin to probe more deeply into the key features of the job. Likely questions could be:

- What do you consider your main pre-occupations?

- What issues cause you the greatest effort?

- How do you tackle this kind of problem?

- What help can you call on?

- To what extent do you share this duty with others?

- How would you describe this particular aspect of your work?

- Why do you approach this issue in the way you do?

- Who is authorised to make this decision?

17. One problem that the analyst is likely to come across is that the job-holder provides far too much information, much of which is not sufficiently relevant. In this situation, the interviewer has to be prepared to cut the job-holder short with a comment such as 'Yes, that's fine. Let's now move on to …' Another tactic here would be to ask closed questions rather than the open questions listed above. Closed questions would tend to begin with 'Are you …?' 'Did you …?' 'Have you …?' and would produce Yes/No answers or some specific piece of information.

18. As well as trying to obtain detailed information about the nature and scope of the job in question, the analyst is also trying to get the 'feel' or 'flavour' of the job. Therefore, one or two relevant anecdotes can be quite informative as well as 'facts' about the job. It is regarded as preferable by some writers that the job interview should take place at the job-holder's normal place of work rather than in a separate room. McBeath & Rands (1976)[3] comment that

> The advantage of privacy in a specially requisitioned office, is outweighed by seeing the actual situation, the tools, papers, ledgers and so on which go to make up the job; also by hearing events and telephone calls that come up during interview.

Generally speaking, it is up to the analyst concerned to decide where he or she would prefer the interview to take place.

19. Some analysts prefer to tape-record their interviews. Most prefer to listen and take notes. In the first situation it is vital to obtain the agreement of the job-holder beforehand. In the second situation, which is the more likely, it is important to let the job-holder know that you will have to take notes. It would be quite impossible for any analyst to recall all he had heard in an interview. Note-taking is therefore essential. This task can be somewhat easier for the analyst if he or she structures the job interview under a number of key headings or questions. This tactic does not

prevent additional questions being put nor other issues explored, but it does help to provide the main framework of the event. It also enables analysts to adopt a consistent line of questioning between different job-holders.

JOB QUESTIONNAIRES

20. For many organisations the time and cost involved in employing skilled members of staff as analysts is considered excessive. Such organisations may well turn to the questionnaire as the principal means of acquiring relevant information about jobs. The length and content of the questionnaire will depend mostly on the purpose for which the analysis is required. If, for example, the analysis is to provide information for a job evaluation programme, then the information sought must be in line with the job factors that form the basis of the system to be used. If skill and effort, for example, are to be key factors, then the questionnaire must be designed to elicit this information. If the analysis is required mainly for organisational planning purposes, then a broader range of questions may need to be asked.

21. Questionnaire design is a difficult task. Questions need to be appropriate and unambiguous, otherwise the quality of information obtained will fall short of expectations.

It is generally a good policy to test out the initial draft of a questionnaire to see if it does elicit the responses required. Once a sample of questionnaires has been tested out, and any relevant amendments made, then the main batch can be prepared and distributed. It is important to ensure that questionnaires have a deadline stated on them and an address for return. Invariably some progress-chasing will have to be done, but eventually those responsible for analysing the returns and writing up the consequential job descriptions will have a good deal of useful material to work on.

ANALYSING DOCUMENTS

22. Some organisations carry out a kind of document study as part of their job analysis programmes. This approach utilises existing documentation as a rich source of information about jobs in the structure. Typical documents for study would include organisation charts, budget statements, letters of appointment and statements of objectives for units. Although other methods also make some use of document study, this particular approach is more likely in an organisation planning or job redesign exercise.

OBSERVATION

23. This approach to job analysis is derived from the techniques of work study, and is usually applied to routine manual jobs. Observation is not likely to form a large part of the job description writer's armoury in a white-collar situation.

Observation techniques are invariably highly skilled, especially in attempting to describe what is essentially social behaviour rather than mechanical behaviour.

THE WRITING-UP PROCESS

24. Once the initial information has been collected, the person responsible for producing a realistic and readable job description has a formidable task on his or her hands. From out of a mass of notes and supporting materials a recognisable job description has to emerge. Whatever the reason for introducing job analysis, the expectations of the senior management concerned will be that accurate, concise and clear information about jobs will be available.

25. What then are the steps that a job analyst might take to produce a credible job description? They could be considered in the following sequence:

1   Assemble the key facts about the job, excluding irrelevant or unclear pieces of information.

2   Sort the key facts into clusters of related issues or responsibility areas.

3   Commence writing up the initial sections of the job description (title, relationships, etc.).

4   Write up the main responsibilities as they appear to the analyst.

5   Then draft out a statement of the overall purpose of the job.

6   Complete rest of description, focusing on the need for accuracy, clarity and conciseness.

7   Review the first draft to see if it has a completeness about it/that it rings true.

8   Send draft to job-holder and/or his senior manager for perusal and comment.

9   Make alterations only if they are judged to be fair to the facts.

10 Draw up final version and submit to the senior person concerned in the exercise.

26. Job analysts are sometimes put under pressure by job-holders or their superiors to amend features to fit in with their view of the job. If this would compromise the analyst's own integrity, then he or she should submit the final document as originally written, but explain that the parties concerned were not entirely in agreement with it. Then it is up to the senior management concerned to decide which version of the 'truth' they prefer.

REFERENCES

1. Ungerson, B. (1983), *The Recruitment Handbook* (3rd edn), Gower.

2. Roff, H. & Watson, T.E. (1961), *Job Analysis*, IPM.

3. McBeath, G & Rands, D.N. (1976), *Salary Administration* (3rd edn), Business Books.

CHAPTER 13

Job evaluation

INTRODUCTION

1. Job evaluation is the name given to any activity which sets out to make a systematic comparison between jobs to assess their relative worth, for the purpose of establishing a rational pay structure. In essence, job evaluation aims to reduce reliance on arbitrary methods of pay determination by introducing an element of objectivity in the way jobs are compared. Every job evaluation method requires at least some basic job analysis in order to provide factual information about the jobs concerned. Nevertheless, as with many other aspects of personnel management, judgement has to be exercised in the final analysis. As Kempner (1980)[1] points out:

   > Job evaluation methods do ... depend to some extent on a series of subjective judgements made in the light of concepts like logic, justice and equity and the progressive refinement of job evaluation techniques is ... an attempt to minimise the subjective ... element.

2. The purpose of job evaluation is to produce a defensible ranking of jobs on which a rational and acceptable pay structure can be built. There are a number of important features of job evaluation which need to be recognised at the outset.

   1 Job evaluation attempts to assess jobs, not people.

   2 The standards of job evaluation are relative, not absolute.

   3 The basic information on which job evaluations are made is obtained from job analysis.

   4 Job evaluations are carried out by groups, not by individuals.

   5 Job evaluation committees utilise concepts such as logic, fairness and consistency in their assessment of jobs.

   6 There is always some element of subjective judgement in job evaluation.

   7 Job evaluation does not determine pay scales, but merely provides the evidence on which they may be devised.

3. Job evaluation methods can be divided into two basic categories:

   1 non-analytical methods

   2 analytical methods.

   The primary difference between these two categories is that the non-analytical methods take whole jobs and rank them, whereas the analytical methods break jobs down into their component parts and then compare them factor by factor. The implication is that analytical methods provide a more refined means of measurement than non-analytical methods. This point is particularly relevant for equal pay legislation, since only analytical schemes are considered to provide an acceptable means of identifying 'work of equal value' (see para. 13 below). Examples of some of the leading methods of both analytical and non-analytical approaches will be described in the rest of this chapter.

NON-ANALYTICAL METHODS

4. The two most widely-used non-analytical methods are *job ranking* and *job grading* or *job classification*.

JOB RANKING

5. The basic process in job ranking is to select a representative sample of jobs (so-called benchmarks), prepare basic job descriptions for them, compare them on the basis of the information in the job descriptions and rank them in order of their perceived importance. Each evaluator's ranking is discussed in a job evaluation committee, compared with the results obtained by other evaluators, and eventually a final rank order is drawn up. The remaining jobs in the organisation are then slotted in to the evaluated rank order on a like-for-like basis. The advantage of this form of evaluation is that it is relatively simple and cheap to operate. Its main disadvantage is that it relies heavily on the subjective assessments of the evaluators, and in particular on their personal knowledge of the benchmark jobs.

6. An example of job ranking, in this case using paired comparisons, is shown in Figure 13.1 below. In this example each job in the listing is compared with every

	Chief A/C	Sales Mgr	Jnr Progr	Recep	Comp Op	Pers Off	Cost Clerk	Snr Sec
Chief Accountant	–	2	3	3	3	3	3	3
Sales Manager	2	–	3	3	3	3	3	3
Junior Programmer	1	1	–	3	3	1	2	2
Receptionist	1	1	1	–	1	1	1	1
Computer Operator	1	1	1	3	–	1	1	1
Personnel Officer	1	1	3	3	3	–	3	3
Cost Clerk	1	1	2	3	3	1	–	2
Senior Secretary	1	1	2	3	3	1	2	–

Scores awarded = 1 if considered less important
2 if considered equally important
3 if considered more important

Figure 13.1 *Job ranking by paired comparisons*

other job and a score is allocated on the basis of whether the first job is estimated to be less important, more important or of the same importance than the job it is being compared with. Totalling up the scores enables an evaluated rank order to be drawn up.

7.   In the above example, the Chief Accountant and the Sales Manager come out with equal scores at the head of the ranking. It would have been quite possible for either job to have outranked the other by a small margin, depending on the nature of the job and its importance to the organisation. What is unlikely, however, is that these two jobs would have been outranked by any of the others on the list. With jobs such as the Junior Programmer, Cost Clerk and Senior secretary, which all achieved the same score in this example, it is quite likely that individual judges would produce somewhat different scores, depending on their knowledge of the jobs concerned and their personal views as to which are the more important.

In essence, what we are seeing with the paired comparisons approach is an attempt to reduce the subjective element to a limited extent by at least forcing judges to make comparisons in a systematic way. Nevertheless, in the final analysis, such a system of evaluation relies considerably on personal judgement.

JOB GRADING

8.   This form of evaluation, also known as job classification, attempts to distinguish between work levels by establishing a small number of general criteria against which specific jobs may be compared. The most well-known, and widely used, system of job grading is the scheme developed by the Institute of Administrative Management. This scheme now has eight grades, each with their statement of general criteria, into which almost 1000 typical office tasks can be slotted. As Figure 13.2 shows, Grades A and B contain jobs at the elementary level of office work, while grades F, G and H contain work of a high professional level. In a survey of job evaluation methods conducted by Thakur & Gill (1976)[2], about one third of clerical, administrative and supervisory jobs were evaluated using some form of grading or classification.

Grade A – Tasks requiring no previous clerical experience; each individual task is either very simple or closely supervised. Examples include: simple sorting and filing, and messenger work.

Grade B – Simple tasks carried out in accordance with a limited number of well-defined rules; fairly short period of training; tasks closely directed and checked. Examples include: simple copying work, and straightforward adding operations using a machine.

Grade C – Tasks of a routine nature and following well-defined rules, but requiring some experience or special aptitude. Examples include: simple calculating machine operations, preparing routine invoices, and shorthand typing of routine work.

Grade D – Tasks requiring considerable experience, but only a limited degree of initiative, and which are carried out within an existing procedure. Work is not subject to same amount of direction as in lower grades. Examples include: shorthand typing of non-routine work, routine administration of a group of sales or purchase accounts.

Grade E – Tasks requiring a basic level of professional knowledge or the performance of clerical/administrative work requiring the occasional use of discretion and initiative, or the supervision of two to six clerical staff. Examples include: routine computer programming, supervision of a section of typists.

Grade F – Tasks requiring intermediate professional or specialised knowledge, or the performance or control of complex clerical or routine administrative work requiring occasional non-routine decisions and some use of judgement on routine matters, or the supervision of five to twelve clerical staff. Examples include: supervision of a print room, conducting routine O & M or systems analysis surveys, complex computer programming, full secretarial service to chief executive

Grade G – Tasks requiring professional or specialised knowledge to first degree standard or advanced professional qualification, or the performance or control of work of wide complexity or importance requiring regular non-routine decisions and exercise of discretion, or supervision of nine to twenty clerical staff. Examples include: supervision of large wages office, computer programming of complex sets of programs, and tutoring on clerical training courses for staff in grades A–F.

Grade H – Tasks requiring professional or specialised knowledge to degree or final qualification level, or performance or control of complex and important work, requiring extensive use of judgement or initiative and some contribution to policy-making, or supervision of twenty or more clerical staff together with their supervisors. Examples include: supervision of a customer accounts office with responsibility for credit control within agreed policy, leading complex O & M or systems analysis projects, and control of complex computer programming projects and their staff.

Figure 13.2 *Summary of IAM job grading scheme (IAM 1976)[3]*

9.   As well as being given the broad parameters described above, users of the IAM system have access to some 1000 task definitions against which they can compare practically every office task they are likely to incorporate in their business. Any management using this system will be able to work out appropriate salary scales for each of the grades identified, and thus devise a reasonable structure of pay differentials. The main advantage of job grading lies in its relative simplicity and cheapness.

However, it is a relatively crude means of distinguishing between jobs, and is not as widely used for managerial, supervisory, professional and other white-collar jobs as the Points Rating Method, which is the most popular form of analytical job evaluation.

ANALYTICAL METHODS

10.   As explained earlier, analytical methods of job evaluation examine jobs in terms of their principal components, and not as whole entities. The most widely-used analytical methods are the Points Rating Method and the Hay-MSL Guide Chart System. Both of these methods enable fairly subtle differences between jobs to be identified and measured. Thus a complex range of jobs in an organisation can be described, distinguished and measured in relative terms, with a fair degree of credibility. Such methods require much more time and effort than non-analytical methods, and are therefore more costly to operate, but many organisations prefer them because they provide a sounder and more defensible basis for wage and salary administration than non-analytical methods.

11.   The basic procedure for introducing an analytical method is as follows:

1   The aims/objectives of the exercise are agreed.

2   The organisation appoints its own job evaluation team from amongst its own staff, or hires consultants; employee representatives are elected to the team, as appropriate.

3   Relevant job factors are agreed upon.

4   Each factor is sub-divided by 'degrees' or 'levels'.

5   Each factor (and its sub-divisions) is given a weighting.

6   Points are then allocated to each factor and sub-divisions.

7   Benchmark jobs are identified.

8   Detailed job descriptions are written for these jobs.

9   Each benchmark job is evaluated in accordance with the points system.

10   Benchmark jobs are ranked according to its score.

11   The initial ranking of benchmarks is reviewed to identify any anomalies.

12   The final benchmark ranking is agreed.

13   The remaining jobs are slotted into the bench-mark ranking.

14   Jobs are grouped within the ranking to isolate possible salary grades, or may be allocated a salary scale on the basis of their individual points total.

POINTS RATING METHOD

12.   The most frequent factors employed in points systems are as follows.

Skill:

•   education and training required

•   breadth/depth of experience required

- social skills required
- problem-solving skills
- degree of discretion/use of judgement
- creative thinking.

Responsibility/Accountability:

- breadth of responsibility
- specialised responsibility
- complexity of the work
- degree of freedom to act
- number and nature of subordinate staff
- extent of accountability for equipment/plant
- extent of accountability for product/materials.

Effort:

- mental demands of job
- physical demands of job
- degree of potential stress.

Working Conditions:

- timescale of operations
- turbulent or steady-state
- amount of necessary travelling
- diversity of subordinates
- pressures from other groups
- difficult or hazardous surroundings.

13. Most points methods incorporate the above factors in one form or another. When devising an 'in-house' system, the inclusion of particular factors, and the decisions about their weightings will be the subject of negotiation between various interested parties. Where trade unions are involved, they will want to be consulted about these matters and to have some influence over the choice of factors and their weightings. Additionally, where significant numbers of women are employed, care needs to be taken to ensure that the job factors selected do not implicitly favour one sex against the other, for example by giving higher weightings to length of service and physical demands (which favour men) in comparison to mental complexity and accountability for others (which may be considered as neutral). In a leaflet on the amended Equal Pay Act, the Equal Opportunities Commission[4] provides examples of such 'neutral' factors. Neutral factors provide a fairer basis for ensuring 'equal pay for work of equal value'.

Different management groups also have their preferred weightings. Line managers tend to stress the importance, and therefore weighting, of responsibility, whereas specialist managers tend to emphasise skills. Ideally, whatever the eventual choice of factors/weightings, one standardised set of criteria should emerge to be applied consistently to all the jobs in the population concerned.

14.   An example of a points rating system applied to manual workers in a manufacturing company is shown in Figure 13.3 below. This relatively uncomplicated matrix highlights some of the key features of this method of job evaluation.

Job Factor	Degree							
	1	2	3	4	5	6	7	8
SKILL								
1. Education	15	30	45	60	75	90	–	–
2. Experience	20	40	60	80	90	100	–	–
3. Initiative	15	30	45	60	75	90	105	120
EFFORT								
4. Physical	10	20	30	40	50	–	–	–
5. Mental	5	10	15	20	25	30	35	40
RESPONSIBILITY								
6. Supervision	5	10	15	20	25	30	35	40
7. Equipment/plant	5	10	15	20	25	–	–	–
8. Safety	5	10	15	20	25	–	–	–
WORKING CONDITIONS								
9. Hazards	5	10	15	20	–	–	–	–
10. Noise/dirt	10	20	30	40	50	–	–	–

Figure 13.3 *Points rating matrix for manual jobs*

15.   The above matrix emphasises aspects of skill, interpreted in a general manner, a rather specific choice of areas of responsibility, working conditions and physical effort. Office jobs by comparison would tend to be measured in terms of knowledge and skill, responsibility for people and procedures, and mental rather than physical effort. In our example, the weightings in the matrix give highest points for factors such as skill, physical effort and noisy/dirty working conditions. Such weightings enable job evaluators to make distinctions between particular jobs. For example, under Education, it is possible to distinguish between a job requiring a BTEC Higher award and one requiring a Final Craft qualification. The former might represent the 6th degree, and the latter the 5th degree. The whole drift of a matrix such as the above is that a lesser degree of a factor means fewer points, and vice versa for jobs requiring a higher degree of a factor.

16.   After a job has been evaluated in accordance with the matrix, the points attained for each factor are totalled to give a score for the job. This score is slotted into the ranking of all the other benchmark jobs. Invariably, the picture that emerges is of a number of job-clusters around particular groups of scores. This useful phenomenon can simplify the basis for allocating wage grades or other differentials. For further discussion of this issue, see Chapter 21 (Pay, Benefits and Incentives).

17. Individual scores will always be subject to some further scrutiny if they appear to be at all anomalous. If a particular job attains a score that appears to be out of place in relation to other, related jobs, then it will be 'red-circled', discussed and awarded a different, i.e. 'correct' score by the evaluation judges. This is an important consideration when dealing with a points system, since the use of numbers, by degrees, does give an air of exactitude about the exercise. Unfortunately, points systems cannot achieve such a degree of accuracy. An element of subjectivity is frequently necessary, and even desirable, in order to achieve a fair evaluation of a job.

GUIDE CHART METHOD

18. A variation of the usual points method is the widely-used Hay-MSL Guide Chart method. In this method the basic points matrix is a standard one, which is applicable across organisational, and indeed national boundaries. This is an important feature for organisations that wish to adopt a unified approach that can be applied company-wide, and who are prepared to make full use of Hay consultants in setting up the exercise and seeing it through to its conclusion. The basic structure of the Hay system is as follows.

1   Three-broad factors are employed for the analysis: Know-how, Problem-solving and Accountability, each scored on a Guide-Chart.

2   Each factor is considered by breadth and depth.

3   Know-how refers to the knowledge and skills required to attain 'average acceptable performance'

4   Problem-solving refers to the analytical and evaluation aspects of the job, and is seen in two dimensions the extent to which thinking is prescribed and the nature of the thinking challenge (variability, creativity, etc.).

5   Accountability refers to 'the answerability for actions and the consequences of that action'. It has three dimensions: (a) the extent of freedom to act, (b) the job impact on end results, and (c) the magnitude of the job primarily seen in terms of responsibility for financial results.

19. A simplified example of the layout of one of the Guide Charts – Know-How – is shown in Figure 13.4.

20. The scores allocated to each part of the matrix are standardised throughout the Hay system. The step differences between the points are intended to reflect just noticeable differences between aspects of a particular factor.

21. An important point to make is that, although the system looks extremely quantified and objective in the light of the subtleties of the matrix, nevertheless a good deal of subjective judgement still has to be exercised in the light of the job description, the evaluators' knowledge of the job in practice, and the scores given to other jobs already. The Hay system, as with any other points rating system, cannot measure jobs with complete and objective accuracy. What it can do is to reduce the subjective and arbitrary elements by a substantial margin, and thus achieve a fairer

	Breadth of management know-how											
	None/ minimal			Specific area			Specialist co-ordination			Broad		
Human relations skills*	1	2	3	1	2	3	1	2	3	1	2	3
PRIMARY	57	66	76	76	87	100	100	115	132	132	152	175
ELEMENTARY VOCATIONAL	76	87	100	100	115	132	132	152	175			
VOCATIONAL	100	115	132	132	152	175						
ADVANCED VOCATIONAL	132	152	175	175	200	230						
BASIC PROFESSIONAL/ SCIENTIFIC, etc.	175	200	230	230	264	304						
SEASONED PROFESSIONAL/ SCIENTIFIC, etc.	230	264	304									
SCIENTIFIC/ PROFESSIONAL MASTERY	304	350	400									
UNIQUE AUTHORITY												

Depth of know-how

*1 = Basic   2 = Important   3 = Critical

Figure 13.4 *Hay-MSL guide chart – simplified model*

result than with a non-analytical method. After evaluation, the Hay system ranks benchmarks jobs in accordance with their points totals. The final rank order is agreed after any red-circling anomalies have been put right, and salaries are then derived from the application of a tailor-made formula agreed between the individual organisation and the Hay consultants.

22.   There are other job evaluation variants available for use by organisations, and these are mainly non-analytical methods. For a clear and comprehensive account of these and other aspects of job evaluation, the reader is recommended to consult Thomason (1980)[5] *Job Evaluation – Objectives and Methods*.

CONCLUSION

23.   Job evaluation can play an important role in the development of systematic and equitable pay systems. Analytical systems, in particular, provide a means of identifying key job factors, weighting them as appropriate, and then comparing jobs against them, and eventually arriving at an understanding of the relative value of all the jobs in a particular population. On the basis of this evidence of relative worth, pay differentials can be worked out in a way that is demonstrably fairer than the arbitrary decisions of individuals or powerful sectional groups. To the extent that job evaluation bureaucratises the formulation of pay scales, it reduces

the negotiating power of both trade unions and other influential groups by robbing them of the possibility of appealing to emotional considerations, which have very little to do with the nature, scope and contribution of jobs in the organisational hierarchy.

24. Non-analytical methods, popular though they may be, lack the credibility of analytical methods. No employer, for example, can resist an equal pay demand with any confidence if he or she is employing non-analytical methods of job evaluation. The Equal Opportunity legislation will not consider such methods as 'proper job evaluations'.

REFERENCES

1. Kempner, T. (ed) (1980), *A Handbook of Management*, Penguin.

2. Thakur, M. & Gill, D. (1976), *Job Evaluation in Practice*, IPM.

3. Institute of Administrative Management (1976), *Office Job Evaluation*, IAM.

4. Equal Opportunities Commission, (1984) *Equal Pay for Work of Equal Value: a Guide to the Amended Equal Pay Act*, EOC.

5. Thomason, G. (1980), *Job Evaluation – Objectives and Methods*, IPM.

CHAPTER 14

Recruitment policies and practice

INTRODUCTION

1. This chapter focuses on one of the most crucial activities of personnel specialists in the organisation, that of securing the organisation's human resources: recruitment. It is in this area that personnel staff play the major role. Whereas selection is shared widely throughout the organisation, recruitment is very much a specialised activity.

2. The principal purpose of recruitment activities is to attract sufficient and suitable potential employees to apply for vacancies in the organisation. The principal purpose of selection activities, by comparison, is to identify the most suitable applicants and persuade them to accept a position in the organisation. The key role of recruitment and selection can be seen at its simplest level in Figure 14.1.

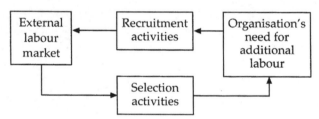

Figure 14.1 *Linking role of recruitment and selection*

This chapter examines recruitment activities whilst the following chapter deals with selection matters.

3. The importance of having efficient and effective procedures for recruitment and selection can hardly be exaggerated. If organisations are able to find and employ staff who consistently fulfil their roles and are capable of taking on increased responsibilities, they are immeasurably better placed to deal with the opportunities and threats arising from their operating environment than competitors who are always struggling to build and maintain their workforce.

RECRUITMENT: POLICIES AND PROCEDURES

4. One of the first steps in planning for the recruitment of employees into the organisation is to establish adequate policies and procedures. A recruitment policy represents the organisation's code of conduct in this area of activity. An example of a typical policy statement for recruitment is as follows:

In its recruitment activities the Company will:

1   advertise all vacancies internally

2   reply to every job applicant with the minimum of delay

3   aim to inform potential recruits in good faith about the basic details and job conditions of every job advertised

4   aim to process all applications with efficiency and courtesy

5   seek candidates on the basis of their qualification for the vacancy concerned

6   aim to ensure that every person invited for interview will be given a fair and thorough hearing.

The Company will not:

1   discriminate unfairly against potential applicants on grounds of sex, race, age, religion or physical disability

2   discriminate unfairly against applicants with a criminal record

3   knowingly make any false or exaggerated claims in its recruitment literature or job advertisements.

5.   Within the context of such a policy the detailed plans and procedures for recruitment can be devised and put in place. These are necessary to ensure that recruitment practices are systematic, consistent and responsive to internal needs. Plans typically contain references to quantity, quality, time and cost as well as identifying those responsible for achieving the required results. In recruitment planning there is a range of questions and issues that can be addressed, as the example in Figure 14.2 shows.

6.   In terms of procedures one way in which managers engaged in recruiting staff can ensure a systematic approach is to adopt a checklist such as the one shown in Figure 14.3. A systematic procedure makes for internal discipline and control in recruitment matters, especially in organisations that are engaged in heavy or regular programmes of recruitment.

7.   Whilst a systematic approach with clear procedures is important for cost-effective recruitment, so also is responsiveness. In other words, recruitment procedures should be flexible enough to permit personnel staff, in particular, to respond flexibly to demands made on them both by recruiting departments and by potential candidate.

Thus, personnel staff should be capable of rearranging their advertising campaigns to meet particular short-term needs of user departments, and of being prepared to negotiate interview times to meet the convenience of shortlisted candidates for key posts. However, it needs to be acknowledged that recruitment is a marketing activity as well as a resourcing one. When recruiting staff, organisations are going out into their external environment and competing with others for suitable recruits. It is important, therefore, that such activities are conducted in a manner that sustains or enhances the public image of the organisation. Applicants who are treated both fairly and efficiently will pass on this experience to others, even if they have been unsuccessful in their application. Conversely, people who feel that their

Question	Issue	Action
1. What additional jobs are being created this year?	New vacancies	Check state of demand with departments/ budget returns
2. What labour turnover is forecast this year?	Loss of current staff	Monthly check & report
3. What categories of employees are likely to be required?	Type of staff needed	Check staffing estimates
4. How many current staff are ready for promotion now?	Availability of own staff	Check training/appraisal reports
5. What is the state of the external labour market (a) locally and (b) nationally?	Availability of new recruits	Personnel's contacts with agencies/ newspapers, etc.
6. How much can we spend on recruitment action this year?	Size of recruitment budget	Monitor budget
7. What time-scale is required to meet both known and estimated forecasts of demand?	Timeliness of recruitment	Agree with departments
8. How many personnel staff will be required to meet this programme?	Efficiency/credibility of the personnel department	Personnel budget

Figure 14.2 *Basis of a recruitment plan*

application has been dealt with inefficiently or unfairly are quick to spread their criticisms around.

8. In order to illustrate the significance of a systematic, yet responsive approach to recruitment, we can turn to the checklist in Figure 14.3 overleaf and consider some of the implications (Figure 14.4).

Item	Question to be considered
1.	Has the vacancy been agreed by the responsible manager?
2.	Is there an up-to-date job description for the vacant position?
3.	What are the conditions of employment (salary, hours, holidays etc.) for the vacant position?
4.	Has a candidate specification been prepared?
5.	Has a notice of the vacancy been circulated internally?
6.	Has a job advertisement been agreed? Have details of the vacancy been forwarded to relevant agencies?
7.	Do all potential candidates (internal or external) know where to apply and in what form?
8.	What arrangements have been made for drawing up a shortlist of candidates?
9.	Have the interviewing arrangements been agreed, and have shortlisted candidates been informed?
10.	Have unsuitable candidates, or candidates held in reserve, been informed of their position?
11.	Have offer letters been agreed and despatched to successful candidates? Have references been taken up, where necessary?
12.	Have suitable rejection letters been sent to unsuccessful shortlisted candidates, thanking them for their attendance?
13.	Have all replies to offer letters been accounted for?
14.	Have the necessary procedures for placement, induction and follow-up of successful candidates been put into effect?

Figure 14.3 *Recruitment checklist*

Item	Comments
1.	Personnel staff may need to confirm that there is in fact a vacancy. Sometimes a new post has not been given clearance by senior management; sometimes an existing post is not, after all, going to be filled now that the previous job-holder has moved on.
2.	Job descriptions should be available for vacancies. With established posts, this may be a mere formality, but for new posts the details may not have been made explicit.
3.	For routine jobs the conditions of appointment will almost certainly be clear; for managerial and specialist appointments the situation could be remarkably vague. From the point of view of maintaining internal equity in terms of conditions of appointment, it is vital to ensure that these conditions are agreed beforehand.

4.	What steps have been taken by the user department to inform personnel about the knowledge, skills and other attributes required by prospective candidates? Such information is critical to the success of eventual interviews.
5.	Where there is a policy of advertising vacancies within the organisation, a brief check should be made to ensure that the procedure has been activated. There is nothing so damaging to employee morale than to see an unexpected advertisement for some highly sought-after post, which no existing employees had been informed about.
6.	Advertisements for jobs are usually left to the personnel staff or their sub-contractors to handle. User departments, having stated their requirements, will normally be happy for their personnel colleagues to deal with the wording and placement of suitable advertising material. Personnel staff frequently make use of specialised agencies to help them prepare copy and locate the best sources of potential recruits.
7.	All candidates need to know where and how to apply for a vacancy, and every job advertisement should indicate this information as clearly as possible.
8.	Who is going to decide on the initial selection of candidates? Personnel? Line managers? or both? In a well-established personnel unit, it is often left to them to draw up a shortlist. Sometimes this task is delegated to recruitment agencies or consultants.
9.	The interviewing arrangements should ensure that all those concerned are informed about the details of the interview schedule.
10.	It is important to decide how unsuitable or reserve candidates are to be dealt with, since it creates a very unsatisfactory image if applicants are not informed of the success or otherwise of their application.
11.	In non-routine cases, it is important to ensure that the terms to be offered have been agreed by the senior manager or director concerned, before personnel send out the offer letter. If references are to be taken up after the interviews have been held, then any offer must be subject to satisfactory references.
12.	It is very important from the marketing point of view, as well as being a courtesy, for unsuccessful interviewees to be thanked for their interest and attendance.
13.	Where a large number of offer letters have been sent out, then personnel need to keep a check on the replies received and to follow up if necessary.
14.	Many organisations have a systematic approach to induction and initial training, and this is usually co-ordinated by the personnel unit, even though the activities concerned are shared between them and the user-departments.

Figure 14.4 *Implications of recruitment checklist*

A number of these items will be examined further in this chapter. As we have already spent some time looking at job descriptions (Chapter 12), it would be appropriate now to focus on the personnel specification.

PERSONNEL SPECIFICATIONS

9. The purpose of a personnel specification, or candidate profile as it is sometimes called, is to make explicit the attributes that are sought in candidates for the job in question. Thus the personnel specification becomes a summary of the most important knowledge, skills and personal characteristics required by the successful candidate in order to be able to carry out the job to an acceptable standard of performance. The specification depends for its relevance on the nature and scope of the job, as described in the job description, amplified where necessary by comments from the manager concerned. Naturally the nature of the job will determine the type and level of knowledge and skills required, but the job will be performed in a particular social context, and so it is important to have the manager's view as to the sort of personal qualities that would permit the newcomer to fit into to the team.

10. Drawing up adequate specifications is not easy. As Munro Fraser (1978)[1] puts it:

    > Each human being is unique and can only be understood as a complete entity. Ill-conceived attempts to force him into classifications usually lead to essential elements being either concealed or missed out altogether. But when trying to select from among a group of candidates, we want to be able to compare one with another. Thus we must describe each in terms which have a common application.

    Fortunately for current practitioners in personnel work, there have been several useful attempts to draw up a practicable if not ideal classifications of personal attributes for the purposes of selection. Two of these classifications are discussed below.

11. The Seven Point Plan. This plan was devised by Professor Alec Rodger[2] of the National Institute of Industrial Psychology in the 1950s, and has proved to be the most popular model for personnel specifications in the United Kingdom. Its seven points are as follows:

    1   Physical Make-up
        What is required in terms of health, strength, energy and personal appearance?

    2   Attainments
        What education, training and experience is required?

    3   General Intelligence
        What does the job require in terms of thinking and mental effort?

    4   Special Aptitudes
        What kind of skills need to be exercised in the job?

    5   Interests
        What personal interests could be relevant to the performance of the job?

6 Disposition
What kind of personality are we looking for?

7 Circumstances
Are there any special circumstances that the job requires of candidates?

12. The use of the Seven Point Plan can best be explained by means of an example. Figure 14.5 shows how it might be applied in the case of a cabin crew member for a national airline.

Feature Sought	Essential	Desirable
Physical Make-up	Weight in proportion to height; eyesight, hearing, etc., perfect; neat, clean appearance; age between 21–28	None
Attainments	GCSE level education	Experience in nursing/catering
Intelligence	Alert, quick-thinking	None
Aptitudes	Social skills adequate to deal firmly but politely with passengers	Fluency in relevant languages
Interests	None	Travel, flying, First-aid
Disposition	Friendly personality; ability to remain cool and calm in an emergency; ability to work short periods under intense pressure	Sense of humour
Circumstances	Must be able to work irregular hours; must be willing to stand for long periods; must be willing to live near the airport	Flexible domestic situation

Figure 14.5 *Personnel specification – cabin crew*

13. As can be seen, it is possible to categorise the candidate specification under Essential and Desirable features. Clearly the more items that appear under Essential, the tighter the specification, and the more restrictive its effect. In the example just quoted the requirements for physical make-up clearly rule out a large number of possible applicants right at the outset.

14. The relationship between the Essential and Desirable features is a factor (a) of the job itself, and (b) of the labour market. If a job requires specific knowledge or skills at a particular level to ensure that new recruits will be able to fulfil their duties acceptably, then these levels must be stated as essential. If the job only requires commonsense levels of know-how, then the specification can be written in broad terms with few essential features. However, the recruitment situation is inevitably linked to the state of the labour market. If labour of a particular kind is plentiful,

then specifications can be made more exclusive than if there is a shortage of the relevant labour, in which case employers loosen their personnel specifications, so as to ensure that at least some candidates will be caught in the net.

15.   In recent years the labour market has swung back in favour of employers. Now the problem is not so much of attracting candidates, but in deciding how best to select them. Lewis (1985)[3] sees the problem in these terms:

> In practical terms, attracting applicants is less of an issue, but administration and deciding whom to offer employment to are more difficult with large numbers.

The present situation encourages employers to set tight specifications for all but the scarcest of jobs. Even with this strategy employers are being faced with large numbers of well-qualified candidates, and so selection processes become more time-consuming and problematic.

16.   Another well-known classification of human characteristics for personnel selection is Munro Fraser's Five Point Grading, which is described in detail in his book *Employment Interviewing* (1978)[1]. Briefly, the five aspects of the individual are as follows:

1   *Impact on Others* – this embraces Rodger's physical make-up and also aspects such as dress, speech, manner and reactions. Fraser emphasises 'the importance of looking at an individual quite objectively from this point of view'.

2   *Acquired Knowledge or Qualifications* – this part deals with general education, work experience and training, and is similar to Rodger's Attainments category.

3   *Innate Abilities or 'Brains'* – this heading refers to the individual's ability to exercise his or her intelligence in a range of situations, and is especially applicable in cases where the individual has few formal qualifications. Fraser suggests that 'from this point of view, we are perhaps mainly concerned with his potentialities'.

4   *Motivation* – this is concerned with the 'goal-directed' aspect of human personality. Fraser sees this more in terms of how the individual has achieved his or her personal needs and ambitions, rather than with trying to identify these needs.

5   *Adjustment* – This aspect concerns the emotional status of the individual stability, maturity, ability to cope with stress, for example. Fraser suggests here that the qualities under discussion are basically aspects of 'the individual's reaction to pressures'.

Fraser is aware of the over-simplification of personal characteristics implied by his model: 'We cannot chop a human being up into five separate sections ...'. However, he justifies his position as follows:

> Separating out these five groups of characteristics is no more than a means to an end. Its justification is its utility in concentrating attention on one facet at a time, each of which is a reasonably self-contained and distinct pattern of traits or personal qualities.

179

17. Fraser's model, like Rodger's, does make an important contribution to the recruitment and selection processes in organisations. It provides a practical framework for enabling selectors to make reasonably consistent comparisons between one candidate and another. Many organisations have adapted one or other of these two models to meet their particular needs for defining the personnel specification and then measuring candidates against it.

The important point here is that the organisation is at least trying to introduce a greater element of predictability and control into an aspect of personnel management in which personal judgement and individual prejudice blend rather uneasily together in a situation where objective information may be in short supply.

JOB ADVERTISING

18. Personnel specifications and job descriptions form the basis of every job advertisement. When labour is in short supply, advertisements need to be able to entice potential applicants as well as to inform them about the basic features of the job in question. Even when labour is plentiful, advertisements need to be able to attract candidates for, as Plumbley (1985)[4] points out:

> ... both at times when unemployment is exceptionally high or exceptionally low, advertisers can receive a poor response: it appears that people prefer to live on state assistance than to risk further redundancy and that those in employment ... stay put unless the new job offers an exceptional opportunity ...

19. Advertising is a crucial part of the recruitment process. It is intended to reach out into the labour market with an attractive offer of employment aimed at producing an adequate response in terms of (1) enquiries/requests for details, and (2) numbers of suitable applications submitted. The main sources of job advertising outside the organisation are:

- local newspapers
- national newspapers
- technical/professional journals
- via the internet (employer's website or on agency's)
- via Jobcentres
- via other agencies
- posters at the factory gates.

Generally speaking, manual and clerical vacancies are filled by local advertising, whereas managerial and professional vacancies are filled by advertising in the national press and in the specialist journals.

20. The national dailies, in looking to their own market position in recruitment advertising, have tended to adopt certain days of the week as their day for promoting particular categories of jobs. So, for example, *The Times* advertises

managerial posts on a Thursday, as does the *Daily Telegraph;* the *Guardian* publishes educational posts on a Tuesday and public sector posts on a Wednesday. This situation is helpful both to organisations seeking recruits and to those looking for new employment, since they know which day is 'market day' for their particular job category. Journals are usually published monthly, and are directed towards specific interest groups. With their predictability and access to special groups of potential recruits, they are an important source of job advertising. Newspapers have one distinct advantage over journals – their speedier throughput of advertisements. The lead-time for a journal is probably about four to five weeks, whereas for a newspaper it is only one to two weeks. The lead-time is the time elapsing between the submission of the advertisement by the organisation (or its agents) and its appearance in the newspaper or journal. Now, however, jobs can be posted on an internet website the next day.

21. The effectiveness of an advertisement for a job vacancy can be judged by:

1   the number of enquiries it stimulates

2   the number of applications submitted

3   the suitability of the applicants.

Even in times when labour is readily available, it is always good practice to aim to produce attractive and informative advertisements. When placing an advertisement in the press, whether local, national or specialist, the organisation is 'going public'. Therefore its public image and reputation are at risk to a certain extent. This is why some organisations, public sector as well as commercial, spend a good deal of effort on establishing a high-quality, standard format for all their job advertising.

22. Advertisements are basically of two kinds – display and classified. *Display* advertisements are given their own box on a page, and this allows the advertiser to include the company logo and some general comment on the job or company before describing the job and person sought in greater detail. Most managerial, professional and technical jobs are advertised in this format.

Classified advertisements are short listings of job vacancies each having about five column centimetres of space, giving brief details of job and salary. Such advertisements are used mainly for clerical and manual jobs. They are more common in local/regional papers than in the nationals. Not surprisingly, the display type of advertisement is several times more expensive than the classified advertisement due to the amount of page space taken by the advertiser.

Journal advertisements tend to be of the display type.

23. An effective job advertisement is one which

- identifies the organisation and/or its industry with a few brief references

- provides brief but sufficient details about the salient features of the job

- summarises all the essential personal features required by the job-holder

- refers briefly to any desirable personal features

- states the main conditions of employment, including salary, for the job

181

- states how and to whom the enquiry or application made
- presents all the above points in a concise but attractive form
- conforms to legal requirements
- attracts sufficient numbers of suitable applicants.

RECRUITMENT VIA THE INTERNET

24. Increasingly, employers are recognising the value of the internet as a means of communicating with potential applicants. Some print-based advertisements now offer applicants the choice of applying on-line. The number of on-line agencies is growing fast, offering services to employers and prospective applicants. Efficient on-line services will undoubtedly speed up the early stages of the recruitment process.

CONCLUSION

25. So far we have been concerned with the basic recruitment tasks of the organisation in its efforts to acquire sufficient and suitable human resources. These have focused on:

1 the development of recruitment policies

2 the establishment of routine procedures

3 the use of job descriptions (Chapter 11)

4 the development of personnel specifications

5 the advertising of job vacancies.

REFERENCES

1. Fraser, J.M. (1978), *Employment Interviewing* (5th edn), Macdonald & Evans.

2. Rodger, A. (1970), *The Seven Point Plan* (3rd end), NFER.

3. Lewis, (1985), *Employee Selection*, Hutchinson.

4. Plumbley, P. (1985), *Recruitment & Selection*, IPM.

CHAPTER 15

Staff selection

INTRODUCTION

1.   Once the organisation's recruitment activities have succeeded in attracting sufficient numbers of relevant applicants from the external labour market, the aim of the subsequent selection activities is to identify the most suitable applicants and persuade them to join the organisation. Even in times of high unemployment, selection is very much a two-way process, with the candidate assessing the organisation as well as the other way round. From the organisation's point of view, selection is just as much a 'selling' operation as the initial recruitment.

2.   The salient features of the selection process are:

1   the application details (forms, CVs and letters)

2   the interview, and

3   selection tests, where applicable, and other supporting evidence, such as references.

The relationship between these features can be shown diagrammatically as in Figure 15.1.

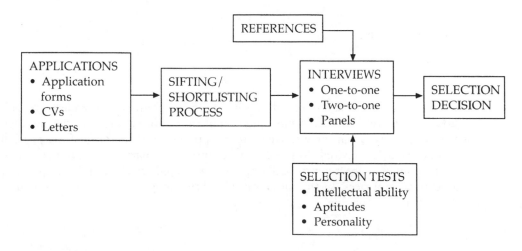

Figure 15.1   *Salient features of the selection process*

The key stages in the selection process are:

1   sifting through application forms or CVs

2   drawing up a shortlist of candidates

3   inviting these candidates for interview

4   conducting interviews (supported by tests where appropriate)

5   making a decision about choice of candidates

6   making an attractive offer and confirming it

7   writing to unsuccessful candidates

8   notifying appropriate managers of decisions.

We shall look at these stages in turn.

SORTING APPLICATIONS

3.   Applications for jobs arrive in four ways:

1   individuals turn up in person

2   an application form is returned by post or email

3   a letter of application is sent

4   a CV (curriculum vitae) is submitted.

Of these four the application form is the most likely source of information about an applicant, although CVs are becoming increasingly popular. Essentially a CV is an application form designed by the candidate. On-line applications are becoming more widespread with the increasing use of the internet.

4.   Applications are usually sorted in the following way: applications are divided into three groups:

1   clearly suitable

2   possibles

3   unsuitable.

Clearly suitable applicants are called for interview, possible contenders are held temporarily in reserve, while unsuitable applicants are rejected. If the numbers accepting the invitation for interview are disappointing, then some of the possible contenders may be invited. In the current economic climate it is more than likely that personnel departments will be overwhelmed with applications from prospective employees. In this situation, only two categories are likely to be used – suitable and unsuitable.

APPLICATION FORMS

5.   One of the biggest advantages of using application forms is that the information about candidates comes in a standardised format. Every applicant is more or less obliged to complete all sections of the form, and any omissions are fairly obvious. A well-designed application form should enable applicants to give a full and fair account of themselves, and thus be provided with an opportunity to demonstrate their suitability for the vacancy in question. The application form can be used as the basis for the job interview since it is the fullest evidence about the candidate available prior to the interview.

6.   Most organisations find that they need to have two or three different application forms to meet the differing demands of major employee groups, e.g. managers, clerical and manual staff. For example, an ACAS advisory booklet (1981)[1] pointed out that

> Some people who might wish to apply for manual work are frightened by forms and may be demoralised by having to leave large areas blank, where details of qualifications, etc., are asked for.

7.   One way of differentiating between application forms is to employ 'closed' forms, requiring only routine information, for unskilled manual and clerical posts, and 'open' forms, requiring candidates to express opinions and judgements as well as providing some routine information, for managerial, executive and professional grades. An example of a 'closed' form is shown in Figure 15.2.

8.   As can be seen, this form merely asks applicants to supply basic factual information about themselves. It does not ask why the applicant changed jobs, what work roles he/she prefers, what attracts them about the new job, and other probing questions. The merit of such a form is that it is simple to complete and the resulting information is standardised between applicants.

9.   By comparison, an 'open' application form asks for questions that provide clues to the applicant's motives, personality and communication skills. An example of an 'open' form is given in Figure 15.3.

10.   The 'open' form enables applicants to supply sufficient routine details about themselves, but then encourages them to reflect on their experience so far, and to explain something of their motives and aspirations. Such a form presents quite a challenge to a prospective applicant-those who are motivated will complete it to the best of their ability, those who are not sufficiently interested will pass by the opportunity. Hence this kind of form encourages a fair amount of self-selection to take place in the labour market, which, of course saves time and effort on the part of the organisation's selectors. Another advantage of the form is that it produces distinctive replies between candidates, which may also be very useful in deciding whom to shortlist. The slight disadvantage of this kind of form lies in the extra and varied amount of detail that selectors need to absorb before deciding on the shortlist.

Job applied for:

Surname: First Name(s):

Address: Telephone No.:

Date of Birth: Place of Birth:

Marital Status: Children:

Educational Qualifications:

School:

College:

Training Courses Attended:

Work Experience:

Present/Last Job:

                    Employer: Weekly Pay:

                                    Bonuses:

Previous Jobs:

Notice required in present job:

Referee:

Signed: Date:

Figure 15.2 *An example of a 'closed' form*

Post Applied For:

Surname:	First Name(s):
Address:	Telephone No.:
Date of Birth:	Place of Birth:

Educational/Professional Qualifications:

School:

College:

University:

Other:

Career Details:

Current Position & Salary:

Brief Details of Previous Posts:
(commencing with most recent)

Principal Interests/Hobbies

What attracts you to this post?

What contribution do you think you can make?

What has given you the greatest satisfaction at work to date?

How do you see your career developing in the next few years?

Notice required by present employer:

Referees: Please supply the names of two persons able to provide a reference on your behalf.

Signed:	Date:

Figure 15.3 *An example of an 'open' application form*

THE CURRICULUM VITAE

11.   The Curriculum Vitae, or CV as it is usually known, is a candidate's own description of how he/she sees their personal history in relation to a job application.

Most CVs are a combination of two elements (1) standard/routine information about the candidate and (2) personalised information. The first describes basic details such as:

1   name, address and telephone number

2   age, marital status

3   education: secondary school/college/university, etc.

4   qualifications: GCSE's, 'A' levels, certificates S/NVQs, diplomas and degrees

5   professional memberships, e.g. ACCA, ARICS, MCIPD, etc.

12.   The second element is a personalised view of such matters as the candidate's job history, personal interests and motivation. Thus the candidate may choose the order in which he/she describes previous experience, and can decide how much or how little to say about time in particular posts, or in developing particular interests. A candidate has the scope to elaborate on his/her experience rather as in the open application form described above.

13.   Since CVs, unlike application forms, do not come readily prepared and printed it is important for candidates to realise that they must make a good presentation of their information. Thus, a neat and clear print-out is usually required by recruiters.

14.   In the final analysis, application forms and CVs are the core of the selection process. Without them the selection process can make little headway. With them candidates can be shortlisted, interviewed and assessed. For many posts the main selection is made on the basis of the application form and Lewis (1985)[2] called this phenomenon 'selecting out', which he prefers to 'pre-selection' as others have called it. He notes that 'As economic conditions ... mean that more and more people will be chasing fewer and fewer jobs ... the existence of an unmanageably large pool of applicants will become much more common.' One response to this situation by employers is to set about pre-selection on a systematic basis. Thus, 'The information on the application form ... becomes the essential data for pre-selection decisions.'

In earlier research Lewis (1980)[3] suggested that a carefully-designed pre-selection procedure could be very reliable, although he was less confident about the validity of the procedure.

15.   Once the shortlist has been drawn up and the candidates invited for interview, the application form and/or CV take on a different role, that of aiding the interviewer in the next, interactive, stage of the selection process: the interview. Before looking at the selection interview in more detail, a few points need to be made about referees and references.

EMPLOYMENT REFERENCES

16. References are brief statements about a candidate made by a third party, usually the candidate's superior. These statements are mainly intended to provide confirmation of information supplied by an applicant on his/her application form. Referees are usually asked to provide (a) factual information about the candidate's period of employment in their organisation, and (b) evidence concerning the candidate's personal character (sobriety, honesty, reliability, etc.). Most public-sector organisations take up references before short-listed candidates are called for interview; private sector organisations tend to take them up after the candidate has been interviewed and a provisional offer of appointment made.

17. Little is known about the effects of referees' comments on the outcome of the selection process. In most cases, they are a mere formality. The most likely reasons for their continuing inclusion in the selection process is that they (a) act to encourage applicants to tell the truth about themselves in their application forms, and (b) they provide a 'backstop' in cases of genuine attempts by applicants to mislead prospective employers.

THE SELECTION INTERVIEW

18. If the application form is the core feature of the first stage of the selection process, then the interview is its counterpart in the second stage. What is an interview? Basically it is a formal exchange of facts, impressions and viewpoints between a prospective employer and a prospective employee with a view to their mutual selection or parting. Usually only one applicant is interviewed at a time, but the number of interviewers may vary considerably. The most common options are as follows:

   1   one interviewer

   2   two interviewers (e.g. one line manager and a personnel officer)

   3   a panel of interviewers (e.g. four interviewers and a chairman).

   Generally speaking the greater the number of interviewers at any one time, the greater the formality. Panel interviews are favoured in the public sector, where they are thought to enable all the organisational interests concerned to play a part in the proceedings and to see that justice is done. Most candidates appear to find panel interviews rather daunting. When more than one interviewer is present it is important to agree the allocation of questions beforehand, so far as possible. In a two-to-one situation, there is an advantage to the selectors in that whilst one person is asking a question, or pursuing a point, the other can observe the candidate's responses.

19. The interviews held in the majority of organisations are conducted by people who are amateurs in the role of interviewer. The typical manager and supervisor in an organisation simply does not have the opportunity to exercise his or her skills with any frequency, and may have received little or no training in the requisite skills.

Research studies in recent years have indicated that interviews are neither particularly reliable nor valid. The test of reliability is usually the degree of agreement between different interviewers about a set of candidates. If several interviewers come to distinctly different conclusions about a list of candidates, the reliability of the system is low, and vice versa. The test of validity is the extent to which the interview can predict suitability for the job. Thus, if a number of appointees turn out to be unsuitable in their first few weeks, the validity of the selection exercise must be questioned.

20. Research has also indicated that where selection criteria are employed in a *structured* way in an interview, reliability and validity are increased. This suggests that, if interviewers make full use of the application form and the personnel specification to provide a framework for the interview process, there will be greater reliability in selecting 'the right candidate'. As in any worthwhile task, the more thorough the preparation, the better the chance of completing it successfully.

21. What does this mean in practice? It suggests the following:

   • The interviewer should possess and have read all the relevant documents (job description, personnel specification, application form and other material such as references).

   • The interviewer should establish what precise issues he/she needs to draw out in the interview.

   • The interviewer should prepare crucial questions and comments to put to the candidate.

   • The candidate should be given every opportunity to give a full and fair account of him/her self.

   • The interviewer should nevertheless be in control of the situation.

   • The interviewer should be aware of his/her own prejudices and needs.

22. Where interviewers prepare themselves along the line suggested, they are more likely to reach informed judgements about candidates rather than hopeful 'guesstimates'. Some organisations encourage their line managers to formalise this process of structuring the interview by asking them to complete a candidate assessment form, which is usually based on the personnel specification. An example of such a form, used by a retail organisation, is shown in Figure 15.4.

23. The interviewer who is well-prepared will go into the interview situation with a degree of confidence that is far less likely to be achieved if he or she is pitched into the situation at the last minute. It is important to consider the interviewer's morale since most interviewers are not conducting interviews sufficiently regularly to feel completely at ease in the face-to-face situation that is central to the whole business. It is worth bearing in mind that it is not only candidates who feel nervous before an interview!

Candidate Assessment for position of .... at .... Branch	
Outward Acceptability Appearance Speech Manner	Evidence obtained & comments
Education & Experience Qualifications Job training Work experience Work progression	
Skills Relevant skills Work motives Previous employment Present post Ambition	
Relationships with people Superiors Subordinates Colleagues Customers Others	
Personal circumstances Family Mobility Health Interests Age/sex	
NB. Relevant sections only to be completed by Manager	

Figure 15.4 *Candidate assessment form: a retail example*

INTERVIEWS

24.   At this stage it is useful to consider what skills may be involved in selection interviewing. Among the most frequently suggested skills are the following:

- the ability to prepare adequately

- ability to listen, including picking up points implied in the candidates responses

- questioning skills – the ability to ask relevant questions at the right time

- ability to analyse the picture of the candidate that is emerging during the interview

- ability to summarise and make notes on the candidate's performance

- ability to supply relevant information to the candidate without boring him/her

- skill in building and maintaining a relationship with the candidate ('rapport')

- ability to control the interview with tact, diplomacy and firmness.

25. We have already indicated the importance of preparation, but what of the other skills we have just referred to? We shall look at these briefly in turn.

26. Listening – Basically, listening requires people to give their undivided attention to another. Interviewers usually demonstrate that they are listening by (a) looking at the candidate, (b) nodding the head, (c) making verbal signs (Uh, uh!, 'Yes', 'Umm!'), and (d) asking follow-up questions or making follow-up comments. Interviewers may be distracted from listening by interruptions of one kind or another and by thinking about their next question while half-listening to the answer to the current question. A important aspect of listening is picking up any implied points that the candidates is making. These are often accompanied by changes in voice and/or facial expression. For example a candidate might respond to a question about why he left his previous employer: 'Well, I ... er ... felt it was time to move on.' The candidate's hesitation suggests that there might be something else in his reason for leaving. An effective interviewer would certainly want to follow this point up.

27. Questioning – Unlike listening, which is an essentially passive behaviour, questioning is active. Through questioning an interviewer can select the issues he wants to cover, can elicit relevant information and can control the pace and direction of the interview. Questions can be divided into two broad categories: 'open-ended' and 'closed'. Open questions seek to draw the candidate out. They usually begin with the words 'what', 'how' or 'why', and cause a candidate to give a considered answer. An example would be: 'What attracts you most about this job?' 'Well, I think it could offer me greater scope than my present job, because of the wider range of problems dealt with.' Closed questions require a specific answer, such as 'yes', 'no' or some other specific piece of information. An example would be: 'How many staff are you responsible for in your present job?' 'Five!' Open questions are used to get the candidate talking about key issues, and closed questions are used to redirect the line of questioning, curtail it, or to confirm a point.

28. Analysing and Summarising – It is important that interviewers should be able to make sense of what the candidate is telling them, build up a picture of the candidate and identify any significant blanks in the overall information. Clearly, it is easier to carry out this analysis if you possess a clear idea of what you as interviewer are looking for. Most of this analysis is done by thinking on one's feet, but interviewers also need to make notes immediately after they have seen a candidate in order to assist in coming to a final choice at the end of the interviewing session. As we saw in Figure 15.4 above, some organisations provide an assessment form for use by interviewers, and this provides a prompt to remind interviewers about key areas of information. Where interviewers feel the need to take notes during the interview, they should mention to the candidate that they will be doing so, and should attempt to be as discreet as possible.

29. Supplying Information – Even though a well-organised recruitment procedure will have ensured that candidates received a good deal of information about the job, the personnel specification and the organisation, there will always be important aspects of the job that will be reserved until the interview. For example, an interviewer may want to inform the candidate about the team he or she may be working in, or may want to go into aspects of the job that it is not possible or desirable to publish in the 'further details'. In a lively interview which is generating a good interchange of ideas and impressions, much of the extra information about the job is being revealed quite spontaneously by the interviewer. 'Yes, that's very interesting, and in fact we are very keen on that here too!' or 'Well, actually we don't use that particular system here, we use …' Ideally, interviewers should be able to impart this sort of information 'en passant'. If not, then it is best reserved for the latter stages of the interview. What should be avoided if possible is to treat the luckless candidate to a ten-minute monologue right at the start, when he or she is feeling most ill-at-ease and only waiting for that moment when a response to the first question can be made.

30. Rapport – Any face-to-face encounter poses a challenge to a manager. In an interview situation, it is essential to get the candidate talking, and this means putting him or her at ease first. Good eye-contact, encouraging facial expressions and comments all help to make a candidate feel that this is a constructive and enjoyable experience.

31. Control – An interview is a costly and time-consuming business. It is important that the time available should not be wasted. Tactful control of the situation avoids this pitfall. Interviewers need to be able to interrupt, stop or re-direct the candidate, if necessary, and to do so politely but firmly. Control is maintained primarily by means of questions and interjections.

32. At the end of an interview, it is important that the candidate is thanked for his or her interest and response. Each candidate has invested a good deal of personal effort in the selection process, and if this point is acknowledge it is usually appreciated. Part of the diplomacy involved here is related to the 'company image' aspects of recruitment.

CONCLUDING THE INTERVIEW PROCESS

33. The end-product of an interview is a decision about the best candidate for the post in question. Where a panel has been involved, the members discuss all the candidates between them and arrive at either a unanimous or a majority decision. Where interviewers have seen candidates separately, they confer afterwards and agree on their choice. If a sufficiently strong candidate has not been forthcoming, the decision will be 'not to appoint', but to re-advertise or take other steps. As in other aspects of human life, the ideal person rarely exists, and most selection decisions are a question of agreeing on the best available candidate in the circumstances.

34. Successful selection interviewing is not easy, but generally it is possible for managers and others to improve their skills in this aspect of their work. By

practising the skills involved and by developing systematic procedures, much of the arbitrariness can be excluded from the situation. An example of a guide to good practice in selection interviewing is provided in Figure 15.5.

Be prepared	Obtain available information, e.g. job details, candidate specification & application form.
	Arrange interview room.
	Ensure no interruptions. Plan the interview.
Welcome the Candidate	After initial courtesies, thank candidate for coming.
	Explain briefly what procedure you propose to adopt for the interview.
	Commence by asking relatively easy and non-threatening question.
Encourage Candidate to talk	Ask open-ended question.
	Prompt where necessary.
	Indicate that you are listening.
	Briefly develop points of interest raised by candidate.
Control the Interview	Direct your questions along the lines that will achieve your objectives.
	Tactfully, but firmly, clamp down on the over-talkative candidate.
	Do not get too involved in particular issues just because of your own interests.
	Keep an eye on the time.
Supply Necessary Information	Briefly add to information already made available to candidate.
	Answer candidates questions.
	Inform candidate of the next steps in the selection procedure.
Close Interview	Thank candidate for his responses to your questions.
	Exchange final courtesies.
Final Steps	Write up your notes about the candidate.
	Grade, or rank, him or her for suitability.
	Operate administrative procedures regarding notification, etc.

Figure 15.5 *Guide to good practice in interviewing*

35. On balance, the selection interview is probably at its best when it is being used to assess (a) the candidate's motivation for the job, and (b) how well he or she would fit into the immediate work-group. For these purposes, the interview can yield what Lewis (1985)[2] called 'rich interpersonal data' and it is this which cannot be gained from the documentary evidence available from application forms and similar sources of candidate information.

SELECTION TESTS

36. There is one further selection method that we have not yet considered – the psychological test, or selection test. These tests are usually standardised tests designed to provide an objective measure of certain human characteristics by sampling human behaviour. Tests typically are used to identify an individual's level of verbal, numerical and diagrammatic reasoning, and his or her personality profile. Most employers make use of tests which have been tried and tested over many years, and thus have acquired a reasonable reputation for both reliability and validity. Test reliability requires that a test provides consistent results when used to measure the same phenomena on two or more occasions. This is usually done on a test-retest basis with a typical group. The validity of tests relates to their ability to measure what they set out to measure.

37. Most well-known tests provide tables of norms that enable individuals to know how their results compare with those of other groups. So, for example, a person might see that his or her score placed him in the top 10 per cent of graduate managers. The common practice is for norm to be established by readily identifiable features such as sex, age, occupational status and educational qualifications.

38. Before using psychological tests there are several important issues to consider. For example:

1   Is such a test appropriate in the circumstances and will it provide the information that we are looking for in a candidate?

2   Is a test to be used as an aid to short-listing or as an element in final selection?

3   How will test evidence be weighed in comparison with other elements of the selection process?

4   Is the test a fair one to use with the candidates in question e.g. does it unfairly discriminate against ethnic minorities or women?

5   Should candidates be given an opportunity to prepare for the test beforehand?

6   Will candidates be given feedback on their test results?

7   How will confidentiality of test results be protected?

8   Should the test(s) be administered and/or analysed by the organisation's own staff or by specialist consultants? (NB: The British Psychological Society will award a Certificate of Competence to staff who undertake relevant training and assessment).

9   What steps should we take to monitor the use of tests and to assess their value and effectiveness?

39.   Briefly, tests can be categorised as follows:

1   Tests of intelligence – these are tests designed to measure performance of a number of standardised mental tasks; they are closely-related to the general ability to learn.

2   Aptitude tests – these are tests of special aptitudes, such as mechanical ability, spatial and numerical ability.

3   Attainment tests – these attempt to measure previous learning, and include tests for spelling, arithmetic, typing, etc.

4   Personality tests – these aim to provide a profile of individual personality; Plumbley (1985)[4] described them as 'the most controversial of all psychological tests'; at present their validity is open to question.

5   Occupational preference tests – these tests are designed to bring out individual preferences for certain categories of employment; they can be useful for career counselling.

40.   Since the administration, scoring and, in particular, the interpretation of psychological tests is a skilled operation, only qualified personnel are entitled to use them. Firms either employ professional psychologists or arrange for selected staff to undergo special training provided by the suppliers of standard tests. This avoids situations where misleading results are achieved as a result of employing untrained personnel in the administration and interpretation of tests. It can also avoid claims of unfair discrimination against ethnic minority staff.

41.   For selection purposes, the most useful tests are those which can provide information about reasoning skills, aptitudes and personality. Some examples of widely used tests are shown in Figure 15.6.

42.   When used for specific purposes by trained personnel, selection tests can provide useful additional information about a candidate to supplement information obtained from the application form and from the interview. Tests, however, need to be seen in context as they may give a greater impression of accuracy than is warranted. With these reservations in mind, organisations can make good use of tests in order to provide evidence on which fairly precise differences between candidates can be spotted. In the current employment situation where well-qualified candidates are often in excess of requirements for certain posts, such testing may well be of considerable help to selectors in narrowing down the field to the best potential candidates.

ASSESSMENT CENTRES

43.   An assessment centre, despite its name, is a *process* not a place. It is a process that incorporates multiple forms of assessment – simulation exercises, in-tray exercises, psychological tests and interviews. What especially distinguishes assessment centres

Type of test	Name	Target population	Distributors
Reasoning	Watson Glaser critical thinking	15+ high ability	High ability NFER
	Graded arithmetic test	7–21	Hodder & Stoughton
	Standard progressive matrices	General population	NFER
Special Aptitudes	Spatial reasoning	General	SHL
	Mechanical comprehension	General	SHL
	General clerical test	15+	NFER
	Computer programmer aptitude battery	Potential programmers	NFER
	Morrisby differential test battery	13+	EITS
Personality	Eysenck personality inventory	General	NFER
	Cattell 16PF	16+	NFER
	Survey of interpersonal values	Adults	SRA

Figure 15.6 *Some common selection tests*

from other forms of assessment are: (a) the combination of assessment methods, (b) the central role of simulation exercises, (c) groups of candidates assessed by groups of observers, and (d) extended period of the selection process (typically half to one and a half days) compared with other techniques such as the selection interview, which usually lasts less than one hour.

44.   In planning an assessment centre the following issues need to be considered:

1   What competencies or other qualities are to be assessed?

2   Is it appropriate to use an assessment centre for such competencies?

3   What standards of performance are we looking for?

4   Can the competencies and performance standards be measured affectively by the assessors involved?

5   Who will be the assessors, and how well prepared/trained are they?

6   Should we run a trial programme first?

7   How will the various exercises/activities be scored and what weighting might be given to different exercises?

8   What measures are incorporated into the assessments to ensure so far as practicable that results are consistent and free from bias?

9   How (and how much) feedback is to be given to participants?

45.   The pros and cons of assessment centres can be summarised as follows.

Advantages:

- considerable data about candidates can be collected

- candidates can display a range of knowledge and skills over the course of half to one and a half days

- if successful, can produce valid and reliable choices of candidates

- has the potential for use as a staff development tool as well as for selection purposes

- provides useful experience for assessors who have to test their personal judgements against those of their fellow assessors.

Disadvantages:

- complexities of putting an assessment centre together (selecting tests, devising simulations, organising interviews and assessors, etc.)

- costliness of setting up and then running a centre

- a poorly designed centre, or one which fails a particular group of participants, (e.g. women or minority groups) can bring adverse publicity and ill-will as well as representing poor value for money

- assessment centres cannot accurately measure tacit skills or capability.

REFERENCES

1.   ACAS (1981), *Recruitment and Selection, (Advisory Booklet No.6)*, ACAS.

2.   Lewis, C. (1985), *Employee Selection*, Hutchinson.

3.   Lewis, C. (1980), 'Pre-selection: its Reliability and Validity', *Paper to British Psychological Society Conference*, York.

4.   Plumbley, P. (1985), *Recruitment and Selection*, IPM.

CHAPTER 16

Retirements, redundancies and redeployments

INTRODUCTION

1. The membership of any organisation is rarely static. People move into membership and others move out. The rate of movement of people through the organisation is usually expressed either as 'Labour Turnover' or as 'Labour Stability' (see Chapter 11). External factors such as the economic condition of the industry have a considerable influence on the rate of staff movement. At times of economic difficulty, firms and public sector organisations may have to cut back severely on employee numbers, leading to redundancies and early retirements. However, even in stable times, people leave the organisation for one reason or another – career progression, dissatisfaction with present job, sickness, retirement or dismissal. Indeed, it is important that such voluntary movement takes place, because it creates promotion opportunities for individuals and encourages beneficial restructuring of jobs and departments.

2. As Figure 16.1 shows, there is only one way in to an organisation, but several ways out.

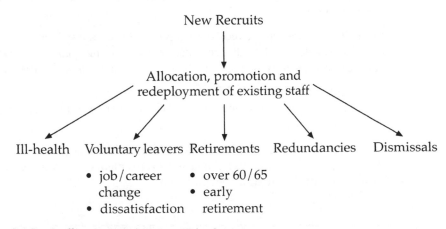

Figure 16.1 *Staff movement in an organisation*

3. Figure 16.1 highlights the flow of people through the organisation. New recruits are appointed and allocated to their initial posts. Existing staff may remain in their current post, be redeployed or promoted. Some, however, will leave, either because

they have to, or because they choose to. In the first group come those who have come to the end of a fixed-term contract, or whose job has ceased to exist. Then there are those who have reached compulsory retirement age, or have been dismissed for one reason or another. People leaving for serious health reasons also fall into this category. Some choose to leave because they have been offered a better job somewhere else, or for a variety of other personal motives. In an expanding or unhappy organisation these elements of change will be ever-present; in a stable or moribund organisation the throughput of staff will be more or less at a standstill. For good organisational health the best scenario is where there is a regular, but controlled, flow of people moving within and through the enterprise.

4.   Human resource managers will always have to be aware of the need to persuade certain key employees with particular skills and talents to stay with the organisation. This may be achieved by offering better resources, greater job challenge, promotion or financial incentives. However, more effort, and heartache, is likely to go into exiting employees, and certainly this is where disputes and grievances can arise. The main grounds for involuntary leaving are as follows:

- Retirement – once men and women have reached their statutory retirement age (65 for men, 60 for women), an organisation is entitled to enforce their retirement, though, of course, it need not do so.

- Redundancy – where employees are employed on work which is no longer required, a firm may dismiss these employees and pay a minimum severance payment to them.

- Expiry of fixed-term contract – the past decade has seen more employees recruited for a fixed term rather than on a permanent basis. The world of higher education is a prime example of a sector which has come to rely heavily on staff appointed on short-term contracts. Public policy is changing on this point, however, and already the *Employment Relations Act 1999* has abolished the waiver to unfair dismissal which individuals on fixed-term contracts were obliged to sign.

- Ill-health – some employees may have to be dismissed because they are no longer capable, on health grounds, of performing their job responsibilities. Such employees may or may not be given financial help by the organisation.

- Dismissal – the type of dismissals we are referring to here are those connected to serious or gross misconduct, for which every organisation needs to have proper procedures.

Issues of dismissal for ill-health or misconduct will be dealt with in a later chapter (Chapter 38). Here we are concerned with retirements and redundancies together with the related issue of staff redeployments.

RETIREMENT AND PENSION

5.   Retirement refers to the time when an employee reaches the end of his working life. To qualify for a State pension in the United Kingdom, a man must be 65 years of

age, and a woman 60. Most employers make provision for an occupational pension in addition to what is provided by the State. An occupational pension is one where the employer makes contributions to a scheme based on a percentage of the individual's salary. This is obviously a very important benefit to the employee. Most employers require the individual to make regular contributions as well by deduction from pay. Not all employers offer a pension scheme, and even those that do so invariably insist on a qualifying period of six months to a year of service before adding the individual to the scheme. Recently the government has decided that all employees should have access to a pension arrangement at work. Employers who do not provide an occupational pension scheme for their staff must now make provision for a so-called *stakeholder pension*. This does not require the employer to make any financial contribution to an individual's pension, but does require the employer to set up a scheme with a pensions provider and to administer it on behalf of those employees who are not in any occupational scheme. In all cases women employees must be given equal treatment with men.

6. The age at which an organisation decides to retire its employees may vary considerably from the State scheme. Some organisations adopt a policy of flexible retirement in which employees may leave early (e.g. after age 50 or 55), or may stay on after normal retirement age, depending on their fitness and their continuing ability to fulfil their employment contract. Firms with a paternalistic style of management tend to prefer a flexible approach, allowing employees to retire when they want rather than when the company itself might do better to retire them and bring on younger staff. Most organisations, however, prefer a fixed retirement age, because this makes human resource planning easier and allows succession plans to be effected. In these cases the usual rule is to follow the State limits, but some employers (e.g. major banks and the Civil Service) set lower age limits.

7. The principal features of an occupational pension scheme are as follows:

   1 A minimum age (e.g. 21) is required.

   2 A minimum qualifying period is required (usually six months).

   3 A retirement pension based on a proportion of final salary combined with length of service.

   4 The proportion of salary converted is based either on 60ths or on 80ths of final salary, subject to a maximum of half-pay.

   5 Part of the pension may be taken as a tax-free lump sum.

   6 A Death Benefit, if the employee dies in service.

   7 A Widows' and Dependants' Benefit on death after retirement.

   8 Both employer and employee pay into the pension fund, usually on a two-to-one basis, respectively.

8. Nowadays, early retirement is becoming a popular method of exiting unwanted employees. Usually a minimum age of 50 or 55 is set, and the employees concerned receive an immediate pension at a lower rate, but with some enhancements to act as an inducement to potential retirees.

9. Organisations that have a comprehensive retirement policy tend to provide pre-

retirement assistance for employees who are approaching their statutory retirement age. Holiday entitlements may be increased during this period, special projects may be allocated to managerial staff to help wean them away from their normal work routine, and free health checks may be provided. Other help may include retirement counselling and pre-retirement courses, covering such issues as health, travel and finance during retirement. Some commercial enterprises also provide favourable arrangements for the purchases of shares by retiring employees.

REDUNDANCY

10. Redundancy arises when the employer (a) has ceased to carry on the business in which the employee was employed, or (b) has ceased to carry on business at the place at which the employee was employed, or (c) no longer has a requirement for the work that the employee was employed to carry out. The fiction is that jobs become redundant not people, but the effect is the same. If there is no work, then there is no need for workers! The most frequent cause of redundancy at the present time is the organisation's intention to reduce its staffing levels in order to cut costs or to take advantage of technological advances which require fewer people to operate the business.

11. In this situation, the State sets minimum rates of redundancy/severance pay and minimum standards of notice to, or consultation with, employees whose jobs may be terminated. However, before any enforced redundancies are considered, many organisations will consider other options. These may include:

   • restrictions on overtime

   • dismissal of part-time or short-term contract staff

   • restrictions on recruitment

   • redeployment within the organisation

   • retraining opportunities

   • retirement of staff over normal retirement age

   • early retirement of staff approaching normal retirement age

   • seeking voluntary redundancies.

12. Some of the above options may not be available in reality. For example, it may not be possible to dismiss all contract staff, because they may be at a crucial stage in the project they are employed on. Similarly, it may not be possible to consider redeployment of staff if their skills are not required elsewhere in the organisation. Thus, most organisations find themselves concentrating on voluntary redundancies and retirements, as the most practicable propositions.

13. If enforced redundancies cannot be avoided, there are several important issues to be decided:

1   Which jobs are to be cut?

2   How are employees to be selected for redundancy?

3   How much advance notice will be given?

4   What degree of consultation with employees or their representatives should take place?

5   What rates of severance payment will be made?

6   Will employees be paid in lieu of notice?

7   What should be done to help employees to find fresh work elsewhere?

14.   In organisations where collective bargaining procedures are well organised, such questions will be thrashed out between management and the trade unions. In other situations employees may find that they have little say in the arrangements that are agreed.

In an ideal situation, redundancy provisions will be planned as a contingency. It is unlikely, however, that the majority of organisations will plan proactively for redundancies in this way. It is much more likely that they will deal with the problem as it arises. Hence, even where unions are involved, the detailed provisions of any redundancy package will generally be worked out in the context of cost-cutting, financial stringency, poor sales and so on. The benefit for the employee of an arrangement agreed well in advance is that the level of benefits has been decided before the organisation is forced to cut costs by reducing its headcount. It does seem odd to consider redundancy arrangements as an 'employee benefit', but in reality there is a security benefit in knowing that if redundancy comes it will be cushioned by the employer.

15.   Decisions about which jobs should be cut tend to be guided by (a) demand for the work concerned, and (b) the need for the work in the light of new machinery or methods. For example, if the demand for programming has slumped, but not disappeared, it may be necessary to cut some jobs from the programming team but not all of them. In this situation, the problem is to decide fairly who should go and who may stay. However, if the need for programmers has disappeared because of the arrival of brought-in software, then all the existing team could be declared redundant. So far as the management is concerned, this is the least complicated situation, as no choices have to be made. In situations where a choice between individual members of staff has to be made, there are certain options available.

1   *Last in, first out* (LIFO) – this means that newcomers will be dismissed before longer-serving employees. This sounds fair to individuals, but may not meet the organisation's needs.

2   *Value to the organisation* – the criterion here is aimed at retaining better performers but dismissing those who are less effective in their jobs.

3   *Volunteers* – some staff will always be willing to discuss redundancy terms in order to take their chances elsewhere.

4   *Enforcing retirements* – of those over normal retirement age.

5   *Early retirement* – persuading employees over 50/55 to take early retirement.

16. Other redundancy issues are affected considerably by the statutory minima required by legislation on redundancy (e.g. Employment Protection (Consolidation) Act, 1978). There are minimum standards set by current legislation in respect of:

    1 the timing and terms of notice to be given;

    2 the amount of redundancy, or severance, pay to be paid to the employee.

17. Notice required to be given – here we are referring to the advance warning of impending redundancies to be given by the employer. The legal position is that where more than 20 employees are to be dismissed within a period of 90 days, then the employer must consult with trade union representatives, where a trade union is recognised, or with other appropriate employee representatives where a union is not recognised, at least 30 days before the first dismissals where 20–99 employees are to be dismissed, or at least 90 days beforehand where 100 or more are to be dismissed. The employer is obliged to notify the Secretary of State of all proposed redundancies involving more than 20 employees, regardless of whether a trade union is involved or not. During this consultation period, the employer is required to disclose:

    • the reasons for the dismissals

    • numbers and descriptions of jobs involved

    • methods and criteria of selection for redundancy

    • the proposed time-scale of the operation

    • the method of calculating any redundancy payments.

18. Redundancy payments – the basic provisions contained in the Employment Rights Act, 1996 are based on age and length of service. The rates are as follows:

    • aged under 22 = ½ week's pay per year of service

    • between 22 and 40 = 1 week's pay per year of service

    • between 41 and 60 (women) or 65 (men) = 1½ weeks' pay per year of service.

19. The maximum number of weeks' pay that can be claimed is 30 weeks, while the maximum amount payable per week is subject to change each year. (£250 in 2002). In order to qualify for a statutory redundancy payment, an employee must have been in continuous employment with the employer for at least two years.

20. Whilst we are considering the statutory provisions, it is worth noting which categories of persons are not entitled to a redundancy payment. These are principally the following:

    • persons with less than two years' continuous service

    • persons over normal retiring age

    • employees who unreasonably refuse an offer of suitable alternative employment with the employer.

REDEPLOYMENT

21. As noted above, an employee under threat of redundancy who is offered redeployment is not entitled to a redundancy payment, unless it can be shown that the new offer was not suitable or appropriate for that person. In cases where the alternative employment is on different terms and conditions, the employee is allowed a trial period of at least four weeks in which to decide if he/she wishes to continue. If he/she decides not to continue, then he/she may claim successfully for a redundancy payment, so long as he/she qualifies in other respects.

22. Redeployment is essentially an offer to be employed elsewhere in the organisation, either at the same or similar work, or on different work. In a redundancy situation, redeployment is a solution to be considered when:

1   alternative jobs are available

2   employees have some of the required skills for the new work

3   retraining facilities are available.

SPECIAL REDUNDANCY TERMS

23. Many large commercial undertakings provide benefits far in excess of the legal minima. They will begin consultations many months ahead of planned reductions in staff levels, and will offer terms well in excess of the basic State requirements. Some organisations enhance the monetary aspect of redundancy by giving employees generous notice periods, which are not required to be worked, thus giving employees extra pay in their pockets. Such organisations may also offer counselling and other advice to employees who are to lose their jobs.

JOB-SEARCH

24. Although unemployment is always present in some parts of the economy in Britain, various services have developed to help the unemployed find fresh work or self-employment. These services are of great importance to the newly unemployed. As Nathan & Syrett (1983)[1] put it at a time of relatively high unemployment:

> Many people who were brought up in times of full employment learned to expect a fulltime paid job ... These people never had to learn the skills of looking for another job, let alone another form of employment.

What are these skills? Briefly they are as follows:

- the ability to locate new employment (or self-employment) opportunities

- the ability to carry out an honest and detailed appraisal of personal strengths and weaknesses

- the skill of writing an attractive CV

- skill in completing application forms and job letters to one's maximum advantage

- skill at handling job interviews.

25.   In addition to the skills just mentioned, there is also the major problem for the unemployed of coping with the disappointment and stress of redundancy. This problem requires a period of redundancy counselling in which the ex-employee is helped to face up to his new situation in a healthy and constructive way. Burrows (1985)[2] identified two approaches to such counselling:

> The traditional emphasis is on the search for jobs, with a sales/marketing orientation to this task. An alternative approach is to emphasise the emotional/psychological aspects of the problem (or opportunity) created by the redundancy.

Burrows distinguished between the two approaches on a number of key issues (aim, focus of concern, etc.) as shown in Figure 16.2.

	Traditional approach	Alternative approach
Aim	To get a job	To feel better
Target group	Successful executives from 'blue chip' firms	Open to all, including the 'hard to place'
Psychological approach	None explicit. Based on individual's track-record	Humanistic psychology approach/therapy
Focus of concern	Individual as jobseeker	Individual as member of family/society
Health	Success in job-hunt will restore psychological health	Psychological health itself is a precondition for a successful job-search

Figure 16.2 *Approaches to redundancy counselling (after Burrows, 1985)*

26.   There are sources of help for the unemployed from both public and private sectors. The principal public sources are (1) the Department of Work and Pensions, via its Employment Service, and (2) the Department for Education and Skills. The Employment Service through its 1000 job-centres handled 2.7 million vacancies in 1999–2000, placed some 1.4 million people in work, and placed over 400,000 in training and employment programmes. The centres not only advertise jobs on behalf of employers, but give active help to job-seekers in identifying suitable vacancies and assisting people with their applications. They also advise on state benefits, such as the Job-seeker's Allowance, and the availability of training. Applicants with disabilities are given special help. The Department for Education and Skills gives guidance to school- and college-leavers, as well as to the unemployed about the various training schemes that are available, including further education opportunities to study for National Vocational Qualifications, possibly as part of a Modern Apprenticeship. Funding, advice and subsidised technical training on all aspects of vocational training is available from regional Learning Skills Councils, which have recently taken over from Technical Education Councils (TECs).

27. Private sector services providing assistance to the unemployed can be categorised as follows:

    1 Redundancy counselling organisations, which also provide careers advice

    2 Careers counselling organisations

    3 Employment agencies

    4 Contract agencies

    5 Management consultants

    6 CV specialists.

28. From the point of view of the unemployed, the public sector sources of help have the enormous advantage of being provided free. In the private sector, some services are free, such as those supplied by employment agencies, who are only permitted to charge employers a fee, not job-seekers. Most other private sector services require a charge for assistance provided, unless they are operating a scheme which is subsidised by the Employment Service.

REFERENCES

1. Nathan, R. & Syrett, M. (1983), *How to Survive Unemployment*, Penguin.
2. Burrows, G. (1985), *Redundancy Counselling for Managers*, IPM.

CHAPTER 17

Personnel records and administration

INTRODUCTION

1. Information about employees is an essential requirement for the successful operation of any business or service. Management need to know what is happening to the human resources available to them, just as much as to the financial and material resources. Indeed, since labour costs invariably represent the largest single element of total costs, it is no surprise that personnel specialists are called upon to create, maintain and make available sufficient and suitable employee records for management purposes.

USES OF PERSONNEL RECORDS

2. The information that resides in a personnel records system may be used (a) for internal purposes such as planning or monitoring or, (b) to meet external requirements such as the provision of statistics to Government agencies. The collection, storage and use of personal data is now regulated by the Data Protection Act 1998, which is summarised later in this chapter.

    Internal uses of personnel records include the following:

    - human resource planning

    - maintaining an inventory of employee skills, etc.

    - employee recruitment

    - monitoring employee performance

    - work planning/scheduling

    - wage and salary administration

    - assessing labour costs

    - employee training and development.

    External uses of personnel data include:

    - provision of statistical data relating to:

    – earnings

    – employment levels

    – sickness rates

    – equal opportunity legislation

    – accident rates.

3.   Traditionally, the bulk of personnel information was kept in manual form, in the shape of files, record cards and other documents. Now, a far larger proportion of employee records are kept on tape or disk in a databank. This chapter will look briefly at what records are kept, why they are kept, and in what form.

TYPES OF RECORD

4.   There are basically two categories of record:

1   personal information, and

2   statistical information.

Most of the internal records of an organisation are composed of personal data about individual employees. Statistical information relates to numbers and categories only, and not to individuals. Information supplied to external sources is normally statistical in nature.

5.   This chapter is primarily concerned with internal records containing personal data about employees. What personnel records are needed in a typical organisation? The most essential are those used for planning and control purposes, such as:

1   *Personal History Records*

    These contain details of the employees' personal background, their job and career history, and include salary details, etc. In a manual system such records are usually kept on a card, an example of which is shown in Figure 17.1.

2   *Application Forms*

    These play a crucial part in the selection process by providing key information about candidates for employment (see Chapter 15).

3   *Job Descriptions*

    These are adaptable for use in recruitment, training, organisation development and job evaluation, for example (see Chapter 12).

4   *Wage/Salary Records*

    These are vital for monitoring the payments made to individuals as well as to the employees as a whole. An example of a salary-change record in a large company is given in Figure 17.2.

PERSONNEL RECORD CARD	SURNAME	INITIALS	SEX (M or F)
ADDRESS			

BASIC WKLY. HRS.	NAT. INS. NO.	MARITAL STATUS

DATE OF BIRTH			DATE OF JOINING			DATE OF LEAVING		
Day	Month	Year	Day	Month	Year	Day	Month	Year

DEPARTMENT	DATE JOINED	JOB TITLE	PAY	ABSENCE DETAILS

EDUCATIONAL BACKGROUND	PREVIOUS EXPERIENCE

TRAINING	REASON FOR LEAVING

Figure 17.1 *Example of a personnel history record*

210

Confidential **staff**	Salary change/bonus recommendation		
Note: Read the Salary Review Procedures supplement before filling in this form			

Group	Division		Region I. II. III.
Name	Staff number	Age	Date joined company
Present job title	Current grade	Min. £ Max. £	Years in present job/grade
New job title (if applicable)	New grade	Min. £ Max. £	Salary Scale Maximum band

	Basic salary £	Increase %	Bonus/allowance £	Gross salary £	
Present salary					Upper band
Proposed increase					Lower band
New salary					Minimum band Tick position of new basic salary

Effective date	Reason code	Next review date

Salary 12 months ago	Salary/bonus changes in the last 12 months (excl. proposal above)	Total percentage increase on salary 12 months ago
£ p.a.	Amount £ Effective date Reason	

Justification of salary change or bonus

Recommended by		Date

Approved by	Controlled by	Authorised by Group Managing Director
Date	Date	Date
	Salary change/bonus authorisation	Authorised by Group Managing Director

Staff number	Proposed increase/ decrease/bonus	New salary £ p.a.	Effective date	

When form has been approved and returned to originating office, this section should be detached and forwarded to the payroll unit.

Figure 17.2 *Example of a salary-change record*

PERFORMANCE REVIEW RECORD – MANAGEMENT

6 Management Review information

The following items will be entered on the Management Development Schedule for Management Review purposes in conjunction with Personnel Division.

Overall performance Comments:	Rating: This rating will be that finally agreed after comparisons have been made across the Laboratory

	1	2	3	4	5
	Excellent	Good	Average	Weak	Unsatis-factory

Potential	Rating

Reasons				
	A	B	C	D
	High potential	Fair potential	Limited potential	Unknown

Employee's own wishes

Comments

This is a précis of the main conclusions, e.g. including anticipated career pattern, recommended development action, development needs for which guidance is sought, etc.

Summary of recommendations

Promotion/lateral transfer

Attachments/visits (excl. courses)

Courses

Special

No action

Immediate Superior	2nd Appraiser
Date	Date

Figure 17.3 *Extract from a management appraisal record*

5 *Staff Appraisal Records*

These are important for assessing training needs, implementing promotion procedures and evaluating efficiency. An example is supplied at Figure 17.3.

6 *Absence, Lateness and Labour Turnover Records.*

These records are useful for assessing morale, employee performance and the effectiveness of personnel policies in general. An example of a form for analysing 'wastage' (number of leavers) is given in Figure.17.4.

ANALYSIS OF WASTAGE BY NUMBERS

COMPANY/UNIT/DEPT: .... PERIOD: 12 MONTHS ENDING ....

JOB CATEGORY	AVERAGE STRENGTH DURING YEAR	LOSSES DURING YEAR		LOSS % FOR PREVIOUS YEAR	NUMBER TRANSFERRED/ PROMOTED
		Number	% of Average Strength		
PRODUCTION SUPERVISORS	30	10	$33\frac{1}{3}\%$	25%	3

Figure 17.4 *Example of a wastage analysis record*

7 *Training Records*

These provide a means of monitoring the various education and training activities undertaken by individuals as well as providing details of training-hours, costs, etc., for statistical and budgeting purposes.

8 *Accident Books*

These and related accident records help to monitor the number and type of accidents occurring, and may form the basis of accident prevention procedures.

6. It is important to bear in mind that, although the computer has made enormous impact on all kinds of record-keeping, there are always certain records that have to be maintained in manual form. For example, it is necessary to retain the originals of such documents as the application form, the offer letter and any other documents relating to individual contracts of employment, appraisal forms, training/first-aid certificates, medical certificates and accident reports.

7. In addition to the typical records for internal purposes referred to above, there are external demands for statistical information, mainly from State bodies. The kind of information collected by organisations includes:

1 Employee numbers (gross)

2 Employee numbers (by category)

- by Department
- by occupation/grade
- by age
- by sex
- by length of service
- by skill/professional qualification
- by ethnic origin

3   Wage and salary figures

4   Labour turnover figures

5   Absence returns

6   Accident rates.

8.   Statistical information provides the organisation with a basis for (a) human resource planning, (b) costing, and (c) monitoring employee performance. It also provides the figures required by national and local government for the purposes of their planning. This kind of information, unlike most of the organisation's own records does not contain personal information. It is utilised mainly to discover trends in labour matters, for example, employment levels, wage rates, sickness levels and accidents.

CONFIDENTIALITY

9.   Whereas raw statistics can be passed over to third parties without too much protocol, personal records are generally subject to a considerable degree of confidentiality. This aspect of personnel practice was recognised in the former Institute of Personnel Management's *Code of Professional Conduct*[1], which stated, among other things, that:

> Personnel practitioners must respect their employer's legitimate needs for confidentiality and ensure that all personnel information (including information about current, past and prospective employees) remains private.

The use and protection of personal records are matters directly affected by the Data Protection Act 1998, which gives important guidance to professionals such as personnel/HR managers.

10. In practice, personnel departments have developed a centralised system of personnel records over which they exercise control. Thus it has never been easy for an unauthorised person to have access to another individual's personal records. With physical documents such as cards or files, which can be kept under lock and key, security of information is maintained at an acceptable level in most organisations. However, with the increasing use of decentralised computer systems, enabling access to central databases, the question of security becomes problematic. In recognition of this fact, most computerised personnel records systems contain security codes which are known only to authorised users. Without a knowledge of the codes, it is difficult, if not impossible, for unauthorised persons to gain access to the files on which personal information is stored.

11. In a survey into the use of computerised personnel information systems in 400 British firms (Richards-Carpenter, 1985)[2], it was found that 44 per cent of the systems employed allowed access only to headquarters staff while 23 per cent allowed access only to operating units. Thus almost 70 per cent of the systems greatly restricted access to their files. An important factor here is that mainframe systems are centralised and controlled by the data processing department, and desktop systems are in the hands of the end users.

DATA PROTECTION ACT 1998

12.   The Data Protection Act 1998, which came into force in March 2000, supersedes the former Data Protection Act 1984. The new Act is a complex piece of legislation, and its provisions are being introduced in stages to enable organisations to set up the required systems for handling data in our increasingly information-dependent society. Oversight of the Act is the responsibility of the Information Commissioner, an independent officer appointed by the Queen and reporting directly to Parliament. The Commissioner's duties include promoting good practice in observing the Act's provisions, maintaining a register of data controllers (see below), and prosecuting those in breach of the legislation. The Act covers *manual* records as well as electronic (digital) files, which for personnel administrators is an important change from the previous Act. The new Act introduces a new system of notification which replaces the old registration scheme. Notification is the process by which a data controller informs the Commissioner of certain details about the processing of personal data carried out by that data controller. Those details are used by the Commissioner to make an entry describing the processing in a register, which is available to the public for inspection. The principal purpose of having notification and the public register is transparency or openness, so that the public know or can find out who is carrying out processing of personal data and for what purposes the processing is carried out. The Act places obligations on data controllers in order to achieve transparency.

13.   There are several important definitions in the Act, including the following:

- *Data* – refers to information that is processed by means of equipment operating automatically, is recorded with the intention that it should be processed, or that it is recorded as part of a relevant filing system (manual records). In all cases the references to files mean sets of information about individuals that are structured in such a way as to be readily accessible, even though they are not accessed automatically. These sets need not be in the same location or in the same format.

- *Personal data* – defined as '*data which relate to a living individual who can be identified from those data, or from those data and other information which is in the possession ... of the data controller*'. These data need not only be specifically related to one individual, but sufficiently relevant to enable that individual to be identified. For example, where a specific department of an organisation is singled out for praise or criticism, the individual manager in charge can be identified, and therefore part of the information that is recorded can amount to personal data.

- *Data subject* – this refers to the person who is the subject of personal data, and who must be living. A corporate body (legal person) may not be a data subject.

- *Data controller* – the person who '*determines the purposes for which, and the manner in which, any personal data are ... processed*'. In this situation the data controller *can* be a corporate body. All data controllers have a duty to comply with certain data protection principles embodied in the Act.

215

14.   There are eight *Data Protection Principles*, which can be summarised as follows:

First Principle – *'Personal data shall be processed fairly and lawfully and, in particular, shall not be processed unless* ... (at least one of the extra conditions in Schedules 2 and 3 are met)'. Schedule 2 conditions include the following: (1) the data subject has given consent to the processing, or (2) the processing is necessary for the performance of a contract, or to comply with a legal obligation or to protect the vital interests of the data subject, or (3) is necessary for the administration of justice. Schedule 3 conditions apply to *'sensitive personal data'*, that is data about racial origin, political views, religious beliefs, trade union membership, physical or mental health, sexual life, or the commission or alleged commission of any offence. In these instances (1) the data subject must have given *explicit consent* to the processing of the data, or (2) the processing is necessary for fulfilling a legal duty in respect of employment, or (3) to protect the vital interests of the subject, or (4) is carried out legitimately by a political, philosophical, religious body or trade union, which is non profit-making and where the processing relates only to members, and is not passed on to a third party without consent of the subject. The only exceptions to the above are (1) where legal proceedings are being taken against the subject, (2) for certain medical purposes carried out by a health professional, (3) where the processing is necessary for equal opportunities requirements, and (4) where there is substantial public interest.

Second Principle – *'Personal data shall be obtained only for one or more specified and lawful purposes, and shall not be further processed in any manner incompatible with that purpose or those purposes.'*

Third Principle – *'Personal data shall be adequate, relevant and not excessive in relation to the purpose or purposes for which they are processed.'*

Fourth Principle – *'Personal data shall be accurate and, where necessary, kept up to date.'*

Fifth Principle – *'Personal data processed for any purpose or purposes shall not be kept for longer than is necessary for that purpose or those purposes.'* To comply with this Principle, data controllers will need to review their personal data regularly, and to delete the information which is no longer required for their purposes.

Sixth Principle – *'Personal data shall be processed in accordance with the rights of data subjects under this Act.'* The rights applicable to employees are essentially the following:

- Right of access to data held about them, provided the request is in writing and an appropriate fee paid to the data controller (e.g. to a credit reference agency or a health professional)

- Right to prevent processing likely to cause damage or distress

- Right to rectify, block, erase or destroy inaccurate data

- Right to compensation if individual suffers damage by any contravention on the part of the data controller.

Seventh Principle – '*Appropriate technical and organisational measures shall be taken against unauthorised or unlawful processing of personal data and against accidental loss or destruction of, or damage to, personal data.*' The data controller must take reasonable steps to ensure the reliability of staff having access to the personal data. With regard to the technical and organisational measures to be taken by data controllers, the requirement is that such measures should be taken '*both at the time of the design of the processing system and at the time of the processing itself, particularly in order to maintain security and thereby to prevent any unauthorised processing.*' Data controllers are, therefore, encouraged to consider the use of privacy enhancing techniques as part of their obligations under the Seventh Principle.

Eighth Principle – '*Personal data shall not be transferred to a country or territory outside the European Economic Area, unless that country or territory ensures an adequate level of protection of the rights and freedoms of data subjects in relation to the processing of personal data.*' This principle is only likely to affect human resource management operations that have a global dimension, as in a multinational organisation.

15. Questions about data security under the Seventh Principle are very important to human resource professionals. The following is a checklist of points that may need to be raised.

General issues:

- Does the data controller have a security policy setting out management commitment to information security within the organisation?

- Is responsibility for the organisation's security policy clearly placed on a particular person or department? (This could be the Personnel Department.)

- Are sufficient resources and facilities made available to enable that responsibility to be fulfilled?

Controlling access to information:

- Is access to the building or room controlled or can anybody walk in?

- Can casual passers-by read information off screens or documents?

- Are passwords known only to authorised people and are the passwords changed regularly?

- Do passwords give access to all levels of the system or only to those personal data with which that employee should be concerned?

- Is there a procedure for cleaning media (such as tapes and disks) before they are reused or are new data merely written over old? In the latter case is there a possibility of the old data reaching somebody who is not authorised to receive it (e.g. as a result of the disposal of redundant equipment)?

- Is printed material disposed of securely, for example, by shredding?

- Is there a procedure for authenticating the identity of a person to whom personal data may be disclosed over the telephone prior to the disclosure of the personal data?

- Is there a procedure covering the temporary removal of personal data from the data controller's premises, for example, for staff to work on at home? What security measures are individual members of staff required to take in such circumstances?

- Are responsibilities for security clearly defined between a data processor and its customers?

Ensuring business continuity:

- Are the precautions against burglary, fire or natural disaster adequate?

- Is the system capable of checking that the data are valid and initiating the production of back-up copies? If so, is full use made of these facilities?

- Are back-up copies of all data stored separately from the live files?

- Is there protection against corruption by viruses or other forms of intrusion?

Staff selection and training:

- Is proper weight given to the discretion and integrity of staff when they are being considered for employment or promotion or for a move to an area where they will have access to personal data?

- Are the staff aware of their responsibilities? Have they been given adequate training and is their knowledge kept up to date?

- Do disciplinary rules and procedures take account of the requirements of the Act? Are these rules enforced?

- Does an employee found to be unreliable have his or her access to personal data withdrawn immediately?

- Are staff made aware that data should only be accessed for business purposes and not for their own private purposes?

Detecting and dealing with breaches of security:

- Do systems keep audit trails so that access to personal data is logged and can be attributed to a particular person?

- Are breaches of security properly investigated and remedied: particularly when damage or distress could be caused to an individual?

16. Offences under the Act are dealt with by means of criminal proceedings commenced by the Commissioner or by or with the consent of the Director of Public Prosecutions. If a company or other corporation commits a criminal offence under the Act, any director, manager, secretary or similar officer, or someone purporting to act in any such capacity, is personally guilty of the offence in addition to the corporate body, if the offence was committed with his/her consent or connivance, or the offence is attributable to any neglect on his/her part.

COMPUTERISED PERSONNEL RECORDS

17. Various options are available to those organisations wishing to computerise their personnel records. These range from:

1 small desktop based systems, handling basic personnel records and data, through

2 mini-computer systems, using integrated packages, to

3 large mainframe systems in large, multi-site operations producing information on labour costs, manpower requirements, compensation trends, skills categories and organisational charts, as well as maintaining personnel records, details of vacancies and other routine personnel information.

The large systems are usually based on costly software designed specifically for the customer. The smaller systems tend to be based on packaged software designed to cope with routine information processing and analysis.

18. Some computerised systems are designed to improve information flows in a particular element of personnel. For example, a large public corporation handling over 70,000 job applications a year, introduced a computerised recruitment system with much success. The system was essentially a large database-cum-word processing facility capable, among other things, of analysing personal histories/ curriculum vitae, producing shortlists, despatching standard letters, and analysing advertising effectiveness. The benefits for the personnel staff were:

1 speedier and more accurate identification of both internal candidates and external applicants with relevant qualifications and experience

2 reduction in repetitive work in the early stages of the recruitment process and

3 better assessment of advertising media used for vacancies.

In another case, an engineering company with a major absence control problem introduced a sickness absence monitoring package in place of a manually operated system. The benefits of the new computerised system lay in the speed of input and subsequent analysis of absence details. This computer-generated analysis informed the management promptly of where absenteeism was occurring (employee category, sex, age, etc.) and whether any trends were identifiable. The system also saved valuable clerical time over the manual system.

19. The benefits of a computerised system of personnel record-keeping compared with a manual system are as follows:

1 speed of access to individual files

2 speed of compiling relevant labour statistics

3 ease of amending files/changing statistics

4 ease of analysing trends

5 ability to make comparative studies (e.g. of employee performance)

6 ability to maintain a large number of records in a small space.

20. The drawbacks of a computerised system are:

    1   it requires existing manual records to be transferred onto the computer

    2   the software may tend to be expensive, especially where it is custom-designed

    3   staff will need to be trained to use the new system

    4   potentially such a system may be less secure than a manual system, unless specific steps are taken to restrict access to the files.

21. Any change to a computerised system requires staff to be trained. Personnel department staff, who may have had limited experience of using computer software, are likely to require a basic introduction to the operation of a database, at the very least. A programme for the least experienced would probably include the following elements:

    1   introduction to operating systems (e.g. MS-DOS), including formatting disks, accessing directories, etc.

    2   using a standard word-processing package to generate letters, utilise mail-merge, amend documents, etc.

    3   using a standard database to enter data, create files, change information, produce an analysis, etc.

    4   create and use personnel forms within a database

    5   introduction to spreadsheet operations

    6   operating a sick pay records system, using a spreadsheet package

    7   produce personnel statistics using a variety of packages or an integrated package.

22. The general principles of computer operations are best taught off-the-job. Staff can then be introduced to specific in-house packages in an on-the-job environment. The final training together with degree of access to the system must depend on the circumstances of each department and its need for maintaining confidentiality. All the relevant personnel staff will need to be informed about the Data Protection Act and its implications for procedures and practice in their particular department.

REFERENCES

1.   Institute of Personnel and Development (1996), *Code of Professional Conduct*, IPD.

2.   Richards-Carpenter, C. (1985) 'The 1985 Computers in Personnel Survey Results', *Personnel Management*, September 1985.

Useful website: www.dataprotection.gov.u.k

QUESTIONS FOR DISCUSSION/HOMEWORK

1.   What are the links between human resource planning and the corporate plan of an organisation?

2. What would you say are the features of human resource planning which most help the processes of organisational change?

3. To what extent can job analysis be regarded as a 'desk job'?

4. In what sort of circumstances would you consider using a non-analytical method of job evaluation? Why?

5. Why does the Equal Opportunities Commission insist on the use of analytical methods of job evaluation?

6. Explain the difference in emphasis between a job description and a personnel specification.

7. For what jobs would an open application form be preferable to a closed form?

8. How would you justify the use of interview time to a senior manager?

9. What are the pressures on managements when it comes to selecting people for redundancy in a situation where some employees have to leave, whilst others remain?

EXAMINATION QUESTIONS

EQ8 'Unless there is a corporate plan for the organisation, integrated with the manpower plan, manpower planning is worthless.' Discuss.

(IPM)

EQ9 a) Discuss the causes of labour turnover in the hotel and catering industry.
     b) How can management reduce labour turnover, and what factors might limit the effectiveness of their efforts?

(HCIMA)

EQ10 Which do you think is more likely to increase employees' productivity: the introduction of payment by results or the improvement of job design?

(ABC)

EQ11 What do you understand by the term job evaluation? Describe three principal types of job evaluation and identify the particular advantages associated with each type.

(ACCA)

EQ12 In which areas of personnel management will the introduction of information technology have most impact over the next five years? Give reasons for your choice and outline the major changes which you expect.

(IOB)

CASE STUDY 3: KITCO LTD

BACKGROUND

Kitco Ltd is a small manufacturing company, producing a range of stainless steel, aluminium and plastic kitchen implements. The factory consists of three production units and two stores, one for in-coming goods/parts, and one for finished items. The site has been developed in a rather piecemeal fashion as trade has grown. The resulting layout is as follows:

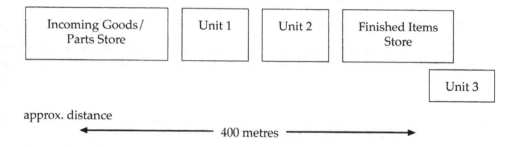

Recently the company has been experiencing excessive delays in getting stores out to the production units, and this has resulted in several disruptions to production. There have also been complaints raised by the Incoming Goods store manager about the difficulties his staff are working under.

The manning arrangements of the Incoming Goods Store are as follows:

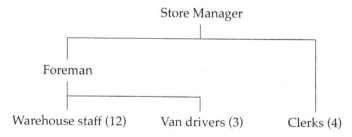

The main work of the store is to:

- receive and record incoming goods/parts
- stack/rack goods in store as assigned using fork-lift trucks
- issue stores in accordance with requisition procedures
- monitor stock levels and re-order in accordance with laid-down procedure
- distribute stores to production units (using van or fork-lift truck)
- recover damaged/reject stores from production units (using van or fork-lift truck).

The drivers are also responsible for collecting finished items from the production units and delivering them to the Finished Items Store (under separate control.)

The warehouse staff and drivers are all long-serving employees, and mostly middle-aged. Their record of lateness and absence is very low, and their reputation for co-operation is well-known.

PROBLEM

The staff of the Incoming Goods Store have indicated in the strongest terms to their manager that they are becoming more and more frustrated and angry with the way work is piling up on them. It always was busy, but now the situation is intolerable – production has grown and with it the pressures on the store have increased. Clerks complain that they are inundated with paperwork and complaints from other units about errors in supply; warehouse staff complain about the activities of the Inspection Department, whose inspection of incoming goods frequently delays the issue of stores to units, and causes periods of waiting with nothing to do followed by periods of intense, almost frantic, activity; van drivers complain that they are kept waiting both to deliver and to return stores; they also feel that the Finished Items manager is beginning to give them more work, and yet he is not their manager.

QUESTIONS

1. How would you summarise the major problems at Kitco Ltd?

2. What suggestions would you make to redesign the work at the Incoming goods Store?

3. What consequential changes would have to be made in respect of other parts of the company?

4. Make a proposal, in the form of a short report, as to how (a) work-flow could be improved, and (b) how the jobs of the Incoming Goods staff could be made more satisfying.

PART IV

CONDITIONS OF EMPLOYMENT

The first chapter (Chapter 18) in this Part outlines the nature of the contract between an employer and an employee, and distinguishes, in particular, between the explicit and implicit terms of the contract. The next three chapters (Chapters 19–21) deal with key aspects of equal opportunities, hours of work and payments systems. Chapter 22 looks at health and safety and Chapter 23 examines issues of stress and welfare at work.

CHAPTER 18

The employment contract

INTRODUCTION

1.   The employment contract can be fairly described as the focal point of all personnel/ HR activity. At the recruitment stage, personnel specialists are concerned with finding a suitable candidate to fulfil a particular contract with the organisation. During the course of employment, they are involved in updating the contract as a result of promotion, job redesign, salary changes, extra employee benefits and the like. At the end of employment, it is the personnel specialists who are responsible for the termination processes associated with retirement, redundancy, dismissal or voluntary departure.

THE CONTRACT OF EMPLOYMENT

2.   The agreement made freely between an employer and an employee is subject to the law of the land. This requires some criteria for establishing just what is employment, and what is not. The principal distinction to be made is whether a person is working under a 'contract of service', i.e. as an employee, or under a 'contract for services', i.e. as an independent contractor. The distinction is important since most legal rights, such as the right not to be unfairly dismissed from one's employment, only apply to employees and not to independent contractors. It should also be stressed that the contract of employment is not a once-for-all phenomenon, but the start of a developing relationship between the two parties concerned.

3.   In recent years the Courts have tended to apply three main tests to establish whether or not a contract of employment exists. These tests are as follows:

   1   *The control test* – the question to be asked here is 'Where does the control of the employment lie?' If the individual is told what to do, and how to do it, he/ she is an employee. If the individual makes his/her own decisions about how to do the work, then he/she is more likely to be an independent contractor.

   2   *The organisation test* – this seeks to discover the extent to which the individual is integrated into the organisation. The more the person appears to be integrated, the more likely he/she is to be an employee, and vice versa.

   3   *The multiple test* – this takes several factors into account: control, organisation and circumstances. By looking at the context of the employment,

for example, how the person is paid, who is responsible for tax and insurance, the Courts can clarify the overall position. Where the individual, in all the circumstances, appears to be carrying out the role of employee, then it is likely that he/she is an employee.

4. On the assumption that a person is entering freely into a contract of service, what conditions must exist if the contract is to be considered valid in law? There are several conditions that are important here, and they are as follows:

1 The persons making the agreement must be competent to do so, in the sense that they are sane, of age, etc.

2 The parties concerned must intend the agreement to be legally binding.

3 The objects of the contract must be legal.

4 There must be offer and acceptance, for example by the offering of wages on the one side, and attendance at the due time on the other side.

5 Finally, some 'consideration' must be exchanged between the parties, e.g. the payment of wages by the employer, and the undertaking of tasks by the employee.

5. The law generally takes the view that two parties to a contract are equal and free. In employment matters, however, it is not as simple as that. For example, there is no doubt that the employer is usually in a stronger position in the labour market than is the individual seeking employment. An employer may lose business if unable to recruit sufficient and suitable staff to meet a particular order, but he or she is unlikely at that stage to go out of business altogether. An individual seeking work, is either in work or out of it! If he or she is already in employment when going for an interview with a prospective new employer, then his or her position is at least reasonably secure. If, however, he or she is a school-leaver, or a person whose previous job became redundant, then any equality in making a fresh contract of employment is clearly out of the question. The employer wants to fill a vacancy, but the prospective employee *needs* the job!

6. This potential inequality in making an employment contract has gradually been recognised by Britain's legislators. Now there are at least two important restrictions imposed on an employer's right to hire whom he or she will. These affect the recruitment process when the employer is making his or her crucial decision as to whether to offer an individual a contract of employment. They are:

1 He/she may not discriminate solely or mainly on grounds of sex or marital status (Sex Discrimination Act, 1975).

The law aims to prevent employers from acting with complete freedom to hire whom they like, if it means that they are consciously discriminating against one sex or against married persons, for example.

2 He/she may not discriminate solely or mainly on racial grounds. The Race Relations Act, 1976, aims to prevent employers from discriminating unfairly on grounds of race in their selection of people for jobs.

7. Employers have other duties placed on them by statute. For example, they may not unfairly discriminate against disabled persons. They also have duties to protect the

health and safety of employees as well as numerous other duties in respect of female employees (see chapter 40). In general terms, however, the employer's position is still much stronger than the employee's especially in a situation of high unemployment.

THE TERMS OF CONTRACT

8. Traditionally, the principal obligations acquired by each party to an employment contract are as follows:

   1 The employer is expected to:

   - pay wages
   - provide work (NB, but only in respect of those employed on a commission-only basis)
   - take reasonable care of the employee
   - indemnify the employee for expenses and liabilities incurred in the course of employment
   - treat the employee with courtesy.

   2 The employee is expected to:

   - render a personal service (by being physically present)
   - take reasonable care in the performance of his or her duties
   - to obey reasonable instructions from his or her employer
   - act in good faith towards his or her employer (e.g. not to secure employment for the purposes of industrial espionage)
   - refrain from impeding his or her employer's business.

9. The above obligations derive from the Common Law, or customary law of the land. They are expressed in very general terms. In many instances, for example in relation to health and safety at work, statutes have been introduced to make certain obligaions clearer and more specific than in the past. Examples of the effects of statutes on the employment relationship are given in numerous other chapters in the book. For the present, the key point is that the contract of employment is subject to a number of internal and external forces, some of which are explicit and some which are implied.

10. Figure. 18.1 indicates the major components of the employment contract divided between its explicit and implicit terms.

   We shall consider first the explicit aspects of a typical employment contract.

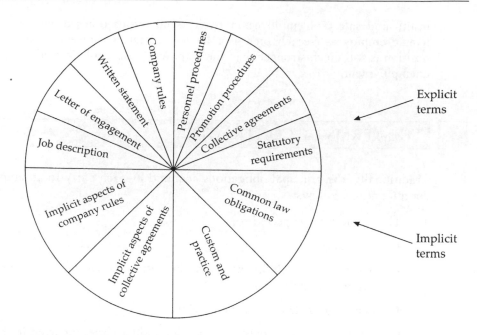

Explicit terms

Implicit terms

Figure 18.1 *The employment contract*

EXPLICIT TERMS

11. The visible features of an employment contract are those that have been made explicit, and they are usually the following:

1   the letter of engagement

2   any job description which accompanied the further information sent to applicants

3   the written statement of terms and conditions of employment

4   the organisation's rule-books

5   the published details of collective agreements made between the employer and the trade unions

6   any subsequent offer or confirmation of promotion after initial appointment.

These written aspects of the contract are very important in deciding the nature or terms of a contract. However, there is no legal obligation to make an offer in writing – it can be effected by oral agreement so, in order to protect employees against possibly unscrupulous employers, the law in Britain requires a written statement of the main terms and conditions of employment to be made available to each employee within fourteen weeks of starting employment.

12. The legal requirements concerning written statements are contained in the Employment Rights Act, 1996. The main requirements are as follows:

1   Within one month of commencing employment, the employee should be given a written statement of the main terms and conditions of his/her employment.

2   The statement must also include some references to disciplinary and grievance procedures.

3   The statement should provide the following information:

- the employee's scale or rate of pay

- the intervals at which he will be paid

- the normal hours to be worked

- the entitlement to holidays

- sick pay arrangements

- pension scheme arrangements

- the terms of notice

- the title of the job

- specify the rules relating to the job, or indicate where they may be found (e.g. in a separate booklet)

- specify the procedure for voicing any grievance and obtaining redress

- state whether there is a contracting-out certificate in force for the job (Social Security Pensions Act, 1975).

13. It should be noted that the above requirements do not apply to certain categories of employees, such as Crown servants, registered dock workers, certain merchant seamen, and certain part-time workers. Independent contractors, i.e. those who are not employees, are, of course, automatically excluded.

14. Much useful information relating to employment contracts can be gleaned from an Employee Handbook. Such a handbook usually contains details of the organisation's general rules and expectations of employee conduct, as well as providing information to employees about benefits and welfare provisions. Many handbooks refer specifically to disciplinary matters, indicating what constitutes misconduct and how it will be dealt with.

15. An example from a well-known company in the motorway catering business includes the following references:

Disciplinary Rules ...

Persistent Minor Misconduct

This is not an exclusive or exhaustive list, but examples of this might be persistent lateness to work, unauthorised absence, incorrect dress, untidy appearance ... gambling on site ... etc.

Gross Misconduct Which Will Lead to Dismissal for First Offence

Theft, unauthorised possession of company property, fighting, criminal damage to company property, clocking cards on or off for another employee, smoking in prohibited areas ... extreme rudeness to a customer, drunkenness

Disciplinary Procedures

Persistent Minor Misconduct

The first step will be a verbal warning

The second stage ... will be either a written or a final written warning depending on the seriousness of the breach of discipline ...

Further breaches of discipline will normally lead to dismissal ...

Gross Misconduct

The above procedure will not apply in the case of gross misconduct. Summary dismissal action may be taken by ... without verbal or written warnings being given.

When supplied with information such as the above, it is easier for employees to understand what is expected of them in terms of their general conduct at work.

IMPLIED TERMS OF CONTRACT

16. Not every situation or contingency can be covered in writing. It is quite usual for organisations to qualify their disciplinary rules with statements such as 'this is not an exhaustive list of offences'. For example, a large County Council makes the following proviso in its 'Disciplinary Procedures' booklet:

> Actions which constitute 'gross misconduct' or 'misconduct' may vary according to the job workplace, and it is not possible in a document of this kind to define and categorise every offence. The lists ... are therefore of an illustrative and not of an exhaustive nature.

What the County Council is suggesting is that, in disciplinary matters at any rate, every case must eventually be judged on its merits. Hard and fast rules cannot be laid down for human behaviour. Therefore, much depends on the way each organisation deals with problems as they arise.

17. When assessing the nature of a contract, the Courts will examine the context concerned, asking such questions as 'what steps have the management taken to ensure that their rules are enforced?' What training has been given to supervisors to help them to play their part in disciplinary matters?' For, if a rule written into a rule-book has been ignored, or blatantly disregarded by the management, it may be considered that *in practice* the rule has been changed. Custom and practice, in fact, provide important clues to the terms of a contract. These constitute the implied (unwritten) terms, and every Court will pay due regard to them.

18. Other examples of implied terms arise from the common law obligations of the parties. An employee, for example, is not expected to divulge his or her employer's secrets to a competitor. On his/her part, the employer who expects his or her employees to use their own cars for company business, or who expects them to travel away on business will be expected, implicitly, to reimburse the employee for reasonable expenses incurred.

19. Another convention which has grown up in recent years is that details contained in collective agreements about terms and conditions of employment will become part

of an individual's contract. Thus, if a trade union successfully negotiates improvements to pay and benefits (e.g. employee purchases, subsidised meals, etc.), then these will be added automatically to an individual's contract by implication. It is not necessary to rewrite an individual's written statement or to notify him or her individually of every change that has taken place as a result of collective bargaining.

VARIATION OF TERMS

20. A further example of the inequality of the parties to an employment contract can be found when considering how terms may be varied. The employee has little or no opportunity to vary the terms of the contract, whereas the employer can impose new conditions quite unilaterally, so long as he or she gives due notice. The 'due notice' is usually the notice period required to terminate the employment. If the change is a radical one, the employee has a number of choices open to him or her:

- agree to the change

- ignore the change and risk being taken through the disciplinary procedure

- operate the grievance procedure (or participate in a dispute, if the change is challenged collectively)

- participate in 'industrial action', i.e. by striking or working-to-rule

- leave and claim 'constructive dismissal' (see Chapter 40)

- claim for breach of contract (through the County Court).

21. If the change is a small one, the employee could also consider some of the above actions. In this case, however, collective action is unlikely, because of the legal implications of industrial action (see Chapter 37) and individual action through the courts is unlikely to succeed, unless the original contract was conceived in a very narrow sense. Since most contracts have a good deal of flexibility in the way they are fulfilled, it is not easy to persuade the courts that the employer is in breach.

22. If the employee refuses to accept the variation in his contract of employment, then the employer is entitled to dismiss him or her. The remedies available to employees who have been dismissed will be dealt with later. However, it is worth pointing out that trade union membership may help to protect an individual against arbitrary dismissal by his or her employer, as the union will undoubtedly make representations on the individual's behalf, or even turn the issue into a collective dispute.

REFERENCES

Note: Readers requiring references to important decided cases in Labour Law are recommended to read the following:

Slade, E.A. (1995), *Tolley's Employment Handbook*, Tolley Publishing.

CHAPTER 19

Equal opportunities policies and practice

1. Equality at work is basically about fair treatment for the individual. Equal opportunity, in particular, is about enabling individuals to have fair access to job opportunities, promotion, training and other employee services. It also encompasses equal pay for work of equal value (see Chapter 21). Achieving equality of opportunity at work is not as simple as it sounds, primarily because, for any *one* opportunity that arises, there will almost certainly be competition among employees to be considered for it. Managers, therefore, have to decide (i.e. discriminate) between individuals. We talk of 'discriminating buyers' in an antique market or an arts fair with approval. We clearly think that such people know what is a quality product and can recognise it. In the arena of human resource management, however, the very word 'discrimination' has a negative ring about it. Thus, there is a view that managers ought not to discriminate between people, and yet that is what they are being paid to do – to optimise the skills and effort of their staff.

2. Where, then, is the problem? It has to be found in the *manner* in which a manager discriminates in favour of one individual, and therefore against the others. If a manager (man or woman) selects a *man* for a promotion primarily because he or she is against the idea of working wives, that is prima facie committing an unfair act. If an interviewing manager ignores, let us say, the patently better qualifications and experience of an Asian accountant over a less-well qualified white candidate and appoints the latter, that is also likely to be unfair discrimination. However, so much depends on the circumstances of each case, and individuals usually have to challenge managers' decisions by seeking external conciliation (e.g. via ACAS).

3. There is a limited amount of statute law governing unfair discrimination in the UK, and leading cases are beginning to appear from the Employment Appeal Tribunal (see Chapter 40) and from the European Court. However, at present only unlawful discrimination on grounds of sex, marital status, disability and race are covered by legal requirements. Issues such as discrimination on account of age are not included, and neither is discrimination on religious grounds (except for Northern Ireland). However, a wider range of issues can always be included in an equal opportunities policy, and the Chartered Institute of Personnel and Development, for example, publishes a code of practice[1] on this matter. This chapter looks firstly at the legal framework and then at equal opportunities policies.

SEX DISCRIMINATION LEGISLATION

4. The principal legislation here is the Sex Discrimination Act 1975, as amended by the Sex Discrimination Act 1986. The purpose of the legislation is to eliminate unfair discrimination against individuals at work on the grounds of their sex or marital status. The Acts cover aspects of employment such as recruitment, working conditions, job evaluation, promotion procedures, hours of work and retirement arrangements. In the principal Act (1975) two kinds of unlawful discrimination are defined:

    1   *Direct discrimination* – where an employer treats a person less favourably than another on grounds of sex or of marital status. Examples of direct discrimination would be where an employer did not allow women to compete for jobs beyond a certain level of seniority, or where single people were always preferred to married persons when new vacancies were filled.

    2   *Indirect discrimination* – where a requirement or condition of employment is applied to both sexes but has the effect of adversely affecting one sex (usually women). In such a case the employer may not have intended to discriminate unfairly against one sex or the other, but the practical effect is unfair. So, for example, when the Civil Service put a maximum age limit of 28 years on applicants for professional posts, this was held by a tribunal to be discriminatory against women, since they would be less able to apply for such posts as they would be in their main child-bearing years. This practice has since been suspended.

5. Discrimination is permitted on grounds of 'genuine occupational qualification', e.g. in acting, a man would be expected to play a man's role. There are other exceptions, relating to childbirth and matters of decency or privacy. As from February 1987, the 1986 Act extended these provisions to previously exempted private households and small companies.

6. The major effect of the 1986 Act is to equalise the retirement age between the sexes. With effect from November 1987, all employers have to set a common retirement date for their employees. At present there is no obligation for employers to harmonise their pension rights, however. Thus, although a woman employee may now be allowed to continue working until 65 years of age, her employer is not bound to give her five extra years of pension benefits after her sixtieth birthday. However, under the Employment Act 1989, a woman over 60 is entitled to a redundancy payment, if her job is no longer required. The State retirement arrangements are still based on unequal treatment of the sexes, with men receiving their pension at 65 and women at 60. The Act does not require employers to set the same retirement age for all employers, so long as the grounds for differential treatment are not discriminatory on grounds of sex. So, managers could be retired at 60, staff at 62 and manual workers at 65, so long as the rules apply to both sexes in each group.

RACE RELATIONS LEGISLATION

7. The Race Relations Act, 1976, aims to prevent unfair discrimination on grounds of colour, race, nationality, and ethnic or national origins. The law defines discrimination along similar lines as described above for sex discrimination, i.e. both direct and indirect forms of racial discrimination can exist, and there are situations where an employer can plead a special case for not employing a person of a particular kind. The practicalities of ensuring equal opportunities for employees from the ethnic minorities are often dealt with by means of an equal opportunities (EO) policy. The Race Relations Amendment Act 2000 extends the original legislation by requiring public authorities to promote racial equality.

RELIGIOUS DISCRIMINATION

8. In the UK the only legislation to restrict unfair discrimination on the grounds of religion is the Fair Employment (Northern Ireland) Act 1989, which places duties on employers to 'monitor their workforce and to submit annual ... returns showing religious composition'. There is no similar law in the rest of the UK, but employers who aim to be 'Equal Opportunity Employers' with a publicly-stated policy on equal opportunities always include a reference to creed in their policy statement e.g. in local government 'applicants for posts in the Authority will be considered regardless of their race, sex, creed, etc. ...'. Also, the introduction of the Human Rights Act 1998 (see Chapter 40) will eventually bring about change here.

DISABLED PERSONS

9. Until the Disability Discrimination Act, 1995, the main legal requirements in Britain for dealing with the employment of disabled persons were contained in the Disabled Persons (Employment) Act, 1944. The requirements were very modest, but represented an example of what would now be called 'positive discrimination'. This took two forms:

   1 Employers of more than twenty employees had to employ a quota of disabled persons up to 3 per cent of the total staff – a figure that was generally well in excess of the total number of registered disabled persons in the population (about 2 per cent)

   2 Certain work was identified as being particularly suited to disabled persons, who should be given such work ahead of other employees.

   The 1944 Act was repealed by the new Act, which introduced some major changes.

10. The 1995 Act introduced a longer, more searching definition of 'disability', and relates it to the ability to carry out the normal day-to-day activities of the employment. The quota provision was repealed and replaced by a requirement not

to discriminate against a disabled person at any stage of employment, thus giving disabled employees some of the rights available under sex and race discrimination laws. Discrimination against a disabled person may take three forms:

1   *Direct discrimination*, i.e. where the disabled person is treated less favourably than other persons on the grounds of his or her disability, when such treatment cannot be justified by the employer.

2   *Discrimination by failure of the employer to make reasonable adjustments to working conditions and procedures* to ensure that a disabled person is not substantially at a disadvantage compared with other employees.

3   *Discrimination by victimisation*, i.e. where a disabled person has brought evidence or made a complaint against an employer, and is treated less favourably on account of complaining.

The *employment* provisions of the Act (i.e. the second of the above forms) do not apply to organisations with fewer than fifteen employees, but otherwise the provisions apply to employers of every size.

EQUAL OPPORTUNITIES POLICIES

11.   Many employing organisations have introduced equal opportunities policies in order to guide employment practices. Such policies spell out what constitutes unfair discrimination (e.g. on grounds of race or sex) and what the organisation hopes to achieve through the policy. Some employers have appointed an Equal Opportunities Officer/Manager to implement the policy. This person is usually a woman, and may be a member of an ethnic minority.

12.   An important aspect of any EO Policy is monitoring. The employer needs to ascertain how many employees fall into the categories concerned and where they work, what jobs they do and what training and career development they might have received. This information can provide the basis for assessing where arbitrary discrimination may be occurring. For example, in a well-known British Bank, studied by Incomes Data Services in 1987[2], 53 per cent of the staff were women, yet only 2.8 per cent of the managers were women, most of whom were employed in clerical roles. This has led to an increase in training and career opportunities for women who wish to take advantage of promotion prospects. Action on improving the number of applications from ethnic minorities has also been taken as a result of ethnic monitoring of the recruitment process. In particular, the Bank's aims have been as follows:

● increase number of women entering the Bank with expectations of being treated as equal with their male counterparts

● women being promoted on the career ladders and being more assertive

● more women in managerial positions

● eradicate the assumption that all men are career-minded and all women are not

- increase the number of black applicants to ensure that the Bank's image in the labour market is one of a genuine equal opportunities employer.

13. Neither the Sex Discrimination Act 1975 nor the Race Relations Act 1976 permit employers to discriminate in *favour* of individuals of a particular sex or racial group. However, employers are allowed to undertake positive action (e.g. by providing training facilities designed to help minority groups or to encourage such groups to take up opportunities in particular areas of work) in the following limited circumstances:

    1   where within the previous twelve months there were no persons of the sex or race in question doing the work; or

    2   where the number of persons of that sex or race doing the work is comparatively small.

    Depending on the circumstances, the individuals targeted in this way could include white males as well as women and members of ethnic minority groups.

14. All positive action programmes need to be carefully thought out if they are not to be counter-productive. Those employees who are selected, or encouraged to join such a programme need to see that they are neither being patronised nor being especially privileged, but are only being given a fair chance to compete with others. Sensitivity particularly needs to be shown in treating racial minorities, who, even when taken all together, make up barely 4 per cent of the working population. If they appear to be receiving privileged treatment, the majority may quietly resent the fact, and the cause of racial harmony can receive a setback. Dealing with prejudice against women and racial minorities at work is no easy task, and few organisations are happy with their attempts to eradicate it. The mere fact that women, who make up *more than 40 per cent* of the workforce, are presently campaigning, through Opportunity Now[3], to increase the quality and quantity of women's participation in Britain's economy is a reflection of the relative lack of success of anti-discrimination legislation over the last fifteen years.

WOMEN IN MANAGEMENT

15. Women are still greatly under-represented in middle and senior management roles. This is neither fair nor sensible, and an aspect of equal opportunities which leading organisations are attempting to address. Davidson and Cooper (1993)[4] estimated that, in the UK, women held less than 5 per cent of senior management posts and perhaps some 26 per cent of all managerial-type positions. This is in a situation where as already mentioned they make up more than 40 per cent of the total workforce. The difficulties faced by women in breaking in to what is still very much a male preserve have been referred to as 'the glass ceiling', an analogy to describe the subtly transparent barrier that prevents women from gaining access to the more senior roles in their organisations. What in these circumstances can organisations do to achieve greater fairness for women and a better balance of the sexes in managerial roles?

16. There are several possible actions that organisations can take to provide a fairer framework of working conditions. These are more likely to succeed (i.e. to be fully

accepted by *both* sexes) if they are open both to men and women, thus avoiding possible charges either of favouring men or of patronising women. They include the following:

- increasing part-time opportunities for *permanent* staff (and thus freeing individuals to attend to domestic and family responsibilities whilst in a permanent/career job)

- permitting flexible working hours, where this approach can be accommodated within the usual demands of the job

- making job-sharing more widely available, if this is practicable, given the demands of the job

- enhancing training opportunities for potential managers, especially in such skills as leadership, assertiveness and time management, whilst encouraging women, in particular, to apply for such training

- providing personal development opportunities in form of secondments, special projects and other opportunities to undertake new challenges and extend experience in managerial roles

- developing senior management's awareness of (a) the *benefits* of more women managers appointed on their merits, and (b) the *potential loss* to the organisation if well-qualified women candidates are not appointed to more senior roles

- introducing career breaks for those who wish to take time out to focus on family responsibilities

- providing, or paying for, crèche facilities for employees with family responsibilities

- ensuring that individuals' accrued rights (e.g. to pensions, holidays, etc.) are not disadvantaged merely because the jobholder is a part-time employee or has had gaps in their service with the organisation.

17. Clearly, some of the above steps require relatively simple practical changes to employment conditions, whilst others imply considerable change in the human resource policies. In either case the possible options are likely to send powerful messages to all the members of the organisation. McDougall and Briley (1993)[5] pointed out that change in general, and change in equal opportunities in particular, requires 'a sound and accepted reason for initiating such change' (p. 22). They suggested that there are increasing external pressures on organisations (i.e. on their senior management teams!) to reconsider women's roles in the work-place, which are giving rise to a number of organisational imperatives, which are likely to benefit women, including:

- the introduction of flatter organisation structures requiring a broader range of skills from each employee

- the demand for flexible working (i.e. more varied job-roles)

- increasing dependence on team-working in organisations – a situation which seems likely to favour *women* managers, since it requires a participative leadership style

- moves to increase individual employees' discretion over their work (*'empower-ment'*), creating opportunities for more women to experience the exercise of authority

- the use of objective external standards in work (e.g. via NVQs/Investors in People, etc.), enabling women to compete with men on equal terms in demonstrating their competence in the job

- the weakening of career structures as organisations develop flatter overall structures, thus causing men as well as women to experience job changes, periods of unemployment, temporary work and the development of a portfolio of jobs as they progress through their working lives; career breaks for women in such circumstances are less likely to be seen as an obstacle to women's employment, and more a fact of life for everyone.

18.   McDougall and Briley concluded that cultural change in itself may not be enough. What is also required is an explicit commitment to equal opportunities from the top management, including statements to the effect that 'The specific contributions that ... the increased representation of women in management positions can make should be identified and communicated to all employees' (p. 94). This commitment also requires the investment of sufficient resources, including a training and development strategy not only for women management trainees, but also for the organisation's line managers. Finally, they stressed the importance of ensuring the establishment of 'systems and structures to support the change (for example, including equal opportunities as a key result area for managers)'.

AGE DISCRIMINATION

19.   Unfair discrimination on grounds of age, sometimes called 'ageism', is not specifically remedied by the law in Britain, although moves towards limiting unreasonable discrimination against people are taking place. In 1999 the government published a Code of Practice on Age Diversity in Employment, aimed at employers and with the intention of reducing the incidence of unnecessary age discrimination at work. The driving factor here is not mere justice, but the fact that Britain's population profile is becoming ever more weighted towards the over 50s. In the next few years it is likely that many people over the present retiring age will have to work to keep the economy going as well as to provide for themselves. As the proportion of young people in the economy continues to fall, so there will be fewer workers to pay for the key services of health, education and social welfare. Nevertheless, at the present time many employing organisations are discriminating against would-be job applicants on the grounds that they are too old, at the same time as they are telling others that they are too young!

20.   In a survey carried out for the CIPD in December 2000[6], it was found that whereas 75 per cent of those aged 45–54 were in paid employment, only 39 per cent of those aged 55–64 were employed. By comparison, at the other end of the age-range, 65 per cent of 16–24-year-olds were in employment. A question relating to early retirements showed that 18 per cent of 55–64-year-olds had taken early retirement, as against 9 per cent in the 45–54 group and 1 per cent in the 35–44

group. Although most respondents over 55 wanted to retire completely by the state pension age, it was significant that one in five wanted to work either full-or part-time after this age, mainly because they found their work enjoyable. Most age groups reported that they had been discouraged from applying for jobs in the previous twelve months because of age restrictions in job advertisements. Surprisingly, these restrictions were felt across the spectrum – 13 per cent of 16–24 age-range, and 35–44 age-range, and 9 per cent 55–64-year-olds. Ageism is not just confined to recruitment practices, but even more so in subsequent employment. Nearly one quarter of all respondents thought that their industry was not interested in employing or promoting people over the age of 40.

CONCLUSION

21. In the final analysis, equal opportunities at work boils down to two key issues: firstly, changing people's attitudes so that they become more objective and less fixed in their ideas about people who are different from themselves; and, secondly, making the fullest use of the organisation's human resources. The best thing about equal opportunities policies is that they have the *potential* to bring out the best in the workforce. In this task personnel and human resource managers have a key role to play.

REFERENCES

1. IPM (1990), *The IPM Equal Opportunities Code*, IPM.

2. Incomes Data Services, *Study 392/August 1987*, IDS.

3. Business in the Community (2002), *Opportunity Now: Towards a Balanced Workforce*, BIC.

4. Davidson, M. and Cooper, C. (eds.) (1993), *European Women in Business and Management*, Paul Chapman.

5. McDougall, M. and Briley, S. (1993), *Developing Women Managers*, HMSO.

6. CIPD (2001), *Age Discrimination at Work* (Survey report, February 2001), CIPD.

CHAPTER 20

Hours of work

INTRODUCTION

1. One of the basic terms of any employment contract, whether explicit or implicit, is that the employee agrees to be available for work for a given number of hours per week. Indeed, the issue of hours of work has always been an important one for trade unions in their negotiations with managements. Since the 1940s there has been a slow but steady downward trend in the basic hours expected to be worked in a week, and on which basic pay would be awarded. Thus the five-and-half day week has given way to the five-day week, and the 48-hour week has given way to the 39-hours-or-less week. Traditionally, manual workers have been expected, as a matter of course, to work longer hours than white-collar employees. This practice, like the working week, has declined, as more firms have harmonised conditions of service between blue- and white-collar workers. Another trend in hours of work is towards the harmonisation of treatment between the sexes. Until recently, women employees were debarred either by law or by custom-and-practice from working similar hours to men. Now, under equal opportunities legislation, there are few distinctions that can be made between the employment conditions of men and women employees. Even the statutory restrictions on night-work for women have been abolished by Parliament. As we start the new century it is clear that legislation such as the Working Time Regulations and other interests will continue to affect employees hours.

THE CHANGING EMPLOYMENT SCENE

2. The traditional picture of employment in Britain up to the 1980s was that of the permanent employee, trained in a relatively narrow range of skills, only moderately paid, rewarded for loyalty and persistence rather than for results achieved, and supported by conservative management on one hand and by conservative trade unions on the other. This picture has changed rapidly over the past twenty years for several reasons:

    • British goods and services have no longer been seen as good value compared with those of competitor nations.

    • This lack of competitiveness appeared to be due to low levels of investment in new plant and machinery, high unit costs, low labour productivity, and lack of attention to quality.

- Several nations in the East, notably Japan, but also including countries such as South Korea, Taiwan and Malaysia, successfully outbid British manufacturers in world markets for a range of goods traditionally made in Britain: electrical goods (especially household goods and leisure items), ships, steel plate, textiles, etc.

- In order first to survive, and second to compete successfully on world markets, British firms had to reappraise their markets, their methods, their investment policies and their human resource management policies.

3. The changes in the nation's external environment forced managements and trade unions to consider new ways of organising and paying for work. The changes also forced politicians to consider how to organise and pay for non-work activities. The over-capacity in what were once Britain's key industries led to massive lay-offs in steel, coal, and the docks, and a substantial thinning out of labour in others (esp. manufacturing). This situation brought about a major transformation of the market which has changed from a sellers' to a buyers' market. The result was that management could afford to be more careful in their recruitment and placing of employees, and that trade unions were no longer in a position to defend traditonal craft and other demarcations between jobs. By the end of the millennium a spirit of enterprise evolved, backed by the expansion of services, especially the so-called knowledge economy, which has enabled the UK to remain competitive.

FLEXIBLE WORKING METHODS

4. Both management and unions have faced up to the consequences of these market changes. One such consequence is that employers have perceived the need to deploy the workforce as flexibly as possible. The reasoning nowadays is that if employees cannot work in a range of jobs, then the prospects are of redundancy, i.e. no jobs. Against this background, trade union negotiators have to adapt, or even reject, earlier tactics for protecting the interests of their members. Some of the key pressures acting on decisions about the size and nature of today's workforce are summarised in Figure 20.1 below.

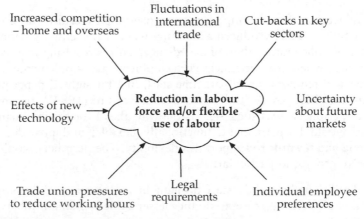

Figure 20.1 *Pressures on size and nature of workforce*

5.   Apart from the increased competition in world markets, which we have already
       mentioned, some comments need to be made about the other pressures referred to
       in Figure 20.1. These are briefly as follows:

- Fluctuations in international trade can have a considerable 'knock-on' effect on a
  business organisation's need for labour, especially in terms of the number of
  hours available for work to be completed. In situations where a large order has
  been placed at short notice, the company will need to take on extra staff, find
  supervisors to train them quickly, and possibly introduce shift-working and other
  restructuring solutions. In the contrary situation of insufficient customer orders,
  the employer may have to reduce hours, even to the extent of short-time working,
  and may seek volunteers to change from a full-time to a part-time contract.

- Whenever there is a cut-back in any sector, public or private, jobs are lost and
  key skills go a-begging. If the adverse pressures on the organisation appear
  temporary, it will try to retain most of its existing workforce, whilst reducing
  their hours. If the situation is permanent, then wholesale redundancies will
  have to be implemented, leaving the remaining workforce to cope with existing
  orders in whatever structure of hours can be agreed with the workforce.

- Information and communications technology in the office and on the shop-floor
  has made some jobs redundant and has changed the requirements for others; it
  has also encouraged developments such as call-centres.

- Firms' doubts about their future prospects have caused them to be less willing
  to commit themselves to an increase in the size of their permanent workforce
  and to seek flexibility instead.

- Trade unions have sought to reduce the standard hours worked during a week,
  but not at the expense of total earnings. Employers conceding a reduction in
  hours have sought greater productivity in return, to pay for the increase in
  labour costs per hour worked.

- Individuals have expressed their desire to have greater control over their
  working hours, and thus flexible working arrangements are seen as a benefit.

- The law also plays a part, and is especially relevant in the rights given to
  individuals for time off, holidays, etc.

6.   The reluctance of many employers to increase their recruitment of permanent, full-
       time employees has produced a situation where firms employ temporary staff as a
       matter of policy rather than of expediency. This is resulting in a 'core-and-cluster'
       workforce where the permanent core employees are supplemented, as required, by
       a cluster of temporary and part-time staff. In a far-sighted paper published by the
       Institute of Manpower Studies and Manpower Ltd (1984)[1], the model of a 'core'
       and a 'periphery' was suggested as the way ahead for flexible manning. The core
       group would be permanent, functionally flexible, and provided with adequate
       training and rewards to support this flexibility. The periphery would consist of two
       or more groups, in particular:

1   Traditionally mobile staff brought in as 'permanent' employees in routine
      areas (clerical, secretarial and lesser-skilled manual jobs) to supplement
      numbers.

NB. High labour turnover amongst this group normally provides a built-in wastage rate that can be advantageous to employers in times of workforce reduction. However, when unemployment is high even this group may stay put and employers may only replace leavers with temporary staff (usually from an agency).

2   'Topping-up' staff, recruited for short-term purposes as fixed-term contract staff, casuals or part-timers.

7.   The whole purpose of such arrangements is that a firm can meet its labour requirements in a flexible way, instead of having to add to its permanent workforce regardless of the volume of work available. Figure 20.2 illustrates the basic problem. The model assumes that from April to September the firm requires more staff to cope with the level of business, and that at the beginning and towards to end of the year it requires *fewer* staff. We can see where the mismatch of requirements occurs.

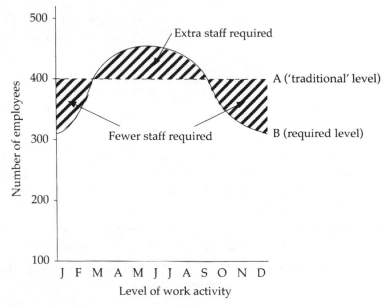

Figure 20.2   *Peaks and troughs – matching work activity and labour requirements*

8.   In the past, firms tended to hoard labour in order to be ready to meet peak periods. Now, however, the tendency is to recruit and maintain a core workforce, which is supplemented by temporaries as the need arises. This alternative model is illustrated in Figure 20.3.

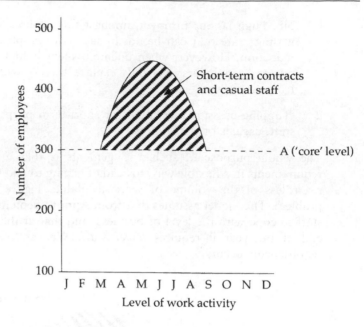

Key: A = Permanent core group
        Shaded area = requirements for short-term
                      and/or casual staff

Figure 20.3   *Peaks and troughs – matching work and labour flexibly*

9.   The assumptions in Figure 20.3 are that a core number of employees approximating to the minimum numbers required throughout the year can be supplemented by staff on six-month contracts and/or employed on a casual basis. Compared with Figure 20.2 above, 100 fewer employees are employed on the permanent staff.

10. What are the main options open to employers who wish to make the best use of their employees' hours of work? They can be summarised as follows.

1	Overtime	Hours worked in excess of standard hours and paid at an enhanced rate.
2	Shift-work	Utilising more hours during a 24-hour cycle by incorporating rating more than one 'working day' (e.g. 3 blocks of 8 hrs, 2 blocks of 8 hrs, 2 blocks of 12 hrs, or some other variant).
3	Flexitime	Enabling employees to vary their working hours within agreed parameters, and provided they attend during a 'core' time (usually 1000–1600 hrs).
4	Annual hours	Rather than negotiating standard weekly hours with trade union representatives, management negotiates an agreement about the total number of hours to be worked during the course of a year, subject to agreed parameters (minimum/maximum hours to be worked in any one week).
5	Use of sub-contractors	Offering work to sub-contract firms in place of employing more staff.

6   Temporary staff   Employing extra staff on short-term contracts of varying length (weekly, monthly, 6-monthly, etc.).

7   Job-sharing   The splitting of an existing job to enable two persons to share it and be paid pro rata.

8   Part-time work   Employing people for a few hours each week (up to 21 hours) usually on a regular/permanent basis.

9   Homeworking/ teleworking   Enabling employees to work at home on a flexible basis, but subject to work achieved or availability for consultation; teleworking involves the use of the firm's computer equipment at home in order to carry out the job.

11.   The principal advantages and disadvantages to employers of these various options can be set out as follows:

Option	Advantages	Disadvantages
Overtime working	Convenient to use existing staff. Can be worked with little/no notice.	Not very cost-effective. May encourage staff to 'save up' work for overtime premium rates.
Shift-work	Can provide 24-hour cover, if required. Enables more man-hours to be worked than the typical day-work system	Not always easy to recruit staff if unsocial hours are involved. Stretches senior management supervision.
Flexitime	Can contribute to staff motivation. Cheap to install.	Key staff may not be available outside the 'core' period.
Annual hour	Enables hours to be distributed more in accordance with patterns (e.g. 3, 4 or 5-day working for up to 9 hours a day, depending on busy/slack periods).	Requires careful negotiation with trade unions for acceptance by workforce.
Sub-contracting	Can be very cost-effective. Offsets total reliance on own workforce. (NB. This is a key policy in most large Japanese manufacturing companies.)	Requires careful selection of subcontractors. Quality control is a critical factor.
Temporary contracts	Provide flexible source of labour to cover: • holidays • sickness absence • temporary peaks in work activity • other emergencies. Cheaper to employ than permanent staff.	If reliance on temporaries is very frequent, unions will press for increase in permanent establishment.

Job-sharing	Might attract experienced staff wanting to work on a part-time basis.	May be difficult to organise 'split' in practice. No real advantage over ordinary part-time working.
Part-time working	Particularly useful for meeting need for short 'bursts' of work activity (e.g. as in shelf-filling in a supermarket). Useful for small business operations. Useful for small business operations.	Employees concerned may have little or no commitment to the organisation.
Home-working/ teleworking	Flexible source of labour. Very cost-effective (i.e. few overheads). Enables experienced workers to combine work with home commitments (the majority of these workers are women). Workers may be employees or sub-contracted (freelances).	Requires close communication with the out-stationed workers. Requires acute attention to project management and to work estimating.

WORKING TIME REGULATIONS 1998

12.   These regulations set limits on the maximum amount of working time, and the way working time is organised. The main limitations are:

- a limit of 48 hours on the working week (i.e. including overtime); however, an *individual* (not a trade union or other collective representative) may opt out in writing of the 48 hour limit

- a daily working limit of eight hours

- compulsory rest periods of at least 24 hours in every seven-day period

- daily rest periods of at least eleven hours in each 24-hour period

- additional rest breaks during work of at least twenty minutes where daily working time exceeds six hours

- annual leave of at least four weeks, and this applies *pro rata* to part-time and casual workers as well

- there is no longer any qualifying period for annual leave, and entitlement begins from day one

- no payment in lieu of holidays is permitted, except on leaving the employer

- the rules do not apply to transport workers, doctors in training and the security services (police, military, etc.).

What such regulations imply is that when managers are looking to cope with extra workloads, seasonal working and changes in the business environment, they must ensure that the legal limits are respected. Most organisations with progressive human resource management policies should find no major difficulty with the new laws, which for the most part reflect good practice.

LEGAL PROTECTION FOR PART-TIME AND FIXED-TERM CONTRACT WORKERS

13. The increased emphasis on employee flexibility as an important means of supplying a competitive advantage has led to a consistently greater use of part-time, casual and sub-contract labour in UK companies. Also, in the public as well as the private sector, there have been pressures from *employees* for more flexible working arrangements. Employee motives for part-time working include the desire to balance home and work responsibilities, to undertake further or different training, and to prepare for retirement. The resulting increase in the number of part-time, casual and fixed-term contract staff has thrown into relief the wide disparity between their conditions of employment compared with those who are full-time, permanent employees. The European Community has decided that conditions for the former should be improved, so as to be roughly comparable to those permanently employed, unless different treatment can be objectively justified. Over the next five years it is likely that part-time workers will qualify *pro rata* for most of the individual rights mentioned in Chapter 40. It is also likely that employees will be able to transfer from full-time to part-time and vice versa without fear of dismissal on those grounds alone.

REFERENCES

1. Atkinson, J. (1984), *Flexible Manning: The Way Ahead*, IMS/Manpower.

CHAPTER 21

Pay, benefits and incentives

INTRODUCTION

1.   The single most important obligation owed by an employer to an employee is to pay him or her wages. The fulfilment of this duty involves most employers in the biggest expense of their business. Typically, wages, salaries and related costs (pensions, etc.) make up about 60 per cent of the total costs of running a major business.

Employers, therefore have more than a passing interest in this aspect of their operations. There are other important influences on this activity – trade unions negotiating a higher price for labour, competitors seeking to attract the best staff, and the State seeking to impose minimum standards of working conditions for all employees.

2.   In these circumstances, therefore, it is not surprising that most organisations, both private and public sector, spend a good deal of time and effort in devising appropriate payments systems to meet all these various pressures. This chapter examines key issues in payments systems, especially (i) their purposes, and (ii) the most important influences upon them. The issue of equal pay is also dealt with. Subsequent paragraphs outline the major policies and procedures required to support wage and salary systems.

POLICY FOR PAY

3.   There are three principal purposes of a payments policy in an organisation:

1   to attract sufficient and suitable employees

2   to retain employees who are satisfactory

3   to reward employees for effort, loyalty, experience and achievement.

These purposes have to be achieved within an agreed budget for wages, salaries and related payments. There are considerable variations in what organisations have to pay to ensure that they do attract, retain and motivate sufficient staff. The two most significant factors are (i) the state of the labour market, and (ii) the nature of their operations. For example, organisations operating in a competitive labour market find that they have to pay a higher price for labour than those operating in a market characterised by a labour surplus, i.e. high unemployment. The nature of the organisation's work determines its requirements for particular categories of employee. Hence, organisations requiring relatively unskilled employees are usually able to pay lower wages than those whose operations require skilled or professional grades of employee.

4. In practice, wages and salaries will be paid for one or more of the following reasons:

    1 to fulfil legal obligations – the 'minimum' reason

    2 to obtain a sufficient share of the relevant labour markets – the 'competitive' reason

    3 to provide a fair reward to those performing specified roles – the 'equitable' reason

    4 to provide an incentive for employees – the 'motivational' reason

    5 to keep pace with inflation – the 'cost-of-living' reason.

5. Organisations that can acquire a plentiful labour supply by paying the bare minimum are free merely to meet their legal obligations under the employment contract and any relevant statute. Every organisation, however, has to compete to some extent in the labour markets. Employers seeking staff who are in scarce supply will find themselves bidding up against other employers in order to secure sufficient numbers of new recruits. Once staff have been recruited, the employer needs to ensure that there are appropriate differentials and other rewards aimed at achieving fairness in pay in relation to effort, responsibility and other factors. In addition to questions of fairness, many organisations find that monetary incentives are needed in order to encourage employees to put in extra effort. Finally, all employers are faced with protecting their employees against the effects of inflation in the economy, so as to at least maintain the purchasing power of individual salaries and pay packets.

MAJOR INFLUENCES ON PAY

6. Payments systems are not devised in an ideal world where every external factor works in the organisation's interest. On the contrary, payments systems, in particular, are subject to major influences from external forces. As Figure 21.1 shows, these external influences, combined with internal issues, such as productivity, produce a complex background against which to construct an effective payments system.

7. These factors represent what might be called the 'facts of life' for both employers and employees. How, then, are they important? Let us consider them in turn.

    1 *The ability to pay*. Organisations vary in their ability to meet their wage and salary commitments. Those which are profitable and which enjoy a good cash-flow, will, other things being equal, find it easier to be generous to their employees. Those which are struggling for survival will find it difficult to meet even their minimum obligations. Both prosperous and weak organisations still have to decide how much of their revenues to set aside for labour costs in

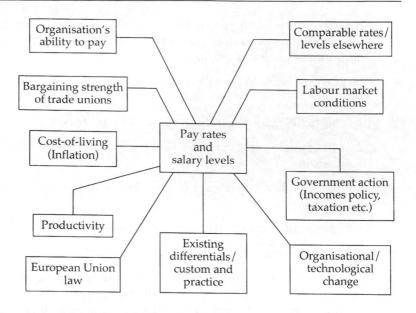

Figure 21.1 *Key factors influencing pay*

comparison with amounts required for investment in new plant and machinery, for example. Thus the ability to pay is as much a question of individual judgement as it is of economic necessity. Hence the arguments that can rage between employers and trade union representatives on this particular issue. Managers have to look at all their resources; employee representatives need only consider the price of their labour. Managers have to consider investment in the future; employee representatives need only focus on the here-and-now.

2   *Comparability.* Both employers and trade unions are bound to consider what comparable jobs are being paid elsewhere. A firm will look at its industry to see what rates are being paid. Unions tend to look at rates for jobs. The public sector tends to look at the private sector for comparisons, especially in terms of occupational groups (e.g. junior clerical, top management, etc.). Pay Review Bodies are one mechanism by which governments can update public sector pay, especially of key groups such as the Services and judges. Comparability is also important when considering equal pay claims (see below).

3   *The bargaining strength of the trade union.* As we have just mentioned, the organisation's 'ability to pay' is as much a question of judgement as anything else. The ability of the trade union to influence this decision depends very much on its bargaining power. If the employer's need for labour is desperate and if the skills he requires are scarce, then, other things being equal, the union's position will be very strong, and certainly strong enough to divert financial resources away from longer term investment to present wage and salary demands. Conversely, where labour is in plentiful supply, the union's position is weaker; and where the organisation is reducing its labour force by means of redundancies, the union's position is at its weakest.

4   *Labour market conditions.* The general economic situation produces changes in the labour markets of an economy. When trade is buoyant, the demand for resources is high. As a major resource labour is also in demand, at least in general terms. The important point for organisations is the state of the particular labour markets that they are drawing upon. Certain skills are always in short supply, even when labour in general is plentiful, and organisations seeking to recruit persons with these scarce skills will have to pay a premium price. Where the skills sought are in surplus, however, then the recruiting organisation is in an advantageous situation.

5   *The cost-of-living.* When the cost-of-living is high, i.e. when inflation is rising, there is enormous pressure on employers to raise wages and salaries by the rate of inflation. Otherwise employees are effectively experiencing a cut in their purchasing power. This problem is often restrained in the short term by government action in the form of an 'incomes freeze' – an event which Britain has seen several times since the mid-1960s. However, it should be recognised that wages and salaries make up only one element, albeit important, in rising prices, and that inflation is triggered by a variety of factors. Other forms of government action to reduce inflation are generally those of a fiscal nature (e.g. taxation).

6   *Government action.* Over the years, governments have intervened actively in pay issues. In a few cases they have legislated to achieve certain ends, by introducing a statutory incomes policy to keep wage levels within defined limits, or by passing acts designed to protect particular groups of employees (e.g. those covered by Wages Councils, and women employees). In other cases, governments have relied on fiscal measures (taxation, interest rates, exchange rates, etc.) to influence wage rates. Government policy is a crucial factor in pay determination. Although, as ministers are the first to point out, governments themselves cannot bring about full employment and prosperity. This can only be achieved by those responsible for providing the goods and services that we need for consumption at home and to pay for the goods and services that we buy from others (i.e. imports).

7   *Productivity.* Ultimately, so long as there are markets (i.e. buyers) for goods and services, it is the efficiency with which these items are produced that determines whether prosperity can be recovered. Wage negotiators can invariably make progress in seeking higher pay, therefore, if the management can see that extra money can be made 'self-financing', i.e. that higher wages can be more than paid for by improvements in productivity, i.e. improved output in relation to inputs. Two key elements here are (a) management's willingness to invest in new plant, machinery and processes, and (b) the employees' (trade unions') willingness to accept greater flexibility in work practices.

8   *Existing differentials/Custom and Practice.* No pay structures can remain free of the influence of existing differentials between groups of employees, and of 'Custom and Practice' (i.e. pay practices that have evolved over time and have come to be accepted). Some differentials will have been established on the basis of job evaluation, others may have been established as a response to the pressures of particular groups at a particular point in time. The former may

still have a certain face validity, the latter may no longer be defensible. In addition to basic pay, many firms have introduced a variety of additional payments to supplement total earnings (overtime, bonuses, etc.), many of which have grown up as a matter of custom and practice. At the present time 'Custom and Practice' arguments are becoming increasingly untenable due to changes in technology, the decline of once – major industries, and the effects of recent labour legislation especially that bearing on equal opportunities.

9   *Organisational/technological change*. An organisation which is in a relatively stable condition, both internally and in relation to its external environment, is able to implement its pay and salary policy with relative ease. Conversely, an organisation undergoing massive change, perhaps as a result of market pressures or of technological change, will probably find that it has to completely restructure its payments system. Few firms have been unaffected by the widespread use of computers in the office and on the shopfloor, which has led to a demand for new skills and new job definitions, whilst reducing the demand for many former skills and jobs.

10   *European Community Law*. It is now a matter of fact that supra-national law-making bodies can influence English Law. This is especially true in the Equal Opportunities arena, which has a major impact in the field of pay (see below).

SEX DISCRIMINATION AND EQUAL PAY

8.   A major issue for employers when deciding on their pay policy is avoiding unlawful discrimination between the sexes on matters of pay and other forms of remuneration. The legal foundations for dealing with this issue were laid down by:

- the Equal Pay Act, 1970

- the Equal Pay (Amendment) Regulations, 1983

- the Sex Discrimination Act, 1975 (see Chapter 19)

- Article 119 of the Treaty of Rome (see Chapter 3)

- Directive 117 of the European Community

- Sex Discrimination Act, 1986 (see Chapter 19).

9.   As the above list indicates, discrimination is an issue in which the law of the European Community takes an interest, and since Community Law takes precedence over UK law in these matters, then any inconsistencies have to be put right. Hence, when the Equal Pay Act was deemed to fall short of Community requirements, Parliament in London was obliged to introduce amending legislation. The current legislation is very complex, as Lord Justice May pointed out in *Leverton v. Clwyd County Council* (TLR 29.3.88), 'The 1970 Act, as amended, is a very difficult statute to construe and its drafting is by no means clear in a number of places.'

10.   The main discussion on sex discrimination legislation is set out in Chapter 19. The legal situation relating to equal pay is currently as follows: Equal Pay Act, 1970.

This Act came into force in 1975 to coincide with the Sex Discrimination Act. Its purpose is to eliminate arbitrary discrimination between men and women in pay and other terms of their contract such as overtime, bonus rates, piecework, holidays, etc. The Act allows an individual to claim equal pay with a member of the *opposite* sex on grounds of either:

1   like work, i.e. work of the same or of a broadly similar nature to that of the other person; or

2   work rated as equivalent as the result of some form of job evaluation. The Act does not require an employer to undertake job evaluation, but where it has been undertaken, it must be based on an analytical rather than whole-job method (see Chapter 13).

Equal Pay (Amendment) Regulations, 1983. These Regulations came into force in January 1984. Their effect is to enable an employee to claim equal pay with a person of the opposite sex on grounds of *work of equal value* in terms of the demands made by the work, i.e. skill, effort, etc. The consequences of the amendment for employers is to require them to use analytical schemes only to ensure fair pay between the sexes, and to apply the same point values and weightings to the factors used.

NATIONAL WAGE MINIMUM ACT, 1998

11.   In responding to trade union lobbying to introduce a national minimum wage, the UK government introduced the above Act to provide for a minimum wage, which will be amended from time to time by secondary legislation in the form of Regulations. The intention of the Act is to provide for appropriate minimum wage rates for (a) younger employees (18–21), and (b) all employees over 22. The current rates are £3.50 per hour for the younger group, and £4.10 for those over 22. The Act also established a Low Pay Commission to deal with claims arising under this legislation.

WAGE PAYMENT SYSTEMS

12.   It is clear from the preceding paragraphs that pay determination is no small matter for an organisation. Quite apart from all the internal pressures on management to set acceptable levels of pay, there are considerable external constraints imposed by legislation. All the more important, therefore, that managers should plan wages and salaries systematically, taking account of external and internal influences on the ultimate costs involved, and ensuring fair and equitable treatment for men and women alike.

13.   The payment of wages is the employer's legal obligation to his or her employees ('consideration'). How much is to be paid, and in what manner, is a matter of judgement or negotiation. In theory, if an employer were free to pay what he or she liked, he or she would probably pay the minimum.

In reality, of course, few employers are free to approach the labour market in this way, since, as we have seen in the previous chapter, there are numerous factors which 'distort' the forces of supply and demand.

14. We now turn to key aspects of wages' policy, pay structures and wage payment systems. 'Wages' are customarily distinguished from 'Salaries' (see paras 42–4). The former are payments made weekly paid to employees, usually in manual grades. The following wage payment systems will be outlined:

- time rate systems
- payment-by-results (PBR) systems
- company-wide incentive schemes
- 'single status' schemes
- skills-based payment systems.

WAGES POLICY

15. A well-considered policy for wages would include most, if not all, of the following points:

The policy of the Company in respect of wages is to pay employees at such a level and in such a manner as to:

1 attract, retain and motivate sufficient numbers of suitable employees to meet production needs

2 encourage the optimum productivity from employees

3 ensure a high level of quality of output

4 recognise the value of jobs in relation to each other

5 enable employees to share in the growth and prosperity of the organisation

6 ensure that labour costs are suitably controlled in relation to other costs, and in relation to revenues.

16. Such a policy is stating clearly that the company concerned is prepared to pay what is necessary to attract the right kinds of employees in the right numbers, and having recruited them, will use its wages system to retain and motivate such employees. Of course, pay is not the only factor involved in attracting, retaining and motivating employees, but it is an extremely important factor. Pay can also be used to encourage employees to work productively and with particular attention to the quality of their work. Here again, money is not the only means of encouraging improved productivity, but for manual workers, in particular, it seems to have a special significance. Goldthorpe et al. (1968)[1], for example, found a distinctly 'instrumental' attitude to work amongst Luton factory workers, i.e. that they saw work mainly as a means to an end – obtaining enough money to enjoy what they really wanted to do.

17. Another important feature of wages policy is the organisation's need to differentiate jobs in line with the value of their contribution to results, both to achieve equity of payment and to provide an incentive to accept greater responsibility. Finally, every policy needs to take account of labour costs in relation (a) to revenues, and (b) other costs, notably investment in new plant and machinery.

WAGES STRUCTURES

18. A wages structure is devised to support the ideas contained in the kind of policy we have just referred to. Essentially, a wage structure is a hierarchy of job grades or rates. Thus, in a factory, for example, there will be a structure consisting of grades or rates for chargehands, skilled fitters, electricians, skilled machinists, semi-skilled operators, storemen, labourers, etc. A grade is a wage band, through which a job-holder passes by virtue of experience or skill; a wage rate is the sum of money attaching to a particular job (i.e.£x per hour, or £x per week). The differences between job grades or rates are called 'differentials'. There are important reasons why both employers and trade unions want to see differentials maintained. Usually differentials will be based on differences in skill or responsibility. Thus, a qualified electrician's rate will be higher than a semi-skilled machine-operator's rate. Managements need to establish differentials in order to be able to attract employees into certain classes of jobs. Trade unions, especially those representing craft occupations need to be able to demonstrate their power to obtain better conditions for time-served employees, or other workers exercising additional skills or knowledge. Differences between one organisation or industry and another are usually called 'relativities'. Relativities are important in wage bargaining because both parties may want to exploit wage trends in 'comparable' industries or relevant sectors, where similar jobs are carried out.

19. Bowey and Lupton (1973)[2] devised a basis for making comparisons between rates of pay in different companies. They selected five factors for comparison between jobs:

1 skill

2 responsibility

3 mental effort

4 physical effort

5 working conditions.

Each factor was subdivided into a number of sub-factors, which were given a weighting, as in the following example:

Skill:

* Education   5 per cent

* Training   5 per cent

• Experience	3	per cent
• Performance	5	per cent
• Initiative	8	per cent
• Mechanical	5	per cent
• Dexterity	5	per cent
Total Weighting for Skill	36 per cent	

20. The objective in Bowey and Lupton's scheme was to identify similarities between jobs, not differences, as in the case of job evaluation (see Chapter 13 above). Having selected relevant criteria for comparing jobs, it is possible to compare like with like in other firms or other sites. This, however, is not as straightforward as it seems:

> If the ... jobs were shown by the procedure to be closely similar ... it would seem to be a ... simple ... matter to compare the pay; and so it would be if the pay packets were made up in the same way. It would be unusual ... if that were the case.

The problem is that pay is made up of several items, which often vary considerably between employers and employee groups.

21. The chief elements of an employee's earnings, in addition to basic pay, are usually as follows:

1 overtime

2 shift premium

3 individual bonuses

4 share of group bonuses

5 special allowances.

Some of these elements are effectively guaranteed by the employer, while others are not. Employers generally aim to reduce the number of guaranteed payments in addition to basic pay. Employee representatives generally seek to raise the number of such payments.

TYPES OF WAGE PAYMENT SYSTEMS

22. There are currently four main types of wage payment system for manual employees in the United Kingdom. These are:

1 time rate systems, where pay is related to hours at work and not to effort

2 payments-by-results systems, geared directly to effort or output

3 company-wide incentive schemes, where pay is linked to overall performance

4 'single status' schemes, where manual workers are paid as salaried employees.

A recent addition to this list is skill-based pay (see below).

23.   Time rate systems – these are the commonest systems to be found in Britain. Payments are made at predetermined rates, per hour or per week, which generally do not vary in accordance with effort made, or results obtained. Figure 21.2 indicates the basic effect of time payment.

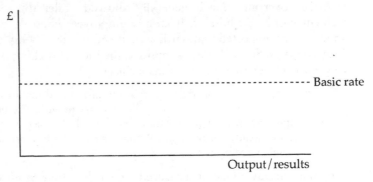

Figure 21.2   *Time payment*

Payment by time systems, according to Shaw and Pirie (1982)[3], are 'consistent with the idea that payments systems should be designed to encourage co-operation between work-people and management to achieve optimum results ...'.

This suggests that as a matter of policy management would prefer a time based system.

24.   The main reasons behind such a policy are:

1   that management rather than employees control the operation

2   that labour flexibility is achieved where people are paid for work as a whole rather than for work as a series of specific tasks (as in payment-by-results).

The wage rates set will usually be subject to the twin influences of work measurement (in this case Time Study) and collective bargaining between the employer and trade union representatives.

25.   The two most common forms of time system are:

1   high day-rate

2   measured daywork.

High day-rate systems involve the payment of a relatively high level of hourly pay with the implied understanding that the work is of a 'high' level or requires 'high' performance, yet where there is no measured attempt to link pay with performance. Under such a system, unlike in measured daywork, overtime and shift premiums are paid at their usual enhanced rates. These systems have been favoured by the chemical industries, where continuous plant operation is the norm.

Measured daywork systems, unlike the high day-rate systems, do include a bonus element in their construction. Under this system pay is fixed on the understanding that the employee will maintain an agreed level of performance set at an incentive level (say 95 or 100 on the BSI scale), which is paid as part of basic pay, i.e. it is paid in advance, and requires an element of trust between management and employees.

26. The advantages of such a system are (i) that management is in control of production, and (ii) that employees receive predictable earnings at an enhanced rate. No overtime rate is generally allowed under this system, and the bonus element can be withdrawn from any employee whose level of performance falls short of the expected standard, where this is due to his or her own failure or shortcomings. Shaw & Pirie supported the idea of making the fixed bonus payable to groups rather than to individuals since:

> ... this encourages cooperation within the group and makes it easier to meet high average performance targets ... it is also less easy to withdraw bonus from a group ... in our opinion (this) is a good feature since the whole objective of time-based schemes is to achieve steady performance. Penalising bad performance does not get the work done. Helping operators to raise it does.

27. The main disadvantage of measured daywork is that employees may slacken their performance without some direct incentive, but this depends on the quality of the supervision. This approach has been used with success in a number of large motor manufacturers.

28. The principal benefits of time-based systems can be summarised as follows:

- they are simple to operate
- they produce predictable earnings
- labour costs can be readily controlled
- they encourage collaboration rather than competition between employees
- they encourage labour flexibility.

PAYMENT-BY-RESULTS (PBR) SYSTEMS

29. These systems relate pay directly to output or effort. They are most applicable to manual operations involving repetitive tasks on a short time-cycle. The most well-known system is that of 'piecework', where an employee is paid on the basis of the number of items produced at an agreed rate per item (see Figure 21.3).

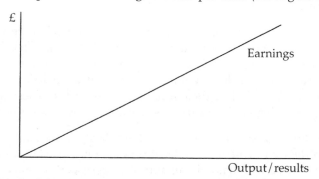

Figure 21.3 *Straight piece-rate*

Piecework is a form of direct incentive, where bonus is related directly to effort, under time-studied standards, and where the employee receives the monetary reward a few days after his or her efforts. The more the operator produces, the more he or she earns. There are several variations of piece-work, for example incorporating a guaranteed rate up to say 75 per cent Standard Performance, followed by enhanced rates for higher performance (see Figure 21.4).

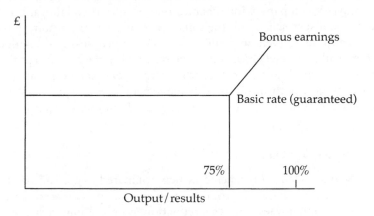

Figure 21.4 *Combined time-rate and piece-rate*

30. The advantages of piecework are primarily (i) that employees can be motivated to put in extra effort, and be rewarded within days, and (ii) that high levels of output can be achieved. The disadvantages are more numerous. They are as follows:

- the rate fixed per item is often subject to argument and haggling

- operators can find ways of achieving high earnings without commensurate effort (i.e. learning how to beat the system)

- production effort is in the hands of the individual employees (i.e. if an operator decides to ease off, having reached a personally satisfactory level of earnings for that day, or that week, the supervisor is hardly in a position to interfere)

- quality tends to suffer in the pressure to attain high levels of output

- support workers, whose efforts cannot be measured in the same way are unable to share in the benefits of increased output, and this can create dissatifaction among such groups.

COMPANY-WIDE INCENTIVE SCHEMES

31. Under a company-wide scheme a bonus is paid to all employees on the basis of productivity achieved within the business as a whole. Usually the bonus payments are based on some key measure of labour productivity, for example the ratio of labour costs per unit of output or output per man-hour. The savings or additional output achieved above an agreed standard are paid out to employees at specified intervals, usually monthly, quarterly or yearly. The important aspect, from management's point of view, is that the productivity measure selected is one that

genuinely reflects labour performance over the period concerned. Thus ratios such as those just quoted are more directly related to employee performance, than such measures as company profitability, much of which may have been attained as a result of non-employee activities, such as selling property, setting an optimum price for company products, etc.

32. Unlike payment-by-results schemes, which tend to encourage competition between employees, company-wide schemes rely on group collaboration. One of the main features of such schemes is their insistence on regular consultation and negotiations between management and employees on the progress and conduct of the scheme. This regular contact ensures that the scheme is generally acceptable to both parties. It is also important to ensure that employees are given adequate feedback on performance, both in terms of management's expectations as well as in terms of results achieved. The two most widely-used company incentive schemes are:

- The Scanlon Plan

- The Rucker Plan.

33. The Scanlon Plan. This scheme, which originated in the United States in the 1940s, is basically a 'share of production' plan, i.e. if increased output from a given number of employees leads to a reduction in unit labour costs, then the savings will be pooled for distribution to the employees on some agreed basis – perhaps all the savings will be made available to employees, or, most likely, some major proportion of them. Lesieur, F.G. (1958)[4], for example, described the experience of one American company, Lapointe Machine Tool Company, in which increases in productivity were allocated on the basis of 75 per cent to the participants (employees) and 25 per cent to the company. Central to such a scheme were plant productivity committees, consisting of both management and employee representatives, whose task was to select productivity criteria monitor performance and make changes in the light of experience. These committees had executive power, which gave the participating employees a genuine opportunity to share in decisions about their work.

34. The Rucker Plan. This is another American idea, dating from the 1950s. The plan is based on the relationship between labour costs and 'added value'. Added value (AV) can be defined as follows:

$$AV = Sales\ Value - Costs\ of\ Materials/Purchases$$

Essentially, added value is the difference between what comes into the factory in the way of raw materials, part finished goods and components, and what goes out in terms of finished products. Sometimes added value is called 'production value' to emphasise this point. As with the Scanlon Plan, a suitable productivity standard is agreed between management and employees. In this case, the ratio of added value to labour costs is the crucial indicator. A typical ratio would be 2:1, i.e. labour costs represent 50 per cent of added value. Thus if, in a given month added value was £200,000, then the anticipated labour share of this would be £100,000. If actual labour costs were only £85,000 in that month, then £15,000 has been 'saved' by improved labour productivity. This latter sum, or an agreed proportion of it, is put aside for the bonus fund.

35. Productivity is the relationship between inputs and outputs. Thus if, for a given

level of inputs, more is achieved compared with an earlier target, then productivity has improved. Or, to look at it another way, if the same amount of output can be achieved using less by way of inputs, then again productivity has improved. Typical measures used in productivity assessment are as shown in Figure 21.5.

Data for the chosen criteria, e.g. production achieved per man-hour, are obtained from routine production and personnel records. Thus such systems avoid getting into detailed studies of individual employees' operating behaviour as happens with most individual incentive schemes.

Input measures	Output measures
Man-hours worked	Production levels
Cost of labour	Production costs
Cost of materials	Added value
Time plant is manned	Time plant is operating at target capacity
	Manufacturing profit

Figure 21.5 *Typical productivity measures*

36.   The advantage of schemes such as the Scanlon and Rucker Plans are chiefly:

- they encourage co-operation between employees and management

- they encourage co-operation between employees

- they produce significant cost savings through improved utilisation of materials/plant

- they avoid the difficulties involved in setting and establishing the performance standards of individuals, i.e. arguing about rates

- they use productivity measures which use cost accounting techniques rather than work study

- they create an awareness at all levels of the interrelated nature of the production process

- they can be applied as much to indirect workers as to direct workers.

The disadvantages are few. They are as follows:

- it is not always clear how much a particular productivity measure reflects the contribution of the labour force rather than other factors

- there is a remoteness of the incentive for the individual employee.

SINGLE STATUS SCHEMES

37.   Single status, or staff status, schemes are those designed to harmonise the payments systems operating in an organisation primarily by removing the distinction between the treatment of manual workers and white-collar staff. Lupton & Bowey (1983)[5] reported that during the 1960s and 1970s 'over a quarter of a million manual

workers changed from hourly or weekly payment systems to some kind of salary scheme'. A salary scheme can vary from merely paying everyone an annual salary paid monthly to completely revising the basis of manual workers' conditions of employment by introducing the same pension, holiday, sickness and other benefits as for white-collar staff. Such agreements as the latter, according to Lupton and Bowey, 'represent more than just a change of payment system and an improvement in manual workers' conditions of work. The employers involved were consciously attempting to change the relationship between workers and management. They wanted to encourage responsibility, pride in work, and cooperation, and hoped thereby to increase efficiency.'

38.   The advantages of single status are:

- organisation saves administration costs

- manual workers' borrowing position is improved by having an annual salary

- industrial relations may well be improved

- wage 'drift' is avoided since there are no extra payments to be made

- manual workers receive a wider range of benefits than previously

- the organisation does not have to pay overtime to manual workers

- pay administration becomes simpler.

The disadvantages are:

- an increase in labour costs as a result of the improvements to manual workers' conditions

- there is less scope for management to make up short-term production losses by introducing overtime working

- manual workers have to wait one month instead of one week before they are paid.

SKILLS-BASED PAYMENT SYSTEMS

39.   In the light of technological change and the influence of Japanese production methods (e.g. flexible working, just-in-time manufacturing, etc.) several firms in the manufacturing sector have introduced skills-based pay (SBP). Such a system links pay with the acquisition of relevant skills and knowledge and is especially applicable where flexible working practices involving multi-skilling are operated.

40.   An important prerequisite of SBP is a clear set of job standards with appropriate performance criteria (e.g. see Chapter 30). These identify what is *required*, to what *standard* and in what *circumstances*. Employees under such a system are more likely to be seen as performing a role which involves a range of jobs and tasks.

41.   SBP schemes also require a sound basis of employee communication and skills training if they are to be effective in practice.

SALARY SYSTEMS AND EMPLOYEE BENEFITS

42.   A salary system can best be considered as a mechanism by which an organisation plans how to attract, retain, reward and motivate its salaried employees, i.e. those who are paid monthly under the terms of an annual rate of pay. It includes 'employee benefits', which were once only associated with salaried staff, but which are now being applied to all grades of employee.

43.   In establishing a salary system, an organisation will enter into a process along the lines of Figure 21.6. The first step is to agree a policy for salaries (and benefits too). As indicated earlier, this will usually be aimed at recruiting, retaining and rewarding staff employees. The second step is either to evaluate jobs and arrange them into job levels, (i.e. grades or scales), or to seek salary comparisons with other employers. Another important step is to assess the performance of staff employees, employing some form of staff appraisal (see Chapter 24).

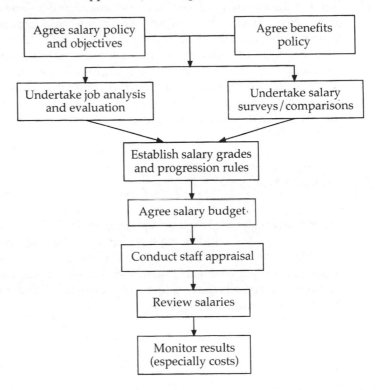

Figure 21.6 *Development of a salary system*

44.   Lupton & Bowey considered a salary system as having the following characteristics:

1   a hierarchy of pay levels

2   a hierarchy of jobs

3   a set of rules and procedures that define:

a) a relation between 1 and 2

b) what qualities are necessary for movement from one level to another

c) who makes choices, or by what process they are made, when there is competition for promotion.

45. The hierarchy of pay levels is a reference to salary grades, or bands, applied to particular groups of jobs. Unlike manual jobs, where the wage is fixed, salaried posts are allotted a range of possible pay-points. Movement from the bottom of a pay-scale to the top depends either on merit or on length of service, or sometimes on both. Generally speaking, the private sector favours the use of merit salary scales, whilst the public sector prefers incremental scales. Cost-of-living increases are usually applied to both types of scale, either on a flat-rate basis, or, more often, on a percentage basis. Thus, the overall salary structure can be maintained relative to external prices.

46. Initially the hierarchy of jobs in an organisation develops organically as numbers grow. Pay scales tend to follow this organic, and possibly haphazard, growth. Subsequently, the job hierarchy may be organised on a more rational basis, using some form of job evaluation to measure and differentiate jobs. Job evaluation techniques were reviewed in Chapter 13. Even where jobs are evaluated, it is still necessary to allocate salary grades to the resulting job clusters. There are two main approaches to this task – one is to apply merit scales to jobs, the other is to apply incremental scales. These approaches are described in the following paragraphs.

MERIT SCALES

47. Merit salary scales are based on a range from £x to £x + y without any fixed points in between. So, for a middle-management post, the range could extend from a base of £30,000 to a ceiling of £50,000. An individual's progress through the scale depends principally on performance in the job, as assessed by his or her senior manager. A typical merit salary scale with guideline points for performance payment is shown in Figure 21.7.

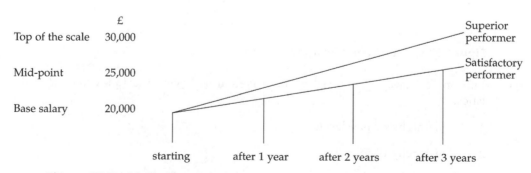

Figure 21.7 *Merit salary scale*

48. It can be seen that this scale is not strictly incremental (see below), but gives guidance to senior managers as to where they might pitch an individual's salary in the light of their performance. The implication in this example is that for satisfactory performance an employee on the base salary should gradually move towards the mid-point, but superior or outstanding performance could be rewarded by early placing near the middle of the range. Progress beyond the mid-point should always be dependent on above average performance. Where several such scales exist in a salary structure, it may help staff motivation to have a significant overlap between scales, so that a thoroughly experienced person at, or near, the top of their scale is earning more than someone who has just started on the next higher scale. Movement through a scale can be based on merit. In order to maintain competitiveness the whole scale can be raised in accordance with cost-of-living pressures or other external influences. Thus, even barely adequate staff will receive some uplift in their salaries.

INCREMENTAL SCALES

49. Incremental Salary Scales. These are salary ranges having a number of pay-points or steps, which every job-holder must alight on as he or she progresses through the range. In 1973, when incremental pay systems were the subject of considerable discussion in the light of national incomes policies, the Office of Manpower Economics carried out a survey of incremental pay systems, most of which were in the public services. The OME report[6] distinguished between 'fixed' systems and 'variable' systems. Fixed systems were those 'with predetermined movement through a scale related to age, service in the company or service in the job or grade …'. Fixed scales were further sub-divided into those with automatic progression, usually on the basis of service in the job or grade, and those with limited flexibility, where increments could be doubled or trebled in the case of good performance, and denied in the case of less than acceptable performance. The OME survey also found that hybrid arrangements combining both fixed and variable features were widely in use, suggesting that there existed 'a spectrum in which essentially fixed systems with different degrees of flexibility shade into essentially variable systems with different degrees of definition'.

50. An example of a traditional incremental scale, taken from the university sector, is shown in Figure 21.8.

This particular scale embodies several of the principles of an incremental system. Movement through the scale is more or less automatic, so that the longer the person is in the post, the more he or she earns, up to the maximum of the scale. To ensure comparability with other grades on age grounds, there is a minimum entry point for research staff over the age of 27. Each year (usually in September) the individual rises to the next point in the scale, thus ensuring a minimum salary growth over a year. In most years (usually in April) a general cost-of-living award raises all scales by a percentage amount. Sometimes the general award is worth more than any single incremental increase. Many academic scales (especially the career post scales) have an efficiency or work-level bar, beyond which an individual may not pass without some management check on either (a) efficiency in the post,

Research and Analogous Faculty Scale (GRADE 1A)

Scales From 1.4.00	Scales From 1.4.01	Scales 1.9.01	Scales 1.3.01
£	£	£	£
16,775#	17,278#	17,451#	17,626#
17,755	18,288	18,471	18,655
18,731*	19,293*	19,486*	19,681*
19,482	20,066	20,267	20,470
20,465	21,079	21,290	21,503
21,435	22,078	22,299	22,522
22,245	22,912	23,141	23,373
23,256	23,954	24,193	24,435
24,227	24,954	25,203	25,455
25,213	25,969	26,229	26,491

\# minimum point for PhD
* minimum point for age 27

Figure 21.8 *Traditional incremental scale*

or (b) level of work being undertaken. Higher scales also provide for limited extra increments for performance on a discretionary basis.

51.   The main benefits and disadvantages of merit and incremental scales may be summarised as shown in Figure 21.9.

Merit Systems

Advantages

- Focus attention on individual performance rather than on length of service

- Provide scope for rewarding extra effort or results

- Enable salaries to be adjusted more flexibly than incremental scales

Disadvantages

- Require an appraisal system

- May not always seem equitable to staff

- Employees do not know in advance how much they will receive for 'merit'

Incremental Systems

Advantages

- Simplicity of operation

- Clearly understood by staff

- No appraisal system required

- Staff can reliably forecast their salary growth

Disadvantages

- Inflexibility

- Tend to reward mediocre performance instead of high performance

---

Figure 21.9 *Advantages and disadvantages of merit and incremental salary systems*

PERFORMANCE-RELATED PAY

52. We have already described several different approaches to performance-related pay, mostly affecting manual grades, which have been used variously by UK employers for many years. Over the last fifteen years, however, there has been a significant increase in the number of employers taking up performance-related payment schemes for management grades as well as for manual grades. A survey into five generic forms of performance pay, conducted on behalf of the Chartered Institute of Personnel Management in October 1997[7], found a wide variety of applications of the five alternatives between and within the two broad categories of 'management' and 'non-management' employees. The five forms of performance pay used by the researchers were as follows:

- Individual performance-related pay – i.e. merit pay or bonuses based on the achievement of individual objectives or targets.

- Team-based pay – i.e. bonuses related to team objectives or targets.

- Skill or competency-based pay – i.e. pay increases linked to acquiring relevant skills, including the development of particular behavioural skills.

- Profit-related pay – i.e. pay increases based on overall organisational performance (mainly in the private sector).

- Employee share ownership schemes – i.e. where employees are rewarded with shares in the business (almost exclusively in the private sector).

53. More than 1150 organisations responded to the survey, covering 1.5 million employees with proportionately more larger than smaller organisations represented. The survey showed, perhaps surprisingly, that just over 500 organisations did not use any of the five forms of performance pay, which suggests that many of the traditional payment methods mentioned above are still very much in use. Of the forms that were being applied in the organisations that operated at least one of them (43 per cent of the total), the most popular form for management employees (40 per cent) was individual performance-related pay, followed closely by profit-related pay (35 per cent). The mean percentage of base salary awarded to managers for individual success was 11 per cent, although this varied substantially between individuals. In this group it was noteworthy that the results for managers in the public sector showed a clear preference for individual schemes. There is a sense here of public bodies wanting to pay their senior executives on a payment-by-results basis to show that their public is getting good value for money. Naturally, there is no prospect of such managers participating in profits, except in a very small number of cases, and no question of share ownership.

54. For non-management employees, individual schemes accounted for only 25 per cent of this group, and in fact almost 200 of the responding organisations provided no individual performance-related pay for the group. The single largest form for the non-management employees as a whole was profit-related pay (34 per cent), suggesting that company-wide 'added value' bonus schemes were being used. This form was not used in the public sector, of course, where the most significant forms were the individual schemes, followed by skill or competency-based pay.

55. The survey suggested that there was greater reservation about performance-related pay forms in the public sector compared with the private sector. Of those reported as having recently given up such forms, a disproportionate number were from the public sector. Reasons given in both sectors for discontinuing performance-related pay were mainly on the grounds of employees discontent and excessive cost. These are serious criticisms of such schemes, since two of the most accepted reasons for introducing performance-related pay are (a) to improve employee motivation, and (b) achieve cost-benefit advantages. The most popular reason is to improve individual and organisational performance by focusing on key objectives and targets. The key is more likely to rest in one of the motivational factors mentioned in Chapter 8 earlier.

EMPLOYEE BENEFITS

56. Employee remuneration is not just about pay, i.e. wages and salaries. It is also concerned with non-pay benefits, or 'benefits-in-kind'. These non-pay benefits are usually known as 'employee benefits', and sometimes as 'fringe' benefits or 'perks'. On balance, the former refer to the more important benefits, such as pensions, and include those which are widely applied in the organisation. The latter refer either to less significant benefits, such as private health insurance, or to benefits provided primarily as a privilege. In this chapter the term 'employee benefits' is used broadly to denote all non-pay items. Originally, employee benefits were only made available to 'staff', i.e. salaried employees. Manual workers were excluded. Nowadays the trend is towards harmonising conditions of employment in respect of benefits – so called 'single-status' arrangements. Hence, although certain benefits are still applied on a differential basis, they are at least made available to all employees and not just for staff.

57. Benefits are usually provided as a package of items, for example pensions, subsidised meals, discounts on company products and the like. Such benefits vary in importance to the individual. An older employee will value a pension scheme much higher than a young employee. Subsidised meals appeal more to some employees than others, who would perhaps prefer luncheon vouchers. All employees would probably welcome the opportunity of having a company car.

    Most benefits plans do not permit an employee to choose his or her preferred range of benefits on a so-called 'cafeteria' basis, i.e. where an employee may select those benefits which are the most valuable personally up to a certain cost-limit. Generally, benefits are offered on a take-it-or-leave-it basis, with the exception of pension schemes in which participation is usually compulsory.

58. The most common benefit offered by organisations is participation in an occupational pension fund supported by the employer to the extent of between 6-10 per cent of the employee's salary. This kind of benefit can fairly be described as a security benefit. Other benefits may be classified as work-related and status-related. Examples of these three categories of benefit are shown in Figure 21.10.

Security Benefits	Work-related Benefits	Status-related Benefits
Pensions (including stakeholder schemes) Life insurance Private health care schemes Bridging loans for house purchase Low-cost mortgages Crèches Profit-sharing schemes Share options Pre-retirement counselling Redundancy counselling	Subsidised meals/meal vouchers Car loans/car allowances (essential users) Cars (for essential users, e.g. sales staff Private car mileage allowance (casual users) Special training opportunities Sabbaticals Prizes (sales staff)	Prestige cars Enhanced pension and life insurance schemes Entertainments allowance Payment of telephone Children's education schemes

Figure 21.10. *Employee benefits*

Note: Most benefits are now generally available to manual workers just as much as salaried employees. As the listing shows, the greatest emphasis in employee benefits is on security.

59. Security benefits are of two kinds: long-term benefits, such as pensions and life insurance; and short-term assistance to meet immediate problems, such as moving house on appointment, when a bridging loan may be financed by the organisation.

Work-related benefits are linked closely to the day-to-day operational requirements of the organisation in relation to its members. Thus, employees need to be (i) adequately nourished during the working day, (ii) properly trained to fulfil their responsibilities, and (iii) provided with adequate means of transport when on the organisation's business.

Status-related benefits are not widely-applicable. They are a rather different type of 'benefit', and some would consider them more as rewards than anything else. Such benefits are applied only to the most senior levels of employee. They are usually considered to be a convenient way of adding to taxable pay as part of total remuneration.

THE STATE AND EMPLOYEE BENEFITS

60. We mentioned earlier that employee benefits are sometimes referred to as 'fringe' benefits. However, this latter term suggests that such benefits are not at all central to total remuneration, that indeed they are seen as 'optional extras' by employers

and employees alike. Nothing could be further from the truth at the present time. Even some 30 years ago, Moonman (1973)[8] could write:

> both (political) parties accept that government has a role to play in the provision of compensation to employees over and above salaries and wages, and that some kind of compulsion must be put on employers to make adequate arrangements apart from those which the State provides.

Today, it is very clear that, in European countries at least, governments are laying down firmer guidelines to employers in matters of employee benefits. Thus, there is an increasing amount of legislation aimed at setting minimum standards of provision for all employees, notably in respect of:

- national insurance/social security

- pensions (see Chapter 16 paras 5–9)

- paid holidays

- sickness payments

- redundancy arrangements.

61. It could be argued that the State has effectively taken over the welfare aspects of employment in order to ensure a minimum level of benefits to employees, which employers can add to if they so wish for any, or all, of their employees. At present, governments seem less interested in non-welfare aspects of employee benefits, although there is a developing interest in stakeholder pension schemes (see Chapter 16) as a means of encouraging employees to provide for their future.

62. One aspect of employee benefits that all governments are interested in is taxation, that is to say whether this or that benefit should be relatively tax-free or not. Salaries and wages can be catered for by means of the 'pay-as-you-earn' (PAYE) system of taxation, whereby the employer deducts tax from source, in accordance with each individual's tax code, and pays it over to the Treasury. Employee benefits, until recently, have been dealt with leniently by successive governments in Britain. Now there is greater interest in examining and implementing ways of taxing various benefits, such as company-provided cars for personal use. Such activity has important implication for employers who see the granting of status benefits as a key element in increasing total remuneration of selected staff, but without their incurring high levels of tax in the process.

BENEFITS POLICY

63. In deciding what benefits policy to adopt an organisation needs to consider several important questions:

1   What is the purpose of the benefits policy?

- meet basic social/legal obligations?

- encourage employee commitment?

- reward employees?

- minimising individual's tax-burden?

- enhance organisation's reputation?

2 What range of benefits should be provided?

- all types of benefit or just security and welfare benefits?

3 To which groups should benefits be applied?

- all groups of employees?

- selected grades of employee?

- selected occupational groups, such as managerial staff only?

- senior managers?

4 What is the estimated cost of the benefits' programme?

- long-term benefits?

- short-term benefits?

5 To what extent should the programme be influenced by the benefits policies of competitors?

6 What is the programme likely to achieve?

- value to individuals?

- cost-effectiveness for the organisation?

- tax implications?

- employee goodwill?

- relations between different groups within the organisation?

- earnings differentials?

- effect on competitors?

COMPARING SALARY LEVELS

64. In considering the practicalities of salary structures (and, indeed, wages too), employers need to know what rates are being paid by other employers. How can they find this out? There are several important sources of information, and these are primarily:

- official statistics (e.g. Department of Employment monthly indices of earnings/ annual New Earnings Survey)

- published reports of Review Bodies (e.g. Armed Forces, Doctors & Dentists)

- published reports/surveys by private organisations (e.g. Incomes Data Services, Regional Reward Surveys)

- informal surveys conducted by individual employers (e.g. exchanging salary information with one or more comparable organisations)

- external surveys (e.g. carried out by professional bodies on members' pay or by management consultants)

- employment agencies (quoted rates/special pay surveys)

- newspaper advertisements.

Whilst most of the above sources can be helpful, employers have to take care that they are comparing like with like. Many sources of information about pay are really too general to be of practical use, but, where like for like comparisons can be made both in terms of comparable jobs and comparable remuneration practices, then surveys and other sources can be of considerable help to organisations wishing to keep up-to-date with the market-place. Several leading pay and salary surveys may now be accessed via the internet upon payment of a fee and allocation of a password.

CONCLUSION

65. It is important for organisations to review their pay and benefits programmes on a regular basis. The continuing ability to recruit, retain and motivate staff is vital to employee resourcing. Salary levels (and wages, too) need to be comparable with competitors. Benefits, in particular, should be carefully examined as they are usually more visible than pay, and can develop into major irritants if their application is seen to be unfair by those concerned. Company cars, executive dining rooms, extra holidays and the like may be as much a source of resentment to the many as they can be of satisfaction to the few, and organisations need to be aware of the impact on non-participating groups of such obviously selective benefits. Generally speaking, it is status-related and work-related benefits which most need diplomatic handling by employers. It is no surprise that Japanese companies with their eye on harmonious employee relations, have avoided potential conflicts in this area by providing single-status schemes for their employees.

REFERENCES

1. Goldthorpe, J.H. *et al.* (1968), *The Affluent Worker: Industrial Attitudes and Behaviour*, Cambridge University Press.

2. Bowey, A. & Lupton, T. (1973), *Job & Pay Comparisons*, Gower Press.

3. Shaw, A.G. & Pirie, D.S. (1982), 'Payment by Time Systems', in Bowey, A. M. (ed.) *Handbook of Salary & Wage Systems* (2nd edn), Gower.

4. Lesieur, F.G. (1958), 'What the Plan isn't and What it is', in Lesieur, F.G. (ed.), *The Scanlon Plan*, M.I.T. Press.

5. Lupton, T. & Bowey, A.M. (1983), *Wages & Salaries* (2nd edn), Gower.

6. Office of Manpower Economics (1973), *Incremental Pay Systems*, HMSO.

7. IPD Survey report (September, 1999), *Performance Pay Trends in the U.K.*

8. Moonman, J. (1973), *The Effectiveness of Fringe Benefits in Industry*, Gower.

CHAPTER 22

Health and safety at work

INTRODUCTION

1. This chapter looks briefly at the current state of public law and private attitudes in relation to matters of health and safety of employees in Britain. In the year 1995/96 in Britain there were more than one million employees who suffered an accident causing more than three days absence from work. This represents an enormous waste of human resources as well as human suffering. The cost of accidents and work-related illness to British employers has been estimated at £2.5 billions at 1995/96 prices (HSE report).[1]

HISTORICAL BACKGROUND

2. Historically, the health, safety and welfare of employees are issues that have been the subject of public debate in Britain since the turn of the century. The resulting work practices in health, safety and welfare today are a product of:

    - the common law

    - employer paternalism

    - public outcry

    - legislation – both UK and European Union

    - decided cases

    - major accidents or disasters

    - employer pragmatism.

3. Where employer–employee relationships are concerned – they were once called 'master-and-servant' – the Common Law of the land has set out the general duties owed to the other by the parties concerned. These general duties have not proved effective enough to provide reasonable protection for employees against the actions of their employers. Whilst a paternalistic regard for employees certainly motivated a number of Victorian employers, the overall picture in the nineteenth century was one of massive disregard for the health and safety of employees.

4. As a result of pressure from a number of well-known public figures, Parliament was forced to define employee protection more specifically by passing a variety of Acts and Regulations, enforced by an Inspectorate.

Challenged in the courts, important legal precedents were established, and these led to further legislation. Major accidents or disasters also made their impact on safety and health at work. Finally, employer pragmatism played a part too. The costs of accidents are an unwelcome addition to production costs, and employers have sought ways of avoiding this additional burden.

5. Welfare has sometimes been dealt with at the same time as health and safety by legislators, but since the time of the Beveridge Report in the 1940s, Britain at any rate has seen the separate rise of a Welfare State alongside activities specifically aimed at occupational health and safety.

HEALTH AND SAFETY AT WORK

6. The current legislation on health and safety in Britain developed largely out of the Robens Committee Report of 1972[2], although there has been a growing European Union influence which will be referred to later (para 31). The Robens Committee was set up to examine the then state of the law and to make recommendations. Briefly, the conclusions reached by the Committee were as follows:

1 Despite the existence of a wide range of legal controls, accidents were still a major problem in British industry.

2 The law on health and safety was often obscure, haphazard and out-of-date.

3 There were too many enforcement agencies involved, which caused confusion.

4 The main reason for the continuing of this unsatisfactory state of affairs was apathy.

7. The chief proposals submitted by the Committee to remedy the situation were threefold:

1 A system should be devised to enable all employers and employees to become aware of their personal responsibility for health and safety.

2 There was a need to set up a unified framework of legislation to cover all work activity, i.e. not just factories, but offices, mines, farms, etc.

3 A unified enforcement agency should be set up, and should be given stronger powers of sanction.

The outcome of these proposals was the passing of a new and important piece of legislation – the Health & Safety at Work, etc., Act, 1974, whose main provisions will be looked at shortly.

8. It is useful for the purposes of getting the new Act into perspective to consider the principal statutes which preceded it. These were as follows:

• the Mines and Quarries Act, 1954

• the Agricultural (Safety, Health and Welfare) Act, 1956

• the Factories Act, 1961

- the Office, Shops and Railway Premises Act, 1963

- the Nuclear Installations Act, 1965.

The above were enforced by a variety of enforcement agencies, such as the Factory Inspectorate, Mines Inspectorate and others. The Acts embraced such topics as cleanliness, sanitary arrangements, lighting and heating, first aid, guarding ('fencing') of dangerous machinery, inspection of lifting gear and a host of other items concerned with health, safety and welfare in the occupational groups involved.

9.   Regulations made under these principal Acts covered specific hazards or machines (e.g. Woodworking Machinery Regulations, Electricity Regulations, etc.). Such Regulations have the effect of superseding or qualifying the requirements of the parent statute. So, for example, the Woodworking Regulations make it possible for dangerous parts of machinery to be exposed, albeit it to a minimum degree, thus qualifying the absolute requirement to securely fence every dangerous part of any machine laid down by Section 14 of the Factories Act, 1961. The making of Regulations in this way enables legislation to be kept up to date as new processes are introduced or new hazards discovered. This concept is taken up wholeheartedly by the Health and Safety at Work, etc., Act, 1974, which makes use of Regulations as a mechanism for replacing earlier legislation in a staged process, which maintains strong transitional arrangements whilst the law is being transformed.

THE HEALTH AND SAFETY AT WORK, ETC., ACT, 1974

10.   As a result of the Robens' Committee recommendations, this Act introduced a number of innovations into legislation on health and safety matters. These were briefly as follows:

- the Act applies to all employed persons wherever they work (factories, farms, mines, etc.)

- the obligations to provide safe conditions or to work in a safe manner apply to employees and self-employed as much as to employers (safety thus is seen as everyone's business)

- regulations are to be introduced to supersede existing requirements under the various statutes still in force

- a unified enforcement agency has been established to embrace the previous fragmented arrangements (Health & Safety Commission, Health & Safety Executive etc.)

- increased powers have been granted to the inspectors concerned

- provisions are made to encourage greater employee participation in health and safety matters at the workplace (safety committees, etc.).

11.   The principal duty laid on employers by the Act is worded as follows:

> It shall be the duty of every employer to ensure, so far as is reasonably practicable, the health, safety and welfare at work of all his employees.

Clearly, what is 'reasonably practicable' in any one situation is open to interpretation in the light of the facts or evidence submitted. Nevertheless, this is a very broad duty and it does mean that employers have to convince the courts that they have acted reasonably.

12. Employers are not left entirely without guidance at this stage, however, for the Act also lays down a number of somewhat more specific duties, which are:

   * to provide and maintain plant and systems of work that are, so far as is reasonably practicable, safe and without risks to health,

   * to ensure safety in use, handling, storage and transport of articles and substances

   * to provide sufficient information, instruction, training and supervision to ensure, so far as is reasonably practicable the health and safety of all employees

   * to maintain a safe place of work, and safe means of access and exit

   * to provide a safe, healthy working environment, including adequate arrangements for welfare.

13. The remaining general duties imposed on employers by the Act are concerned with safety policies and duties in relation to persons not in their employment (e.g. members of the public). There are also Regulations concerning the employer's conduct in respect of employee safety representatives and safety committees.

SAFETY POLICIES

14. Except in very small firms of fewer than five employees, every employer is required to prepare, and keep up-to-date, a written statement of safety policy. This statement should reflect the employer's commitment to safety and health at work, and should indicate what standards of behaviour are to be aimed for in health, safety and welfare matters. The Act requires that the policy statement should be drawn to the attention of all employees. In practice, this is achieved by issuing a safety policy document to all employees via their pay-packets, or by issuing company handbooks which include details of the policy. The important point is that the employer should be able to show that he has done more than just pin up a notice in various parts of his premises.

15. A safety policy statement is likely to be set out under a number of different headings. For example:

General statement

The Company's overall intention is to achieve the highest possible standards of awareness of, and attention to, matters of safety, health and welfare at all levels

The Company will endeavour at all times to achieve standards that will exceed the minimum legal requirements

The Company will accept the spirit of the Health & Safety at Work, etc., Act, 1974, as well as the letter of the law.

Safety organisation

The Company will establish and maintain a structure of responsibility for safety and health matters throughout the Company's premises.

The Company will appoint a Safety Officer to act as co-ordinator of safety and health activities.

The Company will provide all necessary information, training and supervision in safety and health matters.

The Company will encourage the work of employee safety representatives, and will establish appropriate Safety Committees following consultation with employees.

Individual responsibility

The Company will impress on every employee the need to be aware of his or her individual responsibility for taking due care at work, and of co-operating with Company representatives in the implementation of this policy.

Review procedure

This policy will be reviewed at least annually by the senior management of the Company, and any changes will be notified to all employees.

16. To be effective in terms of (a) preventing accidents/ill-health, and (b) obviating sanctions by the Inspectorate, such a policy needs to be spelt out clearly to those involved. This will mean publicising safety procedures, both of a general and of a specific kind. Certain safety hazards such as those concerned with lifting and carrying, connecting up electrical apparatus and blocking passageways, for example, can be dealt with by means of general notices and instruction to all types and levels of employee. Specific hazards associated with particular occupations or particular parts of the premises only may be dealt with by issuing specific instructions to the employees concerned. Thus, warnings about the use of grinding wheels need only be displayed in shop-floor areas, and not in a building dedicated solely to office functions.

SAFETY REPRESENTATIVES

17. As part of the general intention to increase the involvement of ordinary employees in safety and health matters, the 1974 Act provides for regulations to be made concerning the appointment of safety representatives from amongst the employees in cases where an independent trade union is recognised by the management. Such regulations have been made – the Safety Representatives & Safety Committees Regulations, 1977[3] and their requirements in respect of safety representatives can be summarised as follows:

   • Independent trade unions recognised by the employer for the purposes of collective bargaining may appoint safety representatives.

- The employer is obliged to consult with safety representatives on matters of health and safety, and must also provide them with time off to perform their duties and attend training, as well as generally facilitating their work as safety representatives.

- The trade union(s) concerned must notify the employer of the names of representatives, who should normally have been employed in the organisation for at least two years.

- The functions of safety representatives are primarily as follows:

    1   to investigate potential hazards and dangerous occurrences, and to examine the causes of accidents at the workplace

    2   to investigate employee complaints

    3   to make representations to the employer about matters of health, safety and welfare affecting the employees

    4   to carry out inspections in the workplace, subject to certain provisos

    5   to represent the employees in workplace consultations with the health and safety inspectorate

    6   to receive information from inspectors

    7   to attend meetings of the organisation's safety committee.

NB. None of the above functions places any legal liability on safety representatives other than their traditional duty of care towards others.

18.   The original provisions for safety representatives were made during a period of deference to trade union influence in the nation at large. As a result, only representatives of independent trade unions, recognised by the employer, have been granted legal backing for their health and safety roles. More recent regulations – The Health and Safety (Consultation with Employees) Relations, 1996 – require employers to consult directly or via representative employees not covered by a trade union.

SAFETY COMMITTEES

19.   The Regulations relating to safety representatives also include obligations regarding the establishment and operation of safety committees at the workplace. Essentially, the current requirement is that if requested by at least two safety representatives, the employer shall establish a safety committee after consultation with trade union representatives, and post a notice stating the composition of the committee and indicating what areas of the organisation it will embrace.

20.   The overall objective of a safety committee is the promotion of co-operation between employers and employees in instigating, developing and carrying out measures to ensure the health and safety at work of the employees. The safety committee should be separate from other joint committees, which may exist in the organisation.

21.   The functions of a safety committee include:

1   studying trends in accidents, etc., with a view to making suggestions for corrective action

2   examining safety reports and making proposals for avoiding accidents, etc.

3   examining and discussing reports from safety representatives

4   making proposals for new or revised safety procedures

5   acting as a link between the organisation and the enforcement agency (the Health & Safety Inspectorate)

6   monitoring and evaluating the organisation's safety policy, and making proposals for changes, if necessary.

22.   Membership of a safety committee is intended to be jointly agreed between the management and the employee representatives on a consultative basis. The committee should be as reasonably compact as possible in the light of sufficient and fair representation from both sides. The management side should include line and specialist managers, whilst the employees' side should include some safety representatives. Meetings should be regular enough to cope with the demands of the environment concerned. The Regulations do not lay down any firm rules. It is also suggested that the meetings are given a formal framework in the sense of having an agenda, minutes and notes of actions taken or proposed.

23.   Failure by an employer to abide by the Regulations constitutes a criminal offence. This, therefore, is a suitable moment to consider how the present legislation on health and safety at work is enforced.

SUPERVISION AND ENFORCEMENT

24.   The 1974 Act created two major bodies to administer and supervise the legislation on health, safety and welfare at work:

- the Health & Safety Commission
- the Health & Safety Executive.

As Figure 22.1 indicates, the senior body is the Health & Safety Commission, which essentially is charged with establishing the overall framework for revising, maintaining and enforcing legislation on health and safety at work.

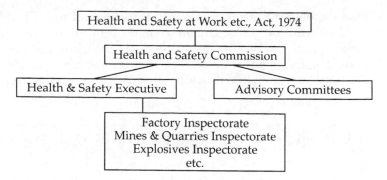

Figure 22.1 *Health & safety – the 1974 structure*

The various bodies mentioned in the diagram are described below, commencing with the Health & Safety Commission.

HEALTH AND SAFETY COMMISSION

25. Membership of the Commission is as follows – Chairman and between six and nine members, drawn in equal proportions from employers, trade unions and third parties (e.g. local authorities).

There are a number of general duties laid on the Commission, and these are as follows:

1 securing the health, safety and welfare of persons at work

2 protecting persons other than employees against risks to health and safety

3 controlling the keeping and use of explosives or highly flammable or otherwise dangerous substance

4 controlling the emission into the atmosphere of noxious or offensive substances from prescribed premises.

26. The Commission also has several specific duties, which are as follows:

1 assist and encourage the furtherance of the above general duties by persons concerned

2 make appropriate arrangements for research into health and safety matters

3 provide an information and advisory service to employers, trade unions and others

4 submit proposals for the making of Regulations

5 maintain regular links with the Minister concerned and carry out his/her directions.

27. The powers of the Commission are wide in relation to all matters of health, safety and welfare at work. These powers include the institution of investigations or enquiries into matters or incidents it believes necessary to pursue. The Commission

has established a number of advisory committees to help with specialised advice and information. These usually contain members drawn from employers, trade unions and specialist bodies, as well as including Health & Safety Executive officials. Examples of current committees include the Advisory Committee on Major Hazards and the Nuclear Safety Advisory Committee.

THE HEALTH AND SAFETY EXECUTIVE

28. Enforcement of the law on health, safety and welfare is carried out by the Health and Safety Executive (HSE), established under the 1974 Act. The HSE is headed by a Director-General and two other Directors appointed by the Health & Safety Commission with ministerial approval. The main branches of the HSE are:

1   the Factory Inspectorate

2   the Explosives Inspectorate

3   the Mines and Quarries Inspectorate

4   the Nuclear Installations Inspectorate

5   the Alkali and Clean Air Inspectorate

6   the Agriculture Health and Safety Inspectorate

7   the Employment Medical Advisory Service.

29. The principal duty of the HSE is to ensure compliance with the legislation on health and safety matters. This is usually done on the basis of persuasion first, followed, if necessary by various sanctions. The powers of Inspectors are considerable and can be summarised as follows:

- inspection at any reasonable time, on any reasonable grounds, of premises within their jurisdiction

- the gathering of evidence (samples, statements, etc.)

- examination of records, registers etc

- issuing of *enforcement notices*:

    – Improvement Notices
      (requiring a person to *remedy* some contravention within a specific period)

    – Prohibition Notices
      (requiring a person to cease an activity, either at once, or within a given period, until or unless the hazard concerned has been remedied – NB. there need not be a contravention for such a notice to be issued)

    – Crown Notices
      (issued in respect of Crown premises, such as NHS hospitals – NB. these are not legally binding, but are a means of exerting moral pressure)

- prosecution of serious or persistent offenders, either summarily through a magistrates' court, or on indictment before a Crown Court. (NB. This is usually considered only as a last resort.)

30. Whilst the above powers may suggest that the emphasis of the HSE is enforcement by sanction, in fact the approach adopted is one of seeking to *persuade* people to take personal responsibility for safety and health at their place of work. The great bulk of the Inspectors' work, therefore, lies in pointing out hazards and contraventions and advising on how they might be dealt with.

EUROPEAN UNION DIRECTIVES

31. As a result of the adoption of a number of new Directives in 1992 by the European Union (EU), the UK is required to introduce further legislation on health and safety. The Health & Safety Commission have therefore introduced several important new Regulations under the 1974 Act. Two aspects of health and safety at work are mentioned below to illustrate the impact on UK practices of EU policy. These arise from the so-called 'framework' Directive, which extends the general duties laid on employers by the 1974 Act, and from the display screen equipment Directive.

32. The framework Directive has led to additional general duties being imposed on employers. In particular these include the following extra obligations:

   1. to carry out risk assessments (e.g. of work in progress as well as of future plans)

   2. to ensure that arrangements are made to plan, organise control, monitor and review protective and preventive measures at work

   3. to appoint 'competent persons' to assist in the event of serious and imminent danger

   4. to adopt procedures that should be followed in the event of serious and imminent danger

   5. to provide appropriate training for employees both on recruitment and when risks change.

33. The display screen equipment Directive has led to VDU (visual display unit) Regulations in the UK. These Regulations cover all workers who habitually use display screen equipment as a significant part of their normal work. The main requirements include:

   1. risk assessment of individual work-stations, especially with regard to visual fatigue, musco-skeletal problems, etc.

   2. work-station design to conform to minimum ergonomic standards (i.e. designing the equipment/facilities around the person)

   3. provision of adequate rest breaks from work at the screen

4   access to eye tests at the employer's expense

5   provision of adequate information and training.

CONCLUSION

34.   In matters of health, safety and welfare at work, the majority of the ground-rules are laid down by statutory regulation in one form or another. It is important to recognise, however, that legal obligations usually aim to set minimum standards. Organisations that are genuinely concerned to protect their employees will accept the spirit and not just the letter of the requirements on health, safety and welfare. This means that much of the provision in practice goes well beyond legal requirements in such organisations. What the 1974 Act and the EU directives are aiming at is to get *all* those concerned with these matters to accept their obligations and fulfil them conscientiously.

REFERENCES

1.   The Costs to Britain of Workplace Accidents and Work-related Ill-health in 1995/96 (2001), HSE.

2.   Robens Committee (1972) *Report of the Committee on Safety and Health at Work* (*Chairman*: Lord Robens), HMSO.

3.   Health & Safety Commission (1977), *Safety Representatives and Safety Committees*, HMSO.

CHAPTER 23

Stress management and employee welfare

STRESS MANAGEMENT

1.   Increasingly, employers are paying greater attention than in the past to the effects of stress on their staff. What is stress? It can best be described as:

      the adverse psychological and physical reactions that occur in an individual as a result of their being unable to cope with the demands being made on them.

      Stress is triggered not so much by the external problems faced by individuals, as by the way they cope (or fail to cope) with those problems. Thus, most people cope with a variety of pressures in their life, some even seem to thrive on 'pressure', especially at work. However, once individuals fail to deal adequately with pressure, then symptoms of stress appear.

2.   The *short-term* symptoms of stress can be manifested as: indigestion, nausea, headaches, back-pain, loss of appetite, loss of sleep and increased irritability. In the *longer-term*, symptoms may include: coronary heart disease, stomach ulcers, depression and other serious conditions. The symptoms of stress, whether triggered by work problems or domestic/social problems, will eventually lead to reduced employee performance, lack of motivation and increased absenteeism.

3.   In a widely-reported study of stress carried out in the 1960s (Holmes and Rahe)[1], most of the life events referred to as potentially leading to stress (e.g. death of spouse, divorce, death of close relative, personal injury or illness, marriage, loss of job, retirement, change in financial state, etc.) occur in a person's *domestic and social life*, not at work. However, since individuals bring their problems with them to work, it scarcely matters in one sense whether the trigger for stress was *work-related* or not, for the effect on individuals is the same and work performance is likely to be adversely affected. Most researchers acknowledge that stress is a personal, subjective reaction to pressure. It depends on individuals' *perception* both of the scale of the problem and their ability to cope with it. Where individuals perceive that a problem is manageable, and are confident of their ability to handle the problem, then stress symptoms are unlikely to appear, whatever the pressures exerted by the problem. However, where individuals perceive the problem as difficult to manage, and are lacking in self-confidence, then stress will result.

4.   A further factor in stress at work lies in the way that individuals perceive the possible outcomes of their work activities, especially in terms of their relative success or failure. Outcomes are often seen to be uncertain. In cases where the outcome is *not* considered to be important to the individual, stress is unlikely. However, where outcomes are seen as both uncertain and important (for example, clinching a major sale, producing a vital report, or just being able to 'please the boss'), then stress is much more likely. Sporting events such as the World Cup often provide the participating teams with situations that are stressful. When a team that desperately needs to win to stay in the competition meets well-matched opponents in a crucial game, there is often evidence of tension and anxiety, e.g. defensive mistakes, uncertain passing in the mid-field, and inaccurate shots at goal by the forwards. Much of this tension may not have been evident in earlier matches against similar opponents, but where the stakes were not so high.

KEY FACTORS IN STRESS

5.   There are several key factors in the work situation that can influence the level of stress that may be experienced by individuals. These are shown in Figure 23.1, which highlights such factors as the external environment, the nature of the individual's job, the organisation's structure and culture, the quality of personal relationships in the workplace, the impact of the individual's domestic situation, as well as such personal factors as the individual's personality type and the nature of their motivation. These groups of factors represent potential sources of stress, depending largely on (a) how individuals perceive their problems, (b) their level of self-confidence, and (c) the relative uncertainty and perceived importance of the outcomes of their work activities.

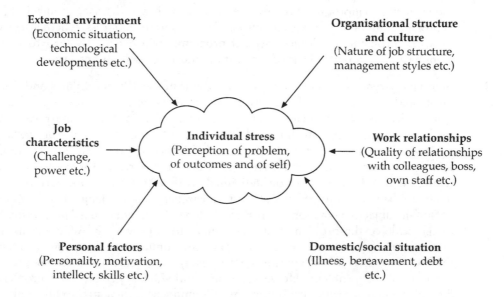

Figure 23.1   *Potential sources of stress*

6.   Some examples to illustrate these potential sources of stress are as follows.

External environment	The nature and/or pace of work is affected by frequent changes in external conditions, e.g. economic, competitive or technological; individuals who are less happy with constant change and its attendant uncertainties are likely to become stressed.
Organisation structure/ culture	The jobholder's place in the job hierarchy and the extent to which individual autonomy is encouraged or restricted are key factors in producing or avoiding stress; the dominant culture may emphasise long hours, maximum effort, etc., and may not tolerate mistakes; team leaders may not always be supportive.
Job characteristics	The way a job is put together can often cause stress, e.g. where conflicting tasks are present or where too much is asked of the individual; jobs that allow little personal discretion tend to increase the potential for stress.
Work relationships	The quality of working relationships with ones superior and colleagues can have a great influence on the relative levels of stress in a job; harassment (see below) is a frequent cause of stress at work.
Personal factors	Every individual's ability to cope adequately with pressure is greatly influenced by personal attributes, such as temperament, level of commitment to the job, particular skills and talents, etc.

HARASSMENT IN THE WORKPLACE

7.   This topic is often dealt with under the banner of equal opportunities provisions since much harassment at work is sexually or racially motivated. However, as the practical consequences of harassment are usually symptoms of stress rather than issues of employee rights, we will examine the topic here.

8.   What is harassment? Clearly, it has to do with an individual's entitlement to respect for their personal dignity at work. If workmates, colleagues or superiors bring excessive pressure to bear on an individual, which is clearly distressing to that person, then prima facie this could constitute harassment. The European Commission puts it this way in its Recommendation on the protection of the dignity of women and men at work (November 1991):

> ... Member States should take action to promote awareness that conduct or a sexual nature, or other conduct based on sex affecting the dignity of women and men at work, including conduct of superiors and colleagues, is unacceptable if:
>
> a) such conduct is unwanted, unreasonable and offensive to the recipient,
>
> b) a person's rejection of, or submission to, such conduct ... is used explicitly as a basis for decision which affects that person's access to vocational training ... employment ... promotion ... or any other employment decisions,

    c)   such conduct creates an intimidating, hostile or humiliating work environment for the recipient ...

9.   Any person who is perceived by work colleagues as being different or somehow vulnerable is liable to harassment. The greatest attention has been focussed on harassment of a sexual nature, mainly, but not exclusively, inflicted on women by men. However, harassment can be triggered by racial or religious prejudice, membership or non-membership of a trade union, and attitudes towards young persons, the disabled and other minority groups. Harassment can take such forms as: unwanted physical contact, suggestive propositions or language, public jokes, offensive posters and graffiti, isolation or non-co-operation at work, shunning an individual at work and socially (sending to Coventry), and pestering a person.

10.   The consequences for employers of not taking action against harassment are primarily two-fold: firstly, they stand to be taken to an industrial tribunal (e.g. under Sex Discrimination/Race Relations legislation) or to a civil court (e.g. for breach of contract), and the costs of such procedures are high; secondly, the work performance of their organisation is likely to suffer adversely due to workplace tension, higher staff turnover, increased absenteeism and generally lower morale. What steps should an employer take in order to minimise the possibility of harassment? The most important steps are as follows:

1   Produce and publish a clear policy statement on this issue to include examples of harassment and its likely effects, and to make clear the standards expected of employees and the penalties available for those who breach them.

2   Ensure that appropriate communication systems exist to enable employees to report harassment in confidence.

3   Ensure that appropriate disciplinary measures are in operation to deal fairly with offenders.

4   Ensure that allegations of harassment are investigated and dealt with without delay.

5   Provide appropriate counselling for recipients and offenders.

6   Through internal communications to give wide publicity to the organisation's intentions regarding the harassment of fellow employees.

INDICATORS OF STRESS IN THE ORGANISATION

11.   When an organisation's employees suffer from stress, the results are likely to take one or more of the following forms:

- high levels of sickness and absenteeism
- reduced productivity and failure to meet targets
- increased accident and error rates
- increased number of internal conflicts between individuals
- undesirably high rate of staff turnover.

Assuming that these *overt* manifestations of stress are probably the tip of an iceberg, then it is likely that the organisation is going to be faced with a range of other symptoms indicating dissatisfaction with work. The costs to the organisation could be substantial and it is in the interests of senior management to implement steps aimed at reducing the levels of stress so that the organisation as a whole can function properly.

12. The steps that managements can take to reduce the experience of stress among their work-force can be considered under two main headings – (1) stress *avoidance* measures, and (2) stress *reduction* measures. The former are aimed at removing the potential for stressful situations, while the latter are aimed at containing stress within reasonable bounds when it does occur. Both sets of measures are implemented at an organisational rather than individual level.

STRESS AVOIDANCE BY ORGANISATIONS

13. It was indicated above (Figure 23.1) that likely sources of stress for individuals include their job characteristics, work relationships, organisation structure and the organisation's culture. Given that a certain amount of pressure can have a positive effect on employee performance, what can organisations do to ensure that, while challenge is to be welcomed, the pressures on individuals do not lead to stress? It is a difficult balance for a healthy, active organisation to achieve. However, there are certain steps that can be taken to provide the necessary incentives for employees without building up chronic stress. Some examples are as follows.

Avoidance counter-measures:

1   Design jobs to permit maximum use of skill and discretion by job-holder; and incorporate sufficient task variety and challenge to maintain employee interest.

2   Design work so as to permit exercise of responsibility by job-holder, giving sufficient authority, and allowing job-holder to share in decisions that affect his or her work and ensuring work goals that do not conflict with those of others.

3   Encourage superiors to develop participative management styles, paying attention to individual needs as well as those of the task and the group.

4   Encourage team-spirit – where team-members support each other, and individuals are valued for their role.

5   Encourage communication *between* departments/sections as well as vertically through the management chain, and provide constructive feedback to individuals (by job results, staff appraisal, etc.).

6   Ensure that decision-making is delegated so that people at every level are able to share in decisions affecting their work and future prospects.

7   Develop an organisation culture in which attitudes towards employees are positive and where attention to product/service quality is reflected in respect for employees' knowledge, skills and contribution, and where mistakes are seen as learning opportunities rather than grounds for criticism.

Stress reduction measures:

1   Reduce the number of changes expected of any one individual or team.

2   Limit the procedural and other complexities associated with the execution of tasks.

3   Permit individuals to express their feelings and anxieties to someone else – boss, colleagues and trained counsellors.

4   Provide sports and social facilities.

5   Provide adequate canteen and rest-room facilities.

COUNSELLING AT WORK

14.   It is becoming increasingly common nowadays for organisations to provide professional counselling facilities for employees. According to the Institute of Personnel and Development, in a Statement on Counselling in the Workplace (1992)[2], counselling at work is 'where one individual uses a set of techniques or skills to help another individual take responsibility for and to manage their own decision-making whether it is work-related or personal'. The individual here is either a professional counsellor or a manager trained in counselling techniques. The IPD statement notes that colleagues while being sympathetic may unwittingly make quite unhelpful suggestions to the person under stress. Therefore trained helpers are required and since most managers do not possess either the talent or the training for counselling, the most they can be expected to contribute is an awareness of when counselling may be appropriate for an employee.

15.   Egan (1990)[3] describes counsellors as 'skilled helpers' who are effective '. . . to the degree that their clients [e.g. people suffering stress], through client-helper interactions, are in a better position to manage their problem situations and/or develop the unused resources and opportunities of their lives more effectively'. The implication that individuals have within themselves the potential to overcome their problems is significant, for counselling can enable people to find their personal reserves, identify external opportunities and then deploy both to work successfully through stressful situations.

16.   Essentially, counselling is a process in which the counsellor helps the client to (1) identify the problem, (2) agree what would be the idea or preferred outcome, and (3) consider ways by which the outcomes might be achieved. So, for example, if an employee seeks help because his marriage has broken down and he cannot concentrate on his work or cope with many of the usual pressures of his work, how might a trained counsellor help such a person? Firstly, it is likely that the counsellor would try to get the client to name the particular issues that are worrying him, both at work and in his domestic situation. Then the counsellor would try to draw out from the client what it is that he now wants from the counselling process, e.g. repair his marriage/accept the inevitability of divorce or separation/contribute fully to his work role once again, etc. The next stage is for the counsellor and client between them to investigate the range of possibilities that could be drawn on to

help bring about the desired outcomes. Counsellors can be very helpful at this stage by extending the range of possibilities for their clients e.g. 'have you considered so-and-so?', 'What about going to a priest, marriage guidance counsellor, solicitor, etc.?' 'How do you think your own manager might to able to help you?' In each case, however, the counsellor leaves the client to decide what he may do and in what order of priority.

17. Organisations that provide counselling services for their employees may provide an in-house service using their own trained counsellor(s), or may hire the services of an external counselling organisation. One approach relying on external assistance is the Employee Assistance Programme, in which an employer contracts a specialist counselling service to provide counselling support for its employees. This usually takes the form of a telephone counselling service which employees can ring at any time of the day or night to seek help for work problems or personal problems. There is usually a limit to the number of occasions that the service can be used by any one employee. Where appropriate the counselling can be of a face-to-face kind in an off-the-job location. Client confidentiality is guaranteed, and the only information that is fed back to the contracting employer is the rate of calls, the type of problems raised and other general information which does not identify individuals in any way.

18. Why do employers provide such a service? The answer is primarily one of enlightened self-interest, i.e. unhappy, anxious or over-stressed employees are not going to be able to achieve high performance in their jobs, they may take more time off work for sickness and may even decide to change their job, leading to increased turnover. It is therefore in an organisation's interests to avoid such uneconomic use of their human resources, and the provision of counselling services may be one way of sustaining employee performance, achieving business targets and showing commitment to employees as individuals.

WELFARE AT WORK

19. The topic of welfare is difficult to isolate from other aspects of employee relations in organisations. Welfare, in the sense of looking after the physical needs of employees, is largely covered by the health and safety legislation referred to in Chapter 22. Thus items such as toilet and washing facilities, seating and eating facilities, first aid and so on are covered by legislation. Welfare, in the sense of financial provision, is covered by pay and salary administration. Thus pensions, sickness benefits, health schemes and the like are provided for as part of the total remuneration of employees. Apart from State social security benefits, which are essentially *national* welfare provisions, what is left to be called 'welfare'? Welfare services fall into two categories:

- individual or personal services to assist with sickness, bereavement, domestic problems, some of which are now covered by the law (see Chapter 40)

- group services consisting of sports and social activities, and clubs for retired staff, generally only provided by very large employers.

20.   Individual services are generally provided as an 'extra' on top of existing services. Thus, in a situation of sickness, while the statutory sick pay scheme will usually take care of the immediate financial demands upon an employee, there may be a need for a company representative to visit the person concerned to reassure them that communication channels with the employer are still open, or that colleagues have not forgotten them.

21.   Other examples of corporate welfare include the following:

- Bereavement – organisations can help the spouses of former employees to sort out pensions and lump sum payments and can organise immediate payments from company benevolent funds.

- Older/retired employees – older employees may be given opportunities to attend pre-retirement courses or provided with additional chances of health checks; retired employees may be given the opportunity of an annual get-together paid for by the previous employer.

- Employment problems – services here may take the form of job counselling, if there is a prospect that the employee's attitude might change or skills be developed; where redundancy is concerned, or dismissal on certain other grounds (e.g. lack of qualification), then career counselling may be provided to help the employee find alternative employment.

- Domestic problems – while most personnel welfare workers do not like getting too closely involved with employees' personal lives, they may be able to give advice about caring agencies who might be able to assist a family or couple going through a difficult period.

22.   In addition to the above, which reflect concern for employees who are in difficulty, there are benefits of a purely beneficial and voluntary nature, such as the provision of routine dental care, chiropody and free hairdressing. Group welfare services usually take the form of canteen facilities, sports and social clubs, and ad hoc activities such as Christmas parties (e.g. for pensioners, children of employees, etc.).

23.   Organisations provide welfare facilities for a number of motives, such as:

- to attract new employees

- to retain the services of existing employees

- to reward employees in a voluntary way

- to satisfy their feelings of paternalism

- to maintain a 'good reputation' in the marketplace.

24.   Employers, it seems, rarely conduct any appraisal of their welfare facilities. If they were to do so, they would need to ask themselves a number of basic questions:

- What are our motives for welfare provision?

- To what extent do our employees want these benefits?

- Should any benefits be incorporated into total remuneration, i.e. as a permanent feature of employee rewards?

- How much do we estimate we are spending on welfare?
- What are the benefits to the organisation and its stakeholders?

Some of the answers will undoubtedly be found among the stress reduction and avoidance measures referred to earlier in this chapter.

REFERENCES

1. Holmes, T. and Rahe, R. (1967), 'The Social Readjustment Rating Scale', *Journal of Psychosomatic Research*, Vol. 11, 213-18.

2. Institute of Personnel and Development (1992), *Statement on Counselling in the Workplace*, IPM (now IPD).

3 Egan, G. (1990), *The Skilled Helper* (4th edn), Brooks/Cole Publishing.

QUESTIONS FOR DISCUSSION/HOMEWORK

1. How useful is it, in practice, to think of an employment contract in terms of the common law duties of the parties concerned?

2. In what ways are employment contracts changed implicity as a result of day-to-day decisions or behaviour in the workplace?

3. What would you expect to learn about conditions of employment from reading a comprehensive company handbook?

4. What issues should be covered in a guide to good practise in equal opportunities?

5. What alternatives are open to employers who wish to optimise working hours in order to accommodate (a) flexible working and (b) seasonal fluctuations in their work-load?

6. To what extent is a trade union's bargaining position affected by the state of the external labour market?

7. What links could be made between an employer's ability to pay and productivity as factors influencing levels of pay?

8. Why might an employer wish to move away from paying wages on a payment-by-results basis to paying on a time-basis?

9. As a personnel manager what factors would you take into account in comparing your wage levels with those of competitors?

10. How would you justify the use of group/company-wide incentive schemes over individual incentives?

11. What are the pros and cons of putting all manual workers on staff conditions?

12. Why do you think incremental salary systems are more popular in the public sector than in the private sector?

13. Which employee benefits are most likely to be seen as the most necessary to each of the following categories of employee:

   - 25-year-old, unmarried sales representative

   - 32-year-old woman office-worker with two young children, aged 3 and 6

   - 55-year-old middle-manager whose children are no longer living at home

14. How can an employer ensure that his or her safety policy is being carried out?

15. To what extent is safety everyone's business rather than just the employer's?

16. In what ways can firms act to limit stress in the work place?

17. What difficulties might a personnel department have to face in helping line management to implement a policy on harassment?

18. How might personnel specialists identify a potential counselling situation in the course of a routine session with an employee?

EXAMINATION QUESTIONS

EQ13 Individual incentive payment methods are less frequently used in large employing organisations nowadays. What are the reasons for the decline of such schemes and in what circumstances might their use become more widespread?

(IPM)

EQ14 To what extent can fringe benefits be systematically applied in an organisation as a partial substitute for direct monetary rewards, as a means of:

   a) attracting potential employees
   b) retaining employees
   c) motivating employees?

(ICSA)

EQ15 a) Discuss the role of safety representatives within a hotel company.
   b) Suggest a suitable training programme for newly elected representatives.

(HCIMA)

CASE STUDY 4: AVICO-MEDICARE

BACKGROUND

Your company, which is a world leader in avionics, has decided to diversify into the medical application of engineering and electronics. As a start, it has recently acquired a small British firm manufacturing specialist equipment for intensive-care units in hospitals, clinics and even ambulances. The current products of the new subsidiary, named Avico-Medicare, depend heavily upon the latest electronic technology, and its associated requirements for high levels of quality, accuracy and reliability in all components as well as in final products. At present there is little competition in the marketplace, although both American and Japanese manufacturers in this field are known to be developing competing products. The forecast demand for Avico-Medicare products is one of sharp growth over the next five years.

One of the terms of the takeover was that the original founder and Managing director of the specialist company would be kept in charge, together with his Director of Research and Development, and the Production Director. These directors would report to the Main Board General Manager of the parent company. Financial, marketing and personnel responsibilities would be met by senior staff from the parent company's head-quarters.

The majority of the present workforce (totalling 30 full-time employees, mostly men, and 20 part-timers, all women) have been with the firm for several years. Most of the work-force lack formal qualifications, having been trained internally. There are also one or two graduates and a small number of qualified technicians.

The present site of Avico-Medicare, which is located in a Midlands development area, is to be tripled in size. Work has already begun on the first stage of a new production area, and plans are well ahead for a new development laboratory. There is a New Town within five miles of the site, but the available employment categories are mostly unskilled or semi-skilled manual workers. The parent company is keen to see an early growth in the existing workforce, but insists that only properly-qualified or fully-trained staff are employed in the key production areas.

QUESTIONS

You are the recently appointed Personnel Manager of the new company. You have been working at the parent company for several years and know their personnel systems well. However, you have been asked to adopt an open mind about the development of personnel practices in the new situation, and need not follow the parent company's procedures. You have a number of immediate questions to think about, and these are as follows:

1. What system of payment would be the most appropriate for the shop-floor employees?

2. Should all employees be paid on a monthly rather than weekly basis?

3. What benefits should the company stress in its recruitment advertising for (i) production employees, and (ii) research and development staff?

4. What steps need to be taken to reassure existing staff about their status, job prospects and possible re-training?

5. How should managers be rewarded for achieving set targets?

Make some initial proposals for responding to these questions and state your reasons in each case.

PART V

EMPLOYEE TRAINING AND DEVELOPMENT

This part considers key issues in the training and development of employees. Broadly speaking, training needs arise from four sources:

1   the requirements of newcomers

2   shortfalls in employee performance

3   organisational change

4   the individual's expressed needs.

To meet these needs effectively requires a systematic approach, commencing with performance appraisal, which is the subject of Chapter 24. The next two Chapter (25, and 26) examine some important issues of learning theory, and highlight some of the main differences in how people are taught and in the way they learn as individuals. Chapters 27–31 look at the principal features of systematic training, from the identification of training (i.e. learning) needs through the design and implementation of training activities and competency-based training to their evaluation. Finally, Chapter 32 outlines the main features of management development systems, and discusses some of the important issues raised by them.

CHAPTER 24

Employee performance appraisal

INTRODUCTION

1. Only a minority of activities in personnel management are concerned with evaluating employees as individuals. These activities are primarily selection and appraisal, but also include grievance and disciplinary matters. In all other cases, the focus of attention is not on individuals but on jobs, structures, procedures or people in groups. Thus, for example, job evaluation focuses on jobs, not on job-holders; job design and organisation development focus on job/task structures; wage and salary administration focus on procedures; whilst human resource planning and collective bargaining focus on people in groups.

2. This chapter considers the evaluation of individuals in terms of their job performance. This is a task requiring a quality of managerial judgement which places a considerable responsibility on the managers involved. It is a task that is delicate as well as complex. The key features of performance appraisal are outlined and a suggested code of good practice in this area is included.

PERFORMANCE APPRAISAL

3. Employee performance appraisal is carried out within a practical context, which is essentially the day-to-day business of the enterprise. What is being assessed in the first instance is the employee's performance in carrying out the general duties of his or her role, together with any specific targets that have been set. Secondarily, appraisal may be used to assess a person's suitability for promotion, either generally or with a specific job in mind. In the appraisal situation, individuals are entitled to ask what aspects of their job are being assessed and against what criteria. An individual will also want to know how the process of appraisal will be carried out, and what opportunities they themselves will have to contribute to it. In most cases the appraisal is conducted by the employee's immediate manager, but for some management posts the appraisal may involve the manager's own staff and colleagues, where so-called 360° appraisal is employed. A basic model of appraisal is as shown in Figure 24.1, which sets out the cyclical nature of the process around the employee's expected work outputs and the criteria, or standards, against which the assessment will be made.

4. In practice there is a good measure of rational thought and emotional intelligence involved in setting the system into motion. The key targets to be achieved need to

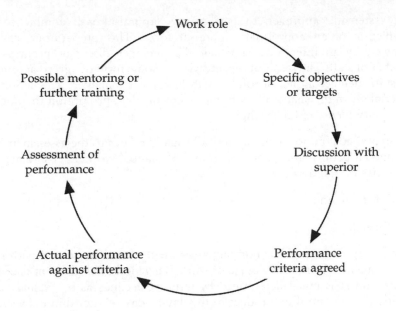

Fig. 24.1 *The context of performance appraisal*

be discussed between employee and manager, so that the former is genuinely able to commit to the challenge. The criteria to be used are frequently a source of discontent, sometimes for both parties. The criteria need to be achievable as well as measurable, and contingency considerations taken into account in case of totally unexpected events affecting the employee's performance. The criteria employed should be such as to encourage the employee to rise to the challenge, and be neither irrelevant nor over-enthusiastic, both of which can be demotivating. The criteria are almost certain to contain some element of timing, and here again the need for results has to be balanced against what is reasonably possible in a given time-frame.

5.   At its simplest, the appraisal process – in terms of assessing individual performance against targets – can be depicted as shown in Figure 24.2.

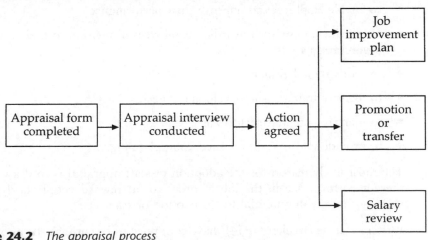

Figure 24.2 *The appraisal process*

Any systematic approach to performance appraisal will commence with the completion of an appropriate appraisal form. This preparatory stage will be followed by an interview, in which the manager discusses progress with the member of staff. The result of the interview is some form of agreed action, either by the staff member alone, or jointly with his or her manager. The action generally materialises in the shape of a job improvement plan, promotion to another job or to a salary increase, for example.

6. The expression 'performance appraisal' usually relates to the assessment of staff or managerial performance, and not to that of manual workers. There are two main categories of appraisal:

1   informal, and

2   formal.

Informal appraisal is the continuing assessment of an individual's performance by his manager in the normal course of work. This kind of assessment is of an ad hoc nature and is as much determined by intuitive feelings as by factual evidence of results. It is a natural by-product of the day-to-day relationship between manager and subordinate. Formal appraisal is altogether more rational and orderly than informal appraisal. In this chapter, when we refer to performance appraisal we mean formal appraisal, that is an assessment of employee performance in some systematic and planned way.

REASONS FOR APPRAISAL

7. There are several reasons why appraisals are carried out in organisations. These may be summarised as follows:

• to identify an individual's current level of job performance

• to identify employee strengths and weaknesses

• to enable employees to improve their performance

• to provide a basis for rewarding employees in relation to their contribution to organisation goals

• to motivate individuals

• to identify training and development needs

• to identify potential performance

• to provide information for succession planning.

The most likely reason for the adoption of staff appraisal is to draw attention to present performance in the job in order to (a) reward people fairly, and (b) to identify those with potential for promotion or transfer.

8. Writers such as Drucker (1954)[1] have continued to be enthusiastic about appraisal:

> To appraise a subordinate and his performance is part of the manager's job. Indeed, unless he does the appraising himself he cannot adequately discharge his responsibility for assisting and teaching his subordinates.

Drucker's view as a whole is that managers are responsible for achieving results. These results are obtained from the management of human, material and financial resources, all of which should be monitored. Monitoring means setting standards, measuring performance and taking appropriate action. In respect of people this entails taking action to improve performance by means of training and help, i.e. 'management development' (see Chapter 32).

9.   Other writers such as McGregor (1960)[2] are critical of formal appraisals:

> Appraisal programs are designed not only to provide more systematic control of the behaviour of subordinates, but also to control the behaviour of superiors ...

He thus sees them as promoting the cause of Theory X, i.e. a management style that assumes that people are unreliable, unable to take responsibility and therefore require close supervision and control.

10.   Whenever the argument is more about practicalities than managerial philosophy, the main issue is not whether performance appraisal, in itself, is justified but whether it is fair and accurate. McBeath & Rands (1976)[3], in discussing salary administration, comment:

> ... equitable salary relationships depend on sound job classification, periodic salary surveys of competitive levels, employee appraisal and effective salary planning.

For them, appraisal is part and parcel of an important personnel activity salary planning and administration. They are keen to acknowledge, however, that

> It is clearly essential to make some attempt at accurate measurement of performance if the appraisal is to be taken seriously into account as a factor which will influence salaries.

11.   If we accept that staff performance appraisal is a legitimate activity in organisations, what are the difficulties concerning both accuracy and fairness? Briefly, they boil down to:

● the construction of the appraisal documents

● the style in which the appraisal is approached

● the culture of the organisation.

Taking the last point first, the 'culture', or value-system, of the organisation will act as the major determinant of both the appraisal scheme adopted and the way it is introduced. For example, if the culture is one which favours control and measurement of people, then it is likely that a system will be imposed on the participants, but that it will at least contain some measurable criteria against which to judge performance. In another situation, where openness and participation are encouraged, any system will be discussed first with those involved, with the result that appraisals are more likely to be joint problem-solving affairs rather than a 'calling to account' by a superior.

APPRAISAL FORMS

12. There are various ways in which appraisal forms can be devised. The key elements, however, are the following:

    1 the focus of the appraisal, i.e. the job or the person

    2 the performance criteria selected

    3 the performance ratings used.

    Where the appraisal focuses on the job, the appraisal form is more likely to ask the appraiser to look for success in achieving job targets or objectives than to comment on the job-holder's personal attributes. Where the focus is on the person rather than on the job, the reverse is true, i.e. the appraiser is expected to give an account of the jobholder's qualities and attitudes rather than of his or her relative success in achieving results. Thus, the focus of the appraisal will determine the nature of the criteria against which individual performance will be judged, as well as of the ratings or measures to be used.

13. Forms which seek information about the person rather than about his performance in the job are typified by an emphasis on:

    1 generalised criteria

    2 generalised ratings of performance

    3 individual qualities rather than results

    4 box-ticking as method of describing performance.

    Figure 24.3 provides an illustration of such a form, employed originally by a medium-sized manufacturing company.

14. The first difficulty with this approach is that of measurement. How can a manager fairly assess qualities of leadership or judgement, for example? The second difficulty is that of relevance. How central to success are diligence and cost consciousness, for example? Hard work is not synonymous with effective work; awareness of costs may be disadvantageous if it discourages initiative or decision-making. The third difficulty is that the managers completing the form have to rely on subjective impressions instead of concrete evidence. Fortunately, the senior management of the company concerned found it too difficult to operate such a generalised instrument and eventually substituted a results-oriented system.

15. The approach just described does not provide a sound basis on which to take decisions about pay and promotion, for example. It clearly deserves the comment made by McGregor (1960)[2] that:

    > If we then take these somewhat questionable data and attempt to use them to make fine discriminations between people for purposes of salary administration and promotion, we can create a pretty picture, but one which has little relation to reality.

    The way forward to reality for many organisations is to take the job duties and responsibilities as the focal point of appraisal. In this approach the emphasis is

Personal Attributes	
Leadership	1 Always at the centre of activity 2 Capable of leading smallish groups 3 Has no real leadership qualities
Initiative	1 Always acts on own initiative 2 Will act on own initiative in minor ways 3 Never acts unless instructed
Judgement	1 Assesses a situation with cool discernment 2 Sometimes confused by strong counter-arguments, but generally makes sound assessment 3 Totally lacks any critical faculty
Decision-making Ability	1 Makes sound decisions at all times 2 Cannot always foresee the outcome of his/her decisions 3 Decisions are more like guesses
Customer Awareness	1 Aware of need for quality, timeliness and price 2 Only partially aware of the importance of the customer during the working day 3 Customers' needs are seen as secondary to his/her own
Self-discipline	1 Has well-balanced attitude towards work and leisure 2 Concentrates on work he/she prefers 3 Needs constant instruction and supervision

Technical Attributes	
Technical Knowledge	1 Wide technical knowledge of Company's products with specialist knowledge of some 2 Limited technical knowledge but useful practical ability 3 Very little required knowledge
Quality of Work	1 Always careful, rarely makes mistakes 2 Sometimes makes mistakes 3 Work characterised by carelessness
Diligence	1 Consistently hard worker 2 Occasionally needs reminding about time-wasting 3 Makes no great effort when working
Cost Consciousness	1 Fully appreciates importance of cost control 2 Gives some thought to costs 3 Tends to be wasteful, rarely considers costs

Figure 24.3 *Appraisal form emphasising individual qualities*

placed on results achieved against standards set, after taking circumstances into account.

16. In any situation what is 'real' depends partly on the perceptions of those concerned, i.e. how they 'see' things, and partly on objective evidence, i.e. information that can be verified by a third party. To build such elements into an appraisal form requires a document such as the one illustrated in Figure 24.4 below. Results-oriented approaches include the growing practice of assessing employees against a 'contract' for a year/six month period in which certain specific targets are agreed between employee and manager.

Company: Office Equipment Sales				
Position: Managing Director				
Key Result Areas	Targets Set for the Period*	Achieved	Evidence	Notes
Profitability	Increase profit:sales ratio by 5%	yes	Annual Accounts	
Market Share	Maintain present market share at 15%	no (13%)	Industry statistics	Price-cutting by all competitors
Sales	Achieve gross sales of £150m	no (£148m)	Annual Accounts	
Delivery	Reduce average delivery time to four weeks	yes	Customer Accounts	
Staff Performance	Ensure staff costs do not exceed 55% of total expenditure *Financial year	yes	Annual Budget Summary	

Figure 24.4 *Results-oriented appraisal form*

17. In an appraisal form set out as above, it is possible to identify the relevant aspects of the job and to set measurable targets against which to assess the individual jobholder's performance in a fair and accurate manner. Humble (1967)[4] saw a performance standard as 'a statement of the conditions which exist when the required result is being satisfactorily achieved'. He suggested then that in setting standards it may help to look for standards which relate to:

- Quantity (how much?)
- Quality (how well?)
- Time (by what time?)
- Cost (at what cost?)

The current approach is to make criteria SMART, as follows:

- Specific

- Measurable

- Achievable

- Relevant

- Timed

Simple acronyms, such as the above, help managers and their staff to remember the basic essentials of performance appraisal.

18. The example in Figure 24.4 illustrates the kind of approach suggested by Humble and other advocates of Management by Objectives. In the example, all the potential criteria of performance are measurable in quantitative terms. Qualitative standards can also be utilised, indeed theorist-managers such as Wilfred Brown (1960)[5] insisted that they are inescapable – 'I cannot wholly assess the work of a general manager ... on figures of output ... etc. ... I must come to difficult intuitive judgements on the relationship of actual to optimum performance.' When such judgements have to be made, they should be based on criteria which, though general, are sufficiently assessable to enable a reasonable manager to measure the extent to which due standards of performance have been met.

19. An example of a general criterion of managerial behaviour could be:

To achieve a major shift in employee attitudes regarding labour flexibility.

Reddin (1970)[6] disliked this latter example: 'If no measurement method is available ... some expression such as "subjective judgement" is added. Try and avoid this.' Brown's (1960)[5] rebuff to this advice is to comment '... the results obtained in any manager's command are a function not only of his own decisions but also of those of his superior manager, and of the policy operated by the Company ...' Thus, to return to the example above, to achieve a major shift in employee attitudes requires the joint efforts of various managers. It also requires meshing together such factors as pay structures, job design, redundancy arrangements and shop-floor supervision in order to achieve any real prospects of change.

RATING SCALES IN PERFORMANCE APPRAISAL

20. We have just seen that appraisal criteria are generally either person-oriented or results oriented. Within each of these orientations appraisers still have to 'measure' individual performance. They do so by using one or more scales for rating performance. The principal options available are:

- *Linear or Graphic Rating Scales*, in which the appraiser is faced with a list of characteristics or job duties and is required to tick or circle an appropriate point on a numerical, alphabetical or other simple scale. Examples are:

Initiative	A	B	C	D	E

(Excellent)   (Non-existent)

Initiative	1	2	3	4	5

(Low)   (High)

Initiative   Excellent .... Good .... Average .... Poor

- *Behavioural Scales*, in which the appraiser has a list of key job items against which are ranged a number of descriptors, or just two extreme statements of anticipated behaviour. One example is shown in Figure 24.2 above. Another scale, dealing with customer relations, could demonstrate a range of possible behaviour from the *best*, e.g. 'Deals politely and efficiently with customers at all time', to the *worst*, e.g. 'Is barely civil to customers, is inefficient'.

- *Results/Targets Set*, as in Figure 24.3 above.

- *Free Written Reports*, in which appraisers write essay-type answers to a number of questions set on the appraisal document.

21. The most common scales currently in use are linear scales, although both results-oriented measures and written reports also have their advocates among several companies. One other approach, which has not been mentioned so far, is that of self-appraisal, where the employees concerned either write an 'annual report' on their work or answers questions set out in an appraisal document. In a survey carried out by the IPM[7] in 1977, over a quarter of firms questioned mentioned that they were making use of self-appraisal forms as part of their appraisal procedures.

22. We noted in paragraph 10 above that one of the difficulties in achieving accuracy and fairness in appraisals concerns the style in which the appraisal is approached. Having considered the effects of (a) the organisation culture, and (b) the appraisal documentation, we can now turn to the appraisal interview conducted by the jobholder's manager.

APPRAISAL INTERVIEWS

23. The appraisal interview is the formal face-to-face meeting between the jobholder and his or her manager at which the information on the appraisal form is discussed, after which certain key decisions are made concerning salary, promotion and training, for example. Judging from research studies into appraisal, the majority of managers do not like conducting annual appraisals of their staff. McGregor (1957)[8] in an article on appraisal interviews commented that 'Managers are uncomfortable when they are put in the position of playing God'.

24. Rowe (1964)[9] in a major British study of six firms found that:

    1 appraisers were reluctant to conduct appraisals, finding ways of evading full completion of the appraisal forms

2   appraisers were extremely reluctant to carry out face-to-face interviews

3   there was inadequate follow-up to the appraisals, in terms of their effect on transfers, etc.

25.   The manner in which a manager approaches an appraisal interview will be strongly influenced by his or her understanding of the purpose of the interview. Appraisal interviews can serve several purposes:

1   to evaluate the subordinate's recent performance

2   to formulate job improvement plans

3   to identify problems and/or examine possible opportunities related to the job

4   to improve communication between superior and subordinate

5   to provide feedback on job performance to the employee

6   to provide a rationale for salary reviews

7   to identify potential performance/possibilities for promotion or transfer

8   to identify training and development needs.

Clearly some of the above purposes involve managers and their subordinate in a joint discussion of common issues, with only a hint of remedial work for the appraisee. A few involve a 'top-down' emphasis in which the manager as representative of the senior hierarchy passes judgement on those lower down the pyramid. Others fall somewhere between these two extremes.

APPRAISAL STYLES

26.   Maier (1958)[10] identified three basic approaches to the appraisal interview. These were as follows:

1   TELL & SELL approach, in which the manager tells his/her subordinate how he/she is doing, and endeavours to persuade him/her to accept what has been decided for him/her in terms of improvement.

2   TELL & LISTEN approach, where the manager tells his/her subordinate how he/she is doing, but then sits back and listens to the individual's point of view both about the appraisal and about any follow-up action required.

3   PROBLEM-SOLVING approach, in which the manager effectively puts aside the role of judge in order to join the subordinate in mutual reflection on progress and mutual discussion about required action.

Maier has in effect described a continuum of interviewer behaviour ranging from a relatively autocratic style to one that is fully participative. The continuum may be described graphically as in Figure 24.5.

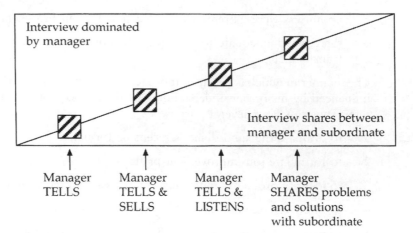

Figure 24.5 *A continuum of appraisal interview styles (after Maier)*

27. The likely success of the varying styles, judging from research into appraisals, can be summarised as follows:

    1 TELL approach – could be counter-productive. Meyer *et al.* (1965)[11] found in General Electric that praise had little effect one way or the other on appraisees. Criticism, however, had a negative effect on subsequent achievement. At least this approach does give the employee some idea of his/her progress.

    2 TELL & SELL approach – unless the manager is very persuasive, it is unlikely that the employee will accept his version of what is required to be done.

    3 TELL & LISTEN approach – this approach has the merit of informing the employee of his/her progress, but then goes further by actively involving him/her in the process of deciding what ought to be done, which is much more likely to produce a positive response.

    4 SHARING approach – this is generally considered to provide the best basis for an appraisal owing to its joint problem-solving approach, in which managers and their subordinates work together more or less as equals. This approach is closer to coaching than anything else (see Chapter 32 below).

The importance of Maier's appraisal model lies in its use as a device for enabling managers to identify their preferred approach and consider how they could improve upon it.

CONCLUSION

28. Employee performance appraisal is an important means by which organisations improve their chances of attaining their key operational goals. Employees who know what, and how much, is expected of them are likely to be more effective than those who are unclear about their role. The process of appraisal itself is an important way for managers and their team-members to work together on the

issues that really matter. If the process encourages a joint problem-solving approach, in which other team-members may be involved, it can contribute to individuals' maturing in experience and obtaining greater job satisfaction. As noted in Chapter 21, in the discussion of performance-related pay, goal-setting as a means of controlling employees' pay may not always be effective. However, as a way of focusing employees' attention on the key priorities of their work, it can make a positive contribution to the way they feel about their work, and the prospects of achieving success in it.

REFERENCES

1. Drucker, P.F. (1954), *The Practice of Management*, Heinemann.

2. McGregor, D. (1960), *The Human Side of Enterprise*, McGraw-Hill.

3. McBeath, G. & Rands, D.N. (1976), *Salary Administration*, Business Books.

4. Humble, J.W. (1967), *Improving Business Results*, McGraw-Hill.

5. Brown, W. (1960), *Exploration in Management*, Heinemann.

6. Reddin, W. (1970), *Managerial Effectiveness*, McGraw-Hill.

7. Gill, D. (1977), 'Towards More Open Performance Appraisal', *Personnel Management*, December.

8. McGregor, D. (1957), 'An Uneasy Look at Performance Appraisal', *Harvard Business Review*, May–June.

9. Rowe, K.H. (1964), 'An Appraisal of Appraisals', *Journal of Management Studies*, March 1964, Vol I, No. I.

10. Maier, N.R.F. (1958), *The Appraisal Interview*, Wiley.

11. Meyer, H. *et al.* (1965), 'Split Roles in Performance Appraisal', *Harvard Business Review*, January-February.

CHAPTER 25

Theories of learning

INTRODUCTION

1. The study of how people learn has fascinated mankind from the ancient Greeks to the present. Influential names such as Plato, Aristotle, Rousseau, Thorndike and Skinner have all left their mark on the way learning is managed in modern organisations. This chapter provides a brief summary of the most influential theories of learning that have affected the way we approach training and development in the workplace today.

LEARNING

2. It is not easy to find a definition of learning that satisfies everyone. For the purposes of this book, however, we shall assume that learning is 'a complex process of acquiring knowledge, understanding, skills and values in order to be able to adapt to the environment in which we live'. Such adaptation generally, but by no means always, involves some recognisable change in our behaviour.

3. A fundamental feature of learning is that it is acquired. How learning is acquired depends on three main factors:

    *   innate qualities of learner (e.g. intelligence)

    *   skills of the teacher

    *   conditions in which learning takes place.

4. The development of innate qualities is outside our control, being part of the process of biological development, or maturation. A person's age, intelligence and disposition, for example, are factors that cannot normally be changed by external influences. Parents, teachers and trainers all have to work with the raw material at their disposal. If a particular individual is neither physically nor mentally capable of making the grade as a commercial airline pilot, then all the tuition and practice in the world will not enable him or her to reach the required standard of competence.

    Where a person does have the basic abilities to perform such a role, then instruction, practice and experience will all combine to develop the required level of performance. The effectiveness of the learning will be tempered by the conditions under which it takes place (e.g. amount of stress present, learning aids utilised, etc.).

EARLY THEORIES OF LEARNING

5.   Our current understanding of learning has been influenced by a variety of past scholars and researchers. Early scholars such as Plato and Aristotle[1], saw that the exercise of mental faculties (reason, memory and willpower) was crucial to the development of the individual and, ultimately, of the community. Today we still talk of the need for people with 'trained minds'. Such an 'athletic' approach to education and training requires extensive self-discipline and control, relying firmly on the belief that learning is fundamentally a matter of innate intelligence. This is the nature of what we might call Thinking People.

6.   The practical effects of this approach are that:

   • learning is structured

   • teaching methods are didactic (telling/directing)

   • the subject-matter is taken to be important in its own right (e.g. maths, philosophy)

   • memorising and rule-learning are seen as crucial.

   Much of the education in Europe and the United States in the first half of the twentieth century was founded precisely on this approach.

7.   The first major reaction to the mental discipline approach came, in the eighteenth century, from the French philosopher, Jean Jacques Rousseau (1712–1778)[2]. He saw people as basically good and active beings, who are free and self-directing. This humanistic and optimistic view of People led Rousseau to emphasise instincts and feelings in education. The Thinking People of the Greeks had been superseded by the Feeling People of Rousseau. Those who followed Rousseau, such as Pestalozzi and Froebel, emphasised the importance of the *learners'* needs in education, and devised a permissive environment in which such needs could be met. At present these liberal ideas have not caught on very widely in education systems, except perhaps at primary school level. Nevertheless, modern trends are returning to concepts of education and training based on *individual* needs, so the legacy of Rousseau and his followers should not be overlooked. Indeed there is more than a resemblance to them in the ideas of self-actualisation expounded by several eminent social psychologists since the 1950s (see Chapter 8).

BEHAVIOURIST THEORIES

8.   The greatest stimulus to modern ideas about learning has undoubtedly been provided by the results of scientific experiments carried out around the turn of the twentieth century by the advocates of what we might term Behaving People. Scientists such as Pavlov, Thorndike and Skinner took as their central theme the *observed behaviour* of their subjects. They made no assumptions about the thinking or feeling processes that might be implied, but merely described, or predicted, overt behaviour. They were especially concerned with connections between stimuli and responses in learning. Their work is important not only for the

direct contribution it made to current training practices, but also for the reactions it caused in theoretical circles, enabling other theories, notably cognitive theories, to emerge (see below).

9.   Some of the notable experiments of the Stimulus-Response (S-R) theorists, or Behaviourists, as they have been called, are described below. For a variety of reasons, of convenience as well as ethics, most of their experiments were carried out on animals rather than on human beings. Although there are drawbacks in experimenting with animals, mainly because of the absence of verbal communication, nevertheless some classic experiments conducted with animals are now firmly part of the history of learning theory.

10.   The experiments described below refer to a number of key learning concepts, which need to be clarified at the outset. These concepts are as follows:

- Drive . . . . .Need; motivation; readiness to respond
- Stimulus . . . . .External prompt or signal
- Response . . . . . . .Reaction of subject
- Reinforcement. . . .Measures designed to strengthen a response.

11.   In the case of animal experiments, the drive was usually hunger. A human example could be the desire to pass an examination. The stimuli used in the animal experiments were typically food or water. For a human, the stimuli could be books or visual aids, for example. Responses in animal experiments were actions of various kinds. Human responses would include saying things or writing them down as well as performing actions. Reinforcers in animal experiments were usually food or water. For humans, reinforcers may include such things as praise, encouragement and achievement. Here feedback of results is a vital factor in reinforcement.

PAVLOV'S EXPERIMENTS

12.   Among the most famous of early learning experiments were those conducted by the Russian physiologist, I. Pavlov (1849–1936)[3]. Pavlov used dogs in his experiments, which were designed to see if the animals could learn to salivate to a neutral stimulus such as the ringing of a bell. Normally, salivation would take place only as an instinctive (unconditioned) response to the sight of food. Accordingly, Pavlov arranged the experiments so that, at the time food was to be presented, a bell would be rung. The animals salivated and the food was presented and duly eaten. After several such combinations of food and bell, the researchers asked themselves, would the animals salivate if the bell were rung, but no food presented? The results were clear – once the animals had begun to associate the ringing of the bell with the arrival of food, they would salivate at the sound of the bell alone! They had made, in effect, a *conditioned* response, i.e. they had learned to react to the sound of the bell (the conditioned stimulus). Dogs do not normally respond in such a way, but Pavlov had 'taught' them to do so, by means of what has come to be called Classical, or Respondent, Conditioning.

13.   We apply the term 'conditioning' to human behaviour when we talk about people

being conditioned to react in a certain way. For example, soldiers are conditioned to move forward under fire, even when their 'instinct' is to take cover, or run away. Hence the need for armies all over the world to spend considerable time and effort on basic training.

THORNDIKE AND OPERANT CONDITIONING

14. Whilst Pavlov was experimenting with dogs, a younger American scientist, E. L. Thorndike (1874–1949)[4] was enquiring into the learning behaviour of cats. In a typical experiment he put a hungry cat into a cage from which there was only one means of escape. Escape could only be achieved if the cat either pulled a wire or pressed a lever, depending on the type of cage used. Outside the cage a plate of food was placed. After a period of apparently random movements, the cat eventually pulled at the wire or pressed the lever and escaped to get at the food. Thorndike found that after a number of repeat experiments the cat would soon go to the wire or lever and perform the necessary action to escape. The animal had apparently learned how to effect its escape from this particular situation.

15. This form of experiment came to be known as Instrumental, or Operant, Conditioning. It differed from Classical Conditioning in two principal ways:

   1 the degree of control exercised by the researcher (e.g. in Pavlov's case, the dogs were passive subjects of the researcher but in Thorndike's case the cats were active participants in the experiment)

   2 the focus of interest (e.g. Pavlov concentrated on a *stimulus* – food, whereas Thorndike was interested in a *response* – escape behaviour).

16. Thorndike's most significant contribution to our understanding of learning was his so-called 'Law of Effect', in which he stated the general principle that when a response is followed by a reward, or feeling of satisfaction, that response is more likely to be repeated in similar circumstances. He firmly established the importance of relevant rewards in education and training, a point we shall consider later.

B. F. SKINNER

17. Following in the same tradition of animal studies as Pavlov and Thorndike, but eventually applying himself to research on *human* learning, came the American psychologist, B. F. Skinner[5]. A Professor at Harvard University, Skinner extended the work of his predecessors but concentrated mainly on Instrumental, or what he termed Operant Conditioning. Skinner's early experiments were conducted on rats and pigeons. In controlled situations, he presented a number of different stimuli, positive and negative, in order to test the animals' ability to adapt. He was particularly interested in the concept of the reinforcement of behaviour. Reinforcement involves the strengthening of a subject's responses. It may be achieved by means of positive stimuli i.e. rewards (food, water, teacher's smile, etc.) or by the removal of threats (negative stimuli). Interestingly, Skinner's view of

punishment was that it is not a reinforcer, since it tends to weaken responses rather than strengthen them, which is the essence of reinforcement.

18. Skinner's principal contribution to human learning has been his development of programmed learning (See Chapter 28), which is based on his ideas of Stimulus-Response-Reinforcement.

BEHAVIOURISM

19. The work of Pavlov, Thorndike, Skinner and others in the same tradition earned them the title of 'Behaviourists' on account of their preference for investigating observable behaviour without making assumptions about how learning took place. Such an approach did not prove acceptable to other researchers investigating animal and human learning. They claimed, in particular, that the behaviourists made no allowance for factors such as 'insight' or 'imagination', and it is partly for these reasons among others that current thinking considers the behaviourists to be unduly narrow in their conclusions about learning.

20. We can illustrate the point that learning and behaviour are not necessarily synonymous by taking a human example. A heavy smoker, exposed to vivid accounts of the damaging effects to health of this habit, may well be able to recount the dangers of smoking, i.e. to indicate that learning has taken place. Yet this selfsame person may be quite unwilling to give up the habit, i.e. unwilling to change his or her basic behaviour. Learning and behaviour are undoubtedly interrelated but this does not mean that they are one and the same thing, as the behaviourists claim. Other psychologists argue that learning is not just a question of doing something, but rather more of reflecting on a situation, sizing it up and then endeavouring to obtain some personal meaning or significance from it.

GESTALT PSYCHOLOGY

21. The first revolt against the Stimulus-Response behaviourists came from a group of German psychologists known as Gestaltists. Led by Max Wertheimer (1880–1943)[6], these psychologists were particularly interested in the subject of perception, i.e. how human beings and animals 'see' their world. From their experiments they demonstrated that learning is a matter of assembling one's world into meaningful patterns rather than just making connections between separate elements. Their model of people was what we might call Perceptive People. Their view of perception was encapsulated in the statement that 'the whole is greater than the sum of its parts'. The word *Gestalt* in German signifies the form or pattern of a whole, hence the title Gestaltist. The exponents of this new approach to learning supported their claims with a number of well-known experiments, some of which are summarised below.

22. Wertheimer conducted a classic experiment in which human subjects were asked to look at two alternately flashing lights and describe what they saw. The overwhelming response was that the light appeared to move from one light to

the other in a single movement. Scarcely anyone described the scene as two independent lights flashing at different intervals. It was the total effect that caught people's attention, not the operation of individual lights. The whole had more significance for human perception than the parts.

23.   In another experiment Wertheimer showed his subjects three dots on a sheet of paper (see Figure 25.1) and asked them what they could see. The response in each case was 'a triangle'.

*

*   *

Figure 25.1 *Typical Wertheimer experiment*

Once again, people had shown that shapes and patterns, i.e. wholes, were more easily perceived than individual parts. Behaving People had been superseded by Perceptive People. Wertheimer argued that our past experience is also used to build up a pattern or network against which we evaluate situations that face us. Such patterns are the basis of the phenomenon of that sudden flash of understanding that we call 'insight'. This particular phenomenon was investigated by another Gestaltist, Wolfgang Koehler (1887–1967) who conducted a series of experiments using chimpanzees as subjects.

WOLFGANG KOEHLER

24.   In a typical experiment, Koehler[7] confined a hungry chimpanzee to a cage, outside of which lay a bunch of bananas, just out of reach, but in full view. Inside the cage a stick had been left. The stick was long enough to reach the food. How would the animal react? At first it tried to reach the food by hand, making several unsuccessful attempts. Then it suddenly grabbed the stick and used it to pull the bananas within reach. There was no evidence of trial-and-error behaviour as in Thorndike's experiments. The animal had just taken the stick and used it to good effect. The researchers claimed that it had shown 'insight' into the problem confronting it. Furthermore, when the same animal was presented with a similar problem at a later date, it invariably 'remembered' what to do in order to retrieve the food. It had been able to transfer its previous learning (see para 29 below).

COGNITIVE THEORIES OF LEARNING

25.   The Gestaltists rank among the so-called cognitive theorists of learning, who were concerned with explaining how understanding occurs in the learning process. Unlike the behaviourists, who saw learning as behaviour only, the cognitive psychologists saw learning as a complex process involving the exercise of problem-solving capacity, mental mapping, intuition, imagination, perception and purpose.

They also held that learning could be latent, i.e. stored away until required for use. Such latent learning did not manifest itself until after it had been acquired. Much of the learning of the smoker referred to earlier was probably latent. It did not manifest itself in an obvious change of behaviour, but could well have produced a slight change in attitude towards smoking, which at some later date could produce a change in behaviour.

BEHAVIOURISTS AND GESTALTISTS COMPARED

26. In comparing the two dominant theories of learning to emerge from the late nineteenth century, we can summarise the key differences between them as shown in Figure 25.2.

Behaviourists	Gestaltists
Learning is basically about making connections between a Stimulus and a Response	Learning is primarily a question of how the environment is perceived
Desired Responses can be elicited by the use of rewards, which can also reinforce behaviour	External rewards are less important than internal 'mapping'
Learning is synonymous with behaviour	Learning can be latent and manifest itself as behaviour
Behaviour can be measured and predicted	Learning is not precise and measurable
Evidence for learning is objective	Evidence for learning is subjective

Figure 25.2 *Key differences between Behaviourist and Gestaltists*

INSIGHT IN LEARNING

27. An important issue in learning is that of 'insight', which is particularly relevant to understanding. E.A. Lunzer (1968)[8] described it in terms of the following characteristics:

- suddenness of solution

- immediacy and smoothness of behaviour

- ability to repeat solution without error on successive presentations of original problem

- ability to transpose the solution to situations exhibiting the same relational or structural features but in a different context.

Insight thus represents the dawning of understanding, when a person grasps the essentials of a problem, can formulate a solution and then make use of the experience on a future occasion. Perceptive People have now given way to Complex People.

28. Whilst acknowledging the importance of insight, it is important to recognise that this phenomenon is not relevant in *all* learning situations. For example, it cannot readily be applied to such activities as memorising lists or rules. In other words, when we are engaged in basic information-gathering, or learning basic skills routines, insight is not called for. Its principal relevance is to situations of a complex, problem-solving nature.

TRANSFER OF LEARNING

29. The ability to utilise previous learning in the service of new learning is called 'transfer of learning'. It is an important factor in any learning, but especially so when basic principles are being learned, or basic skills acquired. Transfer can be of two types: positive and negative.

   1 Positive transfer occurs when something learned previously is helpful in a subsequent situation. For example, if a manager has received training in basic interviewing skills, and is asked to conduct a more complex interview such as a grievance interview, it could be expected that the earlier training will help him or her in this task.

   2 Negative transfer occurs when something learned previously *hinders* performance in a new situation. For example, if a machinist has operated a machine in one particular fashion, but is then required to use a different method, it is likely to be doubly difficult for that person to learn the new method, because he or she has to 'unlearn' a previously-acquired pattern of behaviour.

30. Transfer of learning has been found to occur more readily if the following points are taken into account:

   - introducing identical elements into the old and the new learning, so as to facilitate learning by association

   - generalising from basic principles

   - providing prompts and hints

   - providing opportunities for practice.

   The effectiveness of this approach is, of course, considerably influenced by individual differences in maturity, level of motivation and other personal factors. Nevertheless most training situations would benefit from incorporation of these points.

CONCLUSION

31. Learning is a complex process of acquiring knowledge, understanding, skills and values in order to be able to adapt to the environment. This process depends on a combination of the following factors:

1   our innate (inherited) characteristics, such as intelligence and temperament

2   our readiness to respond to learning opportunities (motivation)

3   the teaching skills of those attempting to assist our learning

4   the conditions under which learning takes place.

32.   Our present understanding of the nature of human learning is derived from four major groups of scholars and researchers, whose work may be summarised as shown in Figure 25.3.

Exponents	Emphasis	Model of People
Plato Aristotle	Exercise of the mental faculties (reason, memory, etc.) Based on an assumption of the predominance of reasoning	Thinking People
Rousseau Pestalozzi Froebel	Permitting full use of individual feelings and inclinations. Based on the assumption that People are basically good, active and free	Feeling People
Pavlov Thorndike Skinner	Observed behaviour is the sole criterion of learning. Based on the assumption that learning is behaviour	Behaving People
Wertheimer Koehler	Importance of perception and insight in learning. Based on the assumption that learning is dominated by perceptual patterning (mental mapping)	Perceptive People and Complex People

Figure 25.3   *Major approaches in learning theory*

REFERENCES

1.   Aristotle: see Schwab, J.J. (1964), 'Problems, Topics and Issues' in Elam, S. (ed.), *Education and the Structure of Knowledge*, Rand McNally.

2.   Rousseau, J.J. (1911), *Emile* (trans. Foxley, B.), Dutton.

3.   Pavlov, I. (1927), *Conditioned Reflexes*, Oxford University Press.

4.   Thorndike, E.L. (1913), *The Psychology of Learning*, Teachers College Press.

5.   Skinner, B.F. (1953), *Science and Human Behaviour*, Macmillan.

6.   Wertheimer, M. (1959), *Productive Thinking*, Harper & Row.

7.   Koehler, W. (1959), *The Mentality of Apes*, Vintage Books.

8.   Lunzer, E.A. (1968), *The Regulation of Behaviour: Development in Learning*, Staples Press.

CHAPTER 26

Modern approaches to learning – the learning organisation

INTRODUCTION

1. Modern approaches to learning theory are best described as based on a complex view of people, since they contain elemnts of all the traditions we have referred to in the previous chapter. The modern image of what we have termed Complex People tends to be closer to Feeling and Perceptive People than to Thinking and Behaving People. This chapter describes the work of several leading contributors to current developments in learning theory as applied to the workplace.

CURRENT APPROACHES TO LEARNING AT WORK

2. Current approaches to learning theory see learning as first-and-foremost an *individual* activity pursued freely within a loose framework of external controls. Thus, current preferences amongst training and development professionals are towards:

   • trainee-centred rather than organisation-centred approaches

   • experiential learning, where 'the person has freedom of choice and action, and the capacity to initiate rather than simply respond to circumstances ...' (Burgoyne & Stuart, 1978)[1]

   • participative forms of training, in which trainees jointly decide with trainers how their needs are to be met, instead of tightly-structured programmes imposed unilaterally by the organisation

   • flexible training programmes, in which trainees work at their own pace rather than in accordance with a rigid timetable.

CURRENT PRACTICE

3. Current *practice* in employee development is still some way behind the theorists of Complex People. Most organisations still adopt styles that are dominated by the collective needs of the organisation rather than by the personal needs of

individuals. Most organisations still tend to emphasise a behaviourist approach in their training and development practices. For example, identifying and measuring suitable behavioural objectives (i.e. trainee responses) are still important features of training provision in organisations (see Chapter 29).

4.   Since training and development policy in organisations is directed primarily towards organisational goals, and only secondarily towards individual goals, there is bound to be some tension between collective and individual priorities. The challenge of modern learning theory as applied to work situations is to find some way of resolving this basic conflict between the requirements of organisations for trained employees and the needs of individuals for personal growth and career development.

5.   Diagrammatically the difference in emphasis between organisational needs on the one hand and individual needs on the other can be shown as follows (Figure 26.1).

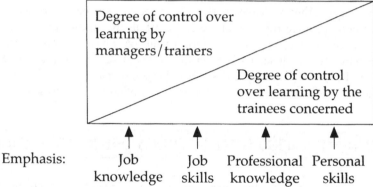

Figure 26.1   *Control over training*

Learning methods are geared towards the principal emphasis or concern. So, if job skills are the focus, then typical methods will include systematic instruction, programmed learning and testing. If the development of broad managerial skills/ professionalism is the priority, then a variety of structured and unstructured approaches could be employed (see Chapter 32).

6.   In the previous chapter we outlined the main alternative theories on which modern approaches to learning have been based. Whilst the rational approaches of the Greeks and the behavioural approaches of the Behaviourists are still significant forces in modern learning practices, there are several significant contributors to newer, less prescriptive approaches allowing greater freedom of choice to individuals in what training they receive, and how they receive it. The first contribution to be described is that of Robert Gagne.

GAGNE – THE CONDITIONS OF LEARNING

7.   Robert Gagne (1970)[2] in a classic work on learning argued that it can be divided into eight different types, ranging from primitive forms to complex forms. His list of categories is useful because it highlights the main alternatives that are available

to those responsible for training and developing employees. Gagne's list can be summarised as follows, commencing with the more primitive types:

Primitive learning

1 Signal learning – i.e. responding to some signal, such as the bell used with Pavlov's dogs. This is a primitive form of learning, closely related to basic emotions and instincts. Classical conditioning is based on signal-type learning.

2 Stimulus-Response (S-R) learning – this involves making a response of a non-instinctive kind to a stimulus. An important factor here is the reward which accompanies a correct response. This type of learning is found in operant conditioning.

3 Chaining – this is a type of learning which involves the linking of two or more previously learned S-R behaviours. For example, linking brake pedal operations with gear change operations when learning to drive a car.

4 Verbal association – this is similar to chaining, but involves links between words. This form of learning is a feature of language development. In work situations it is sometimes manifested in the form of mnemonics (memory aids) to enable people to recall key facts.

5 Discrimination learning – this is the ability to differentiate between a number of different, but related, stimuli. This type of learning is especially relevant to skills development in humans.

6 Concept learning – this refers to the ability to make a common response to a class of objects or events (concrete or abstract). It involves chaining, discrimination and rule-learning. This type of learning and the two which follow are higher forms of learning requiring the ability to assemble and reformulate abstract events and concepts.

7 Rule-learning – this is the acquisition of a chain of two or more concepts, as in 'If ... then ...' type of statements.

8 Problem-solving – this is a learning process that works out new rules and solutions on the basis of previously-acquired rules; it invariably involves the application of insight to a situation.

Complex learning

8. The usefulness of Gagne's list lies in its detailed breakdown of the difficult concept of learning. The list helps to indicate that the complex process of acquiring knowledge, understanding, skills and values cannot be pursued effectively if we adopt a narrow view of learning theory. Gagne's analysis strengthens the modern, eclectic approach that draws upon all the major theories in order to establish the optimum conditions for learning.

CARL ROGERS

9. In another influential text, Rogers (1979)[3], a psychologist, took an essentially humanistic view of how learning can best be facilitated. His main thesis was that the aim of education (and hence the role of educators) is the *facilitation of learning*. Rogers' view of the principles that underlie the successful facilitation of learning can be summarised as follows:

    1   Human beings have a natural potentiality for learning (i.e. curiosity).

    2   Significant learning takes place when the subject-matter is perceived as relevant by the learner.

    3   Learning which involves change in oneself is threatening and tends to be resisted.

    4   Learning which appears threatening can best be acquired, and exploited, when external threats are at a minimum.

    5   Much significant learning is acquired through doing.

    6   Learning is facilitated when the learner participates responsibly in the learning process.

    7   Self-initiated learning, involving the whole person (emotionally and intellectually), is the most lasting and pervasive form of learning.

    8   Independence, creativity and self-reliance are all facilitated when *self*-criticism and *self*-evaluation are encouraged rather than external forms of evaluation.

    9   Learning about the process of learning is essential to enable individuals to cope with change

    10 The task of the facilitator is to provide an environment in which individuals can set their own learning goals.

10. Rogers' ideas are firmly rooted in Rousseau's concept of people as good and active. Rogers comes closest to our model of Feeling People. His general viewpoint is a liberal and humanistic one, which shifts the emphasis of education away from the teacher to the student, and thus from teaching to learning. For many managers and trainers such an approach may be difficult to follow because of the pressures involved in meeting the collective needs of the organisation. Nevertheless, there is a growing body of evidence to suggest that a flexible, trainee-centred approach to employee development contributes more to the achievement of corporate goals than an approach based on predetermined outcomes and the needs of the organisation.

KOLB AND EXPERIENTIAL LEARNING

11. Rogers' theme of the importance of self-initiated, self-directed learning has been taken up by another American psychologist, David Kolb, whose work has been particularly influential in management development. Kolb (1979)[4] claim that classroom-type learning is seen as 'a special activity cut off from the real world and

unrelated to one's life' and where 'learning and doing are separate ... activities'. He believes it is important to distinguish classroom learning from problem-solving. He regards the former as a process, in which the teacher or trainer directs the learning on behalf of a passive learner. The latter, by contrast, involves the learner in an active role, in which the responsibility for achieving a solution rests with the individual and not with the teacher.

12. Kolb has developed a useful model of experiential learning which combines the characteristics of both classroom and problem-solving types of learning. The basic model is shown in Figure 26.2.

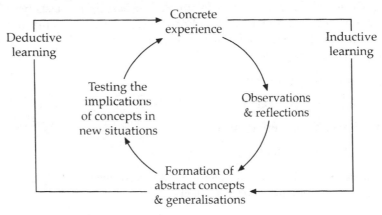

Figure 26.2 *The experiential learning cycle (Kolb, 1979)*

13. The starting-point of the model is a concrete experience of some kind – for example, using a computer keyboard for the first time. Following this experience, the trainee makes several observations, for example about the layout of keys, and begins to make sense of the keyboard, i.e. to formulate abstract concepts. These concepts are then tested in a new situation, in this case by practising on the keys. The practice itself provides a fresh experience and so the cycle begins again. As Boydell (1976)[5] emphasised, experience of itself is not the same as learning, for the experience has to be reflected upon and assessed by the learner before learning (i.e. acquiring and applying knowledge and skills) takes place.

It is also important to point out that Kolb's cycle of learning encompasses both inductive and deductive learning. Inductive learning is the process in which the learner experiences an event or stimulus and draws a conclusion from it, for example some rule or guiding principle. Deductive learning, by contrast, commences with the rule or principle (theory), which is subsequently applied by the learner.

14. Kolb stressed the continuous nature of the learning process, and emphasised the central position of the *individual's* needs in governing the direction of learning. So, the experiences we seek, the way we interpret them and test out our ideas are all strongly influenced by our felt needs and goals. Kolb's model of learning is clearly based on our notion of Complex People. The four stages of the cycle encompass feeling (experiencing), observing, thinking and doing. The implication of Kolb's ideas is that effective learning requires the involvement of the learner at three different levels:

- thinking

- feeling

- doing.

LEARNING STYLES

15. An important development of Kolb's (1979)[4] work is the Learning Style Inventory (LSI), which he described as 'a simple self-description test, based on experiential learning theory, that is designed to measure your strengths and weaknesses as a learner in the four stages of the learning process'. The four stages, taken from Figure 26.2 above, are:

- concrete experience

- reflective observation

- abstract conceptualisation

- active experimentation.

The object of the test is to help individuals to identify their 'learning style', i.e. the way they go about solving problems.

16. According to Kolb the four stages can be combined to form two major dimensions of learning: first, a concrete/abstract dimension; second, a reflective/active dimension. Results can be logged on a chart incorporating these two dimensions, and a dominant learning style allocated to each quadrant, as in Figure 26.3.

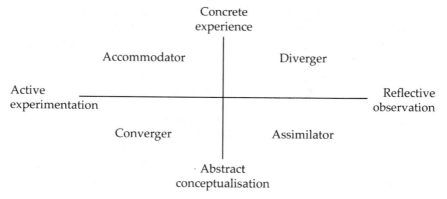

Figure 26.3 *Dominant learning styles*

17. The main characteristics of the four learning styles are:

- *Converger* – favours the practical application of ideas. Things rather than people are preferred. This style is characteristic of many engineers.

- *Diverger* – greatest strength is imagination and the ability to see situations from a variety of perspectives. Interested in people and have broad interests. Personnel managers tend to have this style.

- *Assimilator* – this style is characterised by abstract thinking. Concern is for ideas in themselves. Research and planning staff tend to manifest this style.

- *Accommodator* – this represents the action-centred approach to problems. The emphasis is on personal involvement and risk-taking. In organisations, this style is found in marketing and sales.

18.   Jervis (1983)[6] in applying the LSI to middle and senior managers found similar results to Kolb in terms of the relationship between functional roles and manifested learning styles. Jervis concluded that:

> ... the experiential learning model and the LSI have valid links with individual and organisational processes, including decision-making and problem-solving ... While no one approach will, by itself, provide all the answers, ... the Model and the LSI are valuable additions to the manager's armoury.

LEARNING STYLES – A BRITISH CONTRIBUTION

19.   Honey & Mumford (1982)[7] have developed a separate instrument for assessing learning styles. This consists of 80 statements that individuals are invited to agree or disagree with. The resulting scores are plotted on a two-dimensional chart to give a learning profile. The style types identified by the authors are:

- *Activists* – These are people whose days are filled with activity and new experiences. They thrive on challenge, but get bored with implementation and consolidation.

- *Reflectors* – These are thoughtful, cautious people with a fairly low profile in the organisation.

- *Theorists* – These are the logical thinkers, who like a good theory. They tend to be detached, analytical and rational.

- *Pragmatists* – These are people who like to put ideas into practice. They are essentially action-oriented.

20.   Whether or not one agrees with the learning-styles inventory approach as a method of identifying differences in learning-skills, there is no doubt that the opportunity to discuss in some detail how people appear to learn can be very enlightening for managers by sharpening their awareness of how they are likely to react to particular problem-situations.

21.   Other ideas on learning styles have been put forward by Pask and Marton, for example. Pask (1976)[8] distinguished between 'serialists' and 'holists'. Serialists are people who approach their learning in a step-by-step manner, whilst holists establish an overall framework for their tasks and then tackle the details later. Marton (1976)[9], in a series of studies among Swedish students, found that in approaches to written texts the subjects demonstrated two contrasting styles: deep processors and surface processors. The former tended to probe selectively into a text in order to glean its meaning, whilst surface processors scanned through the entire text with the object of remembering as much as possible.

THE LEARNING ORGANISATION

22. An idea that has emerged recently is that of the 'learning organisation'. Senge (1990)[10] describes such organisations as

    > organisations where people continually expand their capacity to create the results they truly desire, where new and expansive patterns of thinking are nurtured, where collective aspiration is set free, and where people are continually learning how to learn together (p. 3).

    This latter point is particularly important for a learning organisation, and it raises a number of fundamental issues, such as what is being learned, how is it being learned, how is it being applied, and why? Learning at the individual level, as we noted in Chapter 25 (para 2), is essentially a question of acquiring knowledge and skills, and developing understanding and personal attributes. The process of learning may sometimes involve 'unlearning' certain behaviours and attitudes. Indeed, in relation to organisations Hamel & Prahalad (1994)[11] argue that

    > creating a 'learning organisation' is only half the solution. Just as important is creating an 'unlearning organisation' ... To create the future, a company must unlearn at least some of its past. (p. 60)

23. At the heart of the concept of the learning organisation is a perspective that sees work organisations as needing to become more collaborative in the way they perceive problems and opportunities, and how they attempt to answer them or exploit them. Thus everyone throughout the organisation is expected to reflect on practice, raise alternative (better) ways of doing things, and find the will to work together to achieve results more effectively. The underlying philosophy of the learning organisation is to enhance the achievement of collective goals by harnessing the reservoir of knowledge, skills and insights of all the members of the organisation. The goals for a business will include increasing revenue and/or market share, attaining profit targets, increasing the company's standing in the stock market, and establishing a base of satisfied customers who return for repeat business. Arising out of this attention to group goals, individual employees may find opportunities for personal development, increased job satisfaction, and even enhanced career prospects. Depending on the level of commitment of top management to the idea of a learning organisation, the benefits for employees may be regarded as central to the exercise or merely as by-products of it.

24. Senge (*op.cit.*) suggests that the disciplines of the learning organisation are based on five converging strategies that he terms 'component technologies', which can be summarised as follows:

    1 **Systems thinking** – developing a conceptual framework that sees organisations as comprising various interrelated activities and groupings, which together make up more than the sum of the parts; this represents an organic and intuitive view of organisations.

    2 **Personal mastery** – this is the ability to produce results consistently as well as proficiently, and assumes a high degree of personal commitment to learning; Senge sees it as an 'essential cornerstone of the learning organisation'.

3   **Mental models** – what Senge is thinking of here is the importance to a learning organisation of developing people's awareness of their assumptions and prejudices, so that they may be examined for their continued relevance and usefulness.

4   **Shared vision** – this means developing a framework and set of processes which allow a common vision and purpose to emerge around which people at every level can find a sense of destiny.

5   **Team learning** – the discipline involved in this strategy is that of engaging in dialogue with colleagues; Senge defines dialogue as

> the capacity of members of a team to suspend assumptions and enter into a genuine "thinking together"... dialogue ... involves learning how to recognise the patterns of interactions in teams that undermine learning. (p. 10)

25.   Of the five disciplines it is systems thinking that is the most pivotal, because it enables organisations to fuse the others into a coherent body of theory and practice rather than just turning the idea of a learning organisation into a temporary fad or gimmick. The learning required is complex (Gagne), depends on the facilitation of learning (Rogers) and is largely experiential (Kolb). The concept of the learning organisation, therefore, is capable of encompassing the best of modern learning theory.

CONCLUSION

26.   In practice, effective learning requires that trainees (or students) adopt a flexible style, sometimes serialist, sometimes holist. However, this may not be possible for many people. The implication of differing learning styles for course designers is that training methods should be varied to meet the differing approaches of their course members. Thus, although trainers themselves may wish to use experiential and participative forms of training, these may not always be welcomed by their trainees, who may prefer to opt for traditional methods.

REFERENCES

1. Burgoyne, J. & Stuart, R. (1978), 'Management Development Programmes: Underlying Assumptions about Learning', in Burgoyne & Stuart (eds), *Management Development: Context and Strategies*, Gower Press.

2. Gagne, R.M. (1970), *The Conditions of Learning*, Holt, Rinehart Winston.

3. Rogers, C.R. (1979), *Freedom to Learn*, Merrill Publishing.

4. Kolb, D. *et al.* (1979), *Organisational Psychology: An Experiential Approach*, Prentice Hall.

5. Boydell, T. (1976), *Experiential Learning*, Manchester UP.

6. Jervis, P. (1983), 'Analysing Decision Behaviour: Learning Models and Learning Styles as Diagnostic Aids', *Personnel Review*, Vol. 12, No. 2.

7. Honey, P. & Mumford, A. (1982), *The Manual of Learning Styles*, P. Honey.

8. Pask, G. (1976), 'Styles and Strategies of Learning', *British Journal of Psychology*, No. 46.

9. Marton, F. & Saljo, R. (1976), 'On Qualitative Differences in Learning. 1. Process and Outcome', *British Journal of Psychology*, No. 46.

10. Senge, P. (1990), *The Fifth Discipline – the Art and Practice of the Learning Organisation*, Doubleday (British edition, 1992, published by Century Business).

11. Hamel, G. and Prahalad, C. (1994), *Competing for the Future*, Harvard Business School Press.

CHAPTER 27

Systematic training and development

1. The training and development of employees is an issue that has to be faced by every organisation. The amount, and quality, of training carried out varies enormously from one organisation to another. Factors influencing the quantity and quality of training and development activities include:

    - degree of change in the external environment (e.g. technological change, new legislation, etc.)

    - degree of internal change (new processes, new markets, etc.)

    - availability of suitable skills within the existing work-force

    - adaptability of existing workforce

    - the extent to which the organisation supports the idea of internal career development

    - the commitment of senior management to training as an essential part of economic success

    - the extent to which management see training as a motivating factor in work

    - knowledge and skills of those responsible for carring out the training.

2. Many organisations meet their needs for training in an ad hoc and haphazard way. Training in these organisations is more or less unplanned and unsystematic. Other organisations set about identifying their training needs, then design training activities in a rational manner, and finally assess the results of training. Such organisations are engaging in a systematic approach to the training and development of their employees. Organisations achieving a national standard in employee development may be granted an Investors in People award (see para. 13). This chapter discusses what is meant by 'systematic training' and how organisations go about it.

DEFINITIONS

3.   Before proceeding any further, it will be useful to ask ourselves 'What do we mean when we refer to 'training' and 'development'? Are they the same things as 'education', but in a work context? Is 'training' the same as 'development'? These are important questions, because our answers have important implications for the way we approach the training and development of people in their employment.

4.   Throughout this chapter the following interpretations will be applied:

1   *Education* will be taken to mean any long-term learning activity aimed at preparing individuals for a variety of roles in society: as citizens, workers and members of family groups. The focus of 'education' is primarily on the individual and his or her needs, and secondly on the community as a whole, i.e. on society's needs. Examples of individual needs are the need to be literate, the need to be prepared for some occupation and the need to make the most of one's personal gifts and talents. Society's needs can include the need for respect for law and order, the need for a variety of talents to sustain economic activities and the need to protect itself from external aggression.

2   *Training* will be understood as any learning activity which is directed towards the acquisition of specific knowledge and skills for the purposes of an occupation or task. The focus of training is the job or task. Examples of training needs are: the need to have efficiency and safety in the operation of particular machines or equipment; the need for an effective sales force; and the need for competent management in the organisation.

3   *Development* will be seen as any learning activity which is directed towards future needs rather than present needs, and which is concerned more with career growth than immediate performance. The focus of development tends to be primarily on an organisation's future manpower requirements, and secondly on the growth needs of individuals in the workplace. Examples of development needs might be the need for managers to be able to utilise the facilities offered by microcomputers in the operation of the business, the need for replacing senior staff with potential candidates from within the organisation, and the need for preparing employees to accept change.

5.   Each of the three types of learning activity is concerned, in varying degrees, with the acquisition of knowledge, understanding, skills and attitudes. In general, we rely on schools, colleges and universities to provide the bulk of the 'educational' activities carried out in our society. We rely on individual organisations in partnership with the vocational elements of our educational system (technical colleges and the new universities), to provide most of the 'training' in society. The development of National Vocational Qualifications (see Chapter 30.) is important here. Within this framework such developments as Modern Apprenticeships encourage employers to devise skills programmes tailored to their own needs in order to secure well-trained young persons for their workforce. Finally, we rely on individual organisations to create the 'development' opportunities required to prepare individuals for future roles.

THE TRAINING CYCLE

6. A systematic approach to training and development will generally follow a logical sequence of activities commencing with the establishment of a policy and the resources to sustain it, followed by an assessment of training needs, for which appropriate training is provided, and, ending with some form of evaluation and feedback. Figure 27.1 illustrates this basic sequence, or cycle, of events.

Figure 27.1 *Systematic training: the basic cycle*

The key stages of the above cycle of events are the subject of this and the next two chapters.

7. Before moving on, however, we ought to reflect briefly on the advantages to organisations of adopting a systematic approach to training. Generally, the benefits are that with a well-trained workforce, the organisation will turn out a high standard of goods or services, probably in a more cost-effective manner than others, and therefore with a better chance of achieving organisational goals, be they profit-oriented or service-oriented. In specific terms, organisations would expect to enjoy several of the following potential benefits:

- maintenance of a sufficient and suitable range of skills amongst employees
- the development of knowledge and skills in the workforce
- the harnessing of work experience and other forms of on-the-job development in a planned way
- achievement of improved job performance and productivity
- improved product quality
- improved service to customers
- increased motivation amongst employees.

8.   In addition to the above benefits to organisations, there are also benefits to individuals, notably:

- increase in personal repertoire of skills

- increased job satisfaction

- increased value of employee in the labour market

- improved prospects of internal promotion.

It is no wonder, therefore, that organisations recruiting young people, in particular, are keen to point out the nature and benefits of their training programmes.

9.   The rest of this chapter will consider policy and organisational issues in training and development, including the role of training in the organisation, the broad policy options open to organisations and the role of trainers.

TRAINING POLICY

10.   The training policy of an organisation will usually be included in a range of policies dealing with human resources. The policy statement sets out what the organisation is prepared to do in terms of developing its employees. For some organisations a policy statement is a brief sentence such as:

> The Company will provide the means to ensure that every employee will be adequately trained in the basic tasks of his or her employment.

For others the policy statement may be quite lengthy, as in the following example:

1.   The Company believes that it is in its own interests as well as in employees' interests that full support should be given to training and development.

2.   The Company will therefore establish corporate as well as local training organisations.

3.   Systematic assessments of training needs will be carried out before any planned training takes place.

4.   Employees and their immediate manager/supervisor will be consulted about any training identified as relevant to their situation.

5.   The primary objective of training and development will be to support the pursuit of the Company's business goals.

6.   Training and development activities will also be regarded as key elements in an individual's mastery of, and satisfaction in, his principal duties.

7.   The Company will, wherever appropriate, provide opportunities for selected employees to participate in development activities to prepare them for new roles in the organisation.

8.   All training and development activities will be evaluated on a regular basis, including those provided by outside organisations as well as in-company activities.

9.   Training and development activities will be reviewed at least annually by the Company's Joint Consultative Committee, and any proposals for amending this policy will be seriously considered by the Board.

11. The implication of the first, short, example given above is that training will focus on immediate learning needs related to current tasks and duties. The implication of the second, longer, example is that training and development will be closely linked to short, medium and long-term business plans and will be seen as a vital element in the organisation's ability to prove itself with its customers. The discussion in the remaining paragraphs assumes the second position, i.e. that training and development are essential to success in achieving organisational goals. The role of training in the organisation is therefore primarily determined by the overall purpose of the organisation. This provides those responsible for implementing training and development with the best possible *raison d'être* – a direct contribution to corporate goals. Thus in a fast-moving consumer goods company, training will be geared strongly to sales achievements against the competition. In a high-technology manufacturing company, training will be geared to product quality and innovation. In a district general hospital, training will be geared to the provision of a high and reliable standard of patient care.

12. The fulfilment of an organisation's policy can be achieved in a number of different ways. Some organisations have a long tradition of 'growing their own' managers and specialists, and provide a substantial internal training organisation to sustain all their needs. Thus, most of the training and development is provided on an in-company basis with little reliance on outsiders. Other organisations believe in contracting out their training to external providers such as colleges, consultants and private training organisations. In these cases, the internal training organisation may be little more than one or two persons acting as a liaison between the company and its suppliers.

Yet other organisations adopt a midway position, providing induction training and job-training internally, but contracting out management and supervisory training. Whatever option is chosen, it will require funding, and thus justifying, in the inevitable competition between managers for a share of the organisation's financial and material resources.

'INVESTORS IN PEOPLE'

13. 'Investors in People' is a UK national quality standard developed in 1990 to encourage effective investment in employee training and development. It provides 'a framework for improving business performance and competitiveness through a planned approach to setting and communicating business objectives and developing people to meet these objectives.' In particular, the Standard provides 'a comprehensive benchmark of best practice against which an organisation can audit its policies and practice in the development of people.' The Standard is based on four key principles, as follows:

1 A commitment from the top to develop all employees.

2 The regular review of training and development needs.

3 The taking of relevant action to meet these needs throughout people's employment.

4   The evaluation of training and development outcomes for individuals and the organisation as the basis for continuous improvement.

14. Achieving the award of Investors in People requires organisations first to understand the Standard, which has 24 indicators of effective practice against which organisations have to produce evidence for assessment. Once an organisation has committed itself to seek the award, it has to diagnose the gaps between its current practice and that of the Standard and then take appropriate action to meet the requirements involved. This process alone may take many months, and is supported by the local Learning and Skills Council or similar public body. Once the organisation is in a position to seek assessment for the award, it will be visited by one or more independent, licensed assessors, who will review the evidence and give feedback. The final decision to make the award is taken by a recognition panel of senior business people. An organisation that meets the Standard can be publicly recognised, including being allowed to refer to the award in its recruitment or other advertising.

15. The benefits claimed for Investors in People include:

- improved earnings, productivity and profitability

- reduced costs and wastage

- enhanced quality

- improved employee motivation

- greater customer satisfaction

- competitive advantage

- public recognition.

In a nutshell, what the award facilitates is a structured way of improving the effectiveness of employee training and development in the context of business goals.

TRAINER ROLES IN ORGANISATIONS

16. When we talk of the 'role of the trainer', we are usually thinking in terms of our expectations of the way in which the jobholder performs in the job. Morgan & Costello (1984)[1], in a publication for the Manpower Services Commission/Institute of Training & Development, provide an informative definition of 'role':

> ... the essence of 'role' is that it encapsulates the expectations of people about the way in which an 'in-role' person will relate to others. It concerns the manner of performance – some would say 'style' – of the 'in-role' person, rather than what, specifically, he/she does.

Thus, a person's role is somewhat wider in scope than his or her job duties and position in the job hierarchy.

17. The concept of role is clouded precisely because of its closeness to other concepts,

such as the job, the jobholder, and the organisational culture. Graphically, this overlapping of ideas and meanings can be illustrated as shown in Figure 27.2.

Figure 27.2 *The complexities of roles at work*

In the above diagram, the individual's role emerges as a result of the interaction of the job duties, the jobholder's personal attributes, especially his/her perceptions of how these duties should be performed, the organisation's own value-system (culture) and the nature of the organisation's external environment.

18.   What the above diagram does not indicate is that JOB PERFORMANCE, i.e. what is actually done, in itself may affect the individual's role, both in terms of how he/she sees the role, as well as how others see it. We shall therefore be turning shortly to look at the activities engaged in by trainers, since it is these activities which affect the operation of an organisation, not discussions about role, which are in essence academic arguments. However, in the meantime we shall briefly consider two contrasting efforts to describe trainer roles.

DESCRIBING TRAINER ROLES

19.   The first set of descriptions were proposed by Nadler (1969)[2], who isolated three main roles and a number of subordinate roles, as follows:

1   Learning Specialist

    • Instructor

    • Curriculum builder

    • Methods and materials developer.

2   Administrator

    • Developer of personnel

- Maintainer of community relations

- Sponsor of on-going programmes

- Arranger for facilities and finances.

3   Problem-solver

- Advocate

- Expert

- Alternative identifier

- Catalyst

- Process specialist.

Despite the awkwardness of some of Nadler's descriptors, it is certainly possible to see a picture of a trainer as a person who has to combine his specialist knowledge of learning with the specific needs of the organisation, i.e. in terms of its problems, and who is required to perform an administrative role as part of his work.

20.   A more recent attempt to develop a typology of trainer roles has been made by Pettigrew and colleagues (1983)[3]. The model they have developed is based on two major dimensions of trainer perceptions:

1   the trainer's attitude towards training, expressed as either traditionally oriented or interventionist oriented; the traditional view sees trainers in the driving-seat, as it were; the interventionist approach is a responsive one, where the trainer is led by demand

2   the trainer's response to change, expressed as either as maintaining the status quo, or as contributing to organisational change.

21.   The model is shown in Figure. 27.3 below. It includes four ideal types of trainer:

1   *Caretakers* – who use traditional, trainer-centred approaches within a system that is accepted as remaining stable.

2   *Educators* – who use traditional approaches to learning, but accept the need for change.

3   *Evangelists* – who work within the constraints of existing systems and procedures, but who adopt learner-centred approaches in training

4   *Innovators* – who perceive both the organisation and learning processes as subject to change, and adapt to what is essentially a catalyst role.

22.   Pettigrew and colleagues found that most trainers were of the Caretaker type, working within the accepted boundaries of the organisation and using traditional learning methods. Far fewer trainers could be classified as Innovators. Yet this latter type was sought after by many Caretaker managers. They found few trainers who fell into either of the remaining two categories. The extent to which role-holders could become Innovators depended on their level of influence over others in the organisation. As with other specialist roles, power and influence come from a variety of sources, such as position power (authority to act), the organisation's urgency for training, and the personal skills and reputation of the trainer.

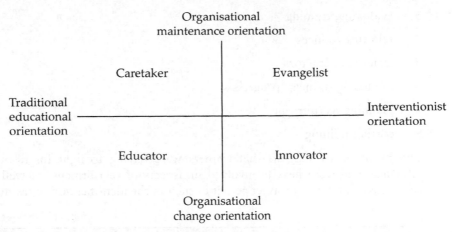

Figure. 27.3 *Trainer types (Pettigrew et al., 1983)*

23.   At a somewhat more practical level, the *Training of Trainers Report* (1978)[4] identified four key job functions applicable to most training specialist posts. These were:

- determining and managing

- planning and organising

- direct training

- consulting and advising.

The four areas indicated suggest a comprehensive role for a training specialist, involving the determination of training requirements, of directing the activities of the training personnel, the planning and organising of training activities, some direct face-to-face training, and, finally, an element of consultancy and advisory work with colleagues. In the event, the Committee concerned focused its attention on the direct training element, which it saw as divided into four sub-functions:

- designing training programmes

- preparing for training

- carrying out training

- assessing the results of training.

These four subsidiary functions are the core-aspects of the work of direct trainers, and will be dealt with in the next three chapters.

24.   It is interesting to compare the ideas of role expressed in the last few paragraphs with a report of an earlier study into the work of the industrial training officer, conducted by Rodger and colleagues from Birkbeck College (1971)[5]. When enquiring about priorities for training officers, the researchers uncovered the following responses. Listed in rank order:

1   selling training to top management

2   identifying training needs

3   evaluating training

4   selecting trainees

5   training instructors

6   discussing trainees' progress

7   planning recruitment

8   costing training.

The Birkbeck list suggests that trainers were having to fight for resources and influence, and were heavily involved in aspects of recruitment, as well as being concerned with typical trainer activities such as the identification of training needs.

CONCLUSION

25.   The stimulus for adopting a systematic approach to training and development arises from the intensity of internal and external pressures for change in the organisation. The first step in a systematic approach is to devise a policy statement to act as a guide to the organisation's intentions concerning the weight and direction to be given to training and development. The second step is to define an initial set of roles for those responsible for implementing the policy, notably trainers. The third step is to set up a suitable structure of training posts and procedures, and to allocate sufficient funds to the training organisation.

23.   Once the above steps have been completed, the trainers concerned can then initiate the cycle of events which commences with an analysis of training needs and ends with an evaluation and review of training carried out (see Figure. 27.1). The next chapter looks at how organisations set about assessing their need for training, and how they plan and execute training activities.

REFERENCES

1.   Morgan, T. & Costello, M. (1984), *Trainer Task Inventory*, MSC/ITD.

2.   Nadler, L. (1969), 'The Variety of Training Roles', *Industrial & Commercial Training*, Vol. 1 No. 1.

3.   Pettigrew, A.M *et al.* (1983), 'Training and Development Roles in their Organisational Setting', *Journal of the Institute of Training and Development*, Vol. 3 No. 6.

4.   *Manpower Services Commission* (1978), *First Report: Training of Trainers*. MSC.

5.   Rodger, A. *et al.* (1971), *The Industrial Training Officer*, IPM.

CHAPTER 28

Training needs and training plans

INTRODUCTION

1. The training cycle referred to in the last chapter begins and ends with the analysis of learning needs. If an organisation has to justify its training expenditure, it must surely do so on the basis of organisational need. This chapter looks at how organisations set about analysing training needs, and concludes by outlining some of the key features of training plans.

TRAINING NEEDS

2. Organisations adopting a systematic approach to training and development will usually set about defining their needs for training in accordance with a well-organised procedure. Such a procedure will entail looking at training needs from a number of different perspectives:

    1   the organisation, i.e. corporate requirements

    2   the department, or function

    3   the job, or occupational group

    4   the individual employee.

3. The particular perspectives chosen will depend on the circumstances. For example, if changes in the external environment of the organisation are exerting pressures for change internally, then a corporate perspective needs to be taken. If, however, the issue is one of improving skills in a particular category of employees, then that occupational group will provide the focus of efforts. Usually organisations analyse training needs in response to operational weaknesses reported in by line managers, or to meet the demands of change. The former reason suggests that there is something of a 'fire-fighting' element in training needs analysis. The latter suggests that it can also be deployed as an element of planned change in the organisation.

4. What is a training need? Basically, it is any shortfall in employee performance, or potential performance, which can be remedied by *appropriate training*. There are many ways of overcoming deficiencies in human performance at work, and training is only one of them. It is important to recognise this fact, since sometimes training staff are asked to meet needs which ought to be dealt with in some other way, such as improving pay, replacing machinery or simplifying procedures, for example.

Figure 28.1 below illustrates the nature of a training need as viewed from the perspective of the individual employee.

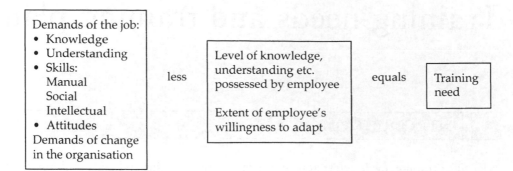

Figure 28.1 *The training need equation*

5.   The diagram shows that the demands of the job will be made up of appropriate proportions of knowledge, understanding, skills and attitudes. Add to these factors the demands for change, and you have a picture of what is required to perform the job in the context concerned. Against these requirements are set the employee's level of knowledge, skill and so on, together with the extent of his or her willingness to co-operate in change. If the two sides match perfectly, there will be no training requirement; if, as is more likely, there is a mis-match between what is required and what is available, then a training need has been identified.

6.   So far as the organisation is concerned, the sources of an individual's training needs are (a) the demands of the job and (b) the demands of organisational change. The former require improvements in, or additions to, knowledge, understanding, skills and attitudes; the latter require attitudinal changes (e.g. personal adaptability) more than anything else. Note that this view of individual training needs appears to take no account of what the employee personally desires. However, as is indicated below, employees' views about training needs are sought by employers in a variety of ways (via questionnaires, job interviews, appraisals).

7.   Most jobs require the jobholders to possess appropriate knowledge and skills. Knowledge on its own may sometimes be insufficient, and understanding is required. Understanding in this context refers to the grasp of underlying principles or workings of a process or procedure. It is a deeper form of knowledge. For example, whilst in most situations a person using a microcomputer needs only to know how to operate it (knowledge), a computer service engineer would be expected to understand the workings of the machine in terms of its circuitry, components and so on. Skills may be subdivided into at least three broad categories: manual, social and intellectual. Manual skills involve the use of the hands combined with other senses to achieve certain tasks; social skills involve the personality in seeking to influence others; intellectual skills involve the higher processes of the brain in analysing and making sense of things.

8.   The exercise of knowledge, understanding and skills in the pursuit of work goals depends considerably on:

- the motivational factors at work in the individual's environment
- the attitudes held by the individual.

For example, where employees are encouraged in their efforts, they will tend to apply themselves more readily to performing at a high level. Conversely, if employees feel dissatisfied with their work, they will not usually perform with the degree of skill and attention to detail required by the job. Some jobs require particular attitudes from their jobholders. For example, cardiac surgery demands patience and attention to detail; fire-fighting demands alertness and courage. The main thrust of any training needs analysis is towards identifying these elements of knowledge, understanding, skills and attitudes in the job, taking account of the context of the particular organisation, or sub-unit, concerned.

TRAINING NEEDS SURVEYS

9. A systematic survey, or analysis, of training needs will progress through a number of key stages. These are likely to be as indicated in Figure 28.2.

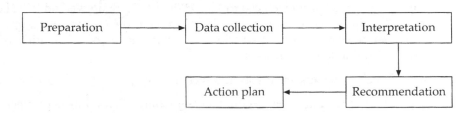

Figure 28.2 *Stages in training needs analysis*

10. The various stages are as follows:

1   Preparatory:

- determining the scope of the survey (e.g. whole organisation? single function?)
- agreeing objectives of survey (e.g. 'improve sales representatives product knowledge', 'improve managers' negotiating skills')
- agreeing time-scale, resources, etc.

2   Data collection:

- organisation-level information
- Occupational-group level
- Job-level
- Individual performance

341

3 Interpretation of data:

- nature of training needs arising
- extent of needs identified
- non-training needs (for referral to others).

4 Recommendations:

- training proposed
- resources required
- time-scale
- evaluation arrangements
- estimated costs.

5 Action plan:

- identify those responsible
- time-schedule.

11. Once the scope, objectives and timescale of the survey have been agreed, the next priority is to collect sufficient and relevant information. The two basic questions at this stage are 'What do we need to know?' and 'Where do we find it?' The answer to the first question arises from the objectives set at the preparatory stage. So, if the principal objective is concerned with improving managers' negotiating skills, then we need to know the following:

1 Which managers are involved in negotiating?

2 At what level are they negotiating, e.g. company level or departmental level?

3 What is the current level of performance of the managers concerned?

4 What standards of performance should we be aiming for?

12. The information necessary for answering the second question may be obtained partly from documentary evidence, such as job descriptions, collective agreements, and personnel manuals, partly from appraisal reports, and partly from interviews with relevant personnel. The most frequent sources of relevant data for a training needs survey are as follows:

Recorded data:

- personnel statistics
- job descriptions
- appraisal records
- Time and Method Study data
- training reports
- production records
- marketing statistics.

Interviews:

- with immediate staff
- with their managers
- with relevant specialist staff.

Questionnaires:

- to immediate staff
- to their managers.

Observation:

- by Work Study or O&M staff
- by managers of those concerned
- by trainers or other specialists.

Aptitude tests:

- for relevant work-groups
- for potential work-group members.

Group discussion:

- via Quality Circles
- via 'brainstorming' sessions
- via other work-groups.

13.   As the above list shows, recorded data form the largest single source of information for those undertaking an training needs analysis. Personnel statistics can provide valuable information about labour turnover, employee categories, absenteeism, sickness and accident rates, for example. Production records can indicate the efficiency with which individual machines are operated. Marketing figures can indicate levels of sales, customer compliants and other useful information. Job descriptions (see Chapter 12) indicate the scope of particular jobs and the standards they are intended to achieve. Work Study techniques provide information about the times and methods required to perform manual or clerical jobs efficiently. Appraisal and training reports (see Chapter 24) provide information about the performance of individual employees.

14   Most training needs surveys have to go beyond the paperwork evidence. Usually employees are asked directly for their views and perceptions either by interview or by questionnaire. Mostly people are asked about their own job and their own performance, but managers and supervisors will also be asked to comment on the performance of their team-members. Some organisations use the group discussion method for bringing out possible training needs in relation to job performance. A few use longer-range methods, such as observation by trained observers and the application of aptitude tests for particular groups of employees.

15.   The methods that can be used to support a survey of training needs are wide-ranging and involve more than just a few training specialists. As the list above

suggests, such a survey can involve production and marketing staff, line managers and personnel specialists too. Thus an analysis of training needs, unless particularly local or small-scale, is likely to have repercussions on all the major activities of the undertaking concerned.

ANALYSING AND INTERPRETING DATA

16. The analysis and interpretation of the information collected for the purpose of assessing training needs straddles two key points: firstly, the standard of performance required; secondly, the level of performance achieved by those concerned. If performance standards have not been found, perhaps because of some recent change in technology, for example, then agreement on an interim standard should be achieved. Where standards are already in force, and are still acceptable, then the analysis of results should be able to distinguish where any shortfalls are occurring and whether these can be made good by training, as opposed to some other solution, such as job redesign. Evidence that may point to a training need could include one or more of the following trends:

- high turnover among new recruits
- increase in materials wastage
- increase in number of reject items
- increase in number of customer complaints
- failure to meet job targets
- increase in accident rate
- reduced productivity
- increase in machine breakdowns.

Standards such as those referred to in Chapter 30 on competence-based training and development can provide a useful basis of evidence for assessing training needs.

17. A systematic survey and analysis of training needs will be concluded by making appropriate training proposals in the form of a plan, indicating what training is proposed, who should conduct it, when, where and at what cost.

TRAINING PLANS

18. Training plans are central to the training process, as Figure 28.3 indicates. A training plan is a systematic statement of training intentions and the means by which they are to be achieved and measured. A plan may embrace the organisation as a whole, or just a small part of it. Either way it will typically contain information under the following headings:

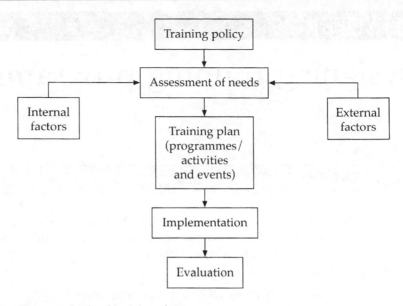

Fig. 28.3 *The central role of training plans*

- *Programme Aims* – a general statement as to what is the intention of the training. (Example: 'The aim of this programme is to improve supervisors' ability to delegate tasks systematically and to spend more time on priority items.')

- *Target Groups* – identification of those for whom the training is intended. (Example: All supervisors of Grade 4 and above employed in production.)

- *Target Numbers* – estimation of likely numbers to be involved.

- *Programme Contents* – details of the topics to be covered, the learning objectives to be achieved, the learning activities to be employed, and the learning methods proposed. (Example: see Chapter 29.)

- *Programme Evaluation* – proposals for estimating the relative success of the training in terms of both objectives achieved and impact on the organisation's activities. (Example: see Chapter 31.)

- *Administration & Costing* – details of timetable for programme, location of activities, release of staff from normal duties, expenses and costs.

- *Training Staff* – identification of staff to be deployed, both specialist trainers and line or departmental staff, as required; also of any external speakers to be employed. (Example: 'The off-the-job training sessions will be conducted by the Company training staff; on return to their normal duties, supervisors will be counselled by their immediate manager; the Company Training officer will be responsible for giving advice as necessary to the managers concerned.')

CHAPTER 29

Designing training programmes

INTRODUCTION

1. Once training needs have been ascertained, the role of the training specialist is to act as a designer of relevant programmes. The design of training is no easy task. It is important, therefore, to take account of the following issues if training is to be both relevant and effective:

   1 What are we trying to achieve in this programme?

   2 What do we expect participants to achieve?

   3 What content is required to achieve these aims?

   4 How should this content be structured?

   5 What learning methods should we employ?

   6 Who should conduct the training?

   7 Where and when should the training take place?

   8 To what extent should participants be consulted about the nature and scope of the programme?

   9 How should we evaluate the success of the programme?

2. With the exception of the last point – evaluation – all these issues will be discussed in this chapter. Evaluation is a topic of sufficient importance to warrant a separate chapter (Chapter 31).

AIMS AND OBJECTIVES IN TRAINING

3. As in many other human activities, it is useful for planners of training to remind themselves of the reason for their planning. Setting clear goals enables planners to structure their activities with relevance and establish a basis for evaluating their efforts. There are several ways of approaching this task, each with its own set of assumptions. Firstly, let us consider what different meanings can be ascribed to the words 'aim', 'goal and 'objectives':

   1 *Goals/Aims* – for the purposes of this chapter, goals and aims will be considered to have the same meaning, that is 'broad statements of purpose or intention on the part of the provider'.

Example: Sales Training in Drugs Company

The aims of this programme are –

- to improve sales' staff product-knowledge

- to improve understanding of Company policy in respect of ethical products

- to inform sales' staff of recent changes in home markets

- to increase confidence in dealing with medical/specialist clients.

Such broad statements help to define the scope of the training.

2   *Objectives* – these are 'statements of specific and intended outcomes of a training activity'. Such outcomes may be expressed in terms of learner-behaviour or in some other way. Objectives develop goals or aims by adding a more precise or measurable element. Effectively an objective states 'we intend to achieve goal 'x' to the extent that, at the end of the activity, such-and-such change will have taken place'.

4.   The place of objectives in training can be seen from Figure 29.1, which looks at the

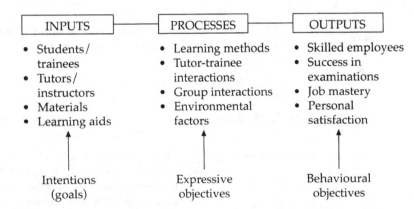

Figure 29.1   *Objectives in learning*

learning process from a systems perspective.

As we shall see below, most course objectives focus on terminal behaviour, i.e. on outputs. Some objectives, especially in the areas of feelings and values focus on processes. These are what have been described by one writer as 'expressive' objectives (see para 15 below). Some objectives focus on inputs, especially those which express intentions of providers more than anything else.

5.   Statements of training aims or goals have aroused little controversy. Statements of objectives, however, have been the centre of heated arguments among theorists and practitioners alike. The basic issue in the argument has been the extent to which it is either practicable, or desirable, to express objectives in precise behavioural terms. The discussion commenced some fifty years ago when Tyler (1949)[1], an American educationalist, in a work on the school curriculum, argued strongly for clear, measurable objectives. Tyler's view was as follows:

347

> ... (a person) can define an objective with sufficient clarity if he can describe or
> illustrate the kind of behaviour the student is expected to acquire so that one could
> recognise such behaviour if he saw it.

This statement is regarded as the classic definition of a 'behavioural objective'. It reflects much of the reasoning behind many modern statements of learning objectives, especially in the training sphere, and in the construction of performance criteria in competence-based standards (see Chapter 30).

BLOOM'S TAXONOMY

6.   Tyler's ideas were taken a stage further by Bloom and colleagues (1956)[2], in a text that has become the standard work for the disciples of behavioural objectives. The taxonomy, or categorisation, of educational objectives devised by Bloom and his associates highlights a number of key areas of learning, commencing with the 'cognitive domain', i.e. the thinking processes. In this area of learning, the different levels of attainment which can be expected can be divided into a number of categories, as indicated by Figure 29.2 below, which lists some examples from the taxonomy.

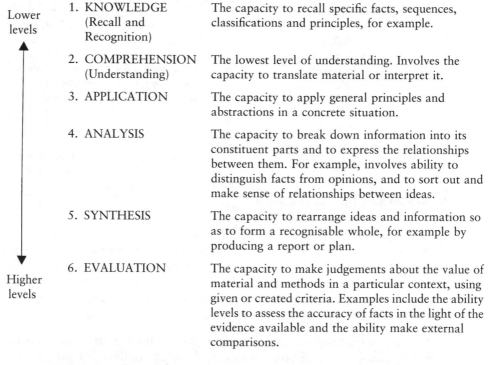

Lower levels	1. KNOWLEDGE (Recall and Recognition)	The capacity to recall specific facts, sequences, classifications and principles, for example.
	2. COMPREHENSION (Understanding)	The lowest level of understanding. Involves the capacity to translate material or interpret it.
	3. APPLICATION	The capacity to apply general principles and abstractions in a concrete situation.
	4. ANALYSIS	The capacity to break down information into its constituent parts and to express the relationships between them. For example, involves ability to distinguish facts from opinions, and to sort out and make sense of relationships between ideas.
	5. SYNTHESIS	The capacity to rearrange ideas and information so as to form a recognisable whole, for example by producing a report or plan.
Higher levels	6. EVALUATION	The capacity to make judgements about the value of material and methods in a particular context, using given or created criteria. Examples include the ability levels to assess the accuracy of facts in the light of the evidence available and the ability make external comparisons.

Figure 29.2 *Levels of thinking (Bloom's taxonomy)*

7.   The value of the above list lies in its provision of a basis for (a) the evaluation of learning activities, and (b) the setting of learning objectives, through its presentation of different cognitive, or thinking, levels. Thus, it is possible to

evaluate test papers using the list to ascertain the thinking levels required by the test and to compare those with the objectives of the test in the first place.

8. The influence of Bloom and colleagues is evident in many statements of learning objectives. The Institute of Personnel Management, for example, in its list of objectives for the Employee development section of its professional examination syllabus includes the following examples:

    At the end of the programme ... the student should be able to:

    a) comprehend the constraints and opportunities presented by the national educational and training environment and how these have developed and apply this comprehension in relation to the selection of appropriate resources to assist employee development ...

    f) design and evaluate programmes of training and development and comprehend the factors which influence these ...

9. In order to assist trainers to devise appropriate objectives, a number of lists of suitable verbs have been prepared. These lists tend to adopt the Bloom approach. Hence typical verbs to be found on such lists are:

comprehend	recognise	state
apply	interpret	analyse
rearrange	propose	describe
evaluate	distinguish	

    If applying such verbs to training objectives it is important not to lose sight of the context of the learning. Objectives which are set in isolation from other aspects of a training programme may well turn out to be meaningless in practice. For example, to set an objective requiring a group of trainees to apply a newly-acquired skill in the workplace, but then to deny them the opportunity to do so, would be a pointless exercise.

PRESCRIPTIVE OBJECTIVES

10. The production of learning objectives can be made even more precise and prescriptive, if the following additional 'rules' are applied:

    1   only observable behaviour is specified (NB. A typical Skinner approach [Chapter 25])

    2   standards of performance are stated

    3   conditions of performance are stated.

    These 'rules' were originated by Mager (1962)[3] in an influential work on instructional objectives. Following these 'rules' means that verbs such as 'comprehend', and 'evaluate' may not be used because it is not possible to observe their processes. Instead the use of 'state', 'propose', 'apply' and other observable forms of behaviour are permissible. Another consequence is that objectives have to be written up with closely-defined standards of performance and conditions of performance. An example of a Mager-type objective would be as follows:

> At the end of a training course of 30 hours' duration, 90 per cent of the participants will be able to undertake the complete range of assembly tasks with an accuracy of 90 per cent in a time equal to 100 BSI as applied in the full production areas.

11. Clearly, it is easier to write up specific, observable objectives for tasks that involve *doing* things rather than employing thinking or judgmental skills. It is also easier to find ways of describing *simple* rather than *complex* forms of behaviour. Thus, a training consultancy's public brochure can describe an objective for a basic report writing course as follows:

> At the end of the two-day course delegates will be able to:
>
> 1. Structure a simple report in a logical sequence.

The emphasis here is on doing and the task is relatively straightforward. By comparison, in the same brochure, an objective for a three-day course on assertiveness in management is stated as follows:

> At the end of the course delegates will be able to:
>
> ... 2. Highlight a range of options that exist in most interpersonal situations, and choose a response that reflects their own, and other people's rights and responsibilities.

This is an altogether more complicated task, and one which is extremely difficult to describe in behavioural terms, precisely because it is concerned with the subtleties of interpersonal behaviour! It would be difficult enough just to observe an individual's response in such a situation. To assess the extent to which the individual selects an appropriate form of response in the conditions described is well-nigh impossible except at a rather introductory and superficial level. This is not to say that the learning experience is invalid, but only that it is not always possible to set meaningful objectives for it.

EXPLORATORY OBJECTIVES

12. Sometimes objectives are set out in terms of aspirations rather than expectations, that is to say they express the hope that, at the end of a learning activity, certain changes will have taken place in the participants. This approach to objectives is suitable for situations in which participants are invited to share in the exploration of an idea or experience, which may lead to the development of fresh insights for the participants. An interesting analysis of objectives set in situations where less observable behaviour may be involved has been carried out by Krathwohl (1964)[4] and colleagues.

KRATHWOHL'S TAXONOMY

13. Krathwohl and colleagues have developed a taxonomy of objectives in the 'affective domain' of learning, i.e. in the emotional and attitudinal aspects of

learning. Following the course set earlier by Bloom, Krathwohl has produced a listing of different levels of attitude, interest and values in responses to learning. The list is shown in Figure 29.3.

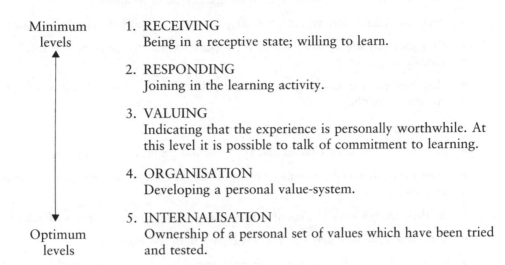

Minimum levels

1. RECEIVING
Being in a receptive state; willing to learn.

2. RESPONDING
Joining in the learning activity.

3. VALUING
Indicating that the experience is personally worthwhile. At this level it is possible to talk of commitment to learning.

4. ORGANISATION
Developing a personal value-system.

5. INTERNALISATION
Ownership of a personal set of values which have been tried and tested.

Optimum levels

Figure 29.3 *Differing levels of attitudinal responses in learning (adapted from Krathwohl, 1964)*

14. The dominant feature of the above listing is its generality. Objectives in this area can only be stated in very broad terms. Little work has so far been done to improve and extend Krathwohl's taxonomy, but until a clearer categorisation exists it will prove difficult to write anything other than general objectives for aspects of learning involving attitudes, interests and values.

15. Eisner (1969)[5], expressing his concern about the use of objectives, sought to distinguish between objectives relating to pre-specified behaviour, in the Tyler tradition, and objectives relating to creative, emergent behaviour, which could not be pre-specified. For the former, he suggested the term 'instructional objective', and for the latter he suggested the term 'expressive objective'. An expressive objective does not specify terminal behaviour, but rather describes a learning encounter. Eisner saw such an objective as allowing both teacher and taught the opportunity to explore and focus on issues of interest to them. This kind of objective can usefully be employed in training situations of an experiential nature, in which the participants are exposed to, and become aware of, particular kinds of interpersonal relationships. A typical objective in these circumstances would be:

> Participants will experience simulated negotiations of an industrial relations nature, and will have the opportunity to explore some of the key issues involved in complex negotiations in a generally combative situation.

16. To sum up, so long as course objectives are not seen as ends in themselves, but rather as guides to practice, or as yardsticks of performance, then their use can be considered profitable. In general, the main advantages and disadvantages of objectives can be summarised as follows:

Advantages

- they clarify the intentions of the providers of the training
- they map out the scope of a learning activity or programme
- they focus attention, where necessary, on the terminal behaviour of trainees
- they can provide a useful yardstick against which to measure the results of training
- they can assist in defining the accountabilities of trainers and learners for the results of training.

Disadvantages

- they tend to be prescriptive, and thus overlook unintended outcomes
- they may introduce an element of rigidity into the management of a learning activity
- as they are not easy to describe, they may focus on trivial aspects of learning
- they stress the provider's intentions rather than the learners'
- by focusing on objectives as ends in themselves, trainers may well ignore the significance of events which occur during the process of a learning activity or programme.

CONTENT AND SEQUENCE IN COURSE DESIGN

17. If objectives help people to define what they wish to achieve by means of a learning activity, they can also help course designers to decide what should make up the content of an activity. The content in this situation means not only the information to be passed on, but also the methods by which it is to be transmitted. Let us first consider the information required, i.e. the substantive content.

18. In deciding what is required in terms of substantive content, trainers will need to ask a number of important questions.

    1 What essential facts, ideas, principles and procedures are needed for the job concerned?

    2 What necessary trainee knowledge, skills or attitudes are implied in the objectives or goals set for this learning activity?

    3 How useful to the trainees (and to the organisation) will this information be?

    4 What would be an appropriate level of content, given the nature of the learners?

    5 How transferable or durable are the knowledge, skills or attitudes we propose to include?

    6 How feasible is the content in the light of the time and resources available?

19. An example of a situation which might face a *clerical* trainer is given as follows:

> In order to move the customer ordering system from a manual to a computerised system, we shall require clerical staff to:
>
> 1) become familiar with the new documentation to be raised
>
> 2) become familiar with a revised procedure for dealing with customer orders
>
> 3) become skilled enough to enter basic information onto a computer via a standard keyboard
>
> 4) become capable of generating hard copies of customer orders via a computer and printer
>
> 5) maintain a high standard of accuracy in entering and recovering data from a computer.

Staff will therefore be required to know the new procedure and its documentation; they will need to develop new skills in keyboard working; they will need to be skilled in generating and/or changing information displayed on a visual display unit; they will need to know how to produce hard copy from a printer; and they will need to 'unlearn' their old ways and become enthusiastic for the new system.'

20. Thus there are knowledge elements, skill elements and attitudinal elements to be included in the training programme. Many existing staff will be highly motivated to learn new skills, especially in relation to the new technology. Others may find the new system unacceptable emotionally and/or technically. Therefore some selection of trainees will need to be made, if the training is to achieve its objectives. In order to allow sufficient time for the selected trainees to acquire the intended levels of knowledge, skills and attitudes, a period of several weeks will probably be required to enable individuals to practise mastery of the new system.

21. Once the relevant boundaries of a training programme have been agreed, the next problem is to decide the sequence of events. What should come first? What should be left until the end? Should general principles be introduced at the outset? Clearly, much will depend on the abilities and needs of the learners, as well as on the skills and knowledge of those responsible for the training. The most likely alternatives available to the trainer are as shown in Figure 29.4.

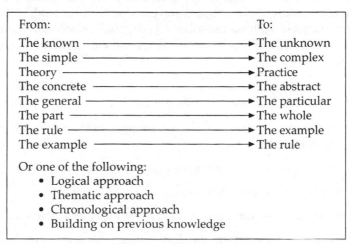

Figure 29.4 *Major alternatives in sequencing training activities*

22. The least risky approach for a trainer would be to work logically (i.e. step-by-step) from the known to the unknown, from the concrete to the abstract and from the simple to the complex, building on previous knowledge wherever possible. Most instructional techniques rely on this kind of approach, and especially programmed learning (see below). The most risky approach would involve moving from the unknown into the known, using examples to illuminate rules and utilising themes rather than logic. Experiential techniques tend to incorporate this less predictable approach. Having briefly considered content and sequence in training, we can now turn to the methods by which ideas and skills are to be transmitted.

TRAINING METHODS

23. When we talk about training methods we are essentially discussing the means by which we intend to communicate information, ideas, skills, attitudes and feelings to learners. Thus methods are a crucial element in the trainer's success. It is common to find methods categorised according to whether they are employed in on-the-job or in off-the-job situations. However, this approach does not make it easy to distinguish the appropriateness of methods for communicating knowledge, rather than developing skills or attitudes, for example. The location, and hence the context, of training is, of course, important and we shall return to it shortly. However, in the meantime we shall look at training methods in terms of their relevance to particular groups of learning objectives, firstly, those groups concerned with extending knowledge and understanding (i.e. objectives in the cognitive domain).

24. For the purposes of passing on knowledge, in the sense of factual information, then lectures or talks, given off-the-job and supported as necessary by handouts will usually be satisfactory. Essentially the object is to enable the learners to recall facts they have been given. Taking things a stage further from factual recall to demonstrating understanding of new knowledge, then lecturing on its own will be insufficient. Some opportunity for questioning and discussion will be necessary, for example by means of discussion group exercises or case-studies. This opportunity is usually available with on-the-job methods, such as job instruction and coaching, where close collaboration between trainer and learner is an essential feature of the method.

25. A list of methods applicable to the development of knowledge and understanding in a work context are shown in Figure 29.5.

26. In an off-the-job location, such as a training centre or educational institution, the emphasis in learning is usually on:

- developing an understanding of general principles

- providing background knowledge

- generating an awareness of comparative ideas and practices.

In an on-the-job location, the emphasis is more on the acquisition of specific, local knowledge in a 'real' situation.

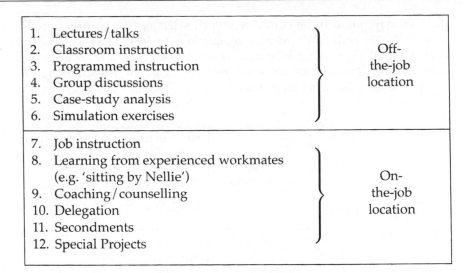

1. Lectures/talks 2. Classroom instruction 3. Programmed instruction 4. Group discussions 5. Case-study analysis 6. Simulation exercises	Off- the-job location
7. Job instruction 8. Learning from experienced workmates (e.g. 'sitting by Nellie') 9. Coaching/counselling 10. Delegation 11. Secondments 12. Special Projects	On- the-job location

Figure 29.5 *Learning methods: knowledge/understanding*

27.   Whilst some of the above methods in Figure 29.5 will be familiar to every reader, there may be others which are less widely known. Some brief explanations of less-familiar methods are provided below:

- *Programmed instruction* – Bigge (1982)[6] describes this as: ' ... a system of teaching and learning within which pre-established subject-matter is broken down into small, discrete steps and carefully organised into a logical sequence in which it can be learned readily by the students. Each step builds upon the previous one.' This is the system introduced by B.F. Skinner (see Chapter 25).

- *Case-study analysis* – in this method an account of a real, or fictional, situation is given, and students are asked to suggest answers to a number of practical and theoretical issues raised by the account. The method is useful for giving participants an opportunity to experience problem-solving in a relevant context.

- *Simulation exercises* – these include interactive exercises in which trainees practise their skills in mock situations based on real work-related situations (e.g. involving interviews/discussion skills, use of information technology, etc.).

- *Job instruction* – this is a method employed in manual and some clerical jobs, by which trainees systematically acquire routine instruction in key processes from a qualified instructor.

- *Coaching* – this refers to a form of management training in which 'a manager, through direct discussion and guided activity, helps a colleague to learn to solve a problem, or to do a task better ...' (Megginson & Boydell, 1979)[7]. This approach is sometimes referred to as 'mentoring', especially where the more experienced manager is not the individual's line manager.

- *Secondments* – these are special arrangements allowing an individual to work for another department or organisation on either his/her speciality or in some new role, with the object of extending the experience of the former to the benefit of the host department or organisation.

28. An important point to be considered when selecting one or other of the above-mentioned methods is the degree of freedom to learn allowed to the trainees concerned. As Figure 29.6 indicates, some methods permit trainees to utilise their own resources and learning styles, whereas others permit no such discretion, a tight control being retained by the trainer.

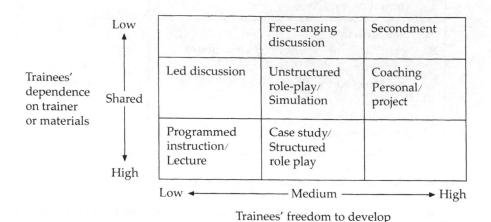

Figure 29.6 *Freedom and Control in Learning*

Lectures and programmed instruction, for example, enable trainers to maintain tight control over learning, but restrict the trainees' freedom to develop their own approaches. By comparison, case-studies and coaching represents a compromise situation, while secondment represents a real opportunity for trying out new approaches.

TRAINING FOR SKILLS

29. When we consider methods used to aid the acquisition of skill, there are two important questions to be asked. Firstly, what is meant by the term 'skill', and secondly, is it reasonable to divide skills into primary and secondary categories? In the present context, 'skill' refers to *the capacity to apply knowledge in a practical, demonstrable way*. Skill is essentially a product of two main factors:

- the individual's store of knowledge

- the individual's personal attributes (inherent aptitudes, maturity, motivation, etc.).

Repetition, i.e. practice, tends to improve skill-acquisition.

30. It is possible to distinguish two main categories of skill:

- broadly based, transferable skills, such as problem-solving and communication skills

- specific, non-transferable skills, such as skill in operating a particular procedure.

The first category can be regarded as primary skills, which form the basis of any skill development. By learning how to learn, so to speak, individuals can then go on to acquire specific, task-related skills, which form the second category. In general, where skills development takes place off-the-job the focus is on the broad, transferable skills. On-the-job skills development focuses primarily on specific, task-related skills.

31. Common methods for developing skills include:

Manual skills:

- job instruction
- 'sitting by Nellie'
- off-the-job instruction.

Thinking skills:

- case-study exercises
- problem-solving exercises
- setting written questions
- project-work.

Communication and social skills:

- effective speaking courses
- report-writing courses
- role-play exercises
- discussion groups
- leadership exercises.

32. In the above list, project work refers to a practical work-related problem or issue, which an individual is asked to investigate, assess and report on, with recommendations. Project work is an effective way of relating theoretical learning to actual practice. Role-play exercises are interpersonal exercises in which individuals act out a role, which may be relatively loosely-bounded or may be tightly scripted. Role-playing is used widely to develop negotiating skills, for example. In these exercises individuals can experience many of the tactical skills and emotional features of a typical negotiation. Leadership exercises can range from situations where no leader is appointed and the group is left to decide how to provide a leadership function, to situations where one individual is assigned to lead and is given a practical task for his group. In developing social and communication skills, the opportunity to discuss performance with those in the group as well as with tutors is a crucial factor in enabling people to assess their personal level of behaviour and to consider what they may need to adapt in order to improve their performance.

33. Whereas a substantial amount of job knowledge can be gained by doing the job in the work context, skills development usually benefits from a period *away* from the normal job pressures, especially in the early stages of learning. Thus, organisations provide a range of resources off-the-job in order to permit skills to be practised in a relatively safe environment, where mistakes will neither prove humiliating for the individual nor costly to the organisation. The links that need to be established between theory and practice, between *'knowing about'* and *'knowing how'* are better developed, initially, away from the job. Once a level of proficiency has been achieved, then practice in the working environment is preferable, for it is that kind of experience which leads to seasoned performance.

34. Another important reason why organisations prefer to tackle skills development off-the-job is to resist some of the effects of the informal organisation at work, i.e. those powerful attitudinal forces at work in the job-context (e.g. 'custom and practice'). Thus, a shop-floor instructor will be influenced by the work attitudes prevalent in his or her particular situation, and this could lead to safety or quality being compromised. Similarly, a manager coaching a subordinate will be implying that his or her approach to the job is the most appropriate. In view of these on-the-job influences, it is not surprising that it is difficult to attain neatly-written learning objectives for such training, compared with off-the-job training. Clearly, the trainers in these circumstances have less control over the process of training, and, so far as results are concerned, the influence of the work group tends to produce a number of unintended outcomes (e.g. learning how to 'cut corners', etc.).

THE RESPONSIBILITY FOR TRAINING

35. Ultimately, the responsibility for training must lie with the senior management of the organisation. Having said that, however, training, in practice, is the direct responsibility of the following people:

1   personnel managers

2   training managers

3   training officers

4   instructors

5   line managers

6   supervisors.

The nature and extent of the involvement of each of the above groups depends on the policy and culture of the organisation concerned. In some instances the personnel manager heads up the training function, whereas in others there is a training manager who fulfils that role. In some organisations training, is centralised with an emphasis on training by qualified trainers; in others, training is decentralised and therefore line managers and supervisors are expected to play the dominant role in training and developing staff. There is no one best way of organising training. What is important is that those who are carrying out the training are themselves prepared for, and committed to, achieving their task.

THE LOCATION OF TRAINING

36. The principal options open to organisations are these:

   - external, off-the-job: at a college, university, or private training agency

   - external, on-the-job: by means of secondment or special project

   - in-company/in-service off-the-job: using the organisation's own training facilities

   - in-company/in-service on-the-job: guided experience in the workplace.

37. The relative advantages and disadvantages of these options can be summarised as shown in Figure 29.7.

Option Chosen	Advantages	Disadvantages
College or University courses	General principles covered; thinking skills developed; leads to qualification	Insufficient practical work; length of the training
Private training agency	Meets special needs in professional way; fills gaps in the organisation's own resources	May have to accept an off-the-shelf package; may be costly
Secondment Special projects	Authentic setting; widens experience Provides useful way of practising problem-solving skills	Employee may not succeed Finding staff to act as mentors
Own facilities	Own standards/customs can be promoted; may be more cost-effective than external provision	Perspective may become too parochial; own staff may lack credibility
Guided experience	Authentic setting; linked firmly to own practices and job requirements	Subject to all the pressures and distractions of the workplace

Figure 29.7 *Training locations – advantages and disadvantages*

38. The final question for this chapter is 'to what extent should trainees be consulted about their training and development?' The answer to this question will undoubtedly vary from one organisation to another, depending mainly on its culture or management style. Organisations adopting an open participative style of management will consult trainees as a matter of course. Organisations with authoritarian or paternalistic styles will tend not to consult trainees. Authoritarian

managements consider that what they are doing is right, whilst paternalistic managements consider that they know what is best for their employees. Trainers, depending on how they see their role, will either conform to the dominant culture of their organisation, or may develop their own sub-culture. Either way, they will have a number of methods to choose from, which as Figure 29.6 above shows, will enable them to permit more, or less, freedom of choice to their trainees.

39.   On balance, it is advisable for those responsible for training to initiate their programmes in the way they think best, and to be prepared to adapt them in the light of trainees' comments and suggestions, as well as of their performance.

REFERENCES

1.   Tyler, R. (1949), *Basic Principles of Curriculum and Instruction*, University of Chicago Press.

2.   Bloom, B.S. *et al.* (1956), *Taxonomy of Educational Objectives. I. The Cognitive Domain*, Longmans.

3.   Mager, R. (1962), *Preparing Instructional Objectives*, Fearon.

4.   Krathwohl, D.R. *et al.* (1964), *Taxonomy of Educational Objectives II. The Affective Domain*, Longmans.

5.   Eisner, E.W. (1969), 'Instructional and Expressive Objectives: their Formulation and Use in Curriculum', in Popham *et al.* (eds), *Instructional Objectives*. AERA Monograph, Rand McNally.

6.   Bigge, M.L. (1982), *Learning Theories for Teachers* (4th edn), Harper & Row.

7.   Megginson, D. & Boydell, T. (1979), *A Manager's Guide to Coaching*, BACIE.

CHAPTER 30

Competence-based training and development

INTRODUCTION

1. In an earlier chapter (Chapter 27, paragraphs 3–6), reference was made to the major focus of Education, Training and Development respectively. If we consider each of these over-lapping aspects of learning in terms of the *outcomes* we are hoping for, we can see that these are all concerned with *behaviour* of some kind. So, for example, pupils in a primary school will be expected to undertake practical writing tasks and do basic addition and subtractions in order to demonstrate that they have learned what their teachers have tried to communicate to them. Later on in school life, and in their experience in further and higher education, students will also be asked to demonstrate what they can do, although at these stages they are more likely to be asked what they *know and understand*. Once they become employees they will be asked to demonstrate especially what they can do, but also to show what they know. In all the above situations those concerned will also be expected to demonstrate certain *general behaviour or attitudes*, e.g. respect for others, attention to tasks, interest in the work, loyalty to the group and so on.

2. When pupils, students and employees are assessed in order to measure their learning, this is often done by testing how much they *know* about a topic or a skill. This is certainly of fundamental importance for assessment, because it is knowledge (in the sense of knowledge about and knowing how to) that provides the foundation for any demonstration of an ability to do something. However, it is also important to test this ability to carry out a task, process or function i.e. to test individual competence. There are arguments about the definition of the word 'competence', but for our purposes we will take it to mean '*the ability to demonstrate to another that you can perform a task, process or function to a satisfactory standard*'. Competence in this sense implies not just that a person can do something, but that they can do it to some pre-determined standard of performance.

3. The difference between *knowing about* and *doing* is recognised in the training of ophthalmic opticians. For example, a student can obtain a BSc degree in Optometry by passing all the necessary examinations some of which are tests of knowledge and understanding and others of practical skills, and yet not be permitted to proceed for professional training as an optometrist because the level of skill shown was not good enough. The student in this situation is not considered as 'competent' in terms of the standards required by the examiners who

recommend who is to go forward to train as an ophthalmic optician.

4.   It was to address this issue of how to deal with the emphasis on testing knowledge rather than ability to perform, especially in vocational education and training, that the UK Government initiated a review in the mid-1980s to investigate the system of vocational qualifications in Britain. The results of the review confirmed the emphasis on the testing of knowledge throughout various trades and professions, and pointed to the excessive number of vocational qualifications and awarding bodies. The outcome of the review was that in 1986 the Government set up a National Council for Vocational Qualifications (NCVQ) to develop a national framework of vocational qualifications. In 1997 the NCVQ merged with its schools' equivalent to form the QCA – Qualifications and Curriculum Authority. The corresponding body in Scotland is the SQA (Scottish Qualifications Authority).

NATIONAL VOCATIONAL QUALIFICATIONS

5.   In addition to increasing and improving vocational education and training, the NCVQs framework of national vocational qualifications would specifically promote a number of key objectives. These were to include:

 • the provision of a coherent structure for vocational training

 • the development of employment-led standards of competence

 • the provision of a system for recognising achievement, including prior achievement

 • the improvement of access to vocational qualifications consistent with the maintenance of standards

 • the rationalisation and simplification of the structure and provision of vocational qualifications

 • the provision of vocational qualifications which are capable of being independent of the mode, duration and location of the learning.

6.   The QCA/SQA does not itself award certificates but approves appropriate 'awarding bodies' who have to (a) demonstrate that they have a recognised standing in their relevant profession or occupational group, (b) agree to work within the QCA framework of qualifications in producing employment-led standards, and (c) seek accreditation for each qualification it seeks to offer as an NVQ (National Vocational Qualification). Several well-known awarding bodies have already had qualifications approved by the QCA/SQA, e.g. BTEC, City & Guilds of London Institute, and the Institute of Industrial Managers (now part of the Institute of Management).

7.   Five levels of NVQ (SVQ in Scotland) have been established, and each denotes a progressively more difficult and/or complex range of competences as follows:

 • Level 1 – Basic Level Includes the ability to perform a minimum number of work activities within realistic time constraints, *to specified standards* and in a restricted range of work conditions.

- Level 2 – Standard Level Ability to perform primarily routine and predictable responsibilities, but where some activities are more demanding; some degree of transfer of competences between contexts is expected; performance judged against specified standards.

- Level 3 – Advanced Level Competence against specified criteria in occupations which are not routine in character; ability to perform a broad range of work activities, including many that are complex, difficult and non-routine.

- Level 4 – Higher Level Ability to perform a comprehensive range of complex, difficult and often specialised activities against specified standards

- Level 5 – Professional Ability to perform a comprehensive range of activities of a largely autonomous nature in which personal judgement and responsibility are critical; suitable standards of performance have to be developed

The above Levels are intended by the QCA/SQA to be indicative rather than prescriptive.

8. Most S/NVQs that have been awarded have been at Levels 1 to 3. Several awards have been made at Level 4 (roughly comparable to a graduate level qualification), and a few at Level 5 (postgraduate level).

9. The principal criteria for an award are as follows:

- it must be based on national standards

- it must be outcomes-based

- it must be awarded on the basis of valid and reliable forms of assessment

- it must allow open access to all who are capable of achieving the required standards by whatever means

- it must be free from covert or covert discriminatory practices.

10. The requirement that awards should be made on the basis of national standards led to a number of industry groups forming their own 'Lead Body' to draw up acceptable standards for the industry. Some Lead Bodies represented fairly homogeneous groups such as the Publishing Qualifications Board, others represented widely varying groups such as the Construction Industry Lead Body, which includes architects, surveyors, civil engineers and building/structural engineers. A few bodies represent management functions rather than industries (e.g. Training & Development Lead Body). The Lead Bodies spent considerable time deciding on the outcomes that are important for employment-led standards, and in the case of the higher levels often struggled to define suitable outcomes. Assessment methods were determined jointly between employers and providers of further and higher education. Since assessment has to focus on competence, the methods selected had to be applied in the workplace (in both on- and off-the-job locations) as well as in education and training centres. The standards setting bodies are mostly employer-led, and are known as National Training Organisations.

11. According to the QCA a 'standard' comprises a coherent set of statements of competence set out as shown in Figure 30.1.

Title
Units of Competence
[The main sub-division of an NVQ, consisting of a coherent group of elements, which can be assessed and certificated in their own right.]

Elements of Competence
[The sub-divisions of a unit, reflecting the things a person should be able to do at work, and be capable of demonstration and assessment.]

Performance Criteria
[Evaluative statements defining acceptable performance, which must accompany each element and be expressed in terms of outcome.]

Range Statement
[A statement of the various circumstances in which each competence is applied must accompany each element.]

NB. QCA also recommends that guidelines should be included as to the kind of evidence to be looked for in support of the performance criteria.

Figure 30.1 *Format of NVQ Statement of Competence*

12. Standards have been developed by a process which has come to be called 'Functional Analysis', which is a top-down approach to job analysis, carried out by practitioners and their advisers, with a view to identifying what people need to be able to do in order to be considered competent in the workplace. Functional Analysis aims to identify the key purpose of a job, the key roles that are needed to support that purpose, and then breaks them down into various job functions, which are described in greater detail at unit and element level. Extracts from two differing sets of standards (Management II and Book Publishing) are given below to indicate how standards have been described to date.

MANAGEMENT STANDARDS – AN EXAMPLE

13. In the standards for Management (MII) developed by the Management Charter Initiative and first published in September 1991, the key purpose of management at Middle Management level was given as:

> To achieve the organisation's objectives and continuously improve its performance.

The key roles (ten in all), together with their associated Units, were stated as follows:

Manage Operations–

Unit 1. Initiate and implement change an improvement in services, products and systems.

Unit 2. Monitor, maintain and improve service and product delivery.

Manage Finance–

Unit 3. Monitor and control the use of resources.

Unit 4. Secure effective resource allocation for activities and projects.

Manage People–

Unit 5. Recruit and select personnel.

Unit 6. Develop teams, individuals and self to enhance performance.

Unit 7. Plan, allocate and evaluate work carried out by teams, individuals and self.

Unit 8. Create, maintain and enhance effective working relationships.

Manage Information–

Unit 9. Seek, evaluate and organise information for action.

Unit 10. Exchange information to solve problems and make decisions.'

14. Each Unit of management was broken down into two or more separate Elements which gave the essence of what managers are expected to be competent in at this middle-management level. Some examples of these Elements are given below:

Unit 2. Monitor, maintain and improve service and product delivery

Elements–

2.1 Establish and maintain the supply of resources into the organisation/ department

2.2 Establish and agree customer requirements

2.3 Maintain and improve operations against quality and functional specifications

2.4 Create and maintain the necessary conditions for productive work ... etc.

Unit 5. Recruit and select personnel

Elements–

5.1 Define future personnel requirements

5.2 Determine specifications to secure quality people

5.3 Assess and select candidates against team and organisational requirements ... etc.

15. Examples of Performance Criteria applied to some of the above Elements include:

Element 2.2. Establish and agree customer requirements

Performance Criteria–

a) The benefits and features of services and products are explained in a manner, and at a level and pace, appropriate to the customer ... etc.

c) Communications with customers are conducted in a manner which promotes trust and goodwill ... etc.

f) Specifications agreed contain all the relevant and essential information to allow operations to meet customer requirements ... etc.

Range Indicators – specifications include quality, price, etc., and conform to legal requirements ... etc.

Element 5.2 Determine specifications to secure quality people

Performance Criteria–

a) Specifications identify job title, responsibilities, key objectives, competences and other details specific to the organisation ... etc.

d) Specifications are written and are clear, concise and comply with legal requirements

e) Final specifications are checked and agreed with appropriate people prior to recruitment action.

Range Indicators – Views and requirements taken into account include Personnel specialists; information in specifications derived from personnel forecasts, departmental plans, etc.; legal requirements, e.g. Sex Discrimination Acts met.

PUBLISHING STANDARDS – AN EXAMPLE

16. The Publishing industry example is the NVQ in Book Publishing Commissioning, as developed by the Publishing Qualifications Board, and accredited at Level 4 by NCVQ in November 1991 (figure 30.2).

Title: Book Publishing Commissioning

Units	Elements of Competence	
1. Identify and assess publishing market	1.1	Identify and assess current and future market trends
	1.2	Plan and use market research techniques
	1.3	Quantify distinct market opportunities
2. Contribute to a publishing programme	2.1	Introduce projects into the publishing programme
	2.2	Maximise financial viability of proposed projects
	2.3	Manage backlist
3. Identify, acquire and develop publishing projects	3.1	Research and commission individual projects
	3.2	Evaluate publishing proposals
	3.3	Present publishing proposals to company for acceptance
	3.4	Commission and co-ordinate production contributions to publishing project
4. Support and develop authors	4.1	Identify appropriate authors
	4.2	Negotiate terms and contracts with authors or agents
	4.3	Liaise with author during project development

	4.4	Maintain post-publication liaison with author
	4.5	Provide creative support to author
5. Process project	5.1	Vet projects for content requiring legal checks
	5.2	Ensure structural editing and copy-editing of projects
	5.3	Monitor design and production of publication
6. Market publications	6.1	Contribute to the marketing and sales of publications
	6.2	Liaise over co-editions of publications

Figure 30.2 *NVQ in Book Publishing Commissioning*

17.　One or two examples of performance criteria, by way of comparison with the MCI standards, are now given from the Book Commissioning NVQ:

Unit 4. Support and develop authors

Element 4.1. Identify appropriate authors

Performance Criteria–

4.1.1　Author networks are established and maintained sufficient to ensure the required supply of projects

4.1.2　Existing authors are matched with projects and encouraged to develop new projects

4.1.3　Contact with existing authors is maintained to ensure sustained and productive author-editor relations.

Range Statement – Author networks to include new and existing authors; projects to include single and series projects

Element 5.3. Monitor design and production of publication

Performance criteria–

5.3.1　Project is handed over for design/production with all necessary information and material

5.3.2　Design and production brieds are clear and comprehensive

5.3.3　Design contributions are monitored for fidelity to original specification, and all deviations promptly reviewed ... etc.

Range statement – Design and production information to include completed final text, title, ISBN, projected price; extent and number of words, format instructions, production schedule and degree of priority, and projected publication date ... etc.

CONCLUSION

18.　Perhaps the biggest single achievement of the competence-based approach to improving vocational education and training may turn out to be the development of a consensus in industry (or industry sectors) as to what constitutes the work of that industry, when looking at it from the perspective of individual jobs. In other words, the creation of a nationwide form of job analysis (i.e. Functional Analysis) may lead to broad agreement as to the basic content of all the typical jobs in any one industry/sector. The resulting occupational standards should lead to benefits for both organisations and individual employees. Firms could benefit from:

- better qualified workforce with industry-relevant skills

- improved quality standards

- ready-made performance assessment system

- basis for staff career development and training

- improved staff motivation due to better training and opportunity to gain qualification from doing their own work effectively.

Individuals could benefit from:

- knowing what standards they have to achieve to become competent

- learning to do their jobs better

- gaining an nationally-recognised qualification (S/NVQ)

- knowing that they can achieve further S/NVQs whilst at work and thus enhance their career prospects.

19. There are nevertheless several problems with a competence-based approach. Due to the breaking down of job functions in the Functional Analysis process, there is a danger, particularly in higher level jobs, that insufficiently flexible, or even inappropriate, standards may be allocated to such jobs. In that situation it is likely that the sum of all the parts will always add up to something *less than the total* of of the job. Another problem concerns keeping up-to-date. A person who is deemed competent at a particular point in time in a range of tasks incorporated in the standards for his/her industry may well become less than competent if taken off usual duties for a period. There are few industries where employees have to go on proving that they are competent. Some exceptions are Air Traffic Controllers and Airline Pilots, who have to 'requalify' at regular intervals (at least every twelve months), and undergo health checks too. The whole issue of Continuous Development will clearly have to be addressed by educational, training and professional groups over the course of the next few years.

20. The status of S/NVQs in the opinion of (a) those who obtain them, and (b) their employers, is still somewhat uncertain. How credible will S/NVQs become, and what advantage might they have over other, existing, qualifications such as BTEC Highers/Degrees and GCE A-levels? It will be some time before these questions can be answered, but in the meantime the standards themselves will undoubtedly prove useful guides to good working practice for both employees and employers. Since 1991 the various standards have been modified and improved in the light of experience. The latest information on particular industries is available on government and professional body web-sites (see the list at the end of this book).

CHAPTER 31

Evaluating training and development

INTRODUCTION

1. This chapter is concerned with the final stage of the training cycle – the evaluation of training. In this context we are considering planned evaluation rather than ad hoc evaluation of courses and programmes. Planned evaluation will be systematic even if it is conducted informally at certain stages. The chapter discusses what is meant by 'evaluation', who is involved in it, and how it can be carried out.

THE MEANING OF EVALUATION

2. At its simplest level, evaluation means 'to assess the value or worth of something'. This is not a particularly illuminating definition, however, because it does not provide any clues as to what is meant by 'value' and 'worth'. Guba & Lincoln (1981)[1], in discussing the concept of value offer a useful distinction between 'merit', which they see as something having value in its own right, and 'worth', which they see as something whose value is determined by its context. As an example of their distinction, they suggest that 'gold might be judged for merit on its inherent beauty ... it is judged for its worth, however, in the mundane trading marts of London, Paris, etc. ...'. For our purposes, we could take the example of a person who studies for an Open University degree, not for any reason of career development, but solely because he or she enjoys the intellectual challenge of part-time study in a subject of personal interest. For this person the course has intrinsic value, or merit. By comparison, a person who pursues a course to qualify for promotion sees the experience as having a tangible outcome, or worth. Generally speaking, merit remains fairly constant; worth, however, varies with the context, and this is a very important point for evaluating training.

3. In addition to assessing training in terms of merit and worth, evaluators are interested in the processes and outcomes of training. When a trainer assesses the training process he or she is basically seeking answers to the question 'did we do things right?' This implies (a) finding out about the training activity, and (b) looking for possible improvements to the training. This step has been called (Scriven, 1967)[2] 'formative evaluation'. If the trainer is assessing the ultimate outcomes of the training, i.e. enquiring 'did we do the right thing in the first

place?', then he or she is attempting to evaluate the worth of the activity. Scriven calls this step 'summative evaluation', because it takes place at the conclusion of an event and reviews it as a whole.

We shall use these two terms in this chapter to distinguish between the two approaches.

4. Hamblin (1970)[3] contributed a well-known definition of evaluation, in a training context, as follows:

> Any attempt to obtain information (feedback) on the effects of a training programme, and to assess the value of the training in the light of that information.

This definition emphasises the importance of information-gathering in evaluation, a point taken up later in this chapter. Hamblin's perspective is nearer to summative than formative evaluation, but as Figure 31.2 indicates, in a later work he combines both in his chain reaction of training.

5. Evaluation is not the same as validation, although the two are sometimes confused. Validation is just one aspect of evaluation, and refers to the assessment of progress towards the achievement of course or programme objectives. It has a much narrower focus than evaluation. The term 'validation' has, in recent years, come to mean 'approval by an external body'. Thus BTEC, for example, is the validating body for colleges and universities wishing to offer courses bearing its qualifications. The validation conferred by these bodies comes, of course, after a thorough evaluation of all aspects of the courses concerned.

6. Validation, in the sense of evaluating objectives, dates back to Tyler (1949)[4], whose ideas were mentioned in a previous chapter. Tyler's view was that evaluation is concerned with the achievement of educational (learning) objectives. This point of view has been challenged on the grounds that it is unduly narrow and prescriptive. It has been described by Guba & Lincoln (1981)[1] as a 'preordinate' form of evaluation, i.e. it is constructed before the evaluation begins, it focuses only on measurable outcomes, it adopts the standpoint of the evaluator, etc. In its place, recent theorists are proposing what Guba & Lincoln call 'responsive' evaluation, which in contrast to preordinate approaches, focuses on the concerns of the parties involved, adapts to changing conditions or new information, and is more concerned with portrayal than measurement. In the context of this book, a preordinate approach to evaluation would be suited to training involving the performance of specific tasks, such as the conversion training of airline pilots from one type of jetliner to another; a responsive approach would be better suited to evaluating social skills training in a management development programme, for example.

EVALUATION IN TRAINING

7. The place of evaluation activities in training can be demonstrated diagrammatically as in Figure 31.1.

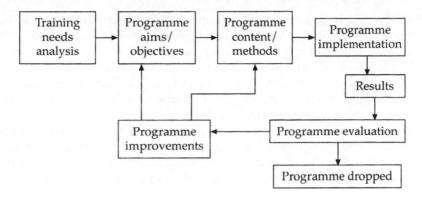

Figure 31.1 *Evaluation in training*

Taking a systems view of the above process, the programme aims, content and learning methods represent inputs, the programme implementation represents the process, and the programme results represent the outputs. The last-mentioned may represent either intended outcomes, as expressed in the programme objectives, or unintended outcomes, which the designers had not anticipated. A preordinate approach could well overlook such unintended outcomes, whereas a responsive approach would actively seek out such outcomes. An unintended outcome could be the improvement of communication or understanding between groups of colleagues on a programme, or an uplift in individual motivation, for example. Following evaluation the programme is either dropped or improved. Improvements are fed back into programme aims/objectives and programme content.

8.   Hamblin (1974)[5], in a classic work on evaluation in training, identified a number of evaluation strategies that are linked to training effects. Hamblin's view is the training can bring about a chain reaction in the organisation and that at each key stage an evaluation strategy can be selected, as indicated in Figure 31.2.

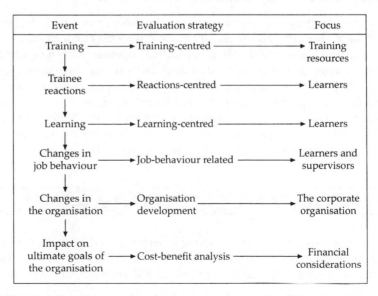

Figure 31.2 *Training effects and evaluation strategies (adapted from Hamblin, 1974)*

9.   Hamblin's analysis is interesting because it shows that evaluation can be carried out at a number of different levels, each with its own evaluation possibilities and often with differing focal points. Generally speaking, the first three levels are likely to be the subject of formative evaluation, whilst the remaining three are more likely to be included in a summative evaluation. The chain of effects with its accompanying strategies highlights the differences of viewpoint concerning training that are possible in a real situation. Training staff, for example, tend to question their training resources and the reactions/behaviour of their trainees. Line managers tend to question the appropriateness of the training for the job, as well as the behaviour of their staff. Senior managers tend to question the cost of training and the benefits it may bring to the organisation as a whole.

10.   Apart, perhaps, from routine formative evaluation conducted by training staff, most evaluation exercises have to be agreed and planned between the trainers and the various interested parties. Figure 31.3 illustrates a possible sequence of events for the implementation of an evaluation exercise.

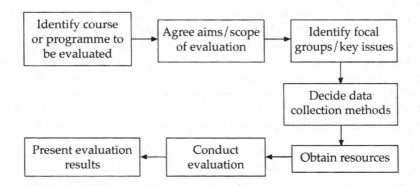

Figure 31.3 *Planning an evaluation exercise*

11.   Having identified the course or programme to be evaluated, the responsible trainer will agree the aims and scope of the exercise with client managers and colleagues. The trainees concerned will be identified together with any key issues raised by their managers, the training staff and the trainees themselves. Then methods of collecting relevant information have to be decided upon. Since this stage usually involves taking up the time of the parties involved, agreement needs to be sought to proceed. The collection of information provides the basic evidence on which the evaluation, i.e. assessment of merit and worth, depends. Finally, the results of the evaluation are made available to one or more of the parties concerned.

THE SUBJECT-MATTER OF EVALUATION

12.   The subject-matter of evaluation is extensive. As Figure 31.4 shows, it embraces not only the trainees and their trainers, but also the learning context, the course content, the learning methods employed and the materials used in the programme.

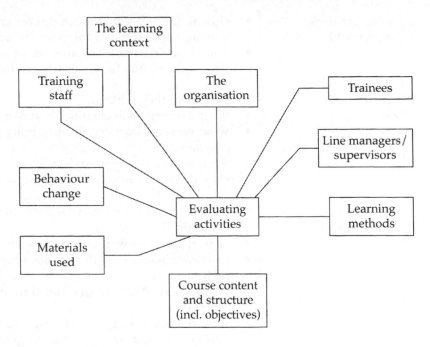

Figure 31.4 *The Subject-matter of evaluation*

Each of the above factors gives rise to further issues for evaluators when assessing the effectiveness of a programme. A comprehensive evaluation would cover most, if not all, of these issues. A partial evaluation would cover selected factors only, e.g. course content and structure.

13. The kinds of issues that might arise from the various factors are illustrated in Figure 31.5 below, which takes a graduate trainee programme in a large retail group as an example.

Factor	Issues for evaluators
The learning context	• What standards of behaviour are expected of graduate trainees? • How are graduates regarded in the organisation? • What is the impact on graduates of all the other factors on this?
The organisation	• How does the management structure cope with graduates on short-term projects in different departments? • What issues are raised by the physical structure of the organisation?
The training staff	• How well-qualified are they? • Are they adequately experienced in handling graduate trainees? • What range of skills is available in the staff group?

Line managers/ supervisors	• How well-briefed are they in respect of their training responsibilities for graduate trainees? • What is their attitude towards such trainees? • How well do they fulfil a coaching or counselling role?
The trainees	• How were they selected? • What are their individual needs and/or motives? • What previous learning did they bring to the programme? • What are their learning styles? • How do they fit in to the organisation culture (its values, etc.)?
Programme content and structure	• On what assumptions was the programme content founded? • How appropriate were course aims and objectives? • How well linked were the various programme elements? • To what extent was theory linked to practice and vice versa • Were the trainees able to influence the nature and direction of their own personal programmes? • How relevant was the course content?
Learning methods	• What range of methods were employed during the programme? • How appropriate or effective were the methods selected? • To what extent did the selection of learning methods take differing learning styles into account? • How well did the training staff and/or line staff apply the learning methods selected?
Materials used	• What handouts were used and what was the basis of their selection? • How useful were the handouts to the trainees? • What documents were used to indicate individual progress or other forms of feedback? • What policy and procedural documents were utilised during the programme?
Behaviour changes	• What changes have been noticed in the development of the trainees? • To what extent have intended changes been noticed? • What unanticipated changes have occurred? • What methods have been used to assess individual progress during the course/programme?

Figure 31.5 *Evaluating a graduate trainee scheme*

COLLECTING DATA FOR EVALUATION

14. There are several methods of data collection available to evaluators. The most important are as follows:

1   *Interviews with relevant parties* – these may be relatively structured, with pre-specified questions asked of each person interviewed, or may be relatively open-ended, with exploratory questions posed as and when appropriate throughout the interview.

2   *Questionnaires* – these are pre-specified lists of questions, which may require a range of responses from box-ticking to considered comments.

3   *Observation* – most observations in training evaluation are conducted by outside observers, such as trainers and line managers/supervisors. The trainers observe the behaviour of those involved in the off-the-job training process, whilst line staff observe the behaviour of individuals on their return to the job.

4   *Tests* – these are practical examinations of knowledge or skill, designed in a closely controlled way so that an individual's results can be compared either with the performance of similar persons undertaking the same test in the same conditions (norm-referenced), or with the number of correct answers given (criterion-referenced).

5   *Materials Analysis* – this refers to any analysis of teaching/learning materials used, such as case studies, role-playing exercises, handouts, statements of objectives, syllabuses, etc.

6   *Records Analysis* – At the cost-benefit analysis level of evaluation, records may be analysed to see what improvements have been made in output, or what reductions have been identified in the wastage rate, level of accidents, production delays, etc.

15. Questionnaires are a very popular method of data collection with training staff. However, the significance of the information collected by questionnaire is directly related to the relevance and wording of the instrument itself. It will be useful, therefore, to consider some important factors in questionnaire design. Firstly, three fundamental questions need to be asked before any questionnaire is prepared. These are as follows:

1   What is the purpose of the survey? (e.g. is it to obtain general impressions of a training activity, or to draw out specific points about detailed aspects?)

2   At whom is the questionnaire to be directed? (e.g. at trainees, line managers, at specialist groups?)

3   What resources are available for conducting a questionnaire? (e.g. designers, word-processing facilities, computer-analysis of results, etc.?)

16. If the above three issues are resolved, then work on the questionnaire itself can begin. This involves decisions about:

1   the *content* of the questions (i.e. their relevance and viability)

2   the *wording* of the questions (i.e. clarity, freedom from bias, etc.)

3   the *sequence* of questions (i.e. logical, arousing interest, etc.)

4   the *form of response* sought (i.e. box-ticking, multiple-choice, open-ended, etc.)

17. It is not easy to pose relevant, clear and viable questions. Indeed, most questionaires have to be redrafted more than once, often utilising a 'pilot' questionnaire, which is a trial set of questions designed to test initial reactions amongst a sample of the target group, with the object of revising questions in the light of the feedback obtained. When assessing a questionnaire, designers need to ask:

- is this question necessary?

- how many questions are needed on this particular topic?

- is the question sufficiently clear in its meaning?

- is this question biased in any way?

- will respondents have the information required to respond?

- how will respondents react to this question?

- is this wording likely to be objectionable in any way?

- can the form of response be quantified?

- how can we deal with qualitative responses?

18. Two examples of typical questionnaires are shown below. Figure 31.6 illustrates the kind of box-ticking response that might be asked of a line manager, reporting on a supervisor returning from a course on leadership and delegation. Figure 31.7 shows an example of the type of questionnaire that college students might be asked to complete concerning the performance of their lecturers.

On the basis of the replies to the questionnaire, the evaluator can make a judgement about the relative changes brought about as a result of the training course. Where a manager's response is not clear, the evaluator can follow this up with the individual concerned in order to clarify the position.

19. The student questionnaire presents a number of statements about lecturer behaviour and asks the respondents to say how closely the lecturer fits the description.

To what extent has the individual's job behaviour changed since attending the course on Leadership and Delegation?					
Key tasks/skills	Greatly improved	Partly improved	No change	Worse	Unknown
Communicating with staff					
Delegating work					
Motivating staff					
Handling grievances					
Making decisions					
Appraising staff etc. etc.					

Figure 31.6 *Questionnaire relating to behaviour change*

PRESENTING THE RESULTS OF EVALUATION

20. Once the material for the evaluation has been collected and analysed, the training staff responsible will need to draw up a suitable report and present it to one or more of the interested parties. If the original aim of the evaluation was to make everyone aware of the possibilities of a particular programme, then the report will be circulated widely amongst past and potential participants and their managers. If the aim was to conduct a discreet enquiry into delicate issues of personal leadership, then the report may be restricted to the client managers concerned and to selected training staff. Many evaluations never go further than the training department in any formal sense, the results being used to modify future courses in the light of the feedback obtained. Where the evaluation is essentially formative in nature, then the latter situation is perfectly justifiable. Where the evaluation is of a summative kind, then senior managers and others will wish to make any evaluation reports widely available among decision-making groups and key individuals.

To what extent does the lecturer's performance fit each of the descriptions listed below?				
Factor	Completely	Partially	Infrequently	Not at all
Gives clear explanations				
Supplies relevant examples				
Provides useful visual aids				
Presents material in a lively manner				
Pitches the material at the right level				
Encourages class discussion				
Is supportive to those with problems etc. etc.				

Figure 31.7 *Lecturer performance: a student view*

CONCLUSION

21.   The evaluation of training activities can be conducted at a number of different levels and in a number of different ways. The most fruitful evaluations are likely to be those which examine a range of factors rather than just one or two. Ultimately, because of its role in promoting organisational goals, training must be seen to have tangible benefits for its constituents. Its worth is more important than any intrinsic merit it may possess.

REFERENCES

1.   Guba, E.G. & Lincoln, Y.S. (1981), *Effective Evaluation,* Jossey-Bass.

2.   Scriven, M. (1967), *The Methodology of Evaluation,* AERA Monograph, Rand McNally.

3. Hamblin, A.C. (1970), 'Evaluation of Training', supplement to *Industrial Training International*, No. 54.

4. Tyler, R.W. (1949), *Basic Principles of Curriculum and Instruction*, University of Chicago Press.

5. Hamblin, A.C. (1974), *Evaluation and Control of Training*, McGraw-Hill.

CHAPTER 32

Management development

1. In the whole field of employee development, management development has become an important issue in its own right. It has developed its own techniques, practices and literature. This chapter reviews the subject of management development, commencing with some definitions, continuing with an assessment of typical management development techniques and practices, and concluding with a consideration of the relationship between management development and corporate policies and culture.

MANAGEMENT DEVELOPMENT – SOME DEFINITIONS

2. The following definitions of management development indicate some of the differences of emphasis that exist:

    1. ... manager development must embrace all managers in the enterprise. It must aim at challenging all to growth and self-development. It must focus on performance rather than on promise, and on tomorrow's requirements rather than those of today. (Drucker, 1955)[1]

    In this statement, Drucker was well ahead of his time, especially in terms of seeing management development as self-development within the total management structure, and of recognising the importance of preparing for change in the organisation.

    2. '... any attempt to improve managerial effectiveness through a planned and deliberate learning process.' (MSC, 1978)[2]

    This general statement emphasises the wide range of options facing organisations wishing to undertake management development, and stresses the need for a systematic approach.

    3. ... development is a continuing improvement of effectiveness within a particular system, which may be a person, but in the case of management development is within the management function of an organisation ...(Morris, 1978)[3]

    Professor Morris sees management development as part of the process of organisational renewal, with the implication that a variety of approaches are possible.

4. In some organisations the focus of management development will primarily be
    upon the training and education of managers. In other(s) ... (it) ... may be seen to
    be aiming to change the managerial style ... In yet others ... the main focus will
    be on formalised systems ... associated with performance appraisal and career
    planning ... (Easterby-Smith et al., 1980)[4]

Easterby Smith and colleagues found a variety of approaches to management
development in their studies of several hundred managers' experience of management development

3. Although by no means the majority of management development systems are
    formalised, the structure of activities implicit in such an approach can be
    illuminating. Figure 32.1 indicates the range of features likely to be present in a
    formal system.

Figure 32.1 *Formal management development system*

In a formal system, management development arises from needs expressed in plans
and manpower reviews, as influenced by (a) the corporate culture, or value-system.
Present and future needs for managers imply recruitment and succession planning
measures. Performance of managers is formally appraised, in terms of present and
potential level of achievement. Improvements in performance are dealt with by a
variety of training and development activities, which are evaluated individually,
and, in some cases, may also be subjected to a management development audit as a
whole.

4. Three underlying trends can be discerned in the variety of possible approaches to
    management development, and these are as follows:

    1   the improvement of individual manager effectiveness (i.e. 'The extent to which
        a manager achieves the output requirements of his position.' [Reddin, 1970][5])

2   the improvement of management performance as a whole

3   the improvement of organisational effectiveness (i.e. the achievement of corporate objectives by means of collaborative efforts throughout the enterprise).

5.   In practice, the first of these three trends results in specific educational and training activities provided to meet individuals' immediate and short-term needs. The second trend is directed more towards common, medium-term needs of *groups* of managers. The third trend emphasises the medium and long-term needs of the organisation as a whole in adapting to the pressures of its environment. If we take the first two trends, a key question is 'What do managers need to know and need to perform to be effective?' This question will be considered in the next few paragraphs. The third trend will be considered towards the end of the chapter.

MANAGEMENT – KNOWLEDGE AND SKILLS

6.   In his classic definition, Fayol (1949)[6] saw the task of management as follows:

> To manage is to forecast and plan, to organise, to command, to coordinate and to control.

Such a definition is always limited by its generality. It does not tell you what managers need to know or do in order to be able to carry out the functions described. In recent years there has been an emphasis on examining what managers actually do in practice (e.g. Mintzberg, 1973, and Stewart, 1982)[7,8]. This approach has led to other developments, where attempts have been made to identify specific areas of knowledge and skill in managerial positions.

7.   A useful example of this last development is provided by Pedler *et al.* (1994)[9] in their list of attributes of 'successful' managers. Their list comprises the following features of an effective manager:

1   command of basic facts

2   relevant professional knowledge

3   continuing sensitivity to events

4   analytical, problem-solving, decision-making and judgement-making skills

5   social skills and abilities

6   emotional resilience

7   proactivity, i.e. the inclination to respond purposefully to events

8   creativity

9   mental agility

10   balanced learning habits and skills

11   self-knowledge

Whilst the list reads rather like a prosaic version of Kipling's 'If', nevertheless it does provoke other questions, as the authors themselves are aware, and these questions can help to direct managers' thinking about their effectiveness as managers.

8.   Pedler and colleagues raise several questions under each of their eleven features to enable managers to assess themselves at the start of a series of self-development exercises built around their list. Rosemary Stewart (1982)[8] takes a rather different approach to analysing manager's jobs. She looks at managers' jobs in terms of the demands, constraints and choices that are present. Jobs were described along these lines, and then managers were encouraged to consider how they could extend their range of choices, as well as learning to cope with those aspects that could not be changed.

9.   Another view of managerial jobs was expressed by Simmons & Brennan (1981)[10]:

> ...managing well means:
>
> 1.   Having frequent reviews of performance as a group...
>
> 2.   ...listening to each individual's views on the situation and how things can be improved...
>
> 3.   Proposing and getting commitment to a solution ... which is in line with the goals ... of the system.

This particular viewpoint emphasises the team-leadership aspects of a managerial position.

10. Taking all these views about the nature of managerial jobs as a whole, four key elements can be discerned in terms of what managers might need to know or be able to do. These are as follows.

- *Managerial knowledge* – what the manager needs to know about the organisation, the job, the procedures involved, etc.

- *Managerial skills* – what problem-solving, social and other skills the manager needs to be able to practise.

- *Managerial attitudes* – what the manager is required to accept in terms of coping with stress, dealing with clients, etc.

- *Managerial style* – the expectations that people have concerning the way the manager exercises leadership.

These four elements can be found in most management development programmes, whether for individuals or for groups. They are also a feature of the occupational standards being developed for managerial posts (see Chapter 30).

MANAGEMENT DEVELOPMENT METHODS

11. The various methods employed in management development can be placed into three main categories, as follows:

    1 *Management education* – qualification-bearing courses run by universities or public sector colleges, for example MBA degrees, Diplomas in Management Studies, and various professional examinations, such as the Institute of Personnel Management; the level of work is regarded as post experience, and the emphasis is on acquiring knowledge and theory.

    2 *Management training* – internal and external courses, off-the-job and focusing on acquiring specific knowledge and relevant job skills; some experiential learning via course exercises.

    3 *Experiential learning* – 'learning by doing'; on-the-job experience usually with guidance from superior or colleague.

12. Of these three categories, the first two have been discredited in many respects. Writers such as Humble (1967)[11] and Hague (1974)[12] criticised off-the-job methods on grounds of their lack of relevance to 'real' needs. Humble proposed the alternative of Management by Objectives (MBO), which in essence is a jointly-planned target-setting exercise, in which a manager and his or her superior identify job priorities, agree targets to be attained, and set up a system for (a) monitoring the manager's progress and (b) providing help when necessary. Such an approach can be an extremely effective way of developing management skills and experience. Hague, on his part, favoured what he called 'executive self-development', which, in practice, means on-the-job guided experience.

    Most modern approaches to management development concentrate on experiential learning on the job, and relegate courses to a secondary role.

EXPERIENTIAL APPROACHES TO MANAGEMENT DEVELOPMENT

13. The most widely-used experiential methods are as follows: coaching/guided experience, mentoring, delegation, projects, secondments/job rotation. We shall briefly examine each of these, and highlight their key points and advantages (see Figure 32.2).

COACHING/GUIDED EXPERIENCE

14. Coaching, according to a management dictionary definition, is:

    Individual or small-group management training characterised by on-the-job training, continuous assessment and personal counselling and tuition.[13]

Method	Salient features	Advantages
• Coaching/Guided Experience/ Mentoring	Planned involvement of the manager in advising and aiding junior manger to develop effective job performance Involves discovery learning with support	Relevant to learner Improves collaboration Good feedback for learner
• Delegation	Manager gives specific responsibility authority and resources Performance is monitored	Individual able to exercise real responsibility for results
• Projects	A specific problem or opportunity is worked on by an individual or a team with the object of producing concrete proposals in a given time-span	May generate a high degree of commitment Utilises problem-solving, negotiating skills
• Secondments	A manager is assigned to a post in another department/unit for a limited period	Valuable experience based on doing the job assigned Tests individual

Figure 32.2 *Experiential methods in management development*

Common general dictionary definitions of '*coach*' and, by implication, '*coaching*' usually refer to intensive training of one or more persons by another who uses instruction, demonstration and practice as his or her prime methods. Unlike other forms of instruction, which are often concerned with passing on *facts* or *theoretical knowledge*, coaching is about helping others to learn *how to do things*. Not surprisingly coaching is most often associated with sports and other practical skills, such as playing a musical instrument. It is centred around a skilled individual who passes on his or her skills in a fairly intimate way to an individual or small group. Coaches, by implication, have to be people who are already skilled to a high level; people who have already proven themselves to their peers and their public.

15. In past times, coaching was a central feature of the system of apprenticeships that grew up all over Europe in order to retain and develop key crafts. The model was a work-based one where a skilled craftsman passed on his knowledge of how to perform the craft to acceptable standards for a lifetime career. Nowadays the idea of apprenticeships is returning with Modern Apprenticeships – open to both sexes – being offered in order to improve standards and quality in key skill areas. The

context of coaching is the job and the workplace, whether for apprentices or, for the purposes of this chapter, up-and-coming managers. Parsloe (1992)[14] identifies four distinct coaching roles, which can be summarised as follows:

1   the 'hands-on' basic instructor (inexperienced learners)

2   the 'hands-off' high-performance developer (experienced learners)

3   the 'supporter' of learners using a flexible learning package

4   the 'qualifier', helping learners to develop specific competencies for a formal qualification.

16.   In management development the 'hands-off' and 'qualifier' roles are the more usual, with the latter often merging into a 'mentor' role (see below). Managers typically need to develop skills and competence in such areas as communication skills, group leadership, staff appraisal, handling grievances, planning and budgeting. These are aspects of the job in which the job-holder often feels exposed and vulnerable, and where constructive help is required to build confidence and ability levels. The presence of a skilled and valued colleague to help talk through how to handle selected situations can avoid embarrassment and major errors of judgement whilst new learning is taking place. Coaches clearly have to be selected rather carefully. As in other areas of teaching-learning, it is not only *what* a person knows and can do that is required, but most important of all the *ability to communicate personal insights and skills to others.*

MENTORING

17.   The expression 'mentor' originates from Greek mythology, where Ulysses (Odysseus), before leaving for the Trojan wars, entrusts his son, Telemachus, to the care and direction of his old and trusted friend, Mentor. Thus, a mentor has come to mean someone mature and experienced who advises (and gives practical assistance where required) to a younger and less experienced person. The term 'protégé' comes nearest to describing the role of the person being mentored (i.e. protected, guided and advised). Mentoring is a learning relationship which is broader than that involved in coaching. The latter is definitely skills or competency focused, whereas the former is concerned with passing on knowledge, insight and attitudes as well as skills. Mentors, it should be pointed out, are not the line managers of those concerned but other senior managers in the organisation. This enables mentoring to proceed in a relatively friendly fashion without the stress of accountability being present.

18.   Organisations that are using mentoring and coaching approaches in their management development are attempting to gain added value from the talents, experience and wisdom of their senior staff by encouraging them to pass on their store of experience to junior colleagues, and to do so in the workplace rather than at a business school, staff college or some other external provider. The development of these approaches has led recently (e.g. Senge, 1990)[15] to the idea of a 'learning organisation', which positively values and builds on the experience of

its own staff as well as using external sources of employee training and development.

DELEGATION

19. Delegation is essentially a power-sharing process in which a manager transfers part of his or her authority to another, more junior person. The amount of power which is shared will depend on such factors as the urgency of the situation, the assessment by the senior person of the other's readiness for power, and the willingness of the senior person to share in the first place. Delegation usually takes place within an operational context and may well be dominated by considerations of urgency or sheer convenience. However, it can also be used as a developmental tool for giving junior managers the chance to practise or apply new skills in a planned way. There are few better ways of assessing someone's suitability for a possible task than giving them a similar task and observing how well they perform. Where delegation is backed up by mentoring and the support of the senior manager, it is likely to prove a powerful development tool.

PROJECTS AND SECONDMENTS

20. The use of special projects and secondments to other parts of the business or to other roles is also a development tool that is rooted in workplace learning. These two forms of management development are usually supported by some of the other development tools referred to above. The assignment of up-and-coming younger managers to special projects, which are usually part-time, means that for one or two periods, or for one or two days a week, these younger staff can leave their normal duties and spend time with colleagues from other parts of the organisation on some project of benefit to all. They thus get to know a wider range of people, learn how to improve their networking skills, and contribute to what is quite likely to be a multi-disciplinary team effort, thus extending their knowledge and understanding of the roles of other managers or specialists.

21. Sending an individual on secondment is usually seen as a full-time job. Depending on the nature of the secondment the individual might be assigned to a team, but is just as likely to be working on their own. Where the individual is taking up a particular post, then coaching and/or mentoring are likely to be provided to ensure that the task gets done as well as to facilitate the individual's learning. Secondment is a good way of testing an individual's capacity for coping with a particular role.

22. The emphasis in the above-mentioned approaches is on gaining experience and developing skills in the context of work. The key players in these approaches, in addition to the learners, are those other members of the organisation's staff who carry out the roles of senior manager, coach or mentor. Such approaches do not have to rule out *off-the-job* training and development for managers. On the contrary, it may be extremely important to ensure some supporting activities are provided in a 'safe' off-the-job environment, either in-company or externally. Some

of the leading methods of providing experiential methods of training off-the-job are described in the next few paragraphs.

OFF-THE-JOB METHODS AND EXPERIENTIAL LEARNING

23. The majority of experiential methods used in management courses are directed at social skills development, e.g. leadership, influencing skills, negotiating, assertiveness etc. A few are directed at cognitive skills development, e.g. problem-identification, problem-analysis, etc. Perceptive use of such methods by trainers can overcome many of the problems of lack of relevance to the job levelled at off-the-job training by its critics. The point here is that skills development in these particular areas extends the range of an individual's competence in his or her whole life, not just in the present job. These particular skills are in fact 'context-free', that is they do not depend on any one situation in order to be of use to the learner, unlike off-the-job activities. An example of one such method is the use of the so-called 'Managerial Grid'.

24. The Grid represents a matrix of potential management styles of leadership, and was first devised as an aid to management development. Using the basic Grid model, managers can identify their current style and, if appropriate, learn what to do to achieve a 'better' style. Learning is achieved by means of structured questionnaires and a combination of group discussion and practical exercises. The basic Grid is set out as shown in figure 32.3.

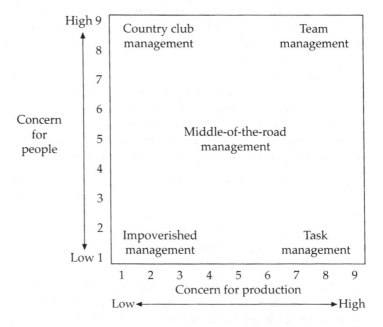

Figure 32.3 *The managerial grid (after Blake & Mouton, 1964)*[16]

The Grid uses two dimensions: *concern for people* and *concern for production (or task)*. By measuring reponses to questionnaires, for example, managers can identify what preferences they have when faced with certain 'context-free' situations. They can then plot their initial positions on the Grid, and begin to see a picture of themselves emerging. The Country Club style is very considerate to people, but shows little concern for the task. By comparison, the Task Management style emphasises getting the task completed more or less regardless of people's feelings or views. Of the five styles, the Team Management style is seen to be the 'best' style, in that it emphasises both the task and people's needs. As a management development device, the Grid has proved very useful. (As a theory of leadership, however, it has not received much support.)

25. Typical methods used in experiential courses are shown in Figure 32.4.

Method	Salient features	Advantages
Group exercise	Group are given a task and certain limits; the results achieved and the process by which they were achieved are examined by the group and a tutor	Definable focus for activities; task provides peg on which discussion can take place; useful for leadership and team-building
Role-playing	Individuals take on a role and experience the nature of an interpersonal encounter; may be tightly or loosely scripted	Participants learn to think on their feet; experience genuine emotions, so long as role is authentic
Sensitivity training	Group exercises in which processes taking place in the group are examined; the focus is on the 'here and now' interactions; requires careful guidance by trainer	Enables groups to explore interpersonal relations and to share feelings
Case-study	A real or imaginary account of an organisational problem is studied by an individual or a small group with a view to diagnosing a situation or proposing solutions	Provides focal point for developing analytical and problem-solving skills
Brainstorming	A group are asked to suggest ways of dealing with an issue/problem; no discussion or criticism of suggestions is made until after the list has been completed	Has proved to be an effective means of stimulating new ideas and creative suggestions

Simulation exercise	This is a combination of a case study with role-play; participants are given a fairly detailed scenario and are asked to undertake a number of decisions within a time-limit	As a kind of enlarged role-play, this can reproduce many real-life situations; useful for developing negotiating and decision-making skills
Simulator/ interactive computer exercise	Sophisticated cockpit simulator for 'realistic' exercises in routine and emergency situations	Participants can practise without endangering others (e.g. passengers)
Workshops	These are practical exercises in which participants work on particular work-based problems as a group	Provide opportunity to share ideas on real day-to-day problems; useful when devising plans/ systems

Figure 32.4 *Experiential methods in courses*

26. These methods try to overcome the problem stated by Schein (1970)[17] that

> The typical training effort therefore faces the problem not only of how to teach a new employee the specifics of a complex job for today, but also how to create a learning situation in which that employee can develop his other capacities by way of preparing for an uncertain future. In management training the latter factor is paramount.

Whilst it is by no means easy to measure the effects of management training courses and on-the-job development, the outcomes that senior management might expect from 'successful' management development activities will include:

1   individual managers performing at a fully satisfactory level

2   improved performance from work-teams as a result of better leadership

3   pool of managers ready and able to take up promotion or stand in for absentees

4   managers working collaboratively together

5   improved communication between managers and their staff, and between managers and colleagues

6   improved problem-solving capacity throughout the organisation.

SUCCESSION PLANNING

27. One of the key features of a structured management development system is a succession plan. This is basically a plan for identifying who is currently in post and who is available and qualified to take over in the event of retirement, voluntary leaving, dismissal or sickness, for example. As Figure 32.5 indicates, a typical

succession chart includes details of key management jobholders and brief references to their possible successors.

Department: Manager:				Date:	
Present management jobholders				Possible successors	Ready
Post	Jobholder	Age	Performance	First choice: Second choice:	

Figure 32.5 *Management succession chart*

AUDITING MANAGEMENT DEVELOPMENT

28. Some important outcomes of management development were referred to in paragraph 26 above. However, the assessment of the effects of management development activities is a complex matter, as the Durham University Business School team discovered when conducting their study into management development in a number of British companies. Part of the Durham remit was to produce an instrument for evaluating management development, and this is described in Easterby-Smith et al. (1980)[4]. The so called Management Development Audit aims 'to ensure that the provisions adopted by any organisation for developing its managers do produce the intended results.' The essence of the Audit approach is 'to ask individual managers to describe their own experiences of, and views about, management development, and then to reflect the collective view back to those responsible for making decisions about the development of managers.'

29. The Audit, which is intended to be a neutral instrument, not preferring any particular approach to management development, attempts to portray a picture which contrasts:

    1   the formal view of what is intended to happen

    2   managers' perceptions of what is happening in fact

    3   what managers would like to see happening in management development.

    The Audit seeks answers to questions such as the following:

    •   What are the main objectives of Management development, and how well are they being achieved?

    •   What are the main forms of training available for managers, and what emphasis is placed on them?

- How is self-development encouraged?

- What discussion takes place before a manager goes on a course, and what happens on his/her return?

- What kind of appraisal system exists?

- Is there a formal system of career development, and is this related to appraisal?

- For what levels of management is succession planning carried out?

- What internal and external resources are made available for management development?

- What are the main problems confronting management development in the organisation at the present time?

30. The Audit represents a thorough review of management development activities, enabling senior management to pinpoint strengths and weaknesses of the current system as well as obtaining a 'feel' for the way the system is operating. Many of the responses to the audit will undoubtedly reflect the various cultural influences at work in the organisation, and these will be considered briefly next.

MANAGEMENT DEVELOPMENT AND CORPORATE CULTURE

31. The approach to management development in an organisation will tend to reflect the dominant value-system of the senior management. They are the persons who, above all, are charged with building a management team and developing their successors. If the top management is centralist and bureaucratic, for example, then its view of management development is likely to produce a logically structured system such as that shown in Figure 32.1 above. In such a system, job descriptions, appraisal forms, succession charts and the like are vital items in the analysis of needs and in decisions about how they are to be met. Such a system would probably favour structured efforts, both on and off-the-job, to supply individual manager needs. Where top management believes in delegation and devolution, then the emphasis in management development is on self-development on-the-job. Where management is considered an elite group, then features such as 'accelerated promotion', 'graduate trainee programmes' tend to predominate. Such systems provide selective support for manager development by concentrating on so-called 'high fliers', i.e. persons with outstanding potential.

CONCLUSION

32. The current mood among writers and researchers on management development suggests that a contingency approach to management development is preferable. A contingency approach in essence adapts to the dominant culture of the organisation concerned, but takes into account a number of forces for change, such as the

influence of new technology. The most successful attempts at management development are likely to be those relying on an appropriate mix of on-the-job experience and off-the-job courses offered in a variety of ways to meet different individual requirements and learning styles.

REFERENCES

1. Drucker, P. (1955), *The Practice of Management*, Heinemann.

2. Manpower Services Commission (1978), *Management Development*, MSC.

3. Morris, J.F. (1978), 'Management Development and Development Management', in Burgoyne & Stuart (eds), *Management Development: Context and Strategies*, Gower Press.

4. Easterby-Smith, M. *et al.* (1980), *Auditing Management Development*, Gower.

5. Reddin, W. (1970), *Managerial Effectiveness*, McGraw-Hill.

6. Fayol, H. (1949), *General and Industrial Management*, Pitman.

7. Mintzberg, H. (1973), *The Nature of Managerial Work*. Harper & Row

8. Stewart, R. (1982), *Managerial Choice*, McGraw-Hill.

9. Pedler, M. *et al.* (1994), *A Manager's Guide to Self-development*, McGraw-Hill.

10. Simmons, J. & Brennan, R. (1981), in Nixon, B.(ed.), *New Approaches to Management Development*, Gower/ATM.

11. Humble, J.W. (1967), *Improving Business Results*, McGraw-Hill.

12. Hague, H. (1974), *Executive Self-development*, Macmillan.

13. Johannsen, H. & Page, G.T. (1992), *International Dictionary of Management*, BCA/ Kogan Page.

14. Parsloe, E. (1992), *Coaching, Mentoring and Assessing*, Kogan Page.

15. Senge, P. (1990), *The Fifth Discipline: The Art and Practice of the Learning Organisation*, Doubleday.

16. Blake, R. and Mouton, J. (1964), *The Managerial Grid*, Gulf Publishing. (See also later edition, 1985.)

17. Schein, E.H. (1970), *Organisational Psychology* (2nd edn), Prentice Hall.

QUESTIONS FOR DISCUSSION/HOMEWORK

1. What are the advantages of conducting performance appraisal on the basis of results achieved rather than on the basis of the qualities of the person appraised?

2. How relevant is self-appraisal in the context of managerial appraisal?

3. How important is the role of the trainer in the learning process?

4. What teaching methods would you employ to enable a group of employees to master certain procedures and practices in your organisation?

5. Why is training important to organisations?

6. What are the arguments in favour of assessing training needs by means of staff interviews?

7. In what aspects of knowledge and skills is it difficult to set measurable objectives, and why?

8. What are the advantages from having clearly-stated aims and objectives for a course?

9. How might you sequence the learning for one or more of the following groups:

   a) instructing till operators in the operation of a computer-linked till?

   b) developing selling skills in newly-recruited sales staff?

   c) developing counselling skills among managers?

10. What factors should be considered when conducting a comprehensive evaluation of a series of on-the-job training activities?

11. To what extent is management development more like 'self-development' than 'manager development'?

12. What are the reasons for suggesting that the most appropriate place for management development activities is on-the-job?

13. What are the likely advantages and disadvantages of employing a competence-based approach to assessing management development needs?

EXAMINATION QUESTIONS

EQ16 'If managers were doing their jobs properly, there would be no need for a performance appraisal system administered by the personnel function.' Discuss.

(ICSA)

EQ17 How would you establish the training needs of a group of supervisors, most of whom have been in post for many years?

(IPM)

EQ18 The evaluation of training is often neglected. Why is this so and how can a more professional approach to evaluation be achieved?

(IPM)

EQ19 Discuss the effectiveness of on-the-job methods for management development compared with off-the-job methods.

(ABE)

CASE STUDY 5: THE MANAGEMENT TRAINEE SCHEME

BACKGROUND

For several years Rosebury's, a steadily-growing retail group, has been recruiting trainees direct from universities and colleges into key management and specialist posts. In the coming year the company intends to recruit 50 such trainees. Most will be graduates, in a variety of disciplines; a few will be BTEC qualified Business students; only a very few will possess a qualification of direct relevance to retailing.

Up until last year, new entrants under the management trainee scheme had been given a broad training in one main segment of the company's business as follows:

either a) in the department stores

or b) in supermarkets

or c) in a central function (e.g. computing or accounts)

It has been decided to extend the scope of the scheme and to design a programme which is truly company-wide.

TRAINING NEEDS

Apart from their graduate and equivalent qualifications, the qualities sought in the trainees have been as follows:

- a lively and flexible outlook
- ability to work well under pressure
- capabilities of leadership
- above-average stamina
- a sense of service to others.

Reports from line departments indicate that the aspects of the current programme most in need of improvement are in leadership development and coping with pressure.

In addition to the above personal attributes, knowledge is required in the following aspects of the work:

- organisation culture and structure
- product range
- merchandising practices
- store/supermarket procedures
- personnel procedures.

Most trainees have no relevant experience in any of these aspects of their work, and therefore require comprehensive briefing.

YOUR TASK

As Management Training Adviser to Rosebury's, you have been asked to design an improved training programme for graduate and college entrants to the company. Submit a report to your Personnel Director as follows:

1. give a brief summary of their training needs, as you see them;

2. draw up a draft training programme for this year's entrants, showing what you recommend, and why.

Your draft should provide information about content, methods, time and location (i.e. on or off-the-job), together with any other information you think is relevant.

CASE STUDY 6: PERFORMANCE APPRAISAL AT MIDSURE LTD

BACKGROUND

Midsure Ltd is a general insurance company offering Life Assurance, and Household, Automobile and Commercial insurance. The company has its headquarters in Birmingham, which directs the activities of eight Branch offices located in major towns in the Midlands and North of England. The headquaters has a range of senior line managers and specialists, all of whom have served for a number of years in the insurance business. Each branch is headed by a Branch Manger, who usually has four or five direct reports, such as the Life Manager, Automobile Manager, etc. Each of these departmental managers has between three and five section leaders or their equivalent.

The Company's policy in matters of promotion and management succession is to identify and prepare existing staff, rather than to recruit outsiders. A major feature of the Company's personnel practice is the Appraisal Scheme. However, in recent years the scheme has come under criticism from both managers and staff on grounds of the vagueness of the performance criteria, and thus the underlying unfairness of eventual assessments. It has also been expressed that as the appraisals are only carried out annually, they are too remote from the fast-changing conditions operating in the branches.

The General Manager has discussed the issue with the Personnel Manager, who has agreed to revise the scheme so that it reflects performance on the job rather than personal qualities. It has also been agreed that the entire appraisal procedure will be reviewed at the same time.

QUESTION

1. As a respected management consultant, you have been called in by the Personnel Manager to advise him/her on a possible new scheme. In particular, he/she has asked you to make recommendations on:

   a) performance criteria to be employed

   b) training proposals for introducing the new scheme

   Prepare a draft report to the Personnel Manager, showing your initial proposals.

PART VI

EMPLOYEE RELATIONS

This final part of the book aims to introduce the main features of the collective relationships between employers and employees. The chapter also considers the role of third parties in this relationship. Chapter 33 introduces the players in the employee relations drama, and considers some of their varying perspectives and objects. Chapter 34 briefly considers some key issues of formal communication in organisations. Chapter 35 discusses the subject-matter and basic processes of collective bargaining between employers (and their representatives) and employees (and their representatives). Chapter 36 introduces the role of trade unions. Chapter 37 outlines some of the important consequences of a failure to agree on a collective issue, and, in particular, describes the activities of third parties, such as the Advisory, Conciliation and Arbitration Service (ACAS), in seeking to fulfil a peace-making role. Chapter 38 deals with issues of individual rather than collective behaviour but which are invariably handled within a collectively agreed set of rules. Chapter 39 provides a basic introduction to the concept of employee participation and the forms it might take in practice. Finally, Chapter 40 summarises aspects of employment law which have not been referred to earlier, and attempts to provide a framework for understanding some of the differences between collective and individual issues in circumstances of considerable legal untidiness.

CHAPTER 33

Perspectives on employee relations

INTRODUCTION

1.   In this text the expression 'Employee Relations' refers to the interrelationships, both formal and informal, between managers and those whom they manage. Thus, employee relations has a wider scope than 'industrial relations', for example, because the former is concerned with all aspects of the interrelationship between management and employees, whereas the latter is confined to the regulation of the relationship principally by means of collective bargaining (see Chapter 35). 'Employee Relations' embraces most, if not all, of the following issues:

- the contractual obligations between employer and employed

- communications policy and practice

- joint decision-making

- joint problem-solving

- collective bargaining

- individual grievance and disciplinary policy and practice

- social responsibility

- employee development

- employee welfare.

2.   In practice, however, 'Employee Relations' is usually confined to the first six issues. In most of these issues, trade unions play an important part, but they are not a prerequisite, for employee relations is as important for non-union organisations as it is for unionised organisations. In recent decades, collective relationships tended to dominate the employee relations scene, even though it is the individual contract which lies at the heart of any system of employee relations. However, there has been a strong trend in the UK recently towards a *reduction* of opportunities for collective rather than individual action.

3.   This chapter considers the roles of the major parties to 'Employee Relations', commencing with a summary of the differing perspectives that are likely to exist among these various stakeholders. Subsequent chapters will examine formal communication in organisations, collective bargaining, disputes and grievances, employee participation and legal aspects of employee relations.

PERSPECTIVES ON EMPLOYEE RELATIONS

4.   The major parties to employee relations are primarily individual employees and their managers. As Figure 33.1 illustrates, however, there are other important stakeholders in management-employee relationships.

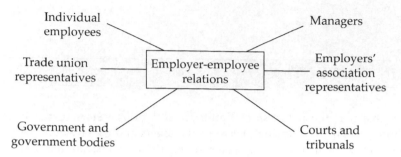

Figure 33.1   *Employee relations: the main parties*

Each of the above parties has a particular perspective to bear on the interrelationship between management and managed. The most significant change since 1980 has been the greatly increased involvement of the law in employee relations. This has taken Britain closer to continental European models of labour relations.

5.   Managers tend to see employee relations in terms of the following activities:

1   creating and maintaining employee motivation

2   obtaining commitment from the workforce

3   establishing mutually beneficial channels of communication throughout the organisation

4   achieving high levels of efficiency

5   negotiating terms and conditions of employment with employee representatives

6   sharing decision-making with employees

7   engaging in a power struggle with trade unions.

Employers' association representatives would tend to share most of these views.

Trade unionists tend to see employee relations as:

1   collective bargaining about terms and conditions of employment

2   representing individuals and groups of individuals in conflict with their management

3   improving the ability of employees to influence events in the workplace

4   regulating relations with other trade unions.

Individual employees tend to see employee relations in terms of the opportunity to:

1   improve their conditions of employment

2   voice any grievances

3   exchange views and ideas with management

4   share in decision-making.

Third parties, such as Government ministers, arbitrators, judges and civil servants may see employee relations more in terms of:

1   creating and maintaining harmonious relationships at work

2   creating a framework of rules of fair conduct in employer employee relations

3   representing the community as a whole in dealing with the repercussions of internal conflicts or decisions made within individual organisations

4   establishing peace-making arrangements to deal with breakdowns in employer-employee relations

5   achieving a prosperous society with justice.

6.   With differing perspectives such as the above, it is not surprising that some degree of conflict is inherent in employee relations. In certain cases, this potential for conflict has broken out with savage and long-lasting results, as the paragraphs on strike statistics indicate (see Chapter 37). Nevertheless, there can also be a substantial amount of common interest, and much of employee relations is concerned with finding out what are these areas and how they can be turned to mutual advantage. We can now turn to the roles of the main parties, commencing with the employers' representatives.

EMPLOYERS' REPRESENTATIVES

7.   In cases where the organisation's own managers do not form the management side in collective bargaining, they are represented by officials of their appropriate employers' association. Such associations are primarily instruments of employee relations (unlike trade associations, which have essentially commercial aims). Their principal objectives are as follows:

1   to represent employers in collective bargaining

2   to develop machinery for the avoidance of disputes

3   to provide information on employee relations matters, and to give advice

4   to represent members on national issues.

The Engineering Employers' Federation, for example, represents a number of important engineering firms. Its main services to members are to:

•   provide advice on employee relations

•   represent collective views of members on Government policies for employee relations

- disseminate relevant information to members
- present the industry's collective views on the economic and social environment to Governments, trade unions and the Public.

The EEF's role in negotiating national agreements has declined as such agreements have been replaced by company-wide agreements. National negotiations between the EEF and the Confederation of Shipbuilding and Engineering Unions (CSEU) ended in 1998. The disputes procedure, however, still stands.

Other well-known employers' associations include:

- Building Employers Confederation
- Newspaper Society
- British Printing Industries Federation
- National Farmers Union.

CONCLUSION

8.   In this chapter we have looked briefly at some of the typical aims and activities of employee and employer representatives. The important role of trade unions is dealt with in a separate chapter (Chapter 36). Other stakeholders in employee relations such as Governments and the Law will be considered in subsequent chapters. The next chapter outlines key aspects of formal communication in an organisation, and these are as important for non-unionised organisations as they are for those with collective bargaining arrangements (see Chapter 35).

CHAPTER 34

Formal communication in organisations

INTRODUCTION

1. The importance of keeping employees informed about general matters affecting their work-role is that it contributes to increased understanding of management's actions, reduces misunderstandings arising from day-to-day activities, and improves trust between employers and employees. Communication, however, is a two-way process – it is a mutual interchange of ideas, feeling and opinions. Thus, in organisations provision needs to be made for upwards as well as for downwards communication. An exemplary employee relations policy on communication could be as follows:

   The Company ackowledges the supreme importance of formal communication channels in the organisation, and will ensure that adequate mechanisms exist to stimulate and channel the exchange of information, suggestions, feelings and opinions between management and employees.

2. In most large organisations the lines of communication are vertical, linked closely to the management hierarchy. The emphasis in these situations is on downward communication by managers and upwards communication by representative groups. Typically both the flow and the weight of communication is biased in favour of the management of the organisation. In small organisations, where relationships are as likely to be lateral as they are vertical, communication flows tend to flow the needs of colleagues rather than lines of authority. These are what Burns & Stalker (1961)[1] called organic organisations, in contrast to 'mechanistic' organisations which emphasise hierarchy.

3. Whether communication channels are vertical, horizontal or both, decisions must be made about the methods of communication to be used. How can employees be kept informed? How can employees' views be gathered? How can major problems be discussed jointly? These are typical issues facing managements. Nowadays there are three principal categories of communication media:

   1 written methods

   2 oral methods

   3 electronic methods.

   We shall look at these briefly in turn.

WRITTEN METHODS

4.   Where detailed information or explanation is called for, written methods are preferable as they are less liable to misinterpretation than oral methods, and have the advantage of being visible. News sheets or discussion documents can be read through at the reader's own pace, difficulties isolated and key points made clear. Employees responding to such written media can refer in a well-informed way to material they have read or studied.

Widely used methods are the use of employee pay-packets to notify important developments affecting the whole workforce or a major segment of it, and notice-boards to communicate information to a wide audience. These two methods are particularly suitable for communicating immediate or current issues. The former is the surest method, but is usually restricted to items of outstanding importance such as announcing major changes in the organisation, or putting forward the management's view concerning a major dispute with trade unions. The latter method is employed much more frequently, being used to keep employees up-to-date about events, meetings and the like.

5.   Some written forms of communication are best presented in booklet form. A booklet can contain detailed, but less immediate, information, which can be referred to as and when necessary. An employee handbook is a typical example of this method of communication. The employee handbook contains many of the terms of the employment contract, and is therefore an important document for employee relations' purposes. The range of information in a handbook may encompass:

- background information about the organisation (brief history, major products/ services, names of directors, managers, etc.)

- basic conditions of employment (hours, pay, bonus arrangements, holidays, etc.)

- sickness arrangements

- absence procedures

- health and safety at work procedures

- particular rules of conduct (e.g. smoking, drinking, gambling)

- disciplinary procedures

- grievance procedure

- life assurance/pension arrangements

- union membership

- termination of employment procedures

- company purchase scheme

Organisations are encouraged to seek advice about such handbooks, and the Advisory, Conciliation and Arbitration Service (ACAS)[2] supply a free advisory booklet on this topic.

6.   Some organisations distribute a popular version of their Annual Report for the information of employees. Others produce a regular journal. These are useful ways of keeping employees informed generally about new contracts and developments, future plans and so on. Over the past decade the law has been used increasingly to encourage consultation and communication with employees. For example, the Employment Protection Act, 1975, requires employers to disclose relevant information to trade union representatives for the purposes of collective bargaining. An ACAS Code of Practice[3] on this topic suggests that information could be supplied on pay and benefits, conditions of service, manpower, performance and financial aspects. The Health and Safety at Work, etc., Act, 1974, also lays certain requirements on employers to

> provide their employees with such information as is necessary to ensure their health and safety at work ... and ... to prepare, and bring to the notice of all their employees, a written statement of their general policy regarding health and safety at work ...

Not only are employers obliged to inform and involve their employees, but now, under the terms of The Employment Act, 1982, they are required, if they employ over 250 employees, to include in their Annual Report to shareholders the initiatives they have taken to develop employee involvement.

ORAL METHODS OF COMMUNICATION

7.   The use of the spoken word constitutes the principal method of communication in any workplace. In the context of this chapter, however, we are thinking in terms of formal communication only. By 'formal' we mean 'planned' communication rather than the day-today use of the spoken word. The most usual forms of communication in this sense are meetings and briefing groups. Meetings may take various forms, but here we will be concerned with (a) management information meetings, and (b) joint meetings. The former are meetings called by the management to enable them to place certain information directly to employees or to put a point of view forward in public. Such meetings may or may not be designed to encourage questions and comment. They are primarily designed to Tell or Sell rather than to Consult (i.e. Listen!). Joint meetings, in contrast, are designed to encourage an exchange of views and perceptions. Management, for example, puts forward a proposal for introducing flexible working hours with the dual objective of (i) informing employees of the proposal, and (ii) obtaining the views of employee representatives, including any counter-proposals that might be suggested. In these situation management are listening as well as talking.

8.   Briefing groups are a form of direct communication between managers and their teams organised on a regular but informal basis. Garnett (1973)[4] argued that the most effective method of communicating what is happening, and why, is 'through small groups on a regular basis'. According to Garnett, briefing groups require a simple checkable routine by which a manager or supervisor can communicate information of relevance to employees at regular (e.g. monthly) meetings which are held in the workplace on an informal basis. This kind of meeting, whilst essentially a downward method of communication using the management hierarchy,

nevertheless does provide an opportunity for managements to *explain* the reasons for decisions and events, instead of just telling employees.

9. Joint meetings between management and employees can range from formally constituted joint committees served by representatives of both parties, to informal joint meetings along the lines of the briefing groups just described. Usually, when reference is made to 'joint consultation' it is the formal committee structure which is intended. Joint consultation refers to joint discussions on matters *of common interest* to management and employees, and is usually contrasted with 'collective bargaining', which is a negotiating process about matters in which the interests of the parties are *not* the same. Clegg (1978)[5] saw three important principles developing in joint consultation from the activities of the Whitley Committee (1917–18):

    > ... there are many topics of concern to employers and trade unions, and to managers and men, which are not suitable for settlement by negotiation and collective agreement; that these topics should be handled by cooperation; and that relations within the plant should be predominantly or entirely confined to cooperation over issues outside the scope of collective agreements.

    By the end of the Second World War, noted Clegg, 'two systems of workshop representation were widely recognised: one, generally through shop stewards, for collective bargaining; a second, usually through elections in which all employees could vote regardless of union membership, for consultation.' Whilst collective bargaining has grown considerably in Britain since that time (see Chapter 35), there is still a great deal of support for joint consultation about matters of mutual interest.

10. The extent to which managers and employees commit themselves to joint consultation depends on a number of important issues:

    - management's view of consultation (i.e. what purpose it serves)
    - employees' views of its purpose
    - the relative strength of the trade unions concerned
    - the state of mutual trust between management and employees
    - the subject-matter of consultation
    - the extent to which joint problem-solving is seen as a legitimate purpose by the parties.

11. Managements tend to see joint consultation firstly in terms of obtaining employee commitment to decisions already taken, or at least well on the way to conclusion. Some managements may see the process as being one by which employees' views can influence, and hence modify, decisions. Yet others see the process as one of mutual problem-solving, even to the point of joint decision-making. The particular position adopted by any one employer depends on the quality of relationships that already exist. The range of options open can be described diagrammatically as shown in Figure 34.1.

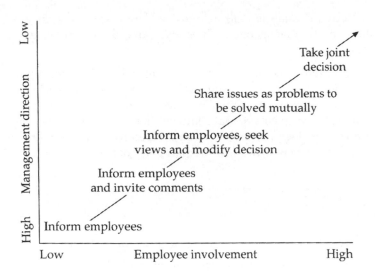

Figure 34.1 *Options in joint consultation*

12. Trade unions tend to see joint consultation as a competing process with collective bargaining. Thus, traditionally, they have attempted to make most topics negotiable in order to reduce the effective power of consultative bodies. The result has been that consultation has not dealt with matters of pay and terms of employment, for example, but has been restricted to welfare, safety and health and productivity. Today's model of joint consultation is nearer to the so-called 'Quality Circle' than anything else. The Quality Circle is a small group of shop-floor employees and their supervisors engaged on shop-floor problems such as quality, safety and efficiency. Whilst many quality circles have powers to institute changes in working methods, they can only operate effectively under management patronage. Hence, while they are useful, they are nevertheless no substitute for employee participation (see Chapter 39) as seen by the trade unions.

13. Individual employees may well see joint consultation as a mechanism for improving the quality of working life by bringing their point of view to bear on discussions of issues connected with day-today working. Where trade union membership or activity is low, joint consultation appears to meet employee needs and management needs effectively. Changes in the mining industry, involving the creation of a new trade union, the Union of Democratic Miners, suggested that union leaders needed to show that they themselves are capable of consulting their members on major issues, or face the consequences of wholesale departures.

ELECTRONIC INFORMATION

14. Now that the dissemination of information and opinions by electronic means is widespread, the upsurge in the use of laptop computers, network systems, satellite communications and other aspects of information and communications technology means that many organisations are now in a position to communicate via these

media. Electronic mail (email) is now widely used as a means of internal communication by managements. It is also possible to send text messages on a mobile phone.

A few organisations make use of video facilities to broadcast information, such as a revised pension scheme or a statement of progress in world markets. Such communication is one-way only. However, interactive methods are available, which will enable recipients to make known their views and impressions by return. Email and Internet facilities are increasingly used for formal communications both locally and between countries for international enterprises.

REFERENCES

1. Burns, T. & Stalker, G.M. (1961), *The Management of Innovation*, Tavistock.

2. *Advisory Booklet No.9 – The Company Handbook*, ACAS.

3. *Code of Practice 2 – Disclosure of Information to Trade Unions for Collective Bargaining Purposes*, ACAS.

4. Garnett, J. (1973), *The Work Challenge*, The Industrial Society.

5. Clegg, H.A. (1978), *The System of Industrial Relations in Great Britain* (3rd edn), Blackwell.

CHAPTER 35

Collective bargaining

1. In Chapter 18 we looked briefly at the individual employment contract, which is still the cornerstone of the employment relationship. In this chapter we examine the main features of 'collective contracts', or collective agreements, as they are more widely known. These agreements, made collectively between employee representatives and managements, are important for individuals because they have the effect of becoming implied terms of the individual employment contract. Thus, if new arrangements for holidays are agreed collectively, then those arrangements will form part of the individual contract of all the employees affected. It is important to mention that by no means all employees are covered by collective bargaining arrangements. In fact, a recent survey found that in almost half of workplaces there were no union members.

    However, where such agreements are made, they do influence the nature of the individual employment contract. Collective agreements will also tend to affect the whole labour market including non-union firms.

2. In this chapter we shall address ourselves to the following questions. What is collective bargaining? What different types of agreements are made, and what subjects do they cover? What happens in the bargaining process? What part does relative power play in collective bargaining?

NATURE AND SCOPE OF COLLECTIVE BARGAINING

3. The following definition of collective bargaining will serve to outline its nature and scope:

    1. In the context of industrial relations, collective bargaining is the process whereby procedures are jointly agreed and wages and conditions of employment are settled by negotiations between employers, or associations of employers, and workers' organisations. (ACAS, 1980)[1]

4. The definition highlights the following important features of collective bargaining:

    1   the emphasis on collective action, not on individual action

    2   the concern both with rule-making and with the settlement of employment conditions

409

Figure 35.1 *Collective bargaining: a basic model*

3   the aim, as in every form of bargaining, is to reach agreement eventually

4   the interests of the parties to collective bargaining are not identical, and therefore conflict of interests is assumed

5   the voluntary nature of the activity, i.e. it is not imposed by law.

5.   The first point is more or less self-evident, since the bargaining process is conducted by representatives of each of the main parties. Trade union representatives act on behalf of the members of the various bargaining units (see below), whilst the management negotiating team act on behalf of their Executive Board. The resulting agreements are drawn up in the context of the particular firm concerned. In some cases, in what are called 'federated' firms, negotiations are conducted by employers' association representatives on behalf of a number of companies. Such negotiations, since they are conducted on behalf of several organisations, have to be more general in outcome and usually result in the establishment of minimum terms of employment.

6.   Collective bargaining, as Figure 35.1 illustrates, takes place against a backdrop of economic, political and competitive events outside 'the organisation', and is not just concerned with improving or agreeing conditions of employment. It is also concerned with drawing up appropriate rules of conduct for management-union relationships. Bargaining over conditions of employment, or what have been called 'substantive' issues focuses on the physical manifestations of the employment contract, such as pay, hours of work and holidays. In recent years there has been a greater focus on including agreement about flexible working practices in substantive agreements. Bargaining about rules, or 'procedural matters', focuses

on the less tangible aspects of employee relations, such as trade union negotiating rights, union membership rights and disputes procedures. This form of bargaining is more a question of defining the context of employee relations than of defining the content of employment conditions. Throughout the 1980s the legal framework of employee relations was greatly extended, and this trend has continued (see Chapter 40).

7. Although the aim of bargaining is to reach agreement eventually, there is usually a degree of conflict between the parties concerning both the means by which agreement may be reached, and the terms on which it is reached. As a general rule, managers, as buyers of labour, seek to achieve agreement at a minimum cost to the organisation and with the maximum pay-off from improved productivity and/or improved employee relations. The trade union representatives, as agents for labour, look for an agreement that incorporates the best possible terms of employment with the minimum number of concessions on working practices. This kind of representation of managers as buyers, and unions as agents, of labour implies a pluralist view of industrial relations. This means that the different, indeed opposing, perspectives of the management and union negotiators are accepted as part of the reality that has to be faced in reaching eventual agreement. A rather less adversarial view is the so-called 'unitary' perspective, which sees common interests, and hence common aims, as paramount. Organisations adopting this perspective emphasise the common interests of employees and management alike, and seek to find mechanisms for enhancing collaboration, such as joint consultation, team briefings and quality circles.

8. These two differing perspectives on management-union relationships have been described by Walton & McKersie (1965)[2] as 'integrative bargaining' in the case of the unitary approach, and 'distributive bargaining' in a pluralist situation. Walton and McKersie see integrative bargaining as essentially a mutual problem-solving exercise to deal with the wage-effort bargain. They see distributive bargaining as a situation where the parties pursue their own interests first. Put simply, integrative bargaining aims for a win/win conclusion, where both management and employees feel that the result is fair and reasonable. Distributive bargaining, by comparison, is more likely to lead to a win/lose outcome, in which one side or the other claims victory, either privately or publicly.

TRADE UNION RECOGNITION

9. The starting point of any collective bargaining is the process of recognising one or more trade unions to act on behalf of the employees affected. Recognition gives trade unions a number of important statutory rights, such as the right to information for collective bargaining purposes, the right to time off for trade union activities, and the right to appoint safety representatives. It also brings other benefits to the union, such as increased membership and revenue. Employers have not been legally obliged to recognise a union unless it can be shown that a substantial number of the employees desire to be represented. Against this background it is not surprising that an official workplace relations survey published in 1999 (the *Workplace Employment Relations Survey 1998*)[3] indicated

that there was no structure for employee representation in 32 per cent of workplaces.

10.   This situation is likely to change in the future, as there is now the possibility of obtaining statutory recognition of a trade union in specified cases. Under the Employment Relations Act 1999 (s.1), there is provision for a trade union to apply to the Central Arbitration Committee (CAC) for statutory recognition in cases where it can demonstrate (a) that it has at least 10 per cent of the workforce in membership, (b) that it has tried unsuccessfully to gain voluntary recognition from the employer. A recent example of this situation is the case of the Honda car company's factory at Swindon, where the AEEU engineering union tried for some time to secure voluntary recognition for the company's 3000 workforce. Honda had been the only non-unionised car manufacturer in Britain since it first opened its factory in 1985. The company adopted a unitary approach to employee relations based upon in-house arrangements between the management and employee representatives, which had produced attractive outcomes for both the company and its employees. This paternalistic situation changed when the AEEU sought CAC support for recognition, and was awarded the appropriate rights. Such a decision is only made after a thorough and independent ballot of all the employees concerned to assess their readiness to be represented by an outside trade union. In the Honda case it was confirmed by the CAC Case Manager that more than 1400 employees had already joined the union, so the 10 per cent minimum was met easily, and the company said they would not oppose recognition.

11.   In cases where the union is seeking a voluntary recognition agreement from an employer, then the latter can ask ACAS to conduct a secret ballot of employees to assess the degree of support for representation by the union concerned. Where there is insufficient support from among the workforce to justify full recognition rights, the employer may nevertheless grant certain representational rights to the union on behalf of those employees who are already members.

BARGAINING UNITS

12.   Trade union negotiators and their management counterparts conduct their discussions at a number of different bargaining levels, typically *national/ industry-wide* or *company-level* or *local/site level*. Bargaining at industry or company-wide levels is usually referred to as centralised bargaining, whilst that at local level is seen as decentralised bargaining. Not surprisingly, centralised forms of bargaining are generally to be found in large public sector organisations and multisite private companies. Use of this approach can enable large organisations to lay down nationally-applicable rules of conduct for employee relations (e.g. regarding union recognition, negotiating structures, grievance procedures, etc.), and the basic framework of pay and conditions to be applied to employees. Thus, a major highstreet bank can ensure that a centrally negotiated agreement with a trade union provides for the proper conduct of management-union relationships on behalf of all its staff regardless of where they are located. It can also ensure that job grading and salary structures are applied consistently across all its branches.

13. The problem with national-level agreements, seen from the perspective of management, is that they lack flexibility in relation to pay and conditions. For example, nationally-agreed wage and salary scales take no heed of local wage/salary rates (except in the case of London, where a special 'London Allowance' is made), and usually provide little or no scope for pay related to an individual's performance. In the current 'enterprise environment', where large companies and even public sector organisations are looking to devolve managerial and budget responsibly to local managers in order to improve business performance, the relative inflexibility of central arrangements is being seen as a stumbling block to growth and efficiency. In its Annual Report for 1991[4], ACAS – the independent conciliation and advisory service (see Chapter 36) – noted that

> The shift towards decentralised bargaining has continued ... This process is intended to encourage variations in terms, conditions and working practices that reflect more accurately local requirements, demands and circumstances.

However, the Report also noted an increase in its conciliation case-load on collective issues, which suggested that decentralising the bargaining process can be a less-than-effective approach to obtaining local flexibility unless those concerned, both local management and trade union representatives, receive adequate training in their negotiating role. This trend has continued, as the latest figures show (see Chapter 37, para 18).

14. Whatever approach is adopted there will be a bargaining structure to support it. Critical, from the unions' point of view, is the issue of *recognition*, i.e. recognition of a union's right to represent the employers' employees (or at least a section of them). Given the historical development of trade unions in the UK, most industrial and public sector organisations find themselves dealing with several unions representing different categories of employee (skilled manual, general workers, clerical staff, technical/professional staff, managers etc.). This has led, for example, to joint agreements between two or more manual workers' unions, and to the making of separate agreements between manual workers, clerical staff and others. However, employers in the new climate of employee relations are looking to streamline their bargaining arrangements, and they are doing so in two ways: firstly by seeking 'single-table bargaining', where one union only negotiates on behalf of the others, which still retain the right to represent their members and carry out typical trade union functions in the workplace; and secondly by seeking a 'single-union agreement' in which one union alone will represent, and negotiate for, all the employees of the company. The first single-union agreement was made between the EETPU and Toshiba. In the last few years, such agreements have slowly but steadily increased in number. One example is the agreement reached in early 1993 between the technical/white-collar union, MSF and Toray Textiles Europe to represent all the workers (i.e. including blue-collar workers) in a new textile plant. This was the first time that the MSF had sought to represent both white and blue-collar employees. This trend keeps up the pressure on unions to merge. The benefit to employers is that they only have to deal with one union in their employee relations instead of many, as in the past.

15. An interesting example of how collective bargaining arrangements can be restructured is provided by a former nationalised industry now privatised – electricity supply. When National Power came into being as a result of

privatisation, all its negotiating machinery and terms and conditions of employment related to its earlier public monopoly status. The new management realised that changes in collective bargaining arrangements would be needed against the background of a competitive environment and a changed business organisation. The previous arrangements were based on a three-tier structure of bargaining at industry, company and local levels. There were also separate collective agreements with each of the three major groups of staff: manual workers, engineering grades and administrative staff. The conditions of employment, and part of the grading structure, were standardised throughout the industry and took no account of local market rates nor of individual company profitability. Salaries were arranged in scales through which individuals moved incrementally on the basis of length of service rather then performance. Also, a number of job demarcations existed between the three principal groups of employees, which prevented the kind of flexible working practices that the management were looking for. Local negotiations were dominated by the agreements made nationally, which left little discretion to either managers or union representatives at site level.

16. As National Power intended to meet its new market challenge by (among other things) giving line managers much greater authority and discretion in devolved operating units, it was decided that new negotiating arrangements would have to be agreed with the unions. The company gave the unions at national level a twelve-month period of notice that they were intending to leave the previously agreed procedure agreements, and that new agreements would have to be made concerning substantive matters. The outcomes were as follows:

1   Two-tier bargaining structures were introduced in separate agreements between the three main employee groups.

2   The two tiers were (i) a company-level committee to discuss and agree terms and conditions, which were to be consistent across the company, e.g. length of working week, basic pay increases, holidays and overtime rates, and (ii) local negotiating committees to discuss and agree local issues, such as shift rotas, call-out payments, annualised hours and local grievances or disputes.

3   Provisions for flexible working (e.g. as between manual grades and engineers) were incorporated into the agreements, and these were accompanied by a revised pay and grading system which reduced the number of grades from about 36 to 12, extended the range of each grade, and allowed overlaps between them.

4   Service-based increments were to be abolished and performance-related pay was to be introduced instead.

5   In order to compensate employees for the loss of incremental progression and other changes in terms and conditions (e.g. flexible working), the company made a lump sum payment to each employee on top of the annual pay award for 1993–4.

17. Although single-table bargaining was urged by the trade unions, led by the Amalgamated Engineering and Electrical Union, the company preferred at this stage to keep separate arrangements for the three main groups. However, as the pay and grading structure applies across the company, it is recognised that this

constitutes a precedent for single-table arrangements at some future date. What is clear is that, at a time of major business restructuring and high unemployment, the management of any company is in a much stronger negotiating position than its trade union counterparts, and can obtain many more concessions than in the past.

TYPES OF AGREEMENT

18. As mentioned above, there are two main types of industrial relations agreement: (a) procedure agreements, and (b) substantive agreements. The basic features of these are described below.

19. Procedure Agreements – These are formal, written procedures that act as a voluntary code of conduct for the parties concerned – managers, on the one hand, and employees and employee representatives on the other. By agreeing a framework of rules, the respective parties are agreeing to abstain from the arbitrary use of their powers.

    Procedure agreements typically encompass the following kinds of issues:

    • recognition of one or more trade unions for the purposes of collective bargaining on behalf of the organisation's employees

    • regulation of membership (e.g. who is to be included and on what terms)

    • representational arrangements (e.g. how many union representatives and what rights they will have?)

    • definition of the subjects for substantive bargaining

    • development of procedures for handling disputes between the parties

    • development of a grievance procedure

    • definition of the rules for dealing with the declaration of redundancies

    • arrangements for the collection of union subscriptions (e.g. by deduction from pay).

    This kind of agreement is usually open-ended in terms of its intended duration, being subject to three or more months' notice from either side if a change is sought. In practice, it is not always feasible to include all relevant issues in one agreement. Thus, it is common to find one agreement on recognition and union rights, another on collective disputes, another on redundancy and so on.

20. Substantive Agreements – These are formal, written agreements containing the terms under which, for the time being, employees are to be employed. Such agreements usually run for a limited period, such as one year, or possibly two. In times of high cost inflation, it is usual for unions to make a formal claim annually, so as to ensure that wages and salaries keep pace with the cost of living. A typical substantive agreement contains details of:

    • revisions to salaries/rates of pay

    • bonus/incentive arrangements

- changes in working hours (e.g. introduction of shiftworking or agreement on a shorter working week)

- holiday entitlement/arrangements

- sick pay entitlement/arrangements

- pension arrangements

- staffing levels

- productivity improvements arising from changes in working practices.

Not all substantive agreements include pay. The reason is that as large companies, in particular, have several levels of negotiations with their unions, pay is usually settled at a corporate level, leaving local units to decide on working practices, hours and holiday arrangements within the framework of a Company Agreement on pay and basic conditions.

THE COLLECTIVE BARGAINING PROCESS

21. The process of negotiating collective agreements does not occur in a vacuum. It forms part of a continuous relationship between rank-and-file employees and their management (also employees!). The aim of the process, so far as employee representatives are concerned, is to achieve a workable relationship with management, founded on mutual respect, in which tangible benefits are realised on agreed terms and not just at management's whim. On their part, management representatives see collective bargaining as one method of attaining corporate objectives relating to pay and the conduct of employee relations. So, by the time bargaining begins, there are already several divergent attitudes at work when it comes to agreeing what is to be negotiated and how. A simplified model of the processes of a typical negotiation is shown in Figure 35.2.

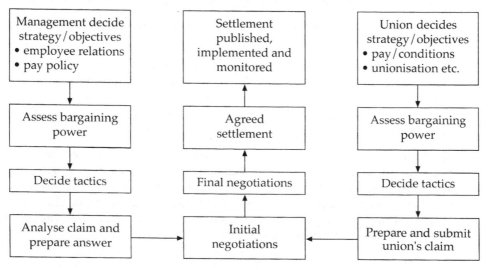

Figure 35.2 *Model of a successful negotiation*

22. Figure 35.2 gives an indication of the extent of preparatory work that has to be undertaken by both sides in a negotiation. Each side has to decide its overall objectives or strategy, assess its relative bargaining strength, and, in the light of that assessment, decide on the tactics to be employed to achieve an optimum result. It is customary for the trade union side to make a claim first, and then for the management to make an initial counter-offer. In practice, the management side will usually be able to concede certain aspects of the claim at the outset, other points will be accepted subject to concessions on the union side, and some features of the claim will be rejected outright. Once management's initial response has been made, then negotiations can commence in earnest. In most cases a settlement is reached without undue delay and acrimony, and the agreed terms of the settlement are published, implemented and subsequently monitored.

So, in a substantive agreement, for example, management will implement new rates of pay and declare new holiday arrangements, whilst the union representatives will co-operate in introducing new working practices and manning levels.

23. It is possible to illustrate the range of options open to each side in a wage negotiation. As Figure 35.3 indicates, each side has its ideal settlement point and a fall-back position. These are set in the light of the objectives sought by each side given their relative bargaining power. For the management side the ideal point is one that represents the *lowest* possible wage increase combined with the *maximum* possible gains in work flexibility and employee productivity. From the trade union side the ideal situation is one where the best possible pay increase is achieved together with acceptable changes in working practices. Recognising that relative bargaining strength and various external factors may affect the equation, each side also has its *fall-back position*. This represents the point beyond which it is not prepared to retreat. If this point is reached, the likelihood of a breakdown in negotiations is considerable. Not surprisingly, therefore, one of the skills of an experienced negotiator is to be able to recognise when the other side is close to its

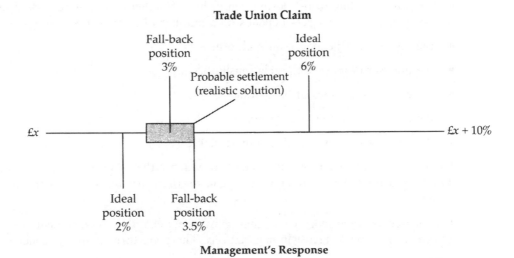

Figure 35.3 *Options in wage negotiations*

fall-back position, and settle before it is too late. A settlement is then likely to be somewhere near what is shown as the 'realistic solution'.

24. In the example given in Figure 35.3, the settlement is likely to be in the 3–3.5 per cent range.

The probable outcome in the above example reflects the tight fall-back position of the management side, probably made in the light of other settlements and the desire to contain labour costs in a highly competitive situation, while still wanting to provide some incentive to employees. The union side, in accepting this level of increase, is probably bowing to general economic conditions, in which their members are lucky to be employed. While the management side is undoubtedly in the more powerful position in the negotiation, they are also under pressure from competitors' behaviour. As is often the case in employee relations, it is usually the external circumstances that have the greatest impact on management-union affairs.

25. Agreements made in the United Kingdom are not usually intended to be legally enforceable against the union. Thus the agreements made rely (a) on the trust that exists between the two parties, and (b) on the authority of each side to carry through its part of the bargain. This raises the whole question of how power affects both the negotiating process and the implementation that follows.

POWER IN BARGAINING

26. Power is the ability to bring about change unilaterally. In industrial relations both parties have a degree of what might be called intrinsic power, that is their ability to influence the other by virtue of their status. For example, a manager has authority granted to him or her by the organisation to reward and to punish employees for whom he is responsible. Handy (1993)[5] calls this 'position power'. An employee may have power in the sense that his or her skills are needed by the employer, who is therefore unwilling to risk losing him or her. Whether or not either side decides to test their power resources depends on a number of factors, for example:

- the degree of dependence on each other
- the amount of trust in the relationship
- the existence of rules of behaviour
- the astuteness of the negotiators
- the extent to which sanctions are available.

These factors will determine the extent to which either side uses coercion rather than persuasion to bring about a settlement, for these are the two main approaches available.

27. The degree of interdependence that exists between the management and the workforce is a major factor in negotiations. There are three main approaches:

either a) employees rely heavily on management, because there is little alternative employment available or   b) management relies heavily on some or all groups of employees, because alternative skills are not available in the marketplace, and because there is no technological alternative available

or   c) both sides recognise their mutual interdependence in the prevailing circumstances.

In option (a) management is in a strong, i.e powerful, bargaining position, because the employees need employment, more than the management need particular employees. In option (b) the employee representatives are in a strong position, because the knowledge and skills of their constituents are not available elsewhere or in other forms. In option (c) both parties can recognise their relative strengths and weaknesses, but because of the influence of external forces which affect them both, they accept a kind of equilibrium in their power relationship.

28. The amount of trust built up between management and trade union representatives, in particular, and between management and workforce generally, is a major factor in the quality of industrial relations of an organisation. Where trust is high, it is less likely that one side or the other will resort to sanctions, i.e. the imposition of penalties on the other. Typical sanctions open to trade unions acting collectively are:

- strikes (withdrawal of labour)
- non-co-operation
- banning extra duties/overtime working
- 'working to rule', i.e. scrupulously observing every detail of safety and operational procedures so as to slow down the entire operation.

Typical management sanctions include:

- dismissal by means of redundancy
- dismissal for strike action
- refusal to implement improvements
- insistence on introducing change regardless of employees views
- ignoring the union's demands.

29. Rules are an important means by which conflict may be institutionalised. Where industrial relations rules exist, then the parties concerned are constrained in their actions.

Typical rules include:

- company rules concerning discipline, etc.
- trade union rules for shop stewards/employee representatives
- custom-and-practice, i.e. 'unwritten' rules
- legal requirements.

Rules of conduct are intended to ensure that if there is a power struggle between the parties it shall only take place after all other efforts have been tried and failed,

419

and it shall be refereed. This point will be discussed at greater length in Chapter 37.

30.   Being in a powerful position by virtue of external events, for example, does not always mean that a negotiating team will exploit its advantage. First of all it has to appreciate that it has an advantageous position, and then it has to be able to use it to good effect. Negotiators do not always recognise the power relationship that exists, and therefore fail to exploit any advantage they might have gained from it, or, worse still, they fail to recognise the limitations on the other side's power and, as a result, get into a confrontation in which dialogue breaks down. An astute negotiator will recognise just how far he or she can go without pushing his or her opponent into an entrenched position. This situation requires careful selection of negotiators and adequate training in the skills of negotiating.

31.   Where coercive power is being threatened by one side, this can only be effective if the other side recognise it as a reality. If one side thinks that the other side is bluffing, they will probably be tempted to call their bluff, and dare them to impose sanctions. For example, if an overtime ban is hinted at by the union side during a firm's peak season, then the management are likely to take it seriously. If, however, an overtime ban is threatened in an organisation that is under-employed in any case, then it is unlikely to carry much weight with the management side. Until recently, the trade unions have enjoyed the negotiating advantage of full employment and a shortage of skills. As a result they have been able to threaten, and, if necessary, enforce strike action and other sanctions with relative impunity. Employers, on their side, have usually been in the position of having to make substantial concessions, or risk a damaging strike. Over the last few years, however, the employment situation has swung away from the unions towards the employers. The consequence is that power to impose sanctions now rests firmly with employers. Thus, if agreement is not reached, the management may enforce redundancies or implement changes without the agreement of the workforce representatives. In a few recent cases, some companies have even withdrawn, or reduced, their original offer to the unions where it was turned down by the trade union side.

CONCLUSION

32.   Collective bargaining is an important element in management–employee relations, enabling agreed rules of conduct to be drawn between the parties. Within those rules terms and conditions of employment can be agreed and implemented with the co-operation of both sides. The benefits which either side is able to obtain from bargaining at any one time depends on (a) the strength of its bargaining position, and (b) its recognition of its position. The intention of the parties to bargaining is to reach agreement on terms that are seen as mutually advantageous. Where this situation is not reached, then the parties are in dispute, and the procedures in such a case are described in Chapter 36.

REFERENCES

1. ACAS (1980), *Industrial Relations Handbook*, HMSO.

2. Walton, R.E. & McKersie, R. (1965), *A Behavioural Theory of Labour Negotiations*, McGraw-Hill.

3. *The 1998 Workplace Employment Relations Survey*, HMSO.

4. ACAS (1992) *Annual Report for 1991*, HMSO.

5. Handy, C.B. (1993), *Understanding Organisations* (4th edn), Penguin.

CHAPTER 36

The role of trade unions

| | INTRODUCTION |

1. Historically, trade unions in the United Kingdom have been viewed as (1) collective employee organisations established to protect employees from arbitrary actions by employers in matters of pay and working conditions, and (2) as promoters of the legitimate interests of people at work. In practice, they have also played an important role in the political life of the nation, and, to a lesser extent, in its social affairs. As with all organisations providing a service to the community, the ability of trade unions to exercise power and influence over users of their service depends on the relative demand for that service. Thus, when demand for skilled labour in the economy is high, trade unions are in a relatively powerful position to negotiate on behalf of that labour. They are also able in such circumstances to employ a wide range of sanctions against employers. When demand for labour is slack and unemployment is high, trade union power to influence events becomes more limited.

2. In Britain the boom period for trade unions was during the 1970s when membership reached a peak of 13.2 million (1979). At that time the demand for labour was high, many skills were in short supply and there were few legal controls over collective action by unions. By 1990 the situation had changed dramatically with a deep recession, record levels of unemployment, changes in working practices brought about by new technology, and, last but not least, a substantial framework of labour legislation designed partly to reduce trade union power in employee relations. The Certification Officer's Annual Report for 1991[1] showed that union membership for 1990 had fallen to 9.8 million. By the year end, 31 December 1995, the decline in membership had slowed with a reported membership of 8.2 million from a total of 256 listed unions[2].

The present level of membership (2000–1) reported by the Certification Officer[3] stands at about 7.9 million, while the number of listed unions has fallen to 218. Thus, the overall decline appears to have stabilised. By the end of the twentieth century, however, the British economy was booming, and what is noticeable is that trade union membership has not recovered despite this high level of economic activity. The *Workplace Employment Relations Survey 1998*[4] showed that in 47 per cent of workplaces there were no union members. This situation may change in the unions' favour given the recent introduction of the statutory right to recognition in prescribed circumstances (see previous chapter).

3. Despite their decline, trade unions still dominate the pay bargaining area and have an important watchdog role to perform, supported by law, to prevent manage-

ments from acting in a purely arbitrary fashion. Nowadays, however, it is more likely that groups of employees in the form of empowered work teams will make the biggest contribution to the control of work and its processes. Employee relations in Britain today is dominated by company/organisation-wide relationships rather than by industry-wide collective arrangements made between trade unions and employers' bodies that were so popular 30 years ago. The legal system now acts to support *individuals* in the workplace as well as collective groups represented by a union. The emphasis in employee relations today is as much on gaining mutual commitment to organisational success as it is to producing joint procedures and rules of behaviour. Wages and other conditions are now more influenced by the competitive situation than by internal power struggles between management and trade unions.

TRADE UNIONS IN BRITAIN

4.   What is a trade union? Essentially, it is an organisation of employees which aims to protect and promote their interests in the workplace, mainly by means of collective bargaining and consultation with employers. Although the last decade has seen a major change in the emphasis of British employment law from collective rights to the rights of individuals in the workplace, there is still a considerable body of law affecting collective activities, especially those of trade unions. The principal legislation on trade unions is contained in the Trade Union and Labour Relations (Consolidation) Act, 1992. The legal definition of a 'trade union' is stated in the 1992 Act, as follows:

> ...an organisation (whether permanent or temporary) which either –
>
> (a) consists wholly or mainly of workers of one or more descriptions and is an organisation whose principal purposes include the regulation of relations between workers ... and employers or employers' associations; or
>
> (b) consist wholly or mainly of –
>
>   (i) constituent or affiliated organisations ... or
>
>   (ii) representatives of such ... organisations;
>
> and in either case is an organisation whose principal purposes include the regulation of relationships between workers and employers or between workers and employers' associations...

5.   The same Act defines what is an *independent trade union*, as follows:

> ...a trade union which–
>
> (a) is not under the domination or control of an employer or a group of employers or one or more employers' associations; and
>
> (b) is not liable to interference by an employer...

In assessing whether a trade union is independent, the Certification Officer (see below) applies a number of guiding principles. These can be summarised in the form of a number of key questions, as follows:

- Is the union financially independent?

- What assistance does it receive from the employer (e.g. premises, offices, extra time off, etc.)?

- How much employer intervention is present?

- What is the union's history (e.g. always independent or started out as a staff association established by the employer)?

- What rules are established to run the union?

- Is this a single-company union (and therefore more liable to employer interference)?

- How is the union organised and financed?

- What is the union's attitude towards negotiations, and what is its record?

CERTIFICATION OFFICER

6. The Certification Officer is appointed by the Secretary of State to supervise the registration and overall conduct of trade unions in Britain. Among his duties are:

- maintaining a list of trade unions

- certifying whether trade unions are independent

- carrying out certain functions regarding trade union amalgamations

- dealing with various complaints made by union members (e.g. regarding breaches of the union's rules relating to internal ballots, disciplinary proceedings, etc.)

- the investigation of a trade union's financial affairs where fraud or some breach of the rules is suspected.

Each year the Certification Officer is required to make a public report on his activities.

7. As mentioned earlier, trade union membership in Britain has fallen over the past years. The decline in membership has been due to several factors, including:

- employment growth has been in white-collar areas not usually known for their interest in trade union representation

- impact of new technology both in manufacturing and service industries, cutting across former job boundaries and leading to requirements for new skills and ways of working

- demise of the 'closed shop' and similar agreements, whereby individuals had to join an appropriate trade union

- less encouragement for collective bargaining, leading to a greater emphasis on individual contracts

- less enthusiasm for trade union membership amongst employees whose fate is now more in the hands of the market-place than in the outcome of collective bargaining

- adoption of single-union agreements in manufacturing firms, leading to the weakening of uncompetitive unions unable to provide credible protection for their members

- de-recognition of trade unions in some cases

- increase in part-time working and short-term contracts in the economy (typically non-unionised).

8.   The number of trade unions has also declined over the past twenty years, mainly as a result of mergers and take-overs. Like their counterparts in management, many unions have had to seek such arrangements in order to expand in some cases, and to survive in others. The 1992 Act, and earlier regulations governing amalgamations, lays down procedures enabling mergers to take place, including arrangements for consulting and balloting the membership. These are of two types – *transfers of engagements* and *amalgamations*. In the former case, a majority of the membership of the transferring union have to agree to the move. In the latter situation, a majority of *both* unions have to agree, and the new union has to be listed and certificated in the usual way.

9.   The difference between the two types are as follows:

1   *Transfer of engagement* – in this situation the transferring union loses its legal identity, whilst the receiving organisation retains its identity. Thus, it is more like a take-over in the business world. A typical example of this type of merger took place in the financial services sector in April 1999, when the Union of Royal and Sun Alliance Staff was absorbed into the NatWest Staff Association.

2   *Amalgamation* – this is more in the nature of a true merger, for it produces a new organisation with a new name. Typical examples of large-scale mergers in recent years include (1) that of the Civil and Public Services Association with the Public Services Tax and Commerce Union to form the Public and Commercial Services Union with a membership of over 245,000 (March 1998), and (2) the amalgamation of three banking unions – Banking Insurance and Finance Union, UniFI and NatWest Staff Association – to form UNIFI.

TYPES OF TRADE UNION

10.   Trade unions have typically been placed into four categories, as follows:

- *Manual workers' unions* – nowadays these are principally the large general workers' unions, although there are still a few craft-based and industrial unions. An example of a general union is the Transport and General Workers

Union with 872,000 members in 1999, making it the largest such union. Examples of craft unions include the Amalgamated Engineering and Electrical Union (727,000) and the Graphical Paper and Media Union (201,000). An example of an industrial union is the Union of Construction Allied Trades and Technicians (123,000).

- *White-collar unions* – these are mostly general unions for clerical, administrative and technical workers, although there are still some specific to certain occupational groups, especially in the public secton. An example of a general white-collar union is Unison (1.27m), which resulted from a merger of three unions representing local government officers, public employees and health workers. It is now the largest of all trade unions. An example of another public sector union is the Public and Commercial Services Union (258,000). An example of a large white-collar union in the private sector is the Manufacturing Science and Finance Union (405,000).

- *Managerial/professional unions* – these tend to recruit from those employed in middle-management and professional occupations. Examples include the Engineers' and Managers' Association (EMA), the Association of University Teachers (AUT), which have fewer than 100,000 members, and other larger unions such as the Royal College of Nursing (RCN) with 327,000 members and the National Union of Teachers (NUT) with 295,000 members.

- *Staff associations* – these are unions which were originally formed from amongst the employees of a single employer, usually in the white-collar sector. Despite their close association with one employer, they were able to demonstrate their independence and were given certificates of independence by the Certification Officer. In the last five years, changing business circumstances have prompted several mergers among this category of trade union. UniFI and NatWest Staff Association have already been mentioned above. Others, such as the Nationwide Group Staff Association have grown by transfers in from smaller groups, such as the Hambro Staff Association, in August 2000.

11. The overall profile of trade unionism in Britain over the past twenty years has changed from one dominated by manual workers to one distinguished by large numbers of white-collar occupations. Of the top 16 trade unions (in terms of size) some 35 per cent of the membership in 1999–2000 were to be found in the white-collar sector. Most trade unions are affiliated to the Trades Union Congress (TUC), which is the central confederation of unions in Britain. With the decline in national collective bargaining and with increased legislation in industrial relations, this body has lost some of its former power and this is reflected in its corresponding employer bodies, at least so far as their industrial relations influence is concerned.

THE TUC

12. The role of the TUC today is primarily to represent the interests of employed people in debates and policy discussions on employment and social security matters (e.g. pensions policy) at national, European Community and international levels.

The organisation's policies (which are not binding on members) are derived from the annual congress of the TUC, while day-to-day operations are administered by a General Secretary and staff directed by a General Council, composed of a cross-section of independent trade union leaders who are elected every year. Most unions are affiliated to the TUC, which currently represents a membership totalling 6.75 million.

EMPLOYERS' ASSOCIATIONS

13. The approximate employers' equivalent to the TUC is the Confederation of British Industry (CBI), which represents all the major industries in Britain. Its aims include acting as a national reference point for those seeking industry's views (e.g. governments, foreign investors, etc.) on a range of economic, social and commercial matters. The CBI also operates a range of information, advisory and training services for its members. In particular, it produces a number of important regular surveys of economic and business trends.

14. Employers' associations, as defined by the 1992 Act (s.122), are primarily intended to handle employee relations issues on behalf of a group or groups of employers. Their main objectives are as follows:

    1   to represent employers in collective bargaining

    2   to develop industry-wide procedures for the avoidance of disputes

    3   to provide information and advice to members on employee relations matters

    4   to represent members on national employee relations issues.

    As mentioned above the role of employers' associations has declined in recent years as collective bargaining has become a company matter rather than an industry matter. It should be noted that employers' associations are not the same as *trade associations*, which are exclusively concerned with furthering their members interests in commercial and competitive matters (e.g. the Publishers' Association).

TRADE UNION REPRESENTATIVES

15. Broadly speaking, trade union officers are of three types:

    • the full-time paid official, employed by the union

    • the part-time, voluntary official, who is elected in a locality to be a Branch officer of his or her union

    • the workplace representative (shop steward/staff representative) who is an employee of the firm or enterprise, but who acts on behalf of a group of his or her fellow employees.

    Full-time officials are employees of the trade union. Their overall task is to carry out the union's policies under the direction of its executive committee. The policies are usually directed towards a two-fold objective: (a) to protect the interests of their members against arbitrary or unfair actions of employers, and (b) actively to promote the interests of their members in matters concerning their terms and conditions of employment. Some examples of typical union objects are as follows:

1. The objects of the Society shall be:

    (a) To act as the negotiating body on all questions affecting the conditions of employment and the relations between members and their employers;

    (b) To protect and promote the interests of members;

    (c) To maintain the professional status of the Public Service or Services;

    (d) To promote the efficiency of the Services in which members are ... employed;

    (e) To provide benefits payable on the death of members...

    (Public Sector Union)

2. The objects of the Association shall be:

    (1) To improve the economic and social well being of the members and to enhance their status.

    (2) To watch over, promote and protect the common and individual interests of its members and to regulate relations between members and employers ...

    (4) To provide financial assistance to members who have withdrawn their labour with the authority of the National Executive Committee or who are locked out as a result of a dispute with their employers ...

    (8) To promote legislation in Parliament for the benefit of the members ...

    (Private Sector White-collar union).

17. The above two examples are quite different in nature and scope from the following example – now consigned to history – taken from a former manual workers' craft union:

> To advocate the socialisation of the means of production, to be controlled by a democratic State in the interests of the entire community, and the complete emancipation of labour from the domination of capitalism and landlordism, with the establishment of a social and economic equality between the sexes.

18. Most unions have a strong central office function, providing leadership, specialised advice and public relations on behalf of all members. Most unions also have regional offices, or their industry equivalent, to coordinate activities amongst a defined group of their membership. Large unions also have offices at local, district level to ensure that the services of full-time officials are available to those members employed by a variety of different employers.

19. Returning to the local level of industrial relations, shop stewards or staff representatives are the key personnel on the union side. Goodman & Whittingham (1973)[5] described a shop steward as:

> ...the representative of union members in the workplace, being acknowledged as such by the management and by his trade union, but who is neither a full-time officer nor a branch official...

Thus, a shop steward is firstly a local representative of a group of employees, e.g. as a local branch official, whatever other office he or she may hold.

20. Shop stewards cannot act as they like, but are constrained by various company and trade union rules. The degree of power they hold depends on several factors, including:

   - the extent to which collective bargaining is centralised at company/industry level
   - the state of the local labour market
   - the nature of the company's wages structure
   - the degree of support for the union amongst employees
   - statutory provisions (e.g. relating to strike ballots, etc.).

   In organisations where the major decisions about conditions of employment are made at a national or industry level, there is little scope for local representatives to bargain. Where delegation of bargaining is encouraged, then local representatives have much more discretion over what shall be negotiated. Shop stewards and staff representatives are less powerful if the labour market is plentiful, but have greater influence in conditions of skills shortage. The nature of the wage structure can also strengthen or decrease the power of local officials. Where wages depend heavily on incentive payments, worked out locally, then shop stewards will be involved in negotiating pay. As this activity will be carried out against the background of immediate production needs, this clearly puts them in a strong bargaining position. Conversely, if everyone is paid annually on an incremental scale, then local representatives will have no influence over pay. Shop stewards and staff representatives also depend on their constituents for support. If this is forthcoming, their power position is strengthened; if it is not, then their position is weakened considerably. The increased role of statute law is another factor, which usually restricts their powers.

21. Trade union representatives, whether full-time officers or voluntary officials, are influenced strongly by the dominant culture of their union. Each union has its own particular set of values and standards. Some pride themselves on their democratic procedures and sense of service to the membership. Others stress their ability to lobby politicians and open key issues to public debate. At the present time, due to the impact of new technology on employment prospects, and the competitive nature of world markets, all trade unions are concerned about their future as viable organisations. It is likely that more unions will amalgamate, if they can find a suitable 'marriage partner', in order to preserve their negotiating strength in relation to employers.

REFERENCES

1   *Annual Report of the Certification Officer, 1991* (1992), Certification Office.
2   *Annual Report of the Certification Officer, 1995* (1996), Certification Office.

3   *Annual Report of the Certification Officer, 2000–2001* (2001), Certification Office.

4   *Workplace Employment Relations Survey 1998*, HMSO

5   Goodman J. and Whittingham, T. (1973), *Shop Stewards*, Pan Books.

CHAPTER 37

Disputes and sanctions

INTRODUCTION

1. No relationships are without their difficulties, and Employee Relations is no exception. However sound the underlying relationship between a management team and their workforce may be, there is always scope for mistakes and misunderstandings on both sides. It is prudent, therefore, to devise an agreed procedure to be followed by the parties if a dispute arises. This chapter describes some of the legal and practical issues that occur when the employer-employee relationship breaks down.

DEFINITIONS

2. For the purposes of this chapter we shall divide all disagreements between employer and employee into two categories:

    1   *collective disputes* (henceforth referred to simply as 'disputes'), involving issues taken up on behalf of groups of employees by their representatives

    2   *individual disputes* (henceforth referred to as 'grievances'), involving individual employees only.

3. This chapter will deal with disputes, since they have a far greater impact on employee relations than individual grievances, and because they are specifically referred to in a number of labour law statutes. The present legal definition of a collective dispute is based on the meaning given to the term 'trade dispute' in the Trade Union & Labour Relations (Consolidation) Act, 1992 (TULRCA). To be considered a dispute the following conditions must be fulfilled:

    • the dispute must be between workers and their own employer

    • the dispute must be wholly or mainly about matters directly affecting their terms and conditions of employment.

LEGAL IMMUNITIES FOR TRADE UNIONS

4. The reason why the legal definition of a dispute is so important to trade unions is that the law provides protection against civil actions for those organising strike

action or other forms of industrial action on behalf of a trade union. If immunity was not provided, the officials concerned would be liable to civil action for inducing employees to break their contracts of employment. In the 1970s in Britain, the legal immunities provided for trade unions and their officials were extremely wide ranging. Over the past 30 years, however, these immunities have been much more closely-defined. If a union or an official organises industrial action which interferes with contracts, including the employer's contracts with his or her customers, there will only be immunity from civil action if the following conditions apply:

1   there is a trade dispute, and the action is in furtherance of that dispute

2   the trade union concerned has previously held a secret ballot of members, and a majority have agreed to support the action.

3   due notice has been given of official action by the trade union to the employee

4   the action does not constitute secondary action or lead to secondary picketing (i.e. the action does not involve an employer who is not a party to the trade dispute)

5   the action is not designed to enforce trade union membership.

Furthermore, a trade union will be held liable for unofficial industrial action initiated by workplace representatives (shop stewards, etc.) unless it repudiates the action in writing at the highest level to the members concerned, their leaders and the employer concerned

5.   Where immunity is not provided, or where it does not apply (e.g. in the case of other civil wrongs committed by strikers), the persons who have suffered loss as a result may sue the union or the officials concerned for damages. The damages that may be awarded are limited by legislation, but could be substantial. Other action that may be taken is for persons affected to seek an injunction (an order restraining somebody from doing something) from the courts. If an injunction is disobeyed, the union concerned may be declared to be in contempt of court and face heavy fines. If the fines are not paid, as happened in the case of the Miners' dispute 1984–5, then the union's funds may be liable to seizure by the courts. The law, therefore, is playing an increasing role in disputes. However, ACAS still considers that 'industrial relations in general continue to rely on the voluntary efforts and co-operation of all those involved'.

6.   It should be noted that there is no protection for unions, or members, taking action to support individuals who have been dismissed as a result of *unofficial* strikes. There are also certain groups of employees who are forbidden by law to strike, notably the armed services and the police force.

PICKETING

7.   Picketing is a tactic that has been employed by trade unions for a century or more. Basically it consists of an attempt to enforce a strike and its effects by placing union members at the gates of the employer's premises in order to persuade fellow

employees and others (e.g. suppliers' employees) not to cross the picket line and go into work. There has never been any legal right to picket, but the practice has not been considered as unlawful in the pursuit of a trade dispute, so long as the picketing did not cause a breach of the peace. Whereas most picketing has been conducted in a peaceful manner, there have been a few notorious cases in past years of mass picketing involving considerable violence to persons and damage to property. Union members who do cross a picket line are now protected by the TULRCA from being disciplined by their union.

8.   Trade unions and union members will be immune from civil action when picketing so long as certain conditions are fulfilled (see TULRCA).

A person acts lawfully if he attends

(a) in contemplation or furtherance of a trade dispute...

(b) at a specified place, namely

   (i)   at or near his own place of work...

   (ii) if he is unemployed and either his last employment was terminated in connection with a trade dispute or if the termination was one of the circumstances giving rise to a trade dispute, at or near his former place of work...

   (iii) if he does not ... normally work at any one place ... at any premises of his employer...

   (iv) if he is an official of a trade union, at or near the place of work or former place of work of a member of that union whom he is accompanying and whom he represents ...

(c) for the purpose only of peacefully obtaining or communicating information or peacefully persuading any person to work or abstain from working.

9.   It is important to note that picketing is only permissible at the place of work, and not, for example, at the private residence of an employer. This restriction also acts to prevent the formation of what were once called 'flying pickets', where groups of individuals would travel from one picketing point to another, regardless of whether they were employed at the sites concerned. The presence of mass pickets often served to heighten tensions and lead to violent scenes. The present law, therefore, protects only *peaceful* actions by pickets in pursuit of their strike. Action outside what is permitted by the TULRCA may lead to criminal charges against individuals, including fines or imprisonment.

10.   The law is supported by a Code of Practice on Picketing, which though not binding in its own right may be taken into account by the courts when considering actions that might be taken against pickets or their union. Among its guidelines the Code includes:

   • organisers should ensure that in general the number of pickets does not exceed six at any entrance to a workplace

   • an experienced person, preferably a trade union official should be in charge of the picket line

- pickets should be properly identified by means of badges or armbands

- organisers should maintain close contact with the police during the picketing

- union members who cross a picket line should not have disciplinary action taken against them by the union

- essential supplies and services (e.g. to hospitals, schools and public health, etc.) should not be impeded.

DISPUTES PROCEDURES

11. One of the principal ways by which the majority of organisations avoid strikes and other trade union sanctions is by drawing up a mutually agreed procedure for dealing with collective disputes. Sometimes the procedure is contained in a negotiating agreement as part of the total arrangements for collective bargaining, union recognition rights, agreements about the content of bargaining and other issues. Sometimes, as in the engineering industry, a separate disputes procedure is agreed. We shall look shortly at the agreement made between the Engineering Employers' Federation and the Confederation of Shipbuilding and Engineering Unions, but in the meantime will examine the kind of procedure that might exist in a medium-sized company in any industry.

12. The stages of a typical disputes procedure for the handling of collective disagreements are likely to be as follows.

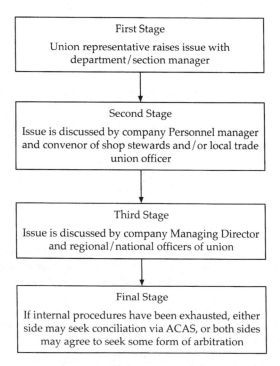

Figure 37.1 *Stages of a disputes procedure*

Stages One to Three are considered as domestic stages, as the dispute still remains within the company. Once all internal stages have been tried to no avail, then outside assistance may be sought. This usually means asking for the Advisory, Conciliation and Arbitration Service (ACAS) to attempt to bring the two sides together and to find some common ground on which further progress might be made, i.e. conciliation. If conciliation fails, then arbitration may be considered, but this can only proceed if both parties agree to this step. What arbitration does is to take the decision for the parties. This decision will generally be regarded as morally binding on both sides. The role of ACAS in industrial disputes will be considered later in the chapter.

13.   The Engineering Employers' Federation agreement with the unions in their industry sets out to draw up the general rules which should be applied by the constituent companies and their union representatives. It identifies two stages of the procedure:

> Where any party has a matter to raise, it shall first be discussed within the DOMESTIC STAGES of procedure. If the matter is not resolved at that level the matter may be referred to the EXTERNAL STAGES.

The domestic, or internal, stage is to be agreed in each of the establishments concerned and should be in written form:

> This [agreement] should cover such matters as the number of stages, the stage at which shop stewards ... and the chief shop steward shall be involved, the level of management to be involved ... and the time limits within which different types of questions shall be discussed.

14.   Thus the domestic procedure is similar to the general model illustrated in Figure 37.1 above. However, there is one significant difference in that the engineering procedure proposes that the domestic stages should incorporate agreed time limits for discussions. This serves primarily to prevent the management side from unnecessary stalling on an issue. A typical procedure might state that 'Once an issue has been raised formally by the shop steward concerned, the appropriate section / department manager shall give a reply within ten days ... '.

15.   The engineering agreement states that where the parties fail to reach a settlement at the final domestic stage, then either one of them may refer the issue to an external conference:

> An EXTERNAL conference shall involve representatives of the employers' association and local officials of the trade union(s) concerned as well as the management representative(s) and the shop steward(s) concerned. An EXTERNAL conference shall be held within seven working days ... of receipt of written application from the party wishing to pursue the reference.

The agreement does not specify the arrangements for such a conference, but does regard this stage as final. In other words, after external conference the procedure is exhausted. The EEF disputes procedure agreed with the CSEU is rarely used nowadays. Only about one case a year proceeds to the national (EXTERNAL) stage.

THE ROLE OF ACAS IN INDUSTRIAL DISPUTES

16. ACAS, the Advisory, Conciliation and Arbitration Service, was established by the Employment Protection Act 1975, when its terms of reference were as follows:

    > The Service shall be charged with the general duty of promoting the improvement of industrial relations, and ... encouraging the extension of collective bargaining and ... the reform of collective bargaining machinery. (EP Act 1975, s.1)

    Employee relations were at a low ebb when these terms of reference were drawn up. Over the next twenty years the situation changed considerably, and ACAS saw a change of emphasis away from collective bargaining to broader issues of organisational effectiveness. In its annual report for 1999/2000, ACAS set out its mission statement as:

    > to improve the performance and effectiveness of organisations by providing an independent and impartial service to prevent and resolve disputes and to build harmonious relationships at work.

    This unitary emphasis derived directly from the Trade Union and Labour Relations Act 1992. This has recently been repealed by the Employment Relations Act 1999, which has restored part of the original terms of reference, so that the present mission of ACAS is 'to promote the improvement of industrial relations'.

17. In relation to collective disputes between employers and trade unions, ACAS offers three main services – conciliation, mediation and arbitration. The distinctions between these three are briefly as follows:

    - **Conciliation** – ACAS offers help and advice aimed at bringing the disputing parties to the point where they themselves can agree a mutually acceptable solution. This approach is voluntary, and the agreements reached are the responsibility of the parties.

    - **Mediation** – ACAS, in the form of an experienced and independent mediator, takes a more proactive role than in conciliation, suggesting possible solutions and drawing up proposals. As with conciliation any decision to agree a way forward is taken by the parties themselves. The mediator does not impose a decision.

    - **Arbitration** – in this situation, the parties acknowledge that they cannot agree a mutually acceptable solution and jointly ask a third party to make the decision for them. ACAS can appoint a single arbitrator or a board of arbitration. It can also refer certain cases to the Central Arbitration Committee. The last named is essentially a senior tribunal. It usually sits as a chairman (legally-qualified) plus two experienced lay arbitrators representing both sides of industry. Its awards are not legally binding, but are always accepted by the parties in practice.

18. ACAS's success in assisting disputing parties towards an early solution of their difficulties can be measured by the number of cases in which a settlement was achieved out of all the requests that were received. Figure 37.2 shows just how successful the Service has been over recent years, and points to the value of building up a core of experienced staff capable of handling the range of issues in dispute. In every sense of the phrase, people are ACAS's prime resource, and their expertise is sought after by employers and trade unions alike.

	2000/1	1999/00	1998
Requests received	1472	1500	1301
Requests withdrawn	58	81	45
Conciliation completed	1226	1247	1214
Settlements	1139	1152	1110
Conciliation unsuccessful	84	95	104

Figure 37.2 *ACAS success in collective conciliation*

(Source: ACAS Annual Reports)

The causes of the disputes dealt with in the completed cases of collective conciliation are categorised by ACAS under the headings listed in Figure 37.3. The percentages show the relative importance of the different causes of dispute year on year.

	2000/1	1999/00	1998
Pay/terms and conditions of employment	604 (49%)	647 (52%)	581 (48%)
Recognition	264 (22%)	147 (12%)	131 (11%)
Changes in working practices	65 (5%)	66 (5%)	77 (6%)
Other trade union matters	56 (5%)	62 (5%)	80 (6%)
Redundancy	98 (8%)	152 (12%)	144 (12%)
Dismissal and discipline	90 (7%)	117 (9%)	157 (13%)
Others	49 (4%)	56 (5%)	44 (4%)

Figure 37.3 *Completed conciliation by cause of dispute*

The figures show a preponderance of cases concerned with the basics of the employment relationship – pay and conditions of employment. The clear implication is that, in their collective negotiations, employers and trade unions are most likely to disagree about the essence of the employment contract – pay, bonuses, hours of work and leave – rather than the complexities of their interaction in the workplace.

20.   The number of situations where conciliation fails and the parties insist on going to arbitration is very small in comparison with the overall number of requests for assistance. In 1994 there were 156 such cases. By 1997 this figure was reduced to 71 cases, and in the year 2000/1 it was down to 62. These cases often occur against actual or potential industrial action by employees, such as strikes, overtime bans and refusal to work on rest days. The subject matter of these disputes is usually one or more of the following:

●   annual pay (not always the most frequent cause in this context)

●   other pay and conditions of employment (bonuses, expenses, shift-work allowances, holiday entitlements, etc.)

●   dismissal and discipline issues

●   job grading issues.

In the vast majority of these cases the parties opt for a single arbitrator. Only one or two cases a year are dealt with by a board of arbitration.

PENDULUM ARBITRATION

21. Pendulum arbitration is an approach applied to disputes of interest where the arbitrator has to make a straight choice between the union's last claim and the employer's final offer. This forces a win/lose outcome, rather than the traditional compromise award, which is what most arbitrators will aim for in order to achieve a fair result for both parties. ACAS, in its 1984 Report expressed its reservation about the pendulum approach:

> Such awards [straight choice] will give a clear result but may not necessarily stand the test of fairness or improve relations in the longer term.

22. In Britain, pendulum arbitration is not common and is usually associated with 'single-union, no strike' agreements (see below). The majority of such agreements make no provision for conciliation or mediation prior to going to arbitration. This means that the parties move directly from a failure to agree to acceptance of a pendulum decision. The advantages claimed for this kind of arbitration are as follows:

1   it encourages the parties to act reasonably in their respective claims and offers, since one of them must lose once the arbitrator has made a choice

2   it restricts the discretion of the arbitrator by obviating any attempt at a compromise decision – hence this approach is sometimes known as 'final-offer arbitration'.

The disadvantages are:

1   there is no flexibility for the arbitrator, who has to treat each party's last position as a total package and a decision made one way or the other

2   it is not always clear exactly what is the final claim or offer

3   there is no prospect of reaching a face-saving formula in a 'Win/Lose' situation, and this may cause one of the parties to lose confidence in arbitration as a means of resolving disputes.

23. The likelihood is that future agreements of this kind will incorporate a conciliation or mediation step in the procedure before any reference to pendulum arbitration. This does give the parties concerned an opportunity to resolve the dispute themselves, albeit with third party help. This alternative may be more attractive to the parties than having decisions made for them by an independent arbitrator.

STRIKES

24. A strike is a form of industrial action taken by employees against their employer by means of stopping work. Most strikes are a result of the parties' inability to achieve

a settlement of some dispute over wages and other conditions of employment. Employees who take strike action are effectively breaking their contract of employment and are liable to be sued by their employer or others affected by their action, such as customers or suppliers. In order to permit strike action under certain conditions, the law provides a degree of protection to employees against actions for breach of contract. So-called 'protected industrial action' can only be called upon after the employees' representatives or their trade union officers have exhausted all the usual disputes procedure. The union then has to ballot its members on the question of strike action, and if the proposed action is supported by the employees, the union has to give appropriate notice of the strike (at least one week) to the employer. This means that the strike is 'official' and protected by the law. It is generally unfair to dismiss strikers in this situation. Where strike action is taken without the above procedures, it is considered an 'unofficial' or 'wildcat' strike and the employees involved are not protected from being sued for breach of contract, nor indeed from being dismissed by the employer.

25. Strikes are only protected where they involve a dispute between employers and employees over terms and conditions of employment. They are not protected where a strike is taken on political grounds, or in support of workers at a different employer. The UK government has kept detailed statistics on the number and nature of strikes for many years. Strikes, whether official, or unofficial, are only recorded where at least ten workers are involved or where the strike lasts for at least one day. The official statistics for strikes produced over the last 30 years provide an interesting picture of the changing nature of employee relations in Britain, as Figure 37.4 indicates.

Year	No. of stoppages	No. of workers involved (000s)	Working days lost (000s)
1970	3,943	1,801	10,980
1974	2,946	1,626	14,750
1980	1,348	834	11,964
1986	1,074	720	1,920
1990	588	237	1,880
1993	211	385	649
1994	180	265	331
1996	244	364	1,303
2000	212	183	499

Figure 37.4 *UK strike statistics 1970–2000 (source: Department for Employment/Labour Market Trends)*

26. The official figures show the sorry state of industrial relations in Britain during the period 1970–80, when there was a rash of lengthy strikes in key industries such as mining, railways and printing. The 1980s saw a significant reduction in the number of working days lost even though the number of stoppages was still in excess of 1000. Since 1990 the situation has improved dramatically with far fewer stoppages and fewer workers involved. Particular strikes can produce a substantial loss of

working days where they linger on even if the numbers taking part are relatively small. By the end of the century, the combined effects of global competition on the UK, and the legal restrictions on industrial action, had produced a much less adversarial spirit between employers and employees.

27. The official statistics published by the Department of Employment use a range of measures of strike activity, of which the following are the most important:

- the number of stoppages

- the number of workers involved

- the number of working days lost

- the number of stoppages by industry

- the incidence of stoppages per 1000 employees per industry

- the geographical distribution of stoppages by region

- the causes of stoppages

- the duration of stoppages in terms of the number of working days lost

- the number of stoppages in terms of the total number of workers involved.

28. Taking the number of working days lost per 1000 employees provides for the relative size of the industry concerned. This indicates how industry-wide are the effects of strike action. Thus, the effects of the miners' stoppages on the issue of pit closures in 1985 was massive, and indeed in that year these stoppages accounted for four million out of the total of 6.4 million working days lost throughout British industry. However, because these particular comparisons take size of industry into account, a low figure does not necessarily mean that the number of working days lost as such was also small. For example, in 1986 some 257 working days per 1000 employees were lost in the public services. However, due to the sheer size of this group, the actual number of working days lost was the highest of any industry group for that year.

29. Strike statistics, therefore, should be treated carefully. Any one perspective on strike activity can be quite misleading. Several perspectives have to be taken together in order to provide a fair picture, especially in terms of overall balance. What, of course, the figures do not provide is any assessment of the social, economic and political background against which strikes occur. Thus, the state of the economy, legislation on collective bargaining, social attitudes towards change and a range of other factors have to be looked for elsewhere, if one is to attempt an explanation of strike activity in any particular year.

30. Although the official statistics provide few clues to the wider context in which strikes occur, they do supply some evidence concerning the *prima facie* cause of stoppages. This is provided by an analysis of the principal causes of stoppages, which have been identified as follows:

- pay – wage rates/earnings levels/fringe benefits

- duration/pattern of working hours

- redundancy questions

- trade union matters
- working conditions/supervision
- staffing and work allocation
- dismissal/discipline.

In 1995, for example, the most frequent causes were pay (70 stoppages), redundancy questions (43 stoppages) and staffing (39 stoppages) out of a total of 212 stoppages involving 145,000 workers.

31. Until the mid-1980s only about 5 per cent of strikes were 'official', in the sense that the trade union's leadership had given its agreement to a strike and had given due notice to the employer(s) concerned. These strikes were usually major affairs compared with the myriad of much more limited actions that took place in the remaining 95 per cent, which, however, were unofficial. Unofficial action is action taken without the authority of the union leadership and without due notice being given to the employer. This state of affairs changed dramatically with the passing of the Trade Union Act, 1984 which required unions to conduct an official ballot of their members before taking strike action and to obtain a majority of those voting, otherwise immunity from civil actions for damages will not be granted by the courts. Successive Employment Acts since 1980 also restricted the scope of trade union immunity. Thus, currently the only strikes that may receive the protection of the law are official strikes. Unofficial ('wildcat') strikes are no longer protected and have effectively vanished from the scene. The principal legislation involved here is the Trade Union and Labour Relations (Consolidation) Act, 1992, as amended by the Employment Relations Act 1999.

BALLOTS

32. In order to encourage the use of secret ballots on proposals for strike action or other important trade union purpose (e.g. the election of officers), the Secretary of State is currently empowered to provide payments towards the costs of a ballot. Qualifying ballots include the following:

1   strike ballots (or other industrial action) in respect of specific actions but not general union policy development

2   ballots for the election of a union's key officers (General Secretary, etc.)

3   ballots on amendments to union rules

4   ballots on decisions about amalgamation with another union

5   ballots on whether to hold a political fund on behalf of members

6   ballots to obtain the views of members concerning proposals made by an employer regarding their pay, hours of work, holidays, etc.

33. Ballots have to be conducted in secret, and proper arrangements must be made for the correct counting of voting papers. Employers, subject to certain conditions being fulfilled, are obliged to provide facilities on their premises to enable voting to

take place properly. Part of the reasoning behind such legal support for ballots is to ensure that trade unions are made accountable to all their members rather than just to their activists. However, the present system of refunding ballot costs to the trade unions is gradually to be phased out.

NO-STRIKE AGREEMENTS

34. A relatively new phenomenon in British industrial relations in recent years has been the so-called 'single-union no-strike' agreement, or what ACAS calls the 'new-style agreement'. The first such agreement was signed between Toshiba Consumer Products, a Japanese-owned company, and the then electrician's union (EETPU), in 1981. Since then a small number of similar agreements have been made, usually involving the Amalgamated Engineering and Electrical Union (AEEU). The key features of a no-strike agreement are as follows:

- sole recognition and bargaining rights are granted to a single trade union

- union agreement that members will not be called on to withdraw their labour in the event of a dispute

- if a dispute occurs both parties agree to go to arbitration (usually pendulum arbitration)

- introduction of 'single-status' across the company (i.e. common conditions of service for both staff and manual employees, including salaried status)

- improved employee consultation and participation arrangements

- complete labour flexibility (i.e. no demarcations between jobs, no restrictive practices, etc.).

35. The underlying aim of such agreements is to encourage a unitary approach to employee relations in organisations rather than the adversarial approach that typified most of British industry in the past. It is not surprising that the majority of agreements signed to date have been in situations where either a previous business has collapsed, or where a completely new enterprise has been established (a 'greenfield' situation). Clearly, these two scenarios are more likely to encourage such agreements than those involving established companies with existing multi-union bargaining arrangement. What is not true is that the companies making the 'single-union no-strike' agreements are invariably Japanese-owned. About half the agreements have been negotiated by British companies and the rest by foreign-owned companies of whom about half are Japanese. Such agreements do have their 'knock on' effect on employee relations attitudes in larger companies. For example, all the major car manufacturers in Britain are aware of the implications of the 'new-style' agreements, which effectively preclude strikes on the one hand and encourage labour flexibility on the other, to produce a very competitive way of assembling motor vehicles.

CHAPTER 38

Grievances and discipline

INTRODUCTION

1. The previous chapter focused on collective disputes. This chapter considers the disputes that arise in practically every organisation between individuals and their managers. Whereas, in strike terms, nine out of ten firms do not experience a strike in a year, in the case of grievances the situation is reversed, with hardly an employer completely free of grievances in the course of twelve months. This chapter will also look at the disciplinary arrangements made by organisations, often jointly with the trade unions concerned.

GRIEVANCES

2. We noted in the previous chapter that a grievance is an individual dispute between an employee and his or her employer. However, since individuals and their problems are as much a part of employee relations as collective issues, then it is in the interests of both management and trade unions to have a written procedure for dealing with grievances. There is also the point, of course, that individual disputes, if left to fester, may themselves lead to a collective dispute. The main object of a grievance procedure is to settle the issue at the earliest possible stage.

3. The stages of a typical grievance procedure are shown in Figure 38.1. The procedure outlined above is intended to inform employees of their rights in the matter of grievances. Whilst the procedure gives the employee the opportunity to raise his or her grievance at the highest possible level, the main aim should be to enable such disputes to be resolved as close as possible to their source. This, of course, depends on the degree of authority given to supervisors and junior managers to resolve grievances at their level. In an organisation that believes in delegation, this will present no problem. Where, however, the organisation reserves disputes of any kind to senior managers only, then inevitably grievances will not easily be settled at the earliest possible stage. A feature of effective grievance procedures is that they include time-limits at each stage. Thus, at stage one five working days is usually the limit within which a supervisor must reply to the aggrieved person. The inclusion of a time-limit helps to speed the entire process, particularly from the management's point of view. A busy manager is much more likely to set aside time for dealing with a grievance if he is subject to an agreed time-limit.

4. In order that justice is not only done, but seen to be done, it is usual for the

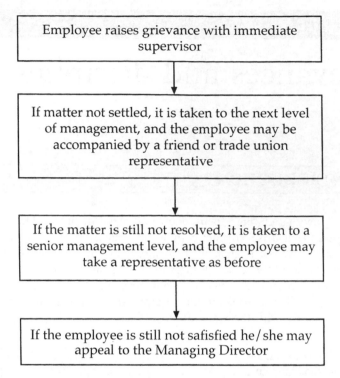

Figure 38.1 *Stages of a typical grievance procedure*

procedure to permit an aggrieved person to take a friend or trade union representative along with him or her to the second and subsequent stages. The presence of this other person helps to ensure 'fair play', not only for the employee concerned, but also for his or her management, for sometimes a flimsy or contrived grievance can be discredited by the employee's representative. The right to be accompanied by a fellow employee or a trade union official is now enshrined in law (Employment Relations Act 1999, s.10).

5. Once a grievance has passed beyond the first stage, it necessarily gathers greater formality. Hence written records should be kept after that stage. Such records will be extremely useful if the grievance turns eventually into a collective dispute, involving the use of the organisation's collective disputes procedure.

6. Whilst grievances are almost inevitable in any organisation, their numbers can be kept to a minimum by maintaining effective communication between employees and their immediate supervisors/managers. It is helpful if conditions of employment, in the broadest sense, are open to discussion at any time on an informal basis, in addition to any formal negotiations that may take place as part of collective bargaining. A firm with a well-motivated workforce and adequate communication procedures can expect little in the way of grievances.

DISCIPLINARY MATTERS

7. Whereas grievances are initiated by the employee, disciplinary matters are initiated by management. At work discipline is a question of (a) devising appropriate rules of behaviour for employees and (b) of providing fair and consistent means of enforcing them. ACAS[1] in its Code of Practice on disciplinary matters suggests the following as model features of a disciplinary procedure.

   The procedure should:

   • be in written form

   • specify to whom it applies

   • provide for the speedy progress of disciplinary hearings

   • indicate the various forms of disciplinary action that may be taken (warnings, dismissal, etc.)

   • specify appropriate levels of authority for exercising disciplinary action

   • ensure that individuals are informed of the disciplinary charges made against them

   • permit such individuals to state their case, and to be accompanied by a friend or trade union representative (See Employment Relations Act 1999, s.10)

   • ensure the proper investigation of every case before disciplinary action is implemented

   • ensure that individuals are informed of the reasons for the action being taken against them

   • ensure that no individual is dismissed for a first offence except in cases of gross misconduct

   • provide for a right of appeal.

8. The standards expected of employees are set out in various documents such as company rule-books, employee handbooks and disciplinary procedures. There will also be 'unwritten', or implied, rules. Since discipline is as much a matter of general behaviour as of specific behaviour, few organisations specify every rule. Whether or not an offence is the cause of disciplinary action also depends on the nature of the circumstances, on management's previous attitudes and on the culture of the organisation generally. What in one firm would be a dismissable offence, could be far less serious in another firm. For example, smoking in certain manufacturing operations is so dangerous that breach of this rule will lead to instant dismissal. In another situation a 'no-smoking' rule, based on the general possibility of a fire hazard would probably be dealt with on the basis of warnings.

9. An example of two approaches to discipline are given below (Figures 38.2 and 38.3). In the first example, taken from local government, the references to discipline are set out in a handbook on disciplinary procedures. In the second example, the references are taken from a nationally agreed procedure in the ceramics industry.

A sound standard of discipline is essential for the efficient and orderly conduct of the County Council's affairs and for the safety and well-being of its employees ...

The procedures take full account of the ACAS Code of Practice on Disciplinary Practice and Procedures in Employment ...

... employees from time to time may engage in actions which can lead to disciplinary proceedings. These actions can be grouped into three broad areas covering poor performance, misconduct and gross misconduct ...

Poor Performance [means]:

(a) consistent failure to perform work to a reasonable and acceptable standard...

(b) evidence of negligence or inadequate attention to the requirements of the job ...

Misconduct [means]:

(a) breaches, infringements or non-observance of any of the general rules ... or of the specific working rules ... e.g. poor attendance, bad time-keeping ...

(b) failure to obey the lawful and reasonable instruction of a supervisor ...

(c) unreasonable or unacceptable conduct, e.g. abusive behaviour, being under the influence of alcohol ...

(d) threatened violence on a colleague or member of the public whilst at work ...

Gross Misconduct [means]:

... behaviour which, in the County Council's view, subject to investigation, warrants immediate dismissal ... Instances could be ...

(d) Falsifying various claim sheets such as time-sheets, bonus sheets, car allowance ... etc. ...

(f) Malicious damage to County Council property ...

(g) Sexual misconduct in work which demands high levels of personal behaviour, e.g. in work with children ...

Figure 38.2 *Extracts from a disciplinary procedure (local authority example)*

10. The above extracts focus particularly on standards of performance and conduct, which form a major part of the procedure concerned. They indicate the detailed nature of this particular approach, which can be contrasted with the national ceramic industry agreement (Figure 38.3). The latter lays down the basic ground-rules of a disciplinary procedure. In this second example we shall highlight the basic process of implementing disciplinary action.

Object:

The purpose of this procedure is to ensure fair treatment of operatives who become liable to disciplinary action because of failure to meet satisfactory standards with regard to conduct, job performance, attendance or time keeping ...

Responsibilities:

It is the responsibility of management to ensure that the rules and standards are fair and reasonable ... to explain them ... and ensure that they are kept
The operatives should familiarise themselves with the rules ... and observe them ...

Procedure:

In all cases, other than instant dismissal, the following procedure will apply:

Stage I   In the first instance the foreman ... will warn the operative verbally. The warning will be recorded ...

Stage II   In the event of failure to meet the agreed standards within a reasonable period of time of the verbal warning a written notice signed by the relevant Manager will be given to the operative ...

Stage III   ... In the event of continued failure to meet the agreed standards, written notice of dismissal will be given by a senior manager ...

Right of Appeal:

In the event of any dispute arising on this agreement, the operatives shall have the right of appeal to a higher level of management ...

Figure 38.3 *Extracts from disciplinary procedure (ceramics industry)*

11.   A key issue in any disciplinary procedure is that of authority to act. In order to achieve fairness and consistency, individual managers and supervisors need to know what the limits of their authority are when it comes to disciplinary action. The options available to organisations are as follows:

- oral warning to employee
- first written warning
- second or final written warning
- suspension of employee with pay
- suspension of employee *without* pay
- dismissal.

It is important that the procedure makes it clear who is empowered to do what. Usually, oral warnings are left to the immediate supervisor or manager; written warnings usually involve the section or department manager, with a copy to Personnel; second or final warnings are usually agreed by the site Personnel

Manager before being issued; suspension (with or without pay) and dismissal are usually authorised by a senior manager or director. As in the case of grievances, an individual who is going through the disciplinary procedure may take a colleague or union representative with him or her.

DISCIPLINE IN THE USE OF INFORMATION TECHNOLOGY

12. The proliferation of personal computers and work-stations in every type of office means that many employees now have ready access both to electronic mail (email) and use of the Internet (via the world-wide web). It is in the interests of the employer as well as the staff that a clear policy on email and Internet use should be available. Data security was referred to in Chapter 17, and any major breach of personal data is likely to lead to large fines being imposed on the data controllers concerned. Personnel staff need to be especially watchful in this regard. However, the general issues of email and Internet abuse potentially affect all staff, and this is why it is important to establish proper disciplinary rules covering this aspect of working life.

13. Email communication has the advantage of enabling written messages to be passed speedily between individuals and around organisational networks, and for responses to be returned just as quickly. The excessive use of email, however, can overload certain individuals, resulting in relatively trivial items being read and replied to as well as more important items. The ready facility for forwarding items to a number of colleagues simultaneously can also produce a situation where many individuals receive mail that is not strictly relevant to them. Such over-enthusiasm for using email may not in itself result in disciplinary action, but could prepare the ground for an over-casual use leading to the dissemination of offensive material which certainly would constitute misconduct. Material of a racial, religious or sexual nature used to make fun of, bully or perhaps titillate colleagues is clearly a disciplinary matter. An advantage here is that unlike a telephone conversation, an email can be stored electronically, which makes it easier for an employer to produce evidence of misconduct. If an organisation has a policy of monitoring emails, it should state this openly, and be aware of possible breaches of individual privacy under the Human Rights Act (see Chapter 40).

14. Employee access to the Internet opens up the organisation's own networks to abuse from external sources. Viruses may be unwittingly imported, junk-mail included in email messages and pornography downloaded, unless steps are taken to restrict the types of addresses accessible from the user's work-station. The careless use of passwords by employees can lead to unauthorised 'hacking' into an organisation's database. These are serious issues for any employer. Add to these the possibility of copyright breaches in respect of downloaded material, and the sheer cost of time-consuming Web-browsing, it is not surprising that many employers are keen to set down clear and fair guidelines on use of IT communications.

15. A policy statement on Internet use is likely to include the following points:

     - *access* – guidance on who should have access to email and use of the Web

- *passwords* – rules to ensure unauthorised use of passwords, and rules for allocating or changing passwords

- *web use* – guidance regarding legitimate sites for access, banning access to sites containing offensive or indecent material, and limiting the amount of time spent browsing; also rules clarifying who is permitted to make adaptations to the organisation's own website

- *email* – guidance concerning disclosure (and non-disclosure) of email addresses, limitations on private use of the organisation's email, restrictions on the content of emails (e.g. banning offensive or salacious gossip), and rules for email distribution

- *disclaimers* – guidance in respect of disclaimers to be attached to emails sent by employees (e.g. regarding any legal references made)

- *monitoring* – a statement to the effect that all or some emails and website access may be monitored on a routine basis

- *disciplinary rules* – a statement setting out the types of breach which constitute misconduct and/or serious misconduct, together with the sanctions that may be imposed on staff.

16. Organisations can do much to minimise the need for the formal punishment of employees. Proper selection, thorough training and effective supervision should all be combined to make poor performance a very rare event amongst employees. So far as misconduct is concerned, effective leadership and adequate communication by managers and supervisors should greatly reduce opportunities for bad behaviour to develop in individual employees. The disciplinary code should be there only as a backstop, when all else has failed. All employees can play a part in setting a good example in terms of job performance and general behaviour at work.

In the light of all the above examples, we can now summarise the basics of disciplinary action in the following diagram (Figure 38.4).

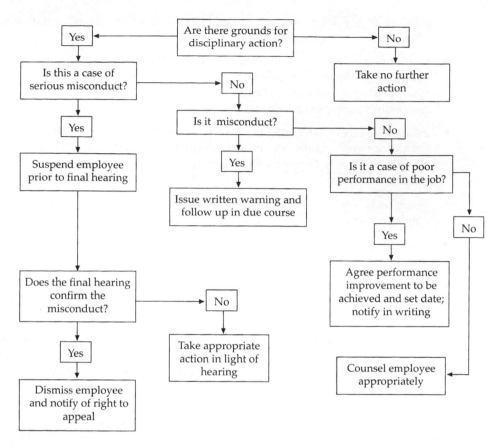

Figure 38.4 *Discipline flowchart*

REFERENCE

1. ACAS (1977), *Code of Practice 1: Disciplinary Procedures*, HMSO.

CHAPTER 39

Employee participation and empowerment

1. The concept of *'employee participation'* refers, in general terms, to the participation of non-managerial employees in the decision-making processes of an organisation. Most writers on the topic agree with this statement. However, there is much disagreement about the degree of employee participation or involvement in decision-making. Almost thirty years ago, Pugh (1977)[1], in an article in *The Times*, distinguished six different meanings of 'increased partici-pation', ranging from improved consultative machinery through wider collective bargaining to workers' control. The British Institute of Management (1977)[2] in that same period described 'participation' as:

    > ... the practice in which employees take part in management decisions and it is based on the assumption of a community of interest between employer and employee in furthering the long term prospects of the enterprise and those working in it.

    Today the options for participation (see below) may also include share ownership and job enrichment. What they will not encompass is anything approaching workers' control. Indeed, it is worth pointing out that 'participation' has been extended in more formal ways to trade union members, who under the Trade Union Reform and Employment Rights Act, 1993 (TURERA) are ensured proper participation in the appointment of senior officials and decisions about strike action, for example.

2. The concept of 'empowerment' is a recent addition to the language of personnel management. Like 'participation' (a) it is usually applied to non-managerial grades, such as team members, and (b) it appears to have several possible meanings. These can range from having increased authority (i.e. legitimate power) and therefore the ability to exercise a wider range of choices at work, to being given a more varied and interesting job – a form of 'job enrichment'. At best 'empowerment' increases individuals' discretion over how they do their work. It may also provide additional opportunities for group problem-solving on operational issues. At its weakest it represents a sham attempt at promising a degree of autonomy that will never be permitted. What empowerment definitely is not is any attempt to hand over unqualified power to junior management or rank-and-file employees. It is probably best thought of as a method of delegation which enables work decisions to be taken as near as possible to the operating units and their customers – both internal and external.

PERSPECTIVES ON PARTICIPATION

3. There are two main reasons why organisations currently take an interest in increasing the role of ordinary employees in decision making: (1) they have been forced into the situation as a result of political pressures (e.g. as in the European Union), or (2) they see 'participation' and 'empowerment' as means of obtaining greater employee motivation and commitment to organisational objectives. We shall look briefly at each of these motives in turn.

4. To date, no legislation on 'employee participation' has been put forward in Britain. Most of the legislative proposals that have been made have come from the European Union. The chief proposal is the draft Fifth Directive, which initially proposed that Community members should adopt two-tier boards in limited companies and ensure worker participation on the supervisory board. Following various objections to these proposals, especially from Britain, which unlike the Continent has unitary (single) boards rather than two-tier boards, they have been revised to allow for several choices as follows:

    • collective bargaining on company decisions

    • two-tier board structure (see below) with workers on the supervisory board

    • single board structure (see below) with workers having non-executive directorships

    • workers' representation on a company council below board level.

5. The last mentioned of the above choices – employee representation on company councils – is moving ahead rapidly throughout the European Union. This arises from a Directive on Works Councils (1994) by which multinational companies employing more than 1000 staff throughout the EU (or more than 150 in at least two of the states) have to ensure the establishment of consultative councils (or similar arrangements) by September 1996. The idea behind these so-called European Works Councils is to provide employees with formal arrangements for information about company progress and prospects, and to encourage an exchange of views between employees and senior management on essentially strategic issues rather than on the more usual operational issues. Britain, having qualified its acceptance of the Social Chapter of the Maastricht Treaty, is not obliged to follow this Directive. Several multinational companies have nevertheless set up such bodies in the belief that they represent 'good practice' in employee relations.

6. An important reason for encouraging greater employee participation in decision-making, even if only through increased consultation, is that it can lead to improved efficiency and effectiveness in delivering goods and services to customers. If the means of participation not only increases employees' contribution to problem-analysis (which may bring a sense of recognition to individuals), but also enhances their ability to make important operational decisions, then increased employee commitment and motivation is likely. This is turn is likely to lead to better product/service quality and enhanced customer satisfaction. Thus, there are sound practical reasons for finding ways of increasing the involvement of ordinary employees in the day-to day running of an organisation. Where real differences of interpretation of

the concept of 'participation' occur is when involvement at a *strategic* level is implied, for here what is at stake is the future direction and nature of the organisation. Most managements are not enthusiastic about sharing strategic decisions with employee representatives, partly because they do not want to alert their competitors to important strategic moves (e.g. a major divestment or a significant take-over), and partly because they often have to face up to some unpleasant decisions about redundancies and redeployments among existing staff.

EMPLOYEE PARTICIPATION – THE OPTIONS

7. As mentioned above, there has been considerable debate over the last twenty years as to the principal meanings of participation, and what these may imply in terms of management–employee arrangements. The range of options currently under discussion is shown on a continuum (Figure 38.1), which reflects the various degrees of participation that may be made available to employees. They range from participation in the ownership of the organisation by means of shareholdings through involvement in day-to-day operations to the appointment of employee directors on company boards.

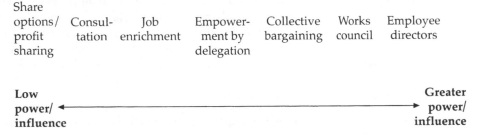

Figure 38.1 *Range of options for employee participation*

8. *Share options/profit-related pay.* These options have been promoted in recent years by Conservative governments in the UK as part of the drive to extend the scope and spirit of private enterprise in the economy. Share option schemes offer employees the chance to own shares in their company and thus participate in its financing, as well as to receive all the information normally made available to shareholders. This option does give employees the chance to take a stake in their employer's business, but is scarcely relevant if one considers 'participation' to involve sharing in decisions. There have also been schemes to link employee effort to overall profitability by permitting profit-related elements in total pay. Part of the incentive for both employers and employees lies in the tax benefits that operate for those who participate in such schemes.

9. *Consultation* This can be seen as 'participation' only in the sense that employees are consulted about decisions affecting their working lives. This does not imply that employers need take any notice of employees' views. However, there have been efforts in recent years to give communications with employees a higher profile. Companies that make use of workplace consultative groups (e.g. quality

453

circles) are not only engaging in a management–employee dialogue, but in many cases are actively encouraging such consultation in order to improve working methods, quality standards and productivity. This form of consultation comes much closer to real participation in decision-making, at least so far as operational matters are concerned.

10. At a wider level, the Companies Act 1985 places a requirement on companies with over 250 employees to show in their Directors' Report what steps they have taken to inform or consult with their employees on issues that affect them. Certain other Acts also contain consultation requirements. These include the duty on employers to disclose relevant information during collective bargaining or consultation regarding redundancies (Trade Union & Labour Relations (Consolidation) Act, 1992), and certain requirements to consult on safety issues (Health & Safety at Work Act, etc., 1974).

11. *Job enrichment.* This topic, which has been referred to earlier (Chapter 9), is 'participation' in the sense that employees are given greater discretion over immediate work decisions. It can also add to employee motivation by increasing their responsibility for their work outputs and increasing job interest. However, it does not usually offer any real opportunity to participate in even the operational decisions taken in the organisation.

12. *Empowerment through delegation.* A participative management style that encourages real delegation of authority implies that all employees will be encouraged to play a part in the decisions affecting their work. In practice, this may be no more than a paternalistic method of involving employees in day-to-day affairs. However, where a bona fide approach to participation is adopted, then it is likely that employees will in fact become 'empowered' by being able to share fully in decisions affecting their immediate work affairs.

13. *Collective bargaining.* Collective bargaining in the UK is less common now than it was even a decade ago. Managements are currently in a strong negotiating position mainly because of (1) the continuing limits on trade union sanctions, and (2) the increased competitiveness of the marketplace. Employers are therefore less inclined to engage in negotiations with their employees, since this may restrict their flexibility in responding to changes in market conditions. Should labour become a scarce commodity, then unions will be in a more powerful position to insist on joint negotiations before agreeing to major changes in policies or practice. Bargaining by its very nature is adversarial and its outcomes, therefore, depend on the relative power of the parties and the extent to which compromises can be reached. Compared with consultation collective bargaining is an essentially active form of employee participation, but in the past often reflected the views of a minority of employees even in situations where union membership was high.

14. *Works councils.* These are essentially joint bodies of managers and employees established to consider and agree key matters affecting employment within the organisation. They are not for union-only employees, as would be the case in collective bargaining, but must be open to all grades and groupings of employees regardless of any union membership. The EU initiative on European Works Councils is especially concerned with the consultative aspects of participation in multi-sited European Community enterprises. Works councils should be discussing

future plans as well as dealing with important short-term matters of mutual interest. The Toyota Motor Manufacturing Company's Members' Advisory Board (see Case study 8, p. 471) is an example of this form of participation.

15. *Board representation.* The appointment of rank-and-file employees to non-executive directorships on the company's board is another manifestation of employee participation. Where there is a system of two-tier boards, as in Germany, the employee-directors sit on the Supervisory Board, but not on the smaller Executive Board. A few large corporations in the UK, which has unitary boards, have experimented with non-executive employee-directors on the board, and undoubtedly this approach enables employees' views to be heard on key policy issues. However, such employee directors are invariably in a minority and are hardly likely to be able to effect radical policies against the wishes of their colleagues from management. This option ensures that employee's view-points are heard at board discussions, and debated. However, given the nature of all directors' responsibilities as company directors, the actions of employee directors outside the board are strictly limited.

PARTICIPATION – KEY QUESTIONS

16. Organisations considering some form of increased employee participation in decision-making need to ask themselves a number of important questions. These will include raising such issues as the following:

   • Is 'participation' to be interpreted chiefly as consultation (i.e. low employee power/influence) or as shared decision-making (i.e. high employee power/influence)?

   • Should participation be confined to operational processes or extended to include strategic issues?

   • What topics/issues should be the subject of any shared decision-making?

   • How should individuals be selected for participation in relevant bodies?

   • What part should trade union representatives play in any arrangements?

   • How should statutory obligations be dealt with (e.g. disclosure on redundancies/communication on safety matters, etc.)?

   • What standards of behaviour may need to be established for participants (e.g. confidentiality, good faith, etc.)?

   • What employee training and other resources may need to be provided?

   • How can participative groups contribute to the needs of other stakeholders, especially customers?

17. In the current climate of intense competition, reduced public expenditure and the need to create flexible, responsive organisations, it would seem that both private and public sector organisations could gain much from increasing the extent of their

employees' participation in the decision-making processes of the corporation. This could certainly be achieved at an operational level, where the outcomes are likely to be increased efficiency, employee motivation and customer satisfaction. Indeed, the current tactic of reducing the number of organisational levels in the organisation (de-layering) has resulted in greater front-line level discretion over problem-solving and operating decisions. The thrust towards the deployment of flexibly operating, self-reliant work teams inevitably leads to much greater delegation from middle management.

18.   Participation at a more strategic level clearly has less immediate pay-offs for all stake-holders and raises issues of real power in organisations, i.e. the power to decide the future direction and shape of the organisation, the power to close down or open up parts of the organisation, the power to decide who stays and who goes. Decisions about employee participation at this level are less likely to be forthcoming, except in organisations that truly value grass-roots opinions about future plans and options. Even in these cases the senior management has to take account of the whole range of stakeholder interests, and not just those of one group, whether employees, shareholders or customers. Where difficulties arise between employees and management, for example in major proposals for work restructuring or flexible working, then the most likely way forward is by means of collective negotiations conducted on employees' behalf by an effective trade union. In today's enterprise economies it is this ability to represent employees from their external standpoint which is the greatest justification for the continued existence of viable trade unions, which are considerably cheaper to employ as advocates than most lawyers!

PARTICIPATION – TRADE UNION AFFAIRS

19.   Reference was made to union members' participation in major trade union decisions in the opening paragraph of this chapter. The effect of the Trade Union Reform and Employment Rights Act, 1993, is to extend the legal mantle of employment law over key trade union activities such as the election of senior officials and decisions concerning industrial action. The Act is intended to encourage all union members and not just activists to participate in key decisions taken on their behalf. It provides for the following:

- arrangements for the election of the union leadership

- secret ballots where industrial action such as strikes is concerned

- ballots regarding the establishment or maintenance of trade union political funds.

Public funds are currently available to unions undertaking such ballots, although this funding is to be phased out over a three year period. The Act, incidentally, also requires employers to play their part in facilitating union ballots on their own premises.

CONCLUSION

20. Much of the progress on the topic of employee participation has arisen from the enlightened self-interest of many leading companies, who see it as a way of improving customer service as well as possibly enhancing employee motivation and interest. The other major influence has been the European Union, which is increasing the pressure on all member states, whether they have signed up to every protocol or not, to improve employees' access to key decision-making mechanisms in their organisations. For Britain this has led to several large multinational companies setting up their own arrangements for participation, which will not only encompass their employees working in other EU countries, but will also include their UK workforces. Organisations that are interested in establishing formal participation arrangements along the lines of the EU requirements are assisted in the UK by organisations such as the Involvement and Participation Association, and the Chartered Institute of Personnel and Development, which have produced a joint Code of Practice (1990)[3] on employee involvement.

REFERENCES

1. Pugh, D. (1977), 'The Six meanings of Participation', *The Times*, 29/9/77.

2. British Institute of Management (now the Chartered Institute of Management) (1977), *Employee Participation – the Way Ahead*.

3. IPA/IPM (now CPD) (1990), *Employee Involvement and Participation in the United Kingdom*.

CHAPTER 40

Employment law: individual rights

INTRODUCTION

1. This chapter summarises key aspects of individual employment law that have not been dealt with elsewhere in the book. Since this is an area of management that is subject to continuous development, as new statutes come into force and key cases are decided, it is advisable to refer to authoritative updates, such as those contained in *Tolley's Employment Handbook*[1].

2. As illustrated in Figure 40.1, there are four sources of employment law in England and Wales.

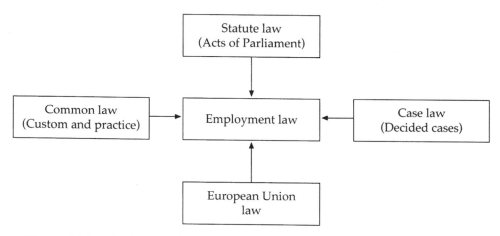

Figure 40.1 *The framework of employment law in the UK*

Statute law – this is the written law arising from various Acts of Parliament passed by the nation's law-makers, and which is the most far-reaching of the legal influences on the workplace. Important examples affecting individual rights include the Employment Rights Act, 1996, and the Sex Discrimination Acts, 1975/1986.

The *common law* – this is the 'unwritten law' that arises from custom and practice. In the context of this chapter it is especially relevant to contracts of employment (see also Chapter 18), and the law of torts (civil wrongs) affecting workplace incidents.

Case law – this is effectively the stock of decided cases issuing from the courts and industrial tribunals in England and Wales, and now also including cases decided in the European Court of Justice and the European Court of Human Rights. The importance of case law is that it interprets statutes as they are applied in particular circumstances. For example, case law has helped to build up an understanding of how statutory rules governing the dismissal of employees should be interpreted. They have also helped to clarify what is, and what is not, unfair discrimination on grounds of race or sex.

European Union law – this is legislation arising from the Treaty of Rome, 1957, and subsequent treaties (e.g. Maastricht). It comprises *Regulations*, which are directly binding on member states, and *Directives*, which are not directly binding but require domestic legislation within a stated period. It also includes decisions of the European Court of Justice. Such decisions are now contributing significantly to case-law in the UK. Effectively, European-wide standards are setting the template for UK Labour Courts.

3.   The main topics covered in the chapter are as follows:

   •   basic human rights

   •   individual rights in the workplace

   •   time off for specified reasons

   •   the role of Industrial Tribunals.

HUMAN RIGHTS ACT, 1998

4.   This act of Parliament is derived directly from the European Convention on Human Rights, and enables British citizens to obtain redress through UK courts and tribunals instead of having to refer to the European Court of Human Rights. The Act came into force in October 2000. It is an overarching law, which means that other relevant pieces of legislation must be interpreted in the light of its principles. The new Act applies *prima facie* to public bodies, such as government departments and local authorities, but its implications stretch much further. In respect of employment matters, it is inconceivable that the Act will not affect all organisations that employ people. There are sixteen basic rights protected in the Act, including the right to life and to liberty and security.

5.   The rights most relevant to public sector organisations and other enterprises are as follows:

   •   *Right to a fair trial* – everyone is entitled to a fair and public hearing within a reasonable time by an independent and impartial tribunal established by law. Disciplinary rules within organisations should make clear provision for a right of appeal to an employment tribunal.

   •   *Right to respect for private and family life* – everyone has the right to respect for their private and family life, their home and their correspondence. Managers need to be aware of possible abuses of this right when monitoring employees' personal telephone calls or emails whilst at work. Clear guidelines will need to be produced to show staff where the limits are to be set. This is especially important when company rules require behaviour to conform to security and other restrictions on personal communications. Employers do not have an absolute right to contact employees at their home, unless such arrangements form part of the employees' contract of employment.

- *Freedom of thought, conscience and religion* – this right includes the right to change one's beliefs. For employers this right has to be considered in relation to the Race Relations Act, and clearly any exercise by individuals of the basic right must not contravene legislation designed to restrict racial or religious abuse. Managers now need to take more notice of religious beliefs than in the past, and should ensure that employees are not *expected* to work on their Sabbath days and on major religious festivals. With an increasing reliance on the provision of services for twenty-four hours a day, seven days a week, such considerations must be given appropriate place in employment conditions.

- *Freedom of expression* – individuals have the right to hold opinions and receive and impart ideas without interference by a public authority. This right extends to dress codes and personal appearance. Managers now have to review disciplinary rules to ensure that any restrictions on an employee's right of expression is a reasonable one in the circumstances (e.g. for safety and health reasons).

- *Freedom of assembly and association* – this includes the specific right to join or not to join a trade union, and to hold union meetings during working hours. The right to take industrial action is not explicit, but is strongly implied. Most of the implications of this basic right are already well catered for in UK businesses and public sector organisations.

- *Prohibition of discrimination* – access to the rights available under the Act should not be denied on any discriminatory grounds unless they can be justified objectively. The effect of this right is to extend the scope of anti-discriminatory measures to religious and political issues as well as those already in force regarding sex, race and disability discrimination. Any such prohibitions in the workplace have to be seen to be lawful and reasonable.

6. All managers in the workplace, and personnel/human resource managers in particular, will have to review their existing practices in relation to grievance and disciplinary codes, and similar codes of behaviour. They will also need to review their agreements with recognised trade unions in order to ensure that they conform to the spirit of the human rights legislation. The Act does not give *carte blanche* to individuals to do or say what they want without any consideration of public unrest or outrage caused by their behaviour. When everyone has rights there have to be arrangements for deciding what is fair when one person's rights conflict with another's. The UK's existing laws affecting employment are still very much in force. The chief difference now is the way in which they are likely to be interpreted by courts and tribunals.

EMPLOYMENT LEGISLATION – INDIVIDUAL RIGHTS

7. It was only about 30 years ago when employees' *individual* rights were first given consideration by statute in the UK. The right not to be unfairly dismissed, contained originally in the Industrial Relations Act 1971, has been retained ever since. Prior to that time employees had to rely on the common law and legal precedent to obtain rights (such as a declaration of wrongful dismissal) under the law. Over the last quarter of the twentieth century the situation for employees has changed dramatically. In a move to reduce industrial conflict, governments in the mid-1970s began to introduce legislation aimed specifically at the employment relationship. Some of this legislation was directed at collective relationships between trade unions and employers, and some towards the individual employment relationship. This process of laying out a legal framework for the conduct of industrial relations was given further stimulus by the requirements of the European Union regarding labour relations. The present situation at the start of the new century is that statute law reigns supreme. There is still a good deal of voluntary action by way of collective bargaining between employers and trade union representatives, but it is now firmly under the auspices of statutes covering both collective and individual concerns.

8. Most, but not all, of the individual rights are now brought together under the *Employment Rights Act 1996*, amended where necessary by the *Employment Relations Act 1999*. The principal rights contained in the 1996 Act are briefly as follows:

   • right to receive a statement of employment particulars

   • Right to an itemised pay statement

   • right not to have unauthorised deductions made from pay

   • right to a guarantee payment (where short-time working imposed)

   • right not to suffer detriment at work

   • right to time off for certain public duties

   • right to time off for ante-natal care

   • right to time off for dependants

   • right to maternity leave and to return to work after childbirth

   • right to parental leave

   • right to time off for trade union responsibilities

   • right to a minimum period of notice

   • right to a written statement of reasons for dismissal

   • right not to be unfairly dismissed

   • right to complain to an employment tribunal regarding alleged unfair dismissal

- right to seek an order for reinstatement, re-engagement or to receive compensation for unfair dismissal

- right to a redundancy payment.

9. The above list confirms that there is a wide range of rights covering key aspects of work. Most of these rights have been available for twenty years or more, but in the current situation are both more widely available and subject to fewer restrictions. In addition to the above, there are also specific rights arising from other legislation on issues such as sex discrimination, racial discrimination and the minimum wage. The principal legislation on these matters tends nowadays to permit the authorities (Secretary of State) to make further Regulations to deal with specific issues and to update monetary limits. The Employment Relations Act 1999, for example, enables such Regulations to be made, and also makes large-scale amendments to earlier legislation, such as the Employment Rights Act 1996 and the Trade Union and Labour Relations (Consolidation) Act 1992. The following paragraphs outline points that need to be taken into account by personnel/HR practitioners in respect of certain key items on the list.

RIGHT TO RECEIVE A STATEMENT OF EMPLOYMENT PARTICULARS

10. The employee has the right within two months to receive basic information about his or her job conditions. The full list of items that should be included can be found in Chapter 18, paragraph 13.

RIGHT TO TIME OFF FOR CERTAIN PUBLIC DUTIES

11. The 1996 Act includes the right of the employee to reasonable time off for the performance of certain public duties. The time off is usually unpaid. The permitted duties include serving as a Justice of the Peace, a local councillor or school governor.

RIGHT TO TIME OFF FOR ANTE-NATAL CARE

12. Maternity rights were first granted under the Employment Protection Act 1975, but have since been extended. The current law on time allowed to attend for ante-natal care is defined by the 1996 Act, as amended by the Employment Relations Act 1999, and permits a pregnant woman to take paid time off work to attend a clinic, provided she has supplied documentary proof of her pregnancy.

RIGHT TO TIME OFF FOR DEPENDANTS

13.   This right was introduced into the 1996 Act (s.57A) by the *Employment Relations Act 1999*, as part of the government's efforts to make work more 'family-friendly'. It permits an employee (man or woman) to take time off to assist a dependant who falls ill, gives birth, or has an accident. The conditions also cover the death of a dependant, the care of a dependant, or dealing with an incident involving a child. In each case, the employee has to notify the employer as soon as practicable as to the reason for his or her absence. There is no requirement on the employer to treat such absence as paid leave, although it would be good practice to do so. A dependant is defined as spouse, child, parent, or someone who shares a household with the person and who is not a lodger or tenant.

RIGHT TO MATERNITY LEAVE

14.   An employee is entitled to ordinary maternity leave (unpaid) for not less than eighteen weeks, including at least two weeks' compulsory maternity leave from the date of childbirth. Although normal remuneration is not required to be paid, a woman may claim Statutory Maternity Pay (SMP) for up to 18 weeks. The first six weeks are payable at 90 per cent of average earnings, and thereafter at a flat rate of £75 per week (from April 2002). To qualify, the employee must have been employed for at least 26 weeks and be earning at least £72 per week. The employer reclaims the SMP from the Department for Work and Pensions. After her childbirth, the employee is entitled to return to the job she held before her absence without suffering any loss of seniority, pension and other rights (1996 Act, s.71–4, as amended), so long as she gave due notice of her intention to return to work. Dismissal of any woman on grounds associated with her pregnancy or childbirth is automatically unfair, regardless of length of service. It is not unlawful for such a woman to be dismissed on other grounds, in which case she is entitled to her normal notice or pay in lieu, together with a written statement of the reason for the dismissal.

RIGHT TO PARENTAL LEAVE

15.   A parent is entitled to a total of thirteen weeks' leave for the purpose of caring for a child up to its fifth birthday. This section applies especially to fathers. The employee has to supply evidence of his responsibility for the child, and has to have been employed by the employer for one year. The law permits employers and employees to agree local arrangements for taking this leave in individual cases. Where no such agreement is in force, a fall-back scheme provides as follows:

● leave must be taken in blocks or multiples of one week

● the maximum amount of leave in any one year is four weeks

● 21 days' notice must be given to the employer

- leave can be postponed by the employer for up to six months, where the employee's absence would be disruptive, except when the leave is to be taken immediately after childbirth.

RIGHT TO A MINIMUM PERIOD OF NOTICE

16. The minimum period of notice to be given to an employee by an employer (1996 Act, s.86) depends on the former's length of service. The current minima are as follows:

   - at least one week's notice if employed between one month and two years

   - at least one week's notice for each year of continuous employment between two and twelve years

   - at least twelve weeks' notice where employed for more than twelve years

   The minima do not apply in cases where the employee's conduct may justify summary dismissal. It should also be noted that an employer may pay an employee in lieu of notice in order to permit him or her to leave without serving the notice.

RIGHT NOT TO BE UNFAIRLY DISMISSED

17. The 1996 Act (s.94) states that '*An employee has the right not to be unfairly dismissed by his employer.*' Dismissal occurs when the contract is terminated by the employer, with or without notice, or where a fixed-term contract is not renewed by the employer. It also includes the few cases in which the *employee* terminates the contract in circumstances in which he/she is entitled to do so on grounds of the employer's conduct (so-called 'constructive dismissal'). Dismissal is considered to be unfair in the following circumstances:

   - solely or mainly on grounds of pregnancy

   - where the employee was not permitted to return to work after her childbirth, having given due notice of her intentions

   - where the employee was selected for redundancy on grounds associated with her pregnancy or childbirth

   - for membership (or non-membership) of a trade union, or for taking part in trade union activities

   - where the employee was unreasonably selected for redundancy

   - where the employee is dismissed for taking part in an official dispute ('protected industrial action') (Trade Union & Labour Relations Act 1992, s.238A, as amended)

   - where the employer has acted unreasonably in the circumstances.

18. Dismissal will only be regarded as 'fair' on the grounds of:

- the employee's (lack of) capability (e.g. skill, aptitude, health) or qualifications (e.g. degree, diploma, etc.)

- the employee's misconduct or gross misconduct

- contravention of a statutory duty or restriction (e.g. regarding safety)

- some other substantial reason.

19. The qualifying period for unfair dismissal claims has been reduced from two years to one year of continuous service, except in cases where no such period applies (e.g. in cases of pregnancy or childbirth). The waiver on unfair dismissal clauses in fixed-term contracts has been abolished, and this leaves it open for the employee to press for a further contract, and, if it is not practicable from the employer's position, then some compensation may be sought on termination of the original contract.

RIGHT TO A REDUNDANCY PAYMENT

20. Where an employee's work is no longer required, or where his or her employer has ceased to carry on business at the employee's place of work, a redundancy situation arises. Redundancy occurs where the work has ended. It is not concerned with the employee's performance at the work, although this may be a factor if only some employees are to lose their jobs. Further details concerning the terms of redundancy payments and the conditions giving rise to redundancy were given earlier in Chapter 16.

THE ROLE OF ACAS AND EMPLOYMENT TRIBUNALS IN INDIVIDUAL CLAIMS

21. Where individuals believe they have a complaint to make against their employer, they are entitled under several Acts of Parliament to complain to an employment tribunal. Where they do complain, ACAS, the Advisory Conciliation and Arbitration Service, has a duty to conciliate. Due to the substantial increase in employment-related legislation, the workload on ACAS and the tribunals has been increasing year on year. In the year 1998/9 there were more than 124,000 cases received. This figure increased in 1999/2000 to over 164,000, and in 2000/1 to more than 167,000.

22. ACAS attempts to conciliate between employee and employer in order to achieve a mutually satisfactory outcome, and part of the Service's performance is judged on its 'clear-up rate', that is the number of cases which are either withdrawn by the complainant or are settled by mutual agreement. The most recent figures (Figure 40.1) show the relative success rate of ACAS's efforts.

	Conciliated settlement	Withdrawn	To tribunal
1998/9	42%	31%	27%
1999/2000	44%	31%	25%
2000/1	43%	28%	29%

Figure 40.1 *Percentage of clearances in individual conciliation*

23. Individuals' claims can be made under several jurisdictions, and ACAS deals with these under the following headings:

	Cases in 2000/1 (round figures)
• Unfair dismissal	50,000
• Equal Pay Act	4,900
• Sex Discrimination Act	9,100
• Race Relations Act	4,100
• Protection of wages	39,000
• Breach of contract	29,000
• Disability Discrimination Act	4,400
• Other	26,000

(Source: ACAS Annual Report 2000–2001)

Year after year the figures show that unfair dismissal cases provide by far the largest group of complaints, followed by wage-related cases and those dealing with breach of contract. The latter are often associated with unfair dismissal claims, and have possibly increased due to the reduction in qualifying time for unfair dismissal claims from two years to one year. Wage-related claims increased substantially between 1998/9 and 2001, probably due to the introduction of minimum wages and legislation concerning working time.

EMPLOYMENT TRIBUNALS

24. The introduction of tribunals into Britain's industrial relations in the 1960s was intended to enable legal disputes to be treated less formally than in a usual court of law. It was also intended that legal representation would not normally be expected. Cases would be presented by lay persons on both sides, and it would be the task of a legally-qualified chairman together with two approved lay members (representing employer and employee interests respectively) to decide on the law and the facts of each case. These tribunals have been a huge success in the sense that they have enabled thousands of ordinary employees to make representations about their employment. The tribunals, now known as employment tribunals, may only allow appeals on a point of law, in which case the appeal is to the Employment Appeal Tribunal, which is presided over by a High Court judge assisted by two lay-people. Subsequent appeals on points of law are to the Court of Appeal and the House of Lords. Tribunals are also within the jurisdiction of the European Court of Justice.

HEALTH AND SAFETY AT WORK

25. The principal *statutory* duties of employers were referred to in Chapter 22. However, it is important to remember that an employer has a *common law duty* to provide a safe place of work for his or her employees and is liable at common law for accidents caused by his or her employees in the course of their employment. The employer's *common law duties* are usually categorised under the following headings:

    1 the provision of a safe place of employment, so far as is reasonable in all the circumstances

    2 the provision of safe means of access to work

    3 the provision of safe systems of working

    4 the provision of adequate equipment, materials and clothing to enable employees to carry out their work safely

    5 the provision of competent fellow workers

    6 a duty of care to ensure that employees are not subjected to any unreasonable risks in the workplace.

26. In each category the courts are likely to assess what is reasonable in the circumstances of a particular employer's safety provision. In cases where an employee is suing an employer for breach of common law duty (a civil action), any relevant breaches of statutory duties can also be taken into account. The remedies for a civil action are, of course, damages for the injured party or their dependants, whereas a breach of a statutory health and safety requirement is dealt with by way of a fine or even imprisonment. Statutory duties, it should be noted, do not supplant common law duties, but supplement them. Thus, a breach of a duty could result *both in a common law claim by the employee and a criminal prosecution by the Health and Safety Inspectorate.* Where an employee makes a common law claim for damages as a result of injury at work, he or she may be liable to a counter claim of contributory negligence, which may reduce any damages awarded by the court.

REFERENCE

1. Slade, E.A. (1995), *Tolley's Employment Handbook*, Tolley Publishing.

QUESTIONS FOR DISCUSSION/HOMEWORK

1. In what ways might an individual employee's view of employee relations differ from (a) that of his/her manager, and (b) that of his/her trade union representative?

2.   On what issues are managers and trade unions likely to share common rather than divergent interests?

3.   What, basically, is the difference between joint consultation and collective bargaining?

4.   What environmental factors tend to produce a favourable negotiating climate for management negotiators compared with their trade union counterparts?

5.   What in your view makes for a powerful trade union? How might such a union exercise its power?

6.   How far would you agree that the **threat** of sanctions is more important in collective bargaining than the sanctions themselves?

7.   What do you see as the principal benefits of having an organisation such as ACAS to help solve industrial disputes?

8.   What is the point of having a disciplinary code for workplace behaviour?

9.   Which model of employee participation would you recommend as the most suitable for British firms at the present time, and why?

10. To what extent and in what ways is it possible to 'empower' employees in the organisation?

EXAMINATION QUESTIONS

EQ20   What steps would you advise management to take to prepare themselves to negotiate over a trade union's claim for an increase in remuneration and a shortening of the working week?

(IPM)

EQ21   In recent years, many organisations have found it necessary to make some of their employees redundant. What have been the principal causes of this phenomenon? How far can the typical organisation plan for the future in such a way as to minimise the number of redundancies?

(ICSA)

EQ22   Joan Greenwell, a recently appointed supervisor in your department, is still under training. It is your job to help her to understand the grievance procedure which is operated in your bank and you are also required to coach her in grievance interviewing. What are the major points you would make to her?

(IOB)

EQ23   Employees can participate in company decision-making at board level, at works council level and at work group level. What are the advantages and difficulties in each of these?

(ABE)

EQ24   Betty has been employed by XYZ Caterers for fifteen years. She recently got into a fight with a fellow-employee, Sally, who has been with the firm for six months. The fight was reported by the head chef to the manager, who has dismissed both Betty and Sally on the spot. Advise Betty and Sally whether they have been treated unfairly, having regard to the legal provisions and the ACAS Code of Practice on Discipline, and discuss what remedies may be available to them.

(HCIMA)

CASE STUDY 7: BRITCO CARS PLC

BACKGROUND

Britco Cars Plc is a major manufacturer of medium-range motor cars, assembled on a mass-production basis. At its Oxbridge plant the firm has its largest production capacity with some 4500 employees and a multi-million pound investment in plant and equipment. The main assembly line incorporates the latest technology, including robots. Another line is to be brought into use over the course of the next ten months. The last two years have seen a modest profit on turnover in the region of 8 per cent. The prospects for the newest range of cars seem good with local dealers pressing for more deliveries, and exports at their highest level for four years. The Managing Director's report to the Board for the previous year commented that

> The overall picture is optimistic – we are winning back markets, we are improving our quality control and we are beginning to see profits emerging. However, we have made major borrowings in order to re-equip, and if we are to take advantage of this substantial investment in the future, we must ensure that our workforce is with us one hundred percent.

COLLECTIVE BARGAINING AND RELATED ISSUES

The Oxbridge plant has several well-established negotiating agreements with a variety of trade unions. At shop-floor level there is a joint trade union committee, which is responsible for co-ordinating the major substantive negotiations with the company, and for supervising the operation of disciplinary procedures and other procedural matters. The manual unions comprise the Engineering and Electrical Workers' Union and the General Workers' Union. Most newcomers join their appropriate union. There are a few persons who do not belong to any union, and their rights have been respected in accordance with the current legislation. Industrial relations at the plant has been described by the Production Director as 'cautious, but better than they were a year or two ago ... there seems to be a greater sense of realism ... I wish we could move forward into a more positive relationship.'

The white-collar employees, working in offices, laboratories, and computer areas are represented by the Scientific, Clerical and Technical Workers' Union. Union membership is about two-thirds of all the grades concerned. Some middle managers are in a managerial union, but most are not.

Quality circles were introduced a year ago, and are working reasonably well. A major effort to introduce labour flexibility into the main production areas, based on multi-skilling, was introduced last year. This has been relatively successful.

ORGANISATION STRUCTURE

The main organisational units are as follows:

- Body Assembly Area

- Engine/Gearbox Assembly Area

- Central Stores

- Principal Production Area

- Paint Shop

- Quality Assurance Department

- Computer/Robotics Department

- Factory Administration

    – Production

    – Personnel

    – Costing/Budgets

    – Purchasing

- Other Administration

    – Marketing/Sales

    – Public Relations

    – Research & Development

    – Accounts.

In broad terms, the plant personnel can be divided into the following horizontal slices:

- Senior Management

- Middle Management

- Supervisory Grades

- Skilled Craftsmen/Technician Grades

- Skilled Specialists (robotics, etc.)

- Semi-skilled Operatives/General Workers
- Administrative/Clerical Grades.

MANAGEMENT'S INTENTIONS

The senior management at the plant, supported by corporate headquarters in London, have decided to set up a pilot Employee Participation Council with the following initial aims:

- increase employee participation in decisions affecting developments over a twelve-month period
- improve the competitiveness of the company's product-range by reducing unit costs
- reduce the number of disputes related to the introduction of changes in production methods and procedures
- improve the effectiveness of the multi-skilling programme
- provide a forum for the discussion of any important matters affecting employee relations.

QUESTIONS

If you were the Plant Personnel Director what proposals would you like to see developed in respect of the following issues?

1. The composition of the Participation Council.

2. The electoral system for the Council.

3. The range of subjects for discussion.

4. The links between the Council and the existing negotiating and consultative machinery.

5. The standards of performance expected from Council members.

6. Training for Council members.

Conclude your report with a summary of what you see as the main risks and benefits involved in the exercise.

CASE STUDY 8: TOYOTA MOTOR MANUFACTURING UK

BACKGROUND

The Toyota Motor Corporation, mindful of the huge potential of the European Union as a market for motor vehicles, took a decision in 1989 to build its first European motor vehicle assembly plant at Burnaston – a 'greenfield' site in Derbyshire, England. Important reasons for the choice of Burnaston included (a) the size of site, permitting further expansion if needed, (b) the excellent transport links within the UK and to the continent of Europe, (c) a labour market containing a workforce experienced in engineering, (d) a large domestic market for motor vehicles, and (e) a positive stance by Government towards inward investment.

The Burnaston development represented a major investment into the UK economy of some £700m, supplemented by the construction of an engine plant in Deeside, North Wales, at a further cost of some £140m. Construction of both plants began in 1990 and was completed for the start of production in 1992 (September for engines and December for cars). Hiring and training began as early as 1990 with the recruitment of about 1000 staff for the start of production. A second wave of recruitment took place subsequently to provide for a second shift, which began in February 1994. Further recruitment has brought the total number recruited and trained to more than 2000 over a period of five years.

Production of the new Carina E model began in earnest in late 1992, working towards the initial target of 100,000 vehicles per annum. By 1995, against a background of weak demand in many European economies, production nevertheless reached 90,000 units. The success of the Carina line has encouraged the Company to commence construction of a second assembly plant at Burnaston, where the smaller Corolla vehicles will be produced. Recruitment for this Phase II development is planned to commence in mid-1997, when up to 1000 additional employees will be required.

In terms of human resource management, the Toyota plant, founded on the Toyota Production System (TPS), has introduced a number of interesting personnel-related practices in the context of distinctly Toyota style personnel policies.

HRM PHILOSOPHY

HRM philosophy at Toyota Motor Manufacturing UK is founded on the following key principle:

> People are the company's greatest asset. Toyota UK recognises the fact that highly competent, motivated people who are treated with respect will show great commitment to the fulfilment of the company's objectives. Fundamental to the 'people' philosophy is a determination to provide to the individual both growth opportunity and stable employment. This is best achieved by securing long term prosperity for the company. (Toyota Information Booklet, April 1996)

As if to underline the prime importance of people, Toyota UK refers to all its employees as '*members*', emphasising the unitary outlook of the company in its internal relationships. There is no sense of '*them and us*' at Toyota plants, and this affects attitudes towards trade union involvement, team-working and individual employee motivation.

EMPLOYMENT AND TRAINING PRACTICES

The respect-for-people outlook has a number of implications for employment and training practices in the two UK plants. These can be summarised briefly as follows:

- the recruitment process involves a variety of job-related exercises to determine an individual's dexterity, teamworking ability and other key attributes

- the average age of the current workforce in the UK (31 years) reflects the newness of the company and its desire to develop an adaptable workforce

- training is seen as an essential and continuing requirement of good performance under the Toyota production system (TPS – see below), in which all employees are required to be multi-skilled

- training for the most part is carried out on the job in such a way that individuals are encouraged to learn their own jobs well enough to be able to train others in due course

- team-building is fundamental to the achievement of goals at every level, and teams have considerable responsibility within a flat organisation structure

- communications, whether organisation-wide, or within and between teams, is seen as critical to employee involvement as well as to efficiency generally

- all employees are salaried and there is a regular organisation-wide performance appraisal system

- given the collective teamworking approach to tasks there is no bonus system, either for individuals or teams

- general work issues may be discussed via the Toyota Members' Advisory Board (see below) composed of management and rank-and-file employees

- a single trade union is recognised for the purposes of representing the employees on a range of work issues.

The company's investment in training has been considerable, totalling more than £19m by the end of 1992. As an example, 100,000 person-days were spent on training *before* production commenced. About 350 key employees received training overseas in Japan, USA and Canada. Since production commenced most of the training effort has been on-the-job, but even so some 20,000 person-days have been spent on specific off-the-job courses. In recognition of its commitment to development, Toyota was awarded both the Investors in People Award and a National Training Award during the course of 1993.

TOYOTA PRODUCTION SYSTEM (TPS)

The Toyota production system, which has proved to be the benchmark system for modern manufacturing systems, combines the best of 'scientific management' methods with modern approaches to team-work and individual motivation. The company sees TPS as having three main goals – product quality and value-for-money for customers; market flexibility, profit from cost reduction and long-term prosperity for the business; and work satisfaction, job security and fair treatment for employees ('*members*'). The basis of TPS is standardisation of work processes and procedures followed by continuous improvement ('*kaizen*'). Two key features of TPS are Just-in-Time (JIT) provision of parts and materials, in which the latter are delivered when needed by the operation concerned, and '*jidoka*', described in English as 'automation with a human touch'. Jidoka includes the ability of members to stop a machine or the production line when a difficulty occurs. At Burnaston, for example, there is an overhead line alongside the assembly track which can be pulled in order to stop the operation by any employee who is in difficulty. If this event happens, the immediate team-leader or other members of the employee's work-team attempt to sort out the problem right away. Importantly, the track does not stop immediately when the overhead line is pulled, but continues until the end-point of that particular part of the assembly process. Thus, every employee knows that there is a short time available to put things right before the track stops. If the problem cannot be overcome, then the line stops until the situation is resolved. The ability to deal with production difficulties quickly, and with minimum disruption, is only possible because of (a) the application of the jidoka system, (b) the high standards of training and preparation required of individuals *before* they commence work, and (c) the supportive nature of the work-teams.

TRADE UNION RECOGNITION AND EMPLOYEE RELATIONS

Like other Japanese companies investing in Britain, Toyota's strategy regarding trade unions has been to select just one appropriate union to represent its employees. At Burnaston and Deesside the union is the Amalgamated Engineering and Electricians Union (AEEU), whose membership is about 45 per cent of the workforce. In return for assurances concerning job security and employee development, the union has given up the traditional trade union role of negotiating about wages and salaries. Whilst it plays a role as external supervisor of employment conditions at Toyota, the main *internal* role of discussing working conditions is conducted by means of a joint management–employee forum called the Toyota Members' Advisory Board. This is composed of ten elected representatives from various segments of the workforce together with six management representatives plus a chairman and secretary provided by management. Issues discussed by the Board include terms and conditions of employment, quality matters, ideas for improving production, questions of employee training and development and other general work issues. The object of the Board is twofold

– to contribute to improvements in meeting company objectives and also to ensure fair and equitable treatment for all employees.

QUESTIONS

1. In terms of personnel/human resource management, what are the *advantages* and *disadvantages* for a company of starting up business in a 'greenfield' site?

2. In what ways does the use of the term '*member*' to describe employees suggest a different approach to employee relations compared with '*them and us*' attitudes?

3. How would you justify the company's expenditure of time and money on employee training?

4. In what ways might the Toyota Production System be said to give encouragement to Anglo preferences for high individualism alongside developing strong team-working attitudes?

5. How far would you agree that trade union membership at Toyota UK is an optional extra rather than an important insurance against arbitrary action by management?

APPENDIX 1

Examination technique

INTRODUCTION

1. It is rarely easy to write an adequate narrative answer to an examination question in the field of Personnel Management. It is usually not enough merely to quote facts or supply descriptions. In most cases, examiners are looking for the ability to discuss ideas, make comparisons and draw conclusions. It is realised that students are working under considerable pressures in trying to achieve what the examiner requires. Nevertheless, given all the constraints, an examiner can invariably pick out the better candidates right away. They stand out from the majority because their answers are relevant, clear and often interesting as well.

2. It is possible to improve one's ability to perform to the standards of examination technique required. These notes are intended to provide advice. The examination questions located at the end of each part of the book are there to provide practice opportunities.

AT THE START OF THE EXAMINATION

3. Read the instructions carefully and follow them. In particular, do ensure that you understand how many questions you are required to attempt.

4. Read through the questions and select those that appeal to you most. These are the questions which trigger off plenty of ideas and which you would feel happy to tackle.

ANSWERING QUESTIONS

5. Read each question carefully. Ask yourself the following questions.

    • Is this just one question or are there several parts to it?

    • What is the examiner getting at?

    • What key issues are raised in this question?.

    Question analysis such as this is vital to ensure that you are responding in a relevant way.

6. Remember to allocate sufficient time to each question at the outset. Then make a rough answer plan. This is best done by 'mapping out' ideas or points that occur to you and linking them as appropriate. If you try to work logically and draw up a list of points you may find that you are less creative. It would be better to generate ideas first and *then* put them into some kind of order. All this rough working may take five minutes or so, but it will enable you to proceed confidently to the answer.

7. Generally speaking, all examination papers are designed to test two or more of the following:

    • the ability to memorise or recall facts

    • the level of understanding of a topic

    • the ability to apply theory to practice

    • ability to analyse a situation or problem

    • ability to make judgements about, or give an interpretation of, an issue.

    This explains why so many questions are in several parts, e.g. 'Describe so-and-so and show how it is relevant to ...' or 'What is so-and-so, why does it occur and how can it be dealt with?'

8. If you are responding to an interpretative type of question, do not be afraid to give several versions where they exist. Bear in mind that there rarely is just one correct answer to a question on Personnel Management. The ideal combination is one where the student identifies relevant issues and discusses them in an interesting way for the examiner.

9. When writing your answer, bear in mind that neatness and tidy layout help the marker to understand what you have written. The use of paragraphs is recommended, possibly with an occasional subheading. Layout is, of course, no substitute for hard thinking, but it does help create a good impression compared with those who have submitted an illegible and untidy script.

10. Once you have completed your answer, quickly scan through it for possible errors or omissions made in the heat of the moment.

TOWARDS THE END OF THE EXAMINATION

11. Make sure that you have made some progress with the final question, even if you have had to leave an earlier answer unfinished. You will tend to earn more marks in the first half of an answer than you will towards the end, so it is worth moving on. Anyone who fails to answer the set number of questions is placing him/herself in an extremely risky position. If you are desperately short of time due to bad planning, then make a few brief notes in lieu of a proper answer. However, it is better not to get into this situation in the first place.

12. If you have some time left in the closing minutes, read through your earlier answers to check them or to add any further thoughts which have struck you.

CONCLUSION

13.   The best way to improve your ability to see what the examiner is looking for and then to supply it, is by practising answers to authentic questions set by the examining body concerned, and then discussing your answers with tutors or colleagues.

APPENDIX 2

Outline answers to selected examination questions

INTRODUCTION

Note: There are 24 representative Examination Questions included in this book. Ten of these have been provided with fairly full outline answers to give guidance to prospective examinees on suggested ways of tackling the various types of questions that examiners have set over recent years. Key points for the remaining 14 questions are available to lecturers only in the separate Lecturers' Supplement obtainable from the publishers.

EQ1

Discuss the effects of social change on a company's personnel policies.

(ABE)

Comments: *This is a question for those who enjoy a discussion on a general topic. The answer should make links between social change and personnel policies.*

Key points:

1.   Social change manifests itself in the following ways:

   •   through changing attitudes and values

   •   through demographic changes

   •   through economic changes

   •   through new legislation.

2.   An example of attitude change can be seen in the way Western men perceive the role of women in managerial positions; another example is how executive health concern has led to a massive decline in smoking.

3.   An example of changing values is the desire for greater leisure, which has led to a shorter working week over the past 30 years.

4.   Demographic changes can encompass factors such as population numbers and population profiles. Britain is experiencing a change in its population profile, which means that there will be more pensioners in society than ever before.

5.   Economic changes mean improvement of the standard of living for some and long-term unemployment for others.

6. New legislation often reflects changing attitudes. For example, attitudes towards strike behaviour have brought about laws to restrict trade union actions or to make them more costly to the union concerned.

7. The impact of the above changes on personnel policies can be summarised as follows:

- women may be positively encouraged to seek training and promotion prospects

- more women graduates may be recruited

- non-smoking offices may be encouraged and a part of total executive remuneration may include preventive health care

- a shorter working week may be introduced for all grades of employee

- pension contributions may have to be raised all round to support the relative growth in the number of employees nearing retirement age

- redundancy terms may need to be reviewed

- pay policies will always need to be competitive in order to keep staff whose skills are in short supply

- dismissal procedures during strikes may be enforced more strictly than in the past as a matter of policy.

EQ2

EQ3
} Lecturers' Supplement

EQ4

'Rational-economic man', 'social man' and 'self-actualising man' are theories that have been advanced successively about the motivation of employees at work. How useful are they in indicating how to manage employees?

(ABE)

Comments: *In order to be able to answer this question the student needs to know the basis of these views of human motivation. This is an evaluative question, which asks you to make the link between theory and practice.*

Key points:

1. These descriptions of human motivation were put forward by Schein (1970) in a review of attitudes towards motivation at work.

2. Rational-economic man implies that people are mainly interested in economic gains; they go to work for money and they will work harder for more money; the dominant feature of this approach is self-interest.

3. Recognition of this viewpoint implies that employee motivation will depend, to some extent at least, on providing adequate financial rewards and incentives in order to get the maximum performance out of people.

4. The application of this approach by management can lead to a measure of job satisfaction, but it appears doubtful that people seek additional monetary rewards on anything other than a short-term basis. On the whole people appear to desire a fair wage for their efforts, rather than a maximum wage.

5. The model of social man implies that people will work more effectively if their social needs are met. Thus the composition of the work-group, the building of teams are seen as key factors in getting extra commitment from employees.

6. This idea is useful in that managements can pay attention to groups so as to meet individual needs.

7. The idea of self-actualising man suggests that people actively look for challenge and personal growth in their work; they see work as an opportunity for enriching their lives.

8. Acceptance of this idea by management would lead them to enrich jobs by adding opportunities for achievement, learning, responsibility and recognition for example.

9. It has proved possible to meet self-actualisation needs for many groups of employees, but it should not be assumed that everyone is looking for it.

10. On balance, each of the three propositions has some relevance and usefulness in the work situation, but to base a motivation policy on any single one could prove self-defeating. What is required is an appropriate combination of these approaches.

EQ5 ⎫
　　　⎬　Lecturers' Supplement
EQ6 ⎭

EQ7

(a) Offer a workable definition of leadership and identify what are currently accepted as the most important types of leader.

(b) Define 'trait theory' and discuss whether there is still some merit in this approach.

(HCIMA)

Comments: *This is a multiple question it has four parts, three of which ask for definitions, and are therefore recall type question. The final part is seeking some evaluation of one approach.*

Key points:

1. Leadership is the ability to persuade other people to work together to achieve a common aim. This ability involves balancing the competing demands of the task, the team and the individual team members.

2. The most important types of leader are:

   • the charismatic leader, who relies on the force of his/her personality

   • the traditional leader, who is born into the role

- the situational leader, who takes the lead on account of particular knowledge or skills required at the time

- the appointed leader, who is given authority as part of his/her position

- the functional leader, who brings integrative actions to bear on a situation.

3. Trait theory of leadership is a concept of leadership based on qualities. It suggests that leaders possess certain special qualities such as determination, courage, intelligence, personal thoughness and so on.

4. There is little merit in this approach. On the contrary, it could be regarded as misleading people about the nature of leadership. It implies that it is not worthwhile training people in leadership since this is mainly a question of having the right personal attributes.

5. There is no agreement amongst theorists as to what precise qualities do make for good leadership.

6. Commonsense suggests that personality and intelligence must play some part in the leadership equation, but the range of people capable of sustaining a leadership role with a fair degree of success is not restricted to those with particular 'leadership qualities'.

EQ8

'Unless there is a corporate plan for the organisation, integrated with the manpower plan, manpower planning is worthless.' Discuss.

(IPM)

Comments: *Sometimes examiners like to make an assertion and then ask you to challenge it. This is such a case. The question is looking for an understanding of the process of manpower planning and, in particular, its relationship with corporate long-term intentions.*

Key points:

1. Like most assertions, this one exaggerates the reality of the situation. It suggests that if there is no corporate plan then manpower planning is a waste of time and effort. However, much depends on the interpretation given to the terms 'corporate plan' and 'manpower plan'. The answer also depends on the extent to which manpower planning is seen as a deliberate, intentional activity springing from the organisation's objectives for the future rather than as an activity, which is a response to marketing pressures caused by the demand for the organisation's goods or services.

2. A corporate plan is a statement on behalf of the whole organisation concerning its objectives and intentions over a period ranging from five to ten years in most cases. Many plans are reviewed annually and the results fed forward over the next five years to form a rolling five-year plan.

3. A manpower plan is much more detailed and shorter term than a corporate plan. The former is intended to provide a picture of the organisation's needs over the next one to five years together with an assessment of the sources of estimated labour supply over that period. Many plans set out their demand

and supply equations in detailed terms for the first two years, in particular, and include approximate estimates for the remainder of the five-year planning period.

4. Manpower planning can be defined as a systematic process aimed at acquiring, retaining, utilising, improving and disengaging employees in order to meet the objectives set out in the corporate plan.

5. If the organisation has a corporate plan, then the process of manpower planning will have a logic to it. Numbers and categories of personnel can be identified, skills requirements gauged, recruitment plans set, training plans prepared and manpower costs elicited. The employee resourcing of the organisation therefore takes place within the guiding limits of an overall plan for people.

6. However, many firms have no long-term plans; they have an annual plan but little more. Thus, any manpower requirements can only be expressed in the short-term. Nevertheless, since manpower planning also has an annual as well as a longer-term perspective, every firm, in theory, could practise a form of manpower planning.

7. This could take the form of an account of present employee numbers and categories, an estimate of forecast needs over the coming year and a brief commentary on the existing workforce. Whilst not at all sophisticated, such a plan would provide the organisation with some guidance for recruitment, training, succession planning and for labour costs. Such a plan would certainly not be worthless.

8. The difference between an organisation with a corporate plan and one without a long-term strategy is that the former can prepare ahead for the development of its personnel requirements to meet growth in the business, whereas the latter can only build up the correct labour force at short notice as a response to, rather than in anticipation of, changing demands in the market-place.

EQ9
EQ10   } Lecturers' Supplement
EQ11

EQ12

In which areas of personnel management will the introduction of information technology have most impact over the next five years? Give reasons and outline the major changes you expect.

(IOB-NOM)

Comments: *This is an evaluative question on a topic of current relevance to personnel management. It requires a certain amount of knowledge about information technology, i.e. what does the expression mean? You are then asked to consider the implications of this for personnel, giving your reasons.*

Key points:

1. Information technology is the term used to describe the application to information processing of the combined technologies of computing, electronics and telecommunications.

2. Manifestations of information technology (IT) are:

    industrial

    –   process control

    –   machine control

    –   performance monitoring

    –   robotics

    • office Systems

    –   personal computing

    –   word processing

    –   information storage/retrieval

    –   electronic mail transmission

    –   tele-conferencing

    –   view data

    –   facsimile transmission.

3. The broad areas of personnel management in which the introduction of IT will have the greatest impact over the next five years are as follows:

    • manpower/organisation planning

    • Personnel administration

    • training.

4. Manpower/organisation planning will be affected (a) in terms of the changes in labour requirements which will be accelerated by the application of IT in the factory and the office; and (b) in terms of the use of IT in the very process of planning.

    The use of computers, for example, linked with wordprocessors enables manpower statistics and personal records to be initiated, amended or recalled with ease and speed. Graphs, tables and reports on manpower figures can be produced with accuracy and speed.

6. These same processes can be used to generate and maintain all the administrative records required by the organisation.

7. The quality of personnel information systems will be matched by the speed of preparation to give line or senior managers up-to-date information on which to base operating and other decisions.

8. IT will itself require old skills to give way to new ones. This fact alone would lead to an increased need for training. However, training as a process can be aided by the application of computers, and computer-based learning will undoubtedly grow over the next five years.

EQ13 Lecturers' Supplement

EQ14

To what extent can fringe benefits be systematically applied in an organisation as a partial substitute for direct monetary rewards, as a means of:

a) attracting potential employees;

b) retaining employees; and

c) motivating employees?

(ICSA)

Comments: *This question is looking for an understanding of the importance of fringe benefits and how they can be applied in practice to achieve ends relating to staff recruitment, retention and motivation. A brief note to define 'fringe benefits' is required at the outset, followed by your assessment of how effective they might be in attaining these ends.*

Key-points:

1. So-called 'fringe benefits' or employee benefits are non-pay benefits which are added to wages and salaries.

2. Benefits can be divided into three major categories:
    - security benefits
        - pension schemes
        - life insurance
        - private health care
        - creche provision
        - bridging loans for staff moving house on company business
    - work-related benefits
        - subsidised meals
        - company cars (essential)
        - mileage allowances for casual users
        - prizes for extra performance
        - sabbatical periods for long service
    - status-related benefits.
        - prestige cars
        - enhanced pension

485

    –   entertainment allowance

    –   children's education schemes

    –   payment of telephone, etc.

3.   Potential employees may be attracted by such measures as company cars, creches and bridging loans. Such benefits may enable a person to take up a new post with confidence, because of the sheer convenience to them personally. It is unlikely, however, that such benefits would displace basic salary or wages as by far the most attractive reason for applying for a job.

4.   Employee retention can be improved by the application of progressive benefits linked to length of service or quality of performance. Participation in share-option schemes or imporved pension arrangements will usually be available only to those with a qualifying period of service. Other benefits such as sabbaticals and special development opportunities may also serve to retain staff. The provision of company cars as a part of total remuneration above a certain salary level can also be a powerful retentive device.

5.   Employees are more likely to be motivated by a combination of what they perceive to be a fair basic wage or salary and a challenging job. However, extra effort or performance could be rewarded by means of benefits such as a bigger car, additional holidays, special prizes and entry to an executive dining room, for example.

6.   It is doubtful if benefits can be used to make up for deficiencies in monetary rewards. All they can do, for newcomers and existing employees alike, is to provide an extra incentive which might just tip the scales in favour of recruiting an employee, retaining others and motivating yet others.

EQ15

EQ16   }   Lecturers' Supplement

EQ17

EQ18

The evaluation of training is often neglected. Why is this so and how can a more professional approach to evaluation be achieved?

(IPM)

Comments: *This question requires an answer that states what is meant by evaluation, analyses why it is often neglected and finally suggests how it can be applied more professionally.*

Key points:

1.   Evaluation of training in this context can be taken to mean any systematic attempt to obtain feedback about the processes and outcomes of training activities in order to assess their merit and worth.

2.   Merit refers to the intrinsic value of the course or its content, i.e. it is important in its own right. Worth refers to the practical value of the course in the particular circumstances.

3. The evaluation of training is often neglected because of one or more of the following:

    - evaluation is difficult

    - it is not seen as vital as the provision of training

    - providers of training may not wish to be exposed to possible criticism of their efforts

    - it is carried out in a half-hearted manner, which merely pays lip-service to evaluation

    - many organisations believe that training is 'a good thing' and therefore need not be questioned.

4. A more professional approach may be achieved by means of:

    a) the adoption of a systematic approach to the business of evaluation

    b) this approach could be based on a framework that ensured that evaluation embraced not only trainees and trainers, but also line managers/supervisors, training materials, training methods, course content, assessment methods, and the context of the training

    c) the use of a variety of means for collecting relevant data about training activities, e.g. interviews with superiors, questionnaires, observation and analysis of learning materials and documents.

5. A professional approach would probably draw a distinction between the evaluation of processes (formative evaluation) and the evaluation of outcomes (summative evaluation). The former focuses on the inputs provided by the trainers, the interaction between trainers and trainees and between trainees. It aims above all to produce suggestions for improving the training. The latter focuses on end-results-improvement in employee performance, cost-effectiveness and trainee satisfaction.

6. Evaluation can be approached in a prescriptive way, emphasising intended outcomes, often expressed as specific objectives, or it can be approached in a responsive way, embracing unintended as well as intended outcomes. A prescriptive approach tends to be dominated by the provider's view of what should be expected as a result of the training. The responsive approach is prepared to accept the expectations of other stakeholders in the training process, especially trainees and their superiors.

EQ19   Lecturers' Supplement

EQ20

What steps would you advise management to take to prepare themselves to negotiate over a trade union's claim for an increase in remuneration and a shortening of the working week?

(IPM)

Comments: *This question hopes to establish the student's general under-standing of the sorts of issues that must be considered by management in their negotiations with trade unions. In this case the emphasis is on the preparatory questions and issues that need to be addressed once the union claim has been lodged.*

Key-points:

1. In broad terms, management need to consider their own position, the trade union's position and any important external issues.

2. Management's own bargaining position depends on factors such as:

   - current employee relations policy

   - current pay policy

   - the company's ability to pay

   - the company's dependence on the union's cooperation

   - the state of the labour market

   - the existence of legal or other external constraints (e.g. Government pay norms).

3. Management need to weigh up the following aspects of the union's position:

   - What is the 'going rate' for the groups represented by the union (i.e. comparability)?

   - What would the union side settle for?

   - What concessions might the union representatives make in return for a generous response?

   - What sanctions might they seek to employ, if our response was disappointing to them?

   - How effective would sanctions be?

4. Management need to ensure they have access to a variety of sources of information, both internal and external, to enable them to answer the above questions.

   Internally this means that they should be able to rely on the Personnel Manager for relevant information about pay policy, labour costs, labour turnover, employee retention rates, the trends in wage rates for comparable groups and the state of the labour market. Management should be able to ensure detailed costings and estimates of various labour and production activities. Marketing department should be able to supply details of forecast sales, likely developments and competitors' pricing arrangements, etc.

5. Management can also prepare by estimating the likely consequences of conceding most or part of the claim. Every agreement has a 'knock-on effect' on other groups of employees in the company, and, if a reduction in the working week were conceded, this could have an effect nationally.

6. Finally, another aspect of preparation is to ensure that the negotiators have received any necessary training in negotiating skills prior to fulfilling their role as a member of the management team.

EQ21

In recent years, many organisations have found it necessary to make some of their employees redundant. What have been the principal causes of this phenomenon? How far can the typical organisation plan for the future in such a way as to minimise the number of redundancies?

(ICSA)

Comments: *This is a question on a topical issue. It asks the student to reflect on the causes of job losses in organisations, and then to suggest how manpower planning can enable employers to maintain an optimum labour force in the light of prevailing economic conditions.*

Key points:

1. The principal cause of redundancy is either that the employer no longer has any need for work of a particular kind or has no need of it at the location where it was previously carried out.

2. This cause is in itself brought about by other causes:

   - poor company performance

   - lack of adequate business planning

   - loss of a major customer

   - sudden increase in costs (e.g. due to a fuel crisis)

   - relocation of firm because of expansion, or need to move to a low-cost area, etc

   - introduction of new technology

   - changes in the company's product-range.

3. In the case of public sector institutions, redundancy may be caused by direct Government action to reduce particular public services, or to seek greater cost effectiveness in the public service.

4. Organisations cannot always avoid declaring job losses, but they can minimise them if:

   a) they have a corporate plan which outlines the organisation's aims over the next five years at least, and the means by which these shall be attained

   b) a product-market strategy is especially important as it identifies the potential size and nature of orders as well as the manner and time of their manufacture/delivery

   c) a manpower plan, based on the product-market strategy, in which future needs are assessed, current supply of labour identified, and plans set for meeting any shortfall or shedding staff by 'natural wastage'

d) a training plan, which can enable appropriate personnel to be re-trained in new skills, or otherwise up-dated in order to cope with change in products, production methods, etc.

5. An organisation's estimate of its current labour force needs to embrace numbers, job categories, age-groups, skills profiles, location, length of service, etc.

6. Future requirements need to be based on a firm idea of the nature and level of production, the outlook for new orders, etc.

7. No workforce is completely static; there are always some people moving in or out of the organisation. So long as this rate of 'natural' change is identified, then proper responses can be made. In some cases employee numbers are allowed to run down, in others leavers must be replaced at once.

EQ22
EQ23 } Lecturers' Supplement

EQ24

Betty has been employed by XYZ Caterers for 15 years. She recently got into a fight with a fellow-employee, Sally, who has been with the firm for six months. The fight was reported by the head chef to the manager, who has dismissed both Betty and Sally on the spot.

Advise Betty and Sally whether they have been treated unfairly, having regard to the legal provisions and the ACAS Code of Practice on Discipline, and discuss what remedies may be available to them.

(HCIMA)

Comments: *This is a question requiring a legalistic answer as much as a managerial answer. It requires the student to have a grasp of the legal features of unfair dismissal and the managerial features of the ACAS code.*

Key-points:

1. This is clearly a case of misconduct, and could be considered as gross misconduct. Punishment of some kind would be expected.

2. Much depends on what the company construes as 'misconduct' and 'gross misconduct'. The former may lead to warnings, but the latter may lead to the dismissal of the employees concerned.

3. Even if this were a case of gross misconduct, the manager should have heard their side of the story, and spoken to any witnesses. They should have been allowed to have a trade union representative, or colleague, present at the hearing.

4. They should have had some right of appeal to a senior manager, such as the Managing director or another director.

5. If a dismissal is shown to have taken place, the employer is required to prove that the reason for the dismissal was permissible, and to show that it was fair

in the circumstances. The latter would include any reference to previous employee behaviour, previous warnings, if any, and length of service, for example.

6.   In this case, Betty would probably be able to persuade an industrial tribunal that she had been unfairly treated by being dismissed. She was a long-serving employee of previous good conduct, so far as we know, and whilst some punishment was in order, it ought to have been restricted to a severe written warning. Also, the manager's conduct in summarily dismissing Betty without a proper hearing or right of appeal was clearly unfair.

7.   Betty could seek reinstatement in her former job, or at least re-engagement in some other work. If these two prospects were not feasible, she could claim monetary compensation for the loss of her employment.

8.   Sally's situation is rather different. She does not qualify for unfair dismissal, since she has been employed for less than one full year. She could perhaps sue for wrongful dismissal on the grounds of lack of notice, but the employer would undoubtedly be able to rebut that claim on the grounds of the seriousness of the misconduct.

Discussion points from two case studies

a)   A case study is a model situation, usually based on real-life experience. Case studies concerning management issues can vary considerably in the amount of information they contain. Some may be extremely brief and sketchy, others full of detailed information. The majority are likely to fall somewhere between these two extremes. What can be said is that students will rarely find (a) that they have all the information they require, and (b) that the key issues are in clear focus. These drawbacks can be considered as part of the challenge involved in unravelling what is essentially a puzzle designed to develop skills in problem-solving and decision-making.

b)   A systematic analysis of a case study can benefit from the following approach:

   • read through the material once with the aim of getting the 'feel' of the situation

   • read through again, picking out salient facts and issues

   • if relevant, draw up an organisation chart

   • group key facts/issues into relevant clusters

   • analyse these clusters, assessing priorities and making any useful links between them

   • draw your conclusions

   • make appropriate proposals.

c)   In order to illustrate the above points, a brief analysis of the first two case studies is provided below. The 'answers' are not intended to be exhaustive, but illustrative. As students will find when analysing cases, there is rarely one correct answer to the problems identified.

CASE STUDY 1: LION OFFICE SYSTEMS PLC

Q1.   The most likely problems during the first few months are:

- establishing the reasoning behind the various pay schemes operated by the divisions

- dealing with problems of pay differentials as certain groups of employees (e.g. sales) become more difficult to retain

- recruitment of sufficient and suitable sales/technical support staff

- negotiation of fresh substantive agreements with the unions in two of the divisions

- difficulty of formulating some common policy on pay systems

- need to consider some form of job evaluation to enable job and pay comparisons to be made.

Q2. The immediate operational aspects of personnel that are most urgent include the following:

- examining the pay and motivational factors surrounding sales, service engineers and technical support staff, because there seems to be a problem of high turnover, requiring frequent recruitment of newcomers

- drawing up proposals for dealing with any pay problems identified in the above groups

- the development of an integrated personnel service, in order to harmonise key personnel practices across the various divisions.

Q3. Over the next 1–2 years possible issues for special attention could include:

- the issue of devising appropriate job evaluation schemes for the major employment categories: manual workers and white-collar employees, in order to provide some rational basis on which to establish fair differentials between jobs, and on which suitable incentive schemes might be provided for some, or all, groups of employees

- the issue of employee retention in certain groups needs to be considered, and this could involve a survey of employee motivation in the various divisions

- the issue of employee numbers, which may need to be reduced if the printing division fails to meet the challenge laid down by the competition, or if the costs in the office machinery/micro-computer division continue to rise

- as a result of the previous issue, retirement and redundancy policies need to be reviewed.

Q4. The amount of authority granted to the Personnel Officer should be commensurate with the responsibility laid on his or her shoulders. In this case greater integration from the centre is sought by the directors, and it would be reasonable to expect the Personnel Officer to be given authority to devise and implement consistent personnel procedures. It would probably be best if the Personnel Officer's authority was exercised firmly but supportively following adequate consultation with line managers at the initial stages. Personnel's authority will undoubtedly be strengthened if the role is seen to be supportive rather than directive.

Q5. The power position of the Personnel Officer over the first few months is likely to rest on senior management support. As the organisation becomes embroiled in the processes of change on the personnel front, then the technical-specialist role of Personnel is likely to grow in importance. Initially, however, it will be top management patronage that will secure the initial power position of the Personnel Officer.

CASE STUDY 2: THE GWYN VALLEY RAILWAY

Q1. The culture of the Gwyn Valley Railway (GVR) can be described as follows: Personal commitment to the venture as a 'good thing in its own right' seems to be the dominant value. Alongside this is the understanding that unless operations are planned and organised, they will not succeed. A high degree of delegation to group leaders by the General Manager is a feature of the current situation.

Q2. The attributes that might work best in these circumstances are:

- good delegation skills

- experience of team leadership participative management style a vision of the future for GVR

- ability to plan overall operation

- ability to act as link with external interests (e.g. tourist boards, sponsors, etc.).

Q3. Possible changes that could be made to the structure of jobs are as follows: separate out the year-round work of restoration and appoint Williams to post, in order to speed up the completion of new exhibits; give Museum manager the responsibility for publicity/PR; appoint new deputies to both Restoration and Operations managers.

An initial new structure might look like this:

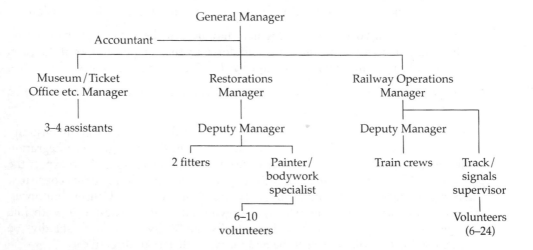

Q4. Taking account of the elderly age-profile of the majority of key staff, the following changes could be considered:

- introduction of Deputy Managers of younger age (e.g. in 50s rather than 60s/70s)

- appoint someone in their 40s/50s to take over the role of General Manager

- promote Williams to new post of Restoration Manager

- look for possible successors to full-time posts from amongst supporters and volunteers.

Q5. The principal implications of having a significant number of volunteer staff are:

- high level of enthusiasm

- lack of experience/expertise (amateurism)

- high turnover of volunteers from one year to the next, producing a basically unstable frontline workforce

- requirement for a firm but tactful style of leader ship from all managers (i.e. no autocrats)

- likelihood that enthusiasts will tend to overlook the commercial realities involved in running the railway.

BIBLIOGRAPHY

The following bibliography represents a selection of leading texts on the range of topics covered in this book. Most are titles written twenty or thirty years ago, but which have provided the basis for much of the modern practice of personnel management in its widest sense.

ACAS (1977), *Code of Practice 1 Disciplinary Procedures*, HMSO.
ACAS (1981), *Recruitment and Selection* (Advisory Booklet No. 6), ACAS.
Adair, J. (1968), *Training for Leadership*, MacDonald.
Adair, J. (1973), *Action-centred Leadership*, McGraw-Hill.
Adair, J. (1986), *Effective Teambuilding*, Gower.
Argyris, C. (1960), *Understanding Organisational Behaviour*, Tavistock.
Armstrong, M. & Baron, A. (1995) *The Job Evaluation Handbook*, CIPD.
Atkinson, J. (1984), *Flexible Manning: the Way Ahead*, IMS/Manpower.
Bales, R.F. (1950), *Interaction Process Analysis*, Addison-Wesley.
Beckhard, R. (1969), *Organisation Development: Strategies and Models*, Addison-Wesley
Belbin, R.M. (1993), *Team Roles at Work*, Butterworth Heinemann
Bigge, M.L. (1982), *Learning Theories for Teachers* (4th edn), Harper & Row.
Blake, R. & Mouton, J. (1978), *The New Managerial Grid*, Gulf.
Bloom, B.S. *et al.* (1956), *Taxonomy of Educational Objectives I The Cognitive Domain*, Longmans.
Bowey, A.M. (ed.), *Handbook of Salary & Wage Systems* (2nd edn), Gower.
Bramham, J. (1982), *Practical Manpower Planning*, IPM.
Brech, E.F.L. (1946), *Management: its Nature and Significance*, Pitman.
British Institute of Management (1977), *Employee Participation – The way ahead*, BIM.
Brown, W. (1960), *Exploration in Management*, Heinemann.
Burns, T. & Stalker, G.M. (1961), *The Management of Innovation*, Tavistock.
Burrell, G & Morgan, G. (1979), *Sociological Paradigms and Organisational Analysis*, Heinemann.
Burrows, G. (1985), *Redundancy Counselling for Managers*, IPM.
Business in the Community (1991), *Opportunity 2000: Towards a Balanced Workforce*, BIC.
Child, J. (1988), *Organisation* (2nd edn), Harper & Row.
Clutterbuck, D. (2001) Everyone Needs a Mentor (3rd edn), CIPD.
Cole, G.A. (1994), *Strategic Management*, (2nd edn), Continuum.
Cole, G.A. (1995), *Organisational Behaviour*, Continuum.
Curson, C. (ed.) (1986), *Changing Patterns of Work*, IPM.
Department of Employment (1980), *Code of Practice: Picketing*, HMSO.
Donovan (1968), *Report of the Royal Commission on Trade Unions and Employers' Associations*, HMSO.
Drucker, P.F. (1954), *The Practice of Management*, Heinemann.
Easterby-Smith, M. (1980), *Auditing Management Development*, Gower.
Egan, G. (1990), *The Skilled Helper* (4th edn), Brooks/Cole Publishing.
Eisner, E.W. (1969), 'Instructional and Expressive Objectives: their Formulation

and use in Curriculum', in Popham *et al.*, *Instructional Objectives*. AERA Monograph, Rand McNally.

Equal Opportunities Commission, (1984), *Equal Pay for Work of Equal Value: a guide to the amended Equal Pay Act*, EOC.

Fayol, H. (1949), *General and Industrial Management*, Pitman.

Fiedler, F. (1967), *A Theory of Leadership Effectiveness*, McGraw-Hill.

Fraser, J.M. (1978), *Employment Interviewing* (5th edn), MacDonald & Evans.

French, W.L. & Bell, C.H. (1978), *Organisation Development* (2nd edn), Prentice Hall.

Gilbreth, F.B. & L.M. (1917), *Applied Motion Study*, Sturgis & Walton.

Gill, D. (1977), 'Towards More Open Performance Appraisal', *Personnel Management*, December.

Goldthorpe, J.H. *et al.* (1968), *The Affluent Worker: Industrial Attitudes and Behaviour*, Cambridge University Press.

Goodman, J.F.B. & Whittingham, T.G. (1973), *Shop Stewards*, Pan.

Goyder, M. (1979), 'The Mondragon Experiment', *Personnel Management*, March 1979.

Guba, E.G. & Lincoln, Y.S. (1981), *Effective Evaluation*, Jossey-Bass.

Hamblin, A.C. (1974), *Evaluation and Control of Training*, McGraw-Hill.

Handy, C. (1993), *Understanding Organisations* (4th edn), Penguin.

Hawkins, K. (1979), *A Handbook of Industrial Relations Practice*, Kogan Page.

Herzberg, F. (1966), *Work and the Nature of Man*, World Publishing.

Hofstede, G. (1980), *Culture's Consequences: International Differences in Work-related Values*, Sage Publications.

Hollyforde, S. & Whiddett, S. (1999) *The Competencies Handbook*, CIPD.

Humble, J.W. (1967), *Improving Business Results*, McGraw-Hill.

IPA/IPM *Employee code on Involvement and Participation in the United Kingdom* (1990).

IPM (1990), *The IPM Equal Opportunities Code*, IPM.

IPM (1991), *Age and Employment – An IPM Statement*, IPM.

Kolb, D., Rubin, I., & McIntyre, J. (1979), *Organisational Psychology – an Experiential Approach* (3rd edn), Prentice Hall.

Krathwohl, D.R. *et al.* (1964), *Taxonomy of Educational Objectives II – The Affective Domain*, Longmans.

Lawrence, J. & Lorsch, P. (1967), *Organisation and Environment*, Harvard UP.

Legge, K. (1978), *Power, Innovation and Problem-solving in Personnel Management*, McGraw-Hill.

Lewin, K. (1951), *Field Theory in Social Science*, Harper.

Lewis, C. (1985), *Employee Selection*, Hutchinson.

Lewis, D. (1994), *Essentials of Employment Law* (4th edn), IPM

Mager, R. (1962), *Preparing Instructional Objectives*, Fearon.

Manpower Services Commission (1978), *Management Development*, MSC.

Maslow, A. (1954), *Motivation and Personality*, Harper & Row.

Mayo, E. (1933), *The Human Problems of an Industrial Civilisation*, Macmillan.

McBeath, G. & Rands, D.N. (1976), *Salary Administration* (3rd edn), Business Books.

McClelland, D. (1961), *The Achieving Society*, Van Nostrand.

McGregor, D. (1957), 'An Uneasy Look at Performance Appraisal', *Harvard Business Review* May–June 1957.

McGregor, D. (1960), *The Human Side of Enterprise*, McGraw-Hill.

Megginson, D. & Boydell, T. (1979), *A Manager's Guide to Coaching*, BACIE.

Mintzberg, H. (1973), *The Nature of Managerial Work*, Harper & Row.

Mintzberg, H. (1979), *The Structuring of Organisations*, Prentice Hall.

Morgan, G. (1986), *Images of Organisation*, Sage Publications.

Morris, J.F. (1978), 'Management Development and Development Management', in Burgoyne & Stuart (eds), *Management Development: Context and Strategies*, Gower Press.

Moss Kanter, R. (1983), *The Change Masters*, Unwin.

Parsloe, E. (1992), *Coaching, Mentoring and Assessing*, Kogan Page.

Paul, W.J. & Robertson, K.B. (1970), *Job Enrichment and Employee Motivation*, Gower Press.

Pedler, M., Burgoyne, J. & Boydell, T. (1993), *A Manager's Guide to Self-development* (2nd edn), McGraw-Hill.

Peters, T. & Waterman, R. (1982), *In Search of Excellence*, Harper & Row.

Plumbley, P. (1985), *Recruitment and Selection*, IPM.

Pugh, D.S. *et al.* (1968), 'Dimensions of Organisational Structure', *Administrative Science Quarterly*.

Purcell, J. (1985), 'Is Anybody Listening to the Corporate Personnel Department?', *Personnel Management*, September.

Rackham, N. & Morgan, T. (1977), *Behaviour Analysis in Training*, McGraw-Hill.

Rae, L. (1985), *The Skills of Human Relations Training*, Gower.

Reddin, W.J. (1970), *Managerial Effectiveness*, McGraw-Hill.

Rice, A.K. (1963), *The Enterprise and its Environment*, Tavistock.

Robson, M.P. (1982), *Worker Participation in the United Kingdom*, MCB Publications.

Rodger, A. *et al.* (1971), *The Industrial Training Officer*, IPM.

Roethlisberger, J. & Dickson, W. (1939), *Management and the Worker*, Harvard University Press.

Roff, H. & Watson, T.E. (1961), *Job Analysis*, IPM.

Schein, E.H. (1969), *Process Consultation: Its Role in Organisation Development*, Addison-Wesley.

Schein, E.H. (1980), *Organisational Psychology* (3nd edn), Prentice Hall.

Scriven, M. (1967), *The Methodology of Evaluation*, AERA Monograph, R and McNally.

Senge, P. (1990), *The Fifth Discipline: The Art and Practice of the Learning Organisation*, Doubleday.

Simmons, J. & Brennan, R. (1981), in Nixon, B. (ed.), *New Approaches to Management Development*, Gower/ATM.

Simon, H.A. (1960), *Administrative Behaviour*, Macmillan.

Slade, E.A. (1995), *Tolley's Employment Handbook*, Tolley Publishing.

Stewart, R. (1982), *Managerial Choice*, McGraw-Hill.

Stogdill, R.M. & Coons, A.E. (1957), *Leadership Behavior: Its Description and Measurement*, Research Monograph No. 88, Ohio State University.

Tannenbaum, R. & Schmidt, W. (1958), 'How to Choose a Leadership Pattern', *Harvard Business Review*, March/April.

Taylor, F.W. (1947), *Scientific Management*, Harper & Row.

Thakur, M. & Gill, D. (1976), *Job Evaluation in Practice*, IPM.

Thakur, M. *et al.* (eds) (1978), *Personnel in Change*, IPM.

Trist, E. *et al.* (1963), *Organisational Choice*, Tavistock.

Turrell, M. (1980), *Training Analysis*, MacDonald & Evans.

Tyler, R. (1949), *Basic Principles of Curriculum and Instruction*, University of Chicago Press.

Urwick, L.F. (1947), *The Elements of Administration*, Pitman.

Vroom, V. (1964), *Work and Motivation*, Wiley.

Walton, R.E. & McKersie, R. (1965), *A Behavioural Theory of Labour Negotiations*, McGraw-Hill.

Weber, M. (1947), *Theory of Social and Economic Organisations*, Free Press.

Woodcock, M. (1979), *Team Development Manual*, Gower.

Woodward, J. (1965), *Industrial Organisation: Theory and Practice*, OUP.

USEFUL WEBSITES

The following selection of websites is included because of the useful information sources it contains for students of Personnel and Human Resource Management. In many cases these sites are the best sources for gaining an up-to-date picture of the current UK law on employment matters. Much of the material is in the public domain and can be downloaded freely; some sources can only be accessed via membership or by the payment of a fee-for-use. Many of the sites provide helpful links to related internet sites. However, it is difficult to find an extensive list of relevant sites, and this is why the following internet addresses have been provided here.

www.acas.org.uk	Advisory Conciliation & Arbitration Service (ACAS)
www.bps.org.uk	British Psychological Society
www.britcoun.org	British Council
www.britishsafetycouncil.co.uk	British Safety Council
www.cac.gov.uk	Central Arbitration Committee
www.cedefop.eu.int	Centre Europeen pour le Developpement de la Formation Professionnelle (Vocational Training)
www.cib.org.uk	Chartered Institute of Bankers
www.cii.co.uk	Chartered Insurance Institute
www.cipd.co.uk	Chartered Institute of Personnel Management
www.dataprotection.gov.uk	Information Commissioner
www.dfes.gov.uk	Department for Education and Skills
www.dti.gov.uk	Department of Trade and Industry
www.dwp.gov.uk	Department for Work and Pensions
www.eoc.org.uk	Equal Opportunities Commission
www.europa.eu.int	European Union information service
www.gateway.gov.uk	UK Government departments' pathway
www.hmso.gov.uk	Her Majesty's Stationery Office (HMSO)
www.hse.gov.uk	Health & Safety Executive
www.ifsis.org.uk	Institute of Financial Services
www.iipuk.co.uk	Investors in People
www.imi.ie	Irish Management Institute
www.inlandrevenue.gov.uk	Inland Revenue
www.managers.org.uk	The Institute of Management
www.instam.org	Institute for Administrative Management
www.iod.com	Institute of Directors
www.ilo.org	International Labour Organisation
www.incomesdata.co.uk	Incomes Data Services
www.indsoc.co.uk	The Industrial Society
www.ismstowe.com	Institute for Supervision & Management
www.learndirect.co.uk	LearnDirect
www.lifelonglearning.co.uk	UK Lifelong Learning
www.lsc.gov.uk	Learning & Skills Council
www.management-standards.org	The Management Standards Centre

www.open.gov.uk	Open Government site
www.qca.org.uk	Qualifications & Curriculum Authority
www.rospa.co.uk	Royal Society for the Prevention of Accidents
www.statistics.gov.uk	Office for National Statistics
www.sqa.org.uk	Scottish Qualifications Authority
www.tiger.gov.uk	Tailored Interactive Guidance on Employment Rights (DTI)
www.tuc.org.uk	Trades Union Congress

INDEX

achievement motivation 98, 100
Advisory, Conciliation & Arbitration
    Service (ACAS) 5, 15, 232, 405, 409,
    436, 465–6
age discrimination 238–9
Alderfer's theory (of motivation) 97
application forms 185–7
appraisal forms 302–5
appraisal interviews 306–9
appraisal styles 307–8
arbitration 436, 438
assessment centres 196–8
autonomous work-groups 116–17

ballots 441–2
bargaining units 412
behaviourist theories 311–14
Bloom's taxonomy 348–9
British Psychological Society 195

Central Arbitration Committee
    (CAC) 412, 436
centralisation see decentralisation
Certification Officer 422, 424
change
    agent 124–5
    resistance to 128–31
Chartered Institute of Personnel &
    Development (CIPD) 3, 8, 15, 232,
    238, 457
closed shop 6
coaching 355, 384–5
collective bargaining
    definition of 409–11
    process 416–18
communication methods 403–8
competence (definition of) 361
computerised personnel records 219–20
conciliation 436–7
conditions of learning (Gagne) 320–1
conditioning 312–14
Confederation of British Industry (CBI)
    427
confidentiality 214
contingency theories (of leadership) 72–4
contract of employment 225–7
    common law obligations 227
    explicit terms 228–30
    implied terms 230–1
    variation of terms 231

counselling at work 290–1
course design 352–4
culture differences (international) 32–5
curriculum vitae (cv) 188

Data Protection Act (1998) 208, 214–18
decentralisation 61–2
delegation 387
demand (for labour) 142–5
development (definition of) 330
disabled persons 234–5
disciplinary procedures 445–50
disputes
    collective 431
    procedures 434–5
    trade union immunities 431–2

education (definition of) 330
email 408
employee benefits 268–71
employee handbooks 404
employee participation
    definition 451
    options 453–5
employee relations
    definition of 399
    main parties 400–1
employers' associations 401–2, 427
Employment Appeal Tribunal (EAT) 232,
    466
employment contract see contract of
    employment
employment tribunals 466
empowerment (definition of) 451
Engineering Employers' Federation (EEF)
    401–2, 434–5
Environment (group) 90
Equal Opportunities Commission 167
equal opportunities policies 235–6
equal pay 252–3
equity theory (motivation) 103
European Union (EU) 27, 452, 459
    directives 27–8, 253, 283, 459
European Works Councils 452, 454
evaluation (of training) 369–70
    data 375–8
    subject matter 372–4
expectancy theory (motivation) 100–2
experiential learning 322–4, 388–90

503